The Vintage Magazine Consumer Guide to

WINE

The Vintage Magazine Consumer Guide to
WINE

BY PHILIP SELDON

Doubleday & Company, Inc., Garden City, New York 1983

Library of Congress Cataloging in Publication Data

Seldon, Philip.
  The Vintage magazine consumer guide to wine.

  Includes index.
  1. Wine and wine making I. Vintage. II. Title.
TP548.S468 1983   641.2'2   79-8505
ISBN 0-385-14961-1
Library of Congress Catalog Card Number 79-8505

ACKNOWLEDGMENTS

I wish to thank the thousands of winemakers, proprietors and other members of the wine trade, fellow wine writers, wine collectors and connoisseurs throughout the world who have, in one way or another, contributed to the information in this book and make the world of wine such a special joy.

I also wish to thank Kathy Borys who assisted in the preparation of the manuscript, my administrative assistant Mildred Walker for transcribing my dictation, Yvonne Montgomery for typesetting, Jami Parker for paste-up and mechanicals, Mary Brittle for proofreading and indexing, my fellow members of the Wine Writers Circle for their encouragement, Daniel Rose for his kind words and my editor, Louise Gault, art director, Alex Gotfryd, and designer, Larry Alexander at Doubleday for their guidance and support.

I especially wish to thank my good friend Lorna Winslow for her inspiration and for making the sharing of a fine wine such a wonderful pleasure.

CONTENTS

Chapter One — Introduction to Wine   1
Why Wine? • What This Book Is About • Learning About Wine • The Winemakers Choice
Jug - Premium - Noble wine • Why Wines Cost So Much

Chapter Two — A Brief History of Wine   9
The Discovery of Wine • Roman Colonization • The Middle Ages • The Role of Religion
Dom Pérignon • Wine in America • *Phylloxera* • Prohibition

Chapter Three — Grapes and Vines   15
Climate and Soil • Balance - Harmony - Breed • Ideal Climate • The Vine • Vine Diseases
The Growing Season • Heat Sumation • Acids and Sugar • New Varieties

Chapter Four — How wine is Made   25
Wine Qualities • The Role of the Grape • Crushing and Destemming • Fermentation
Temperature Control • Yeasts and Bacteria • The Traditional Winery • The Modern
Winery • Chaptalisaton • Adjusting Sweetness • The Centrifuge • Malolactic Fermentation
Racking • Wine Diseases

Chapter Five — Grape Varieties   47
Vitis Vinifera • *Vitis Labrusca* • French/American Hybrids • *Muscadine*

Chapter Six — Wine Regions   61
Argentina • Australia • Austria • Bulgaria • Cyprus • Chile • France • Germany • Greece
Hungary • Italy • Portugal • South Africa • Switzerland • The U.S.A.
MAPS
Worldwide Wine Zones • France • Bordeaux • Burgundy - Côtes de Nuits
Burgundy - Côtes de Beaune • The Loire • The Rhône Valley • Italy • Spain and Portugal
Germany - The Mosel • The Rheingau • The Rheinhessen • The Rheinpfalz • The United
States - California • Napa Valley • Sonoma County • South America • Australia

Chapter Seven — Wine Laws   117
Caveats • France - *Appellation Contrôlée - V.D.Q.S.* • Germany - QbA - Qmp
Italy - D.O.C. - D.O.C.G. • The United States - B.A.T.F.

CONTENTS

Chapter Eight — Everyday Wines   127
Jug Wines • Austria • Germany • France • Italy • The United States • Rumania
Greece • Yugoslavia

Chapter Nine — Premium and Noble Wines   139
Simple-Premium • Mid-premium • Super-Premium • Noble • Harmony - Symmetry -
Color - Complexity - Finesse - Elegance - Breed • Quality Categories of French Wines
The *Appellations Contrôlées* of Bordeaux • The *Appellations Contrôlées* of Burgundy
Germany - The Hierarchy of Quality • Italy - D.O.C - D.O.C.G. • California • New York
The Best Reliable California Wines

Chapter Ten — What Makes A Vintage?   205
The Climate • The Grower • The Vintner • When to Harvest

Chapter Eleven — Sparkling Wines   209
Champagne • *Méthode Champenoise* • *Vin Mousseux* • Charmat Process • Transfer
Method • Yeast Autolysis • *Dégorgement* • Riddling • Dosage • *Spumante* • *Sekt*

Chapter Twelve — Fortified Wines   219
Port - Vintage - Crusted - Late Bottled Vintage - Ruby - Twany - White • Sherry - *Fino*
-Manzanilla - Amontillado - Oloroso - Cream • Madeira - *Sercial - Verdelho - Bual*
-Malmsey - Rainwater • Marsala • Vermouth

Chapter Thirteen — Wine Bottles   233
The Basic Shapes • Rhine • Claret • Burgundy • Magnum • Corks & Closures

Chapter Fourteen — How to Read a Wine Label   239
Vintage • Bottling Terms • Origin Descriptors • Quality Descriptors • Style Descriptors
General Terms • Sample Labels

Chapter Fifteen — Sensory Evaluation   259
Sensory Elements • Smell • Taste • Thresholds • Organaleptic Examination

Chapter Sixteen — Wine in Restaurants   269
House Wine • The Short List • The Familiar List • The Fat Wine List • Bringing Your Own
Bottle • Sending Back a Bottle • Dealing with the "Sommelier"

Chapter Seventeen — Wine Shops and Merchants   279
Finding a Good Merchant • The "Test" • Saving Money • Window Dressing
Discount Stores • Private Labels

Chapter Eighteen — Wine at Home   285
Preparing the Wine • Removing the Cork • Should a Wine Breath • Decanting • Wine
Glasses • Opening and Serving Champagne • Keeping An Open Bottle • Storing Wine
Wine Racks • Your Own Wine Cellar

Chapter Nineteen — Wine Tastings   301
Conducting Your Own Wine Tasting • Testing Your Palate • Keeping Notes
Wine Journal • Scoring Systems

CONTENTS

Chapter Twenty — The Wine Trade 309
The Volstead Act • Repeal • Loopholes • Importers • Distributors • Direct Import
Master of Wine • Boutique Wineries • The Giants

Chapter Twenty-One — Wine Advertising 319
Deceptive Advertising • Worthless Medals • Wine Competitions • "Premium" - "Classic" -
"Rare" - "Vintage Dating Makes It Right" • Off-Vintages

Chapter Twenty-Two — Writers on Wine 327
The Good Writers • The Bad Writers • The "Cub" Reporter • The "Wine Enthusiast"
"Cliffords Disease" • The Experts and the "Not So Expert"

Chapter Twenty-Three — Wine Books 335
Furthering Your Wine Education - Books: Some to Read - Others to Avoid

Chapter Twenty-Four — What Shall I Buy 351
Where To Get The Most Current Information • Wine Magazines • Newsletters
Free Winery • Newsletters • Wine Courses

Chapter Twenty-Five — A Word of Caution 358
The Responsible Use Of Wine and Spirits

Chapter Twenty-Seven - Wine Words 363
The Basic Vocabulary of Wine

Chapter Twenty-Six — Appendix 376
The Best Known Classified Wines of Bordeaux • The Best Known Wines of Burgundy
The Best Known Fine Wines of Germany • Wine Journal

Index 394

FOR MY PARENTS

FOREWORD

When the Psalmist in the Old Testament sang of "wine that maketh glad the heart of man," and when the New Testament commentator in Timothy advised us to "use a little wine for thy stomach's sake," they weren't thinking of vintage charts, expensive decanters, temperature or humidity controls, special glasses and so forth. What they referred to was the straight forward substance of nature produced over the centuries by rugged men and women for the well-being and pleasure of family and friends.

It is to Philip Seldon's credit that he has been able to capture that spirit in this present volume directed to the needs of those who enjoy wine and wish to know more about it; who seek good value for the money they spend; and who in general wish to increase the pleasure they believe wine can add to their lives. Mr. Seldon's approach to the subject is pragmatic; and he is mercifully free from the mystification and mumbo-jumbo that frightens off many potential wine lovers.

We must recognize from the outset, of course, that wine is a highly subjective field. For example, it is a fact of life that the very matching of a luscious Sauternes with a pungent Roquefort cheese which brings cheers in Bordeaux may raise shocked eyebrows in New York. The pairing of red wine with fish, supposedly a classic error, is another instance. Many years ago, it chanced that the great George Lang was examined for membership in the Confrèrie des Chèvaliers du Tastevin at the same session I was; and one of his questions was "under what conditions would it be appropriate to serve a red wine with fish." I was still pondering when George replied briskly, "when the fish is prepared with a red wine sauce, it would be appropriate to serve in the glass the same wine used in the sauce."

On many food and wine questions, opinions legitimately differ, and the late Claude Phillippe (at whose memorable Lucullus Circle dinners Philip Seldon and I shared many pleasant evenings over the years) used to delight precisely in creating lively controversy and in provoking animated discussion over issues of taste. At the wonderful dinners of the Commanderie de Bordeaux, Gregory Thomas, arguably the most impressive figure in the world of American gastronomy, to this day goes to great pains to stimulate good-natured exchanges in which the knowledgeable members enthusiastically lock horns over matters of taste, suitability and preference. If our opinions on this particular wine practice or about the merits of that particular wine writer differ, so much the better; we will all gain entertainment and knowledge in the discussion.

In that context, we all may read with pleasure and profit this useful volume which reflects with grace and candor Philip Seldon's personal views and experiences. The most innocent beginner will not find it intimidating; and the most knowledgeable old hand will find new information and provocative insights.

Daniel Rose

New York City
July, 1983

Daniel Rose is a partner in a nationally prominent New York City real estate firm. He has been active on the international wine and food scene for many years and is a member of many of the nations gastronomic organizations.

INTRODUCTION TO WINE

In the beginning, the new wine lover faces two challenges: how to select a good wine and how to judge the relative merits of comparable wines. In his quest, he turns to the plethora of written material on the subject: books, magazines, articles and newsletters. Then he faces still another new challenge: understanding the technical terms, interpreting the mysteries and sorting the myths which surround the experience of enjoying a glass of wine. Through these books, he is made to believe that the essence of wine's pleasure is found in an esoteric understanding of French Chateaux and vintages, and that checking for clarity is an essential element in drinking a glass of wine. Furthermore, he's bombarded with terms he does not understand and for which he has no use because they are never related to his goal: the intelligent selection of good quality wine.

There is little to be taught about drinking the finest wines of the world...once you know how to appreciate the experience, these wines speak for themselves. Yet, one of the most rewarding aspects of being a wine student is having the know-how to seek out wines which are extremely pleasurable, enjoyable and affordable. Until the wine is open, of course, there is no guarantee to its quality; however, with a little background understanding you can begin to make your own intelligent purchasing decisions. And that's what this book is about.

Making an intelligent wine purchase is a synthesis of two areas of knowledge:

- an understanding of the different quality-levels of wine available

- an understanding of the workings of the wine industry, which has been known to capitalize on a particular wine's popularity — when in fact it doesn't merit the price that merchants are getting.

However, the person who can combine these two areas of knowledge will be well ahead of other consumers, who through ignorance, remain pawns of the wine industry. And that's the backbone of this book: to educate the new wine buyer from the most basic point of reference — to give him the tools he needs to independently purchase wines that appeal to his taste and his wallet.

With every step of this book, I have asked myself "why?" "Why is this question or point important to the reader's understanding of wine?" "Why should he know this?" "How will it help him?" I think you'll find that "why?" is a question too-often over-looked by many wine writers, who prefer that wine maintain its image of mystery and glamour. Consequently, they insist on keeping wines shrouded in mysteries and traditions that have no relationship to wine today. In this book, I hope to put some of those mysteries to rest by explaining their historical, technical or scientific origins.

The second important part of this book is devoted to the experience of enjoying wine. Experiencing all that a glass has to offer. Separately, in Chapter Nineteen, I take you through the complete how-to of tasting wine. This chapter is supplemented by Chapters Seven, Eight and Nine which chart out, more specifically, the characteristics different kinds of wine should take.

Wine is made in many different kinds, flavors, and levels of quality. The vast majority of wine sold in America is well-made, straightforward, relatively neutral, or grapy, in its flavor and relatively inexpensive. Such wine makes for an excellent, healthful and enjoyable everyday beverage. Unfortunately these wines are looked down upon by many wine writers and wine enthusiasts. This attitude has permeated the wine world and consequently, most of the wines written about are beyond the reach or interest of the average consumer. Furthermore, there has been a lot of nonsense written about what is and is not "correct" regarding the service and handling of wine which is inappropriate for most of the wines you will encounter in your everyday drinking. Before reading this book you should try to set aside everything you have already read or heard about the subject of wine. Some of what you may already have learned may be valid; but except for certain wines, much will be incorrect. Together we will examine the subject at its most basic level. In doing so you will develop an understanding of the more esoteric aspects of wine and should quickly be able to put all wines in their proper context.

There are three factors which interact to determine a wine's character: the grape variety and how it's grown, the climate and soil wherein it is grown, and the vintner's creative or commercial objective and his skill in making the wine. There is no question about the importance of the grape for it is the essence of the wine, and without an ideal environment it would only achieve a certain level of quality. Yet, though you can't make a good wine from bad grapes, it is surprisingly easy to turn potentially great wine into very expensive ordinary wine or vinegar.

The vintner (winemaker) has the dual role of scientist and artist. Technological advances over the last twenty years have provided the winemaker with new alternatives, knowledge and analytical techniques that enable him to make good quality wine at even the lowest price level. In his role as scientist he will know when and how to apply that technology. As an artist, the vintner uses his technological background to impart his own hallmark — the subtle differences in flavor and style that act as his signature and differentiate his work from that of another vintner working for the same firm with the same grapes.

Before we continue, we must define the vintner's objective. Simply stated, the vintner's objective is the kind or style of wine he sets out to make. It may be dictated by artistic or commercial considerations, frequently both. To that end, he will apply certain techniques and processes and his success will be measured by whether or not he has achieved his intended goal. The luckiest vintner, of whom there are but a rare handful, can be said to have a total range of choices. For the few that have the opportunity to start their own vineyard, they can, providing the property is available, pick their own site based on determinations of climate, a wine-making tradition, the kind of soil, etc.

Few vintners are so lucky. Most, unable to find or afford their own vineyards, inherit the circumstances of a family or company. Because they cannot choose a location, their choice of suitable grape varieties will be limited and similarly, in most cases, they will have to continue making wine in the style already established by the vineyard which employs them. This is not to say that there is no room for change, experimentation or improvement, or that the parameters of any one vintner are completely limited by the organization that hires him, but rather to help you understand where the winemaker does or does not have choices.

Sometimes the choices are dictated by a wine's style:

To make a true Burgundy, the vintner will necessarily have to follow techniques established by the Burgundy wine making tradition.

- Other times, his choices are dictated by the wine's character. The character of a white wine, for instance, is to be light, fruity, and refreshing. To that end, the vintner would usually not age the wine for long periods in wood casks, or ferment the grape juice in contact with its skins.

• Lastly, his choice may be dictated by economics which in many cases is a function of style and character. A red jug wine for instance, does not require the long, expensive cask aging that a more expensive Burgundy does.

At the same time, the nuances of flavor and bouquet that are characteristic of the Burgundy are not in the true character of a jug wine, therefore in the simplest terms, you can see that with the proper skill, a good, characteristic jug wine can and should be produced less expensively than a good traditional Burgundy.

For the purpose of our discussion, table wines, to which this chapter refers, can be divided into three classifications with the following characteristics:

• JUG WINE can be a good beverage, with good flavor and a vinous (winey) taste. A good jug wine will have a certain amount of body, be balanced, and have a direct, single or neutral flavor, and a short finish or aftertaste.

• PREMIUM WINE has more refinement, more character, the flavors of the grape and a certain texture and complexity not found in other beverages will be apparent. The wine will have a harmonious balance that often transcends one's prior taste experience. The wine's taste will linger in the mouth, and be recognizable as either being from a region or of a particular style.

• NOBLE WINES contain flavor and complexity beyond that found in premium wines, called "breed" or "finesse". The wine will have subtle nuances of flavor and may have a structure that can be called orchestral, but may even be a contradiction in terms, for instance, "assertive yet delicate," "powerful yet subtle."

There is a fourth category of table wine, the Vin Ordinaire — "factory made". It is produced for mass consumption with little regard for quality. It is the everyday cheap carafe wine of ubiquitous cafés and bistros throughout Europe. This wine is frequently the result of haphazard "don't give a damn" winemaking and since it is almost never found in this country, doesn't play a part in our discussion.

As this book progresses we will see how various methods of vinification and aging will be used to produce the desired qualities inherent in each of these categories of wine; but, first, let's look at the relationship of the grape and the vineyard to the winemaking process, and then the winemaking process itself.

A vintner will grow (or purchase) grapes according to the wine he wants to make. For instance:

A varietal wine, like a Cabernet Sauvignon, which relies heavily on the characteristics of the grape variety will require grapes which have been closely grown and selected and which exhibit the best qualities of that variety. The soil, climate, yield and maturity will be very important factors.

Grapes for a jug wine, on the other hand, which by its very nature need not possess the special nuances of a premium or prestige wine, will ordinarily be made from grapes of a lesser quality. Jug wines can be made with a better quality grape, and will have an improved flavor over a comparable wine made with lesser grapes, but there is really no reason to incur the extra cost required by premium grapes.

With the exception of the noble wines, every wine producing country of the world produces wines in my first two categories. Thus the myth that French wine is the best, Italian wines somewhat less good, etc., is a farfetched generalization which has always been untrue. In regions where the finest wines of the world are produced it is not uncommon to find wines which fall into the lowest quality category grown nearby.

Wines come in several basic kinds. Table wines are those which are usually served with a meal and comprise the majority of the wines consumed in the world. Table wines are produced as Reds, Whites, and Rosés and range in alcohol from nine to fourteen and one half percent and are produced to accompany a meal. Many table wines, mostly the reds, improve when aged in the bottle for prolonged periods of times. The frequently touted, "Red goes with meat, White with fish, Rosé goes with everything," axiom, hardly holds true anymore; with an understanding of the varied styles and flavors of all three types, you will soon be able to make appropriate wine/food matches without guidance. Aperitif wines are table wines flavored with herbs, spices or other ingredients to produce a unique flavor. Vermouth is an example. Sparkling wines are table wines which have been carbonated during the fermentation process. Fortified or Dessert wines, are high-alcohol wines ranging from fifteen to twenty-one percent alcohol, usually quite sweet but not necessarily so, and are best-suited for drinking alone or after a meal. Examples are Port and Sherry. Fruit wines are made with fruit other than grapes and will not be covered in this book.

What is often confusing to the wine novice is the vast differences in price for different wines. Even more confusing is the disparity in price between wines which bear the same name, or come from the same region, or are made from the same grape variety. With most products price is usually a good guide as to what you should expect in terms of quality, in other other words, you get what you pay for. Unfortunately, this is often not the case with wine. This book will explain the reasons why. With what you will learn you will be able to determine the worth of a wine yourself, by interpreting its label or by analyzing its taste. The world of wine, and the wine trade is a complex one. Simple rules do not hold. But with a little understanding, you should soon be able to make some wise purchasing decisions.

Many wine novices have gone on to become deeply involved with wine as a hobby, the many fascinating facets of the thousands of wines available are suited to this type of interest. If by chance you get bitten by the "bug" and become a dyed-in-the-wool wine buff, you may look forward to many exhilarating and gratifying taste experiences. There are hundreds of wine clubs which hold organized wine tastings and provide the opportunity to share new wine discoveries with newly found friends. Wine clubs, and wine tasting organization will be reviewed in Chapter Nineteen. Now let us enter the world of wine.

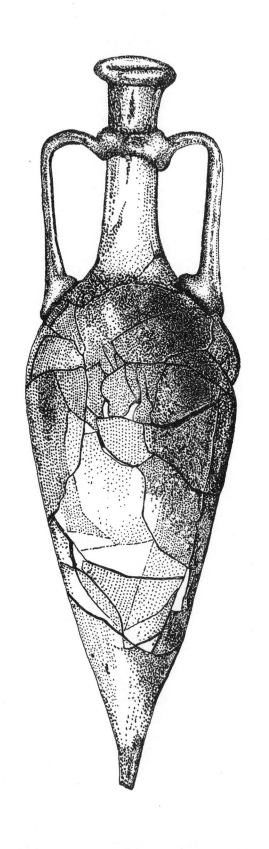

A BRIEF HISTORY OF WINE

Theories abound as to the exact origin of the grape, how long it took man to "discover" wine, how he made it, and what it tasted like. We know from drawings and artifacts found in ancient tombs that the early Egyptians made wine which they often graded and labeled according to vintage, and through the wonderful mythology of Bacchus and Dionysus, it is obvious that wine was part of the Greek and Roman civilizations. Although the history of wine can be traced throughout man's civilization, we may never know the exact origin of the grape or wine, and I'm not sure that's all bad. For one of the nicest enchantments about wine is the wonderful lore and romantic adventure which surrounds its history.

One of my favorite legends takes place well before the birth of Christ at the palace of the Persian King Jemsheed who was so fond of grapes that he hid them, to be savored later, in large ceramic jars marked "poison". As the story continues, one young lady of his harem, distraught over her station in life (or as another version goes, because she fell from the king's favor), attempted suicide by drinking his "poison". She soon fell into a sound sleep, and when she woke, related the wonders of his marvelous potion. She forever remained his favorite. With wonderful stories like this do we ever really need to know the whole truth about the origin of wine?

There are several good books that describe wine's evolution in minute detail and for the interested, they are listed in Chapter Twenty-Three. Whether the Greeks or the Etruscans brought wine to Italy is another point that will be debated long after our current civilization passes; and although early records indicate that the Greeks may have introduced wine to Marseilles in 600 BC, the Roman colonization of Gaul is generally credited for the wide dispersion of vines throughout France — probably because wine tasted good, could be kept long, and could be easily traded. The wines of these bygone eras scarcely resemble the wines of today. The ancients did not understand the chemistry of winemaking, and their wines probably were more closely related to vinegar than to modern wine. Frequently ancient wines were preserved with resins, herbs, or a layer of oil. If we could sample those wines today, I suspect that they would not be to our liking. Yet for their alcohol and vigorous taste, the ancients loved them. Thankfully, history has improved wine.

Wine was universal. Its use spread with every new discovery, exploration or conquest. And wine improved. Fine wine became a sought-after agricultural product. Those who made the best gained fame and fortune. The introduction of grapes and wine to a particular area was an essential element of exploration and colonization. California is a prime example, as the California wine industry can be traced back to Hernando Cortez, conquerer of Mexico. It is said that because space on ships from Spain was at a minimum, and there was consequently a limited amount of space in which to carry wine, Cortez ordered that some piece of every farm be planted with grapes. These were eventually propagated and carried north by missionaries who used them to establish new vineyards. Grapes were easier to transport than wine.

European wine history is inextricably woven with politics and wars which frequently shut down all wine production. The French Revolution for instance, forever affected the wines of France's Burgundy region. The story begins in 581 when Gontran, King of Burgundy bequeathed the vineyards of Dijon to the monks of the Abbey Saint Bénigne. In the next century, the kingdom was reduced to a duchy, and the nobles, following the king's gesture bequeathed some of the great vineyards of Fixin, Chassagne, and Meursault, among others, to the clergy. Under the church wine developed to new heights and the wines of Burgundy became the most renowned, setting the standard for quality wines as we know them today. By the twelfth century, the church had become a major land-holder of vineyards and, in fact, remained so until the French Revolution in the 1790s when the land was divided and put into the hands of the commoners. As they have been handed down from generation to generation, the Burgundy vineyards today are still divided into small plots owned by different people which is why two bottles of Burgundy made in the same year, from the same vineyard, may very well be completely different.

The role of the religious in winemaking is another point that withstands a lot of debate. Some will say that religious communities always in need of sacramental wines were responsible for perpetuating vintners' skills. Yet, for so many this is a moot point. The religious did, however, play two very important roles in wine's history.

Dom Pérignon, cellarmaster at the Benedictine Abbey of Hautvillers in the Champagne region of France during the late seventh and early eighteenth centuries, is credited with having discovered Champagne. Likewise, Father Junipero Serra, whose twenty-one missions stretched the length of California, is credited with hav-

Que mon
F l a c o n
Me semble bon!
S a n s l u i
L ' e n n u i
Me nuit,
Me suit;
Je sens
Mes sens
Mourants,
Pesants.
Quand je le tiens,
Dieux! que je suis bien!
Que son aspect est agréable!
Que je fais cas de ses divins présents!
C'est de son sein fécond, c'est de ses heureux flancs
Que coule ce nectar si doux, si délectable,
Qui rend tous les esprits, tous les cœurs satisfaits.
Cher objet de mes vœux, tu fais toute ma gloire;
Tant que mon cœur vivra, de tes charmants bienfaits
Il saura conserver la fidèle mémoire.
Ma muse à te louer se consacre à jamais.
Tantôt dans un caveau, tantôt sous une treille,
Ma lyre, de ma voix accompagnant le son,
Répétera cent fois cette aimable chanson:
Règne sans fin, ma charmante bouteille,
Règne sans fin, mon charmant flacon!

ing brought the *Vitis vinifera* (the winemaking species of grapes) to the state in the form of the Mission grape. Although it was not ideally suited and produced and coarse wine, in the absence of any other variety, the Mission grape served as the backbone of California wines for over eighty years.

THE AMERICAN SAGA

By comparison to European wine history, the American saga is young. Several species of grapes, notably the *Vitis labrusca* and the Scuppernong, are indigenous to North America. Indeed, Leif Erickson, who tripped across the continent long before Columbus set sail, named the country Vineland. However, while the Concord and Catawba grapes flourished on the East Coast and around the Finger Lakes region of New York State, attempts to plant the fine *Vitis vinifera* vines of Europe were singularly unsuccessful. Scientists from the London Company tried. George Washington tried. Thomas Jefferson tried. No one succeeded. It is often the case that one man's happenstance is another man's fortune, and when a mysterious plague ravaged the French vineyards, the problem with American grape-growing became clear.

The *Phylloxera vastatrix*, indigenous to North America, is a pesky root louse which thrives on vine roots. Native American vines have thick skinned roots and are thus resistant to the burrowing insect; but the European vines, with more delicate root systems, quickly succumb to the pest as did the whole of Europe's most important vineyard districts during the 1870s following the importation of American vines. For a decade the best of France's vineyards were totally devastated until the phylloxera was identified as the cause of the plague. The solution, then as now, was to graft the *Vitis vinifera* vine to the American rootstock, and today *Vitis vinifera* grapes are grown in this way throughout the world. Phylloxera is no longer of concern, although many wine books still dwell on the subject.

The American wine industry really began to take shape in California. During the early 1800s three people were notable:

- Joseph Chapman, a transplanted Missourian arrived in California in 1823, established a vineyard, and was the first person to sell wine.

- Jean-Louis Vignes, a Frenchman from the Bordeaux region of France, emigrated to Los Angeles in the early 1830s and was the first to plant Europe's noble grapes.

- Count Ágoston Haraszthy, the most notorious and notable of them all, is also called the father of American winemaking. A nobleman in his native Hungary,

Haraszthy, for whatever reason, settled in Wisconsin in 1840 where he founded a town, wrote a travel book and established a number of business enterprises. After a brief trip to Europe, where he picked up his wife and a large quantity of vines, Haraszthy settled in California in 1852 and, among other things, planted a vineyard and gave the wine industry the push it needed. Haraszthy firmly believed that the best vines in the world could be grown in California and that the fastest results could be obtained by experimenting with many varieties. To that end, over the years, he imported and grew tens of thousands of different vines, and increased the California wine production by 50 percent. It is said that the adventurous Count met an untimely death in Nicaragua when he fell into the open jaws of crocodiles. The history of wine certainly has its intrigues!

The California wine industry prospered with the Gold Rush and suffered a downturn during the 1875 Depression, but by the 1880s and until 1919, when the Eighteenth Amendment calling for Prohibition was invoked, was very much a part of the fabric of American life, and wineries could be found near most major cities.

Prohibition had a more influential effect on the wine industry than any other law, discovery, or invention of the time. For not only did it set the American wine industry back an entire generation in terms of technology, but it set the stage for the domination and mystique of European wine.

With the exception of sacramental wines, Prohibition put the United States wine industry out of business, and in 1934 when Prohibition was repealed, the few existing wineries produced large quantities of fairly inexpensive dessert wines, high in alcohol, like Sherry and Port. Consequently, when a large quantity of the best quality French and German wines became available on the American market due to a downturn in the European economy, the emphasis of wine writers like Alexis Lichine and Frank Schoonmaker, who were also selling these wines, was, of course, placed on these prestige names. So began an essentially unwarranted emphasis on the prestige wines of Europe, which today is erroneously perpetuated. Although the modern California premium wine industry is only about twenty years old, great strides in technology of wine production have enabled California winemakers (as well as winemakers in other countries) to produce some of the truly fine wines of the world — wines that rival the prestige wines of France and Germany, and it may be said that, even today, we are entering a new period of wine history.

GRAPES AND VINES

The most commonly encountered question from the wine novice is this: "what separates fine wines from those that are merely good?" Or to continue, "what separates the good from the ordinary, and the ordinary from the mediocre?" Most "experts" say the difference lies in the taste: one wine "tastes better" or "greater" than another and then proceed to enumerate their favorite wines in various qualitative groupings. Such responses only lead to more questions, usually asked in silence.

Why for example, do some German Rieslings stand head and shoulders above those made from the same grape variety in California? Why does a Napa Valley Cabernet Sauvignon run circles around most Italian Chianti Classico? Why can't California Pinot Noir compete with the famed wines from Burgundy, for example a La Romanée-Conti, (considered to be the finest red wine in the world) also made from the Pinot Noir. Why doesn't New York State Sparkling Wine rival a great French Champagne? What divine reason can explain the majestic heights reached by the truly great wines of Bordeaux — Château Lafite-Rothschild, Château Latour or Château Mouton-Rothschild, for example.

Simply stated, the factors accounting for the differences between any two wines come from the limitless options exercised in these three fundamental winemaking variables:

- the grape variety (or varieties) used and how they are grown
- the climatic conditions, soil and topography in which the grapes grow
- the creative objective of the winemaker (vintner) and his skill and ability in achieving his intent.

There really is no mystery. No magic. Nobody waving a wand and uttering an incantation. Though at times a winemaker can alter and even enhance the nature of wine through fermentation, blending, and aging, the potential for any good wine begins with the grape itself. The greatest winemakers in the world could not convert poor grapes into fine wines. Winemaking techniques and the vintner's skill will be explored in Chapter Four. For now, let's look at the grape and the climate within which it is grown.

THE GRAPE

So far, approximately eight thousand grape varieties have been identified. While each could probably be made into wine, only about one hundred or so can make a balanced, palatable wine. Of that number, only twelve to fifteen grape varieties can yield wines considered great. The eight thousand grape varieties belong to about ten species, and some of these are suitable only as fresh table grapes or raisin varieties. The *Vitis vinifera* grape species is the wine-bearer of worldwide commercial importance.

Vitis vinifera was cultivated over five thousand years ago and is believed to be native to the regions around the Caspian Sea. It thrived in the Mediterranean Basin, was transported to Greece and Rome and became part of their cultural legacies as their empires expanded throughout Europe.

An American species of grape, called *Vitis labrusca*, is indigenous to the mid-Atlantic states; approximately two thousand varieties have been identified. The Concord grape, the best known *labrusca*, is widely planted in New York State and used to make very sweet wines. Concord is also widely used for grape juice, jellies, and jams.

All of the world's finest wines, especially the great ones, are made from one or more members of *Vitis vinifera*. The majority of the grape varieties yield wines that are "vinous" (wine-like). A certain few are capable of giving elegant, distinctive, identifiable wines, and these attributes have evolved and manifested themselves over hundreds of years of winemaking. For this reason, they are called the "noble" grapes. The noble red grapes include: Cabernet Sauvignon, Pinot Noir, Merlot, and Zinfandel. Among noble white grapes we have: Chardonnay, Riesling, and possibly the Sauvignon Blanc, and Gewürztraminer.

CLIMATE AND SOIL

The grape itself is the prerequisite for quality, but it requires support from both the climate and the soil. *Vitis vinifera* grapes are characterized by their sensitivity to climate and soil. Pinot Noir grown on the upper slopes of Burgundy, where the soil is rich in chalk and limestone and the climate very cool, can yield extraordinary wines like those from tiny vineyards, such as the famed La Tâche or La Romanée, which have qualities that defy description. In the fertile floor soil of the Napa Valley with hot, late-season weather, the resulting Pinot Noir wines are not the same. Cabernet Sauvignon grown in the hot climate and fertile soil of Fresno, California bears little resemblance to wines made in the small commune of Pauillac in the Bordeaux region of France.

The relationship of soil and climate to the quality of the grape is crucial to successful winemaking. Since it is all but impossible to isolate one factor without referencing it to winemaking and aging, we will move from one to the other when needed. The following chapters will focus on vinification and aging. All pieces of this winemaking puzzle are intended to provide an understanding of the factors which contribute to variances in wine quality.

"Balance", "harmony", "breed", "finesse", and "elegance" are words used to describe the qualities of "fine" wines. The potential for these fine wines begins with well-balanced, perfect grapes. Vintners (winemakers) can adjust for deficiencies in a grape, adding sugar to unripe grapes or adjusting a wine's acidity when too high or too low; however, sound ripe grapes picked within the ideal sugar and acid ratio are necessary to produce wines of extraordinary caliber. Sugar and acidity are functions of a grape's maturity at harvest, and optimum grape maturity is a function of climate, soil and vineyard practices.

Under less than optimum conditions, the grape will be out of balance. The sugar development can be either too low or too high affecting the alcohol level of the wine. The acidity can also be too high or low causing a wine to be sharp or dull. The grape's flavor could be either undeveloped or baked by heat; raisined, or with rain and humidity, suffering from rot and mold.

Ideal climatic conditions that enable wine grapes to thrive include:

- cold but not freezing winter months (for dormancy of the vine) and rainy winters to build up the water tables
- mild, frost-free spring weather
- gradually-warm, sunny, long, dry summer months
- mild, Indian summers in the fall.

These are, of course, ideal situations, and the chance for all or most of them to be satisfied is usually probable within the ranges of 34° to 49° North and South latitudes. But, here and elsewhere, exceptions exist. Germany's fine Rieslings grow at 51° North latitude, but the coldness of this northern location is compensated for by planting the vineyards facing south and west for maximum exposure to the sun, and usually near a river which has moderating influences. Conversely, in parts of Napa Valley, located at 39° North latitude, the intense heat during the day is compensated for by cool temperatures in the evening and early morning (aided by fog) which allows the grapes to recover.

THE VINE

The grapevine does not always grow true-to-type when planted from seed; consequently, most vines are propagated as cuttings or begin as cuttings grafted onto an already-growing vine root called a *rootstock*. Either way, the vine, once established, will spend most of its first year developing its root system. During the second, it experiences more top-growth through branches and leaves. By the third year (or third *leaf*) a healthy vine will produce fruit, i.e. grapes, that can be used in wine production. Vines will bear fruit well into their eightieth or one hundredth birthday, but with age production decreases. Consequently, the average life of a commercially productive vine is about twenty or thirty years.

By the second or third year, the grape grower (viticulturist) begins training or trellising the vine and an annual regime of pruning to control the quantity of fruit that the vine will produce, an essential element in producing well-balanced, mature grapes. Pruning normally takes place in mid-winter and involves the removal of old growth in order to regulate growth over the next year. Careful pruning thwarts a vine from wasting its energy on branches and shoots and encourages it to work producing quality fruit. Thus, the yield, or quantity, is regulated by the deliberate, calculated acts of the grape grower — winemaking indeed begins in the vineyard. Wine quality is inversely related to vine productivity; the fewer the grapes, the better the flavor and character .

There's an old axiom in grape growing that says the vine must "struggle". Planted in fertile soils, a vine produces enormous foliage, but grapes of weak character, but plant a vine in poor soil in an appropriate climatic environment, and the grapes are fragrant, balanced, and ideal for making fine wine. The relationship between yield and quality depends upon the type of vine, the climate and the kind of wine to be produced .

Training, trellising, and pruning can also compensate for the vine's environment or climate. In hot regions, vines are trained so that the foliage provides a canopy, or umbrella, to shade the grapes. In cool areas, the vines are stretched out allowing the grapes to be better exposed to the limited sunlight, thus facilitating photosynthesis needed for ripening.

The trunk of the vine bears the branches and the shoots which bear the flower-clusters that are ultimately converted into berries and grapes. In growing quality wine grapes, the root system and the leaves are the most crucial determinants. Depending on the vine's age and the soil, the root system usually bores down six to ten feet (and sometimes more, thirty feet is not unusual in certain soils) to seek out underground water and other nutrients (trace minerals) which add to the subtle nuances imparted to wines made from such grapes. Vines that struggle, that force their roots deep into the earth, produce a better quality grape.

In most wine regions today, new vines are grafted onto American rootstock in order to avoid the devastating root disease known as phylloxera. This is short for the *Phylloxera vastatrix*, a plant louse which was unknowingly transported to Europe in the nineteenth century when native American vines were imported into France. By the 1870s most European vineyards had fallen victim to phylloxera. Since then, the cure has been to graft the varieties onto native, phylloxera-resistant American rootstocks. Despite some unsubstantiated assertions to the contrary, there is no evidence that grafted vines produce wines inferior to those grown on their own roots.

An even more important consideration in the propagation of vines is the viruses which attack the leaf nodes of the vines early in the season, thus depriving the vines of adequate working foliage to bring the grapes to full maturity. Once infected, a vine can not be cured. The solution to this problem is to propagate virus-free vines, an exacting task begun in vine nurseries under the most sterile, scientific conditions. Fortunately, through modern science, grape vine propagation has developed into a fine art and the bright scarlet leaves of a virus infected vineyard will soon be a sight of the past.

The leaves play the most important role in determining a grape's quality. Through photosynthesis, they form and store carbohydrates enabling the plant to produce sucrose which is stored in the leaves. As the ripening period approaches, the leaves translocate the sucrose to the berries, forming larger and more sugar-rich grapes. Thus, by pruning and trellising, growers strive to encourage vines to push leaf development early in the season and then concentrate on the slow, incremental development of the grape sugar which is ideal for winemaking.

If the leaves are diseased, or if heavy rains, frosts, hail storms, or any of the many other possible blights destroy the leaves, the grapes can not properly mature, and even the most noble grapes will be inadequate to produce great wine. Thus, you can see how carefully-tended vines contribute to the quality of the grape, and, with the skill of the winemaker, to the wine.

The growing season of a vine differs with both the specific variety and, again, the climate. The average ripening period is 105 days; however, some grapes require as little as ninety days from budding to maturity, while others may require as many as one hundred and ninety days. The normal pattern is as follows:

> April 1st — bud break
> May 15th — flowering or blooming
> June 1st — berry set
> July 15th — berries begin ripening
> September 15th — maturity is reached

Sometimes nature makes such a pattern hypothetical. Spring frosts can ruin the flowers by stunting or destroying them. Excessive rains during the flowering and before the berry set time will create irregular-sized berries which will not ripen at the same time or at all. Rains occurring in the midst of maturity can swell the berries and thus dilute their sugar and acids or split the skins and rot the grapes; if severe and accompanied by winds, they may knock off or destroy the leaves before the grapes are fully developed and inhibit further ripening. The first late fall rainstorm may ruin the bold gamble of a winemaker shooting for highest possible maturity. High humidity is unwanted, since it encourages molds and mildew.

Aided by technology, the grape growers worldwide have discovered solutions for most normal climatic disasters. To prevent killer-frosts, heaters can be ignited in the vineyards or giant windmill-like fans started to stir the air — both to keep the cold temperatures away from the grapes. A system popular in California came about as an offshoot of an overhead sprinkling system for irrigation. As frost nears, the sprinklers are turned on sending a fine mist over the vines. The mist freezes, and the vine is protected from frost, since the energy needed to convert water into ice creates heat which then insulates the parts of the vine.

HEAT SUMMATION

Heat is the one factor most difficult to control. Without adequate sunshine, grapes do not ripen; with too much, they ripen too fast and in excess and often impart a "baked" taste to the wine. Heat in the early season can sunburn the grapes; longterm heat waves bake the acid out of grapes; and, of course, prolonged warm spells in the winter months prevent the vine from going into needed dormancy.

The importance of sunshine to grape development has long been recognized, but not until the 1930s did scientists plot out a relationship between temperature and the vine's growing season. Professors Amerine and Winkler of the University of California, Davis, completed a study of heat summation units which helps classify areas for grape growing. They analyzed the daily temperatures during the growing season and developed a system of vineyard classification based on degree days (similar to those reported by weather forcasters as a means of measuring the severity of the winter heating season). For the grapevine, 50°F was chosen as the temperature baseline, since the vine becomes inactive below this temperature. The time span chosen was April 1 to October 1, the typical normal growing season. The heat units are the total number of degrees of the mean daily temperature above 50°F, over the growing season. They are multiplied by the number of days in the season to yield total "degree days."

For example, if for a thirty day period the mean daily temperature was 75°F, then the heat summation is expressed as the difference between 75° and 50° degrees, (75° - 50° or 25°) which is multiplied by thirty days equaling 750 degree days for the period.

Amerine and Winkler then categorized climatic regions on the basis of degree days during the growing season. The lower total was the coolest; the highest, the hottest. For convenience they went with a five region scheme. These five regions were broken down as follows:

Region I — Less than 2,500 degree days
Region II — 2,501 to 3,000 degree days
Region III — 3,001 to 3,500 degree days
Region IV — 3,501 to 4,000 degree days
Region V — 4,001 or more degree days

At the time, the system proved helpful by enabling growers to plant varieties where they would fully ripen. Today, this system is a little too crude, too far-reaching, as it does not distinguish between whether the heat comes rather suddenly within a short period of time, or, steadily and constantly over a long time. Also, in some wine–growing regions, budbreak (the awakening of the vines following their dormancy during winter) does not occur until mid-May, and the harvest is just beginning in October.

Modern grape growers look at the heat summation units as they relate to the grape at various stages of development. As a grape ripens, its sugars and acids are constantly changing. Let's look at a few specifics:

- A grape which began as mostly acid, becomes predominantly sugar.
- As the sugars begin to increase, other constituents, notably acids, decrease.

- The chlorophyll in the skin of the grape is diminished, then lost.
- Flavor compounds are formed and for red grapes pigmentation is developed.

The heat summation over the critical periods affects the grape in many ways. First, it controls the rate of maturation — gradual or rapid. (The rates of change are unique to each variety.) Second, high heat can burn the skins and rob the grapes of flavor compounds and, for reds, color. Third, a grape under intense heat *weeps* or respirates, losing not only moisture but also acidity. Loss of the liquid content through dehydration or of acidity through respiration leads to unbalanced wines since the grapes and consequently the wine made from them could be high in sugar, but lacking in other essential components.

Therefore, regions with high heat accumulations can never produce wines of better than average quality. Also, even the best grapes grown in excessively warm climates may yield better than average wines, but never truly fine wines.

The heat summations system of defining grape growing zones has several applications. It indicates where, for example, early-maturing grapes (those needing 1700 to 2000 degree days) should be planted and where the late ripening varieties (needing over 3000 degree days or more) can mature. When applied to smaller sub-regions, or even individual vineyards, it can help locate zones within zones, a *microclimate* within a larger region. Such microclimates often are created by proximity to cooling water, wind breaks, and by elevation.

Now let's relate these back to soil. As mentioned earlier, a rich, fertile soil is usually unsuited to produce quality wine grapes. In fact, French winemakers, for decades, have argued in favor of the merits of gravel over loam, pebbly over sandy soil, and chalk and limestone over neutral soils. What now stands as important is that the soil be relatively infertile, but with some trace minerals to add subtle flavor nuances to the grape required for fine wine, and well-drained to prevent the vine from absorbing too much moisture after the rain. Rocky top soil may be advantageous, since the rocks absorb and then reflect needed warmth in climates which may be too cool; hard rockpan in the subsoil is bad, because the root system is forced outward, not down toward the deep water table.

A fine example of the impact of soil drainage is seen in the wines of France's Médoc, a sub-region of Bordeaux wherein subtle differences in soil composition can be found in many of its premiere wine producing communes. The meager topsoil is very gravelly in one of these small communes, Pauillac; a few miles away in another, Saint-Estèphe, the gravelly soils contain more clay and are heavier; thus, they retain more moisture. From the slightly-less-well-drained soils, the Saint-Estèphe wines lack the aromatic complexity and general finesse of those from Pauillac. Wines from each of these communes share distinctive characteristics and are subtlely but discernably different from those of the communes nearby. Thus, soil plays an important, albeit less crucial, role than that belonging to climate.

During the last forty years or more, scientists, geneticists, and researchers, knowing that climates can't be severely altered to suit wine grapes, have genetically altered wine grapes to better suit certain climates, producing grapes that mature earlier or at different times or with other special characteristics. These vines may be new *clones* of a specific variety; a cross of two varieties from the same species, or a hybrid of *Vinifera* and American (*Labrusca*) varieties. As examples: the widely planted Müller-Thurgau, a German cross between the noble Riesling and the earlier-ripening and less sensitive Sylvaner, retains a good deal of Riesling character but ripens earlier and is less sensitive to soil and microclimates than the Riesling. It has been widely planted in Germany replacing the Riesling in all but the finest vineyards. California's Ruby Cabernet, a genetic cross resulting from breeding the noble Cabernet Sauvignon with the prolific, highly adaptable, heat-loving Carignane, produces grapes for "jug" wines which have some of the better qualities of the more costly Cabernet Sauvignon. Emerald Riesling, a white grape that is a cross between the Riesling of Germany and the Muscat grape that thrives in hot regions, provides for fragrant, yet inexpensive, "jug" white wines. There are many others; undoubtedly there will be more. All are specifically developed to satisify the need for particular types of grapes grown in specific climatic conditions. They are the modern scientific solution to the crucial problems of unpredictable and uncontrollable weather.

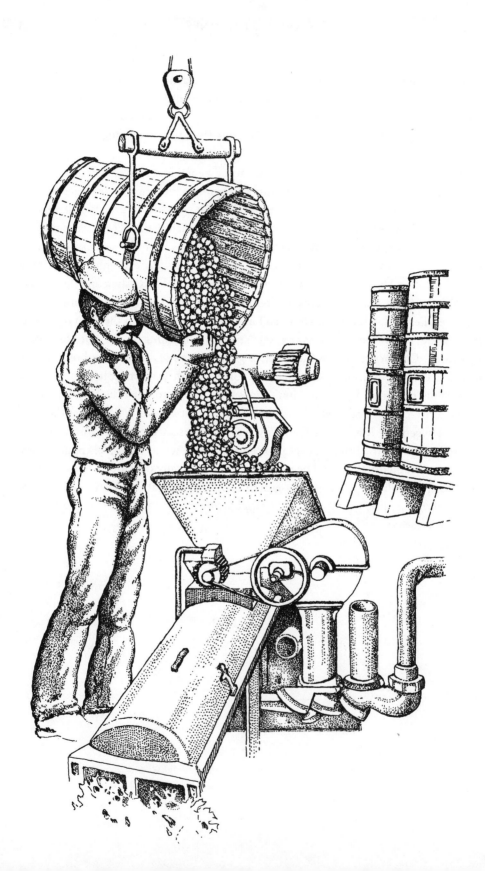

HOW WINE IS MADE

In the previous chapter, I listed the three major factors which interact to determine a wine's character: 1) the grape variety and how it is grown, 2) the climate and soil within which it is grown, and 3) the vintner's (winemaker) intent and expertise in making the wine. The importance of the grape variety, technically known as a *cultivar*, is indisputable, but without an ideal climate its chances of yielding high quality are limited. No winemaker can make top quality wine from bad grapes. Yet it is surprisingly easy to take fine grapes and end up with expensive vinegar or mediocre wine.

The vintner wears many hats, plays different roles. He is a scientist and an artist, a creator and a nursemaid. Over the last two decades technology has advanced and provided the vintner with more alternatives and a better comprehension of and control over the entire winemaking process than he ever had. Thus, good quality wines at low price levels are within the capacity of most winemakers.

As a scientist, the winemaker knows when and how to apply the best techniques; as an artist, he (or she) works to achieve something distinctive, a hallmark of his personal signature. How these two roles interact is determined by the winemaker's and the winery's creative and commercial objectives. Some winemakers are obligated to maintain a tradition, either on the basis of quality or the producer's marketing needs. Creativity is often stymied by external dictates.

Only a few fortunate winemakers in the world are allowed complete creative freedom. Some own the whole show and/or have been allowed to select the vineyard sites, the equipment, and the wine styles. Most others are hired hands inheriting a traditional approach or asked to follow predetermined guidelines. They may be allowed some room for modification and for experimentation, but usually only within certain restrictions. The available winemaking options vary from winery to winery; some winemakers have *carte blanche*, but most are limited.

It is important to be aware of the choices and limitations the winemaker has before him. Sometimes he is restricted by wine type itself, or by the region and its internal regulations, or by the requirements of commercial enterprise. This applies to winemakers in Burgundy, California, Chianti, and, in fact, most places. Those in Burgundy and in Chianti are limited to certain grapes, certain yields, and certain traditional vinification methods; those in California are forbidden to add sugar (*chaptalization*). Makers of top echelon red Burgundy have to maintain high standards. They could make red jug wines, but given the value of their vineyards, they would also go broke rather quickly.

WINE QUALITY

As I briefly described in the Introduction, I have divided table wines into the following three basic quality–tiers as they relate to winemaking options and economics.

JUG WINES

Regardless of bottle shape and size, jug wines can be viewed as a good drink, a beverage. They offer vinous (grape-like) flavor, along with body, balance, and straightforward appeal. They tend to have a short finish and aftertaste.

PREMIUM WINES

Here, the term is not related to price or prestige. Premium wines have more character and offer either the flavors and aromas usually attributed to the named grape variety (or varieties) or to the named region. Both texture and complexity will be apparent, and the taste will linger. Such wines can be recognized by the varietal or regional designations they bear on the label as part of their name.

NOBLE WINES

These offer flavors that are recognizable and distinctive, yet accompanied by more character and complexity. They capture the hard-to-find facets of "breed" and "finesse." Subtle, sometimes compressed; delicate, yet assertive — let's say they offer unique style. They gain complexity with prolonged aging; the reds will live for many years, are basically multi-faceted, frequently defying description, and offer an extremely long, marvelous aftertaste as well. The whites have an outstanding balance, either an exquisite depth of flavor or a harmonious delicacy, and that elusive quality called "breed." They will develop in the bottle and certain types, which I will describe later, will actually improve over many years in the bottle.

VIN ORDINAIRE

This is a fourth category, synonymous with the cheap carafe wine of Europe, so common in French bistros. Mass produced, it is without any personality, and ordinary for sure. The difference is that one can't say with certainty that these wines were made from grapes. Since they are seldom found in this country, they don't play any part in my schematic approach. Plant managers, not creative winemakers, turn out these wines.

My three quality-tiers relate to a winemaker's options, choices, which begin with the grape variety or varieties selected to make a wine. For example, Cabernet Sauvignon is a grape that can be made into jug, premium, or prestige quality wines. In the inappropriate soil and climates, it seldom surpasses jug quality and frequently will produce a lesser quality jug wine than other, more suited varieties. Jug wines need not possess any nuance of flavors and therefore, more ordinary, or lesser quality grapes will generally be used. To use finer grapes in jug wines may improve the wine, but will also add a cost which frequently is significantly greater than the contribution in terms of added quality.

Wine consists of more than simply grape juice and alcohol; otherwise, it could be easily produced by adding neutral alcohol to grape juice. During the process of fermentation, the various substances within the grape are broken down, dissolved into solution, transformed into new compounds, and chemically combined to create an entirely new substance. The nature of the process is so complex that scientists really do not understand every aspect of it. What they do know is that a typical fine wine contains literally hundreds of compounds in minute amounts which add or detract from its flavor and character. The basic constituents of a wine are: 1) water as part of grape juice; 2) alcohol created during fermentation; 3) acids inherent in the grape or produced during fermentation; 4) extract and tannin from the grape; 5) flavors from the grape; 6) flavors from the yeasts used for fermentation, and 7) flavors created by various interactions of the chemical compounds produced during the winemaking process. Aging in wooden casks further adds to the multiplicity of elements in a wine.

In the preceeding chapter I mentioned that fine wine requires quality grapes. Why is this so? To answer this question let's look at what each part of a grape contributes to wine quality. By themselves, the sugar and acid of a grape will produce an ordinary, rather neutral-flavored wine. If the sugar is too high, the wine will be either too high in alcohol or will contain unfermented sugar called *residual sugar* or *sweetness*. If the sugar is too low, the wine will be weak in body. The acidity of the grape must be in proper proportion to the sugar to produce a wine which will taste balanced. If the acidity is too high, the wine will taste too tart or harsh, too low, the wine will be dull or flabby. Besides alcohol and acidity, wine contains flavor and tactile elements which come from the grape's stem, skin, pulp, and even pits. Each makes an essential contribution to the totality of a wine.

THE GRAPE

Each variety of grape has its own exacting requirements. The key is picking the grapes when they have developed the correct level of sugar, acidity, and flavor maturity appropriate to the kind and style of wine into which they will be made. As grapes begin to reach maturity, all three components undergo relatively rapid changes. In warm winegrowing regions, the principle concern is the changing sugar-acidity ratio — ideally seeking good sugar without loss of necessary acidity. In the coolest regions of the wine world, the vintners are more preoccupied with achieving both adequate sugar and flavor ripeness. Frequently, grapes grown in cool climates ripen with an inadequate level of sugar. Fortunately this can be corrected, as we will see later. Grapes signal ripeness by changes in their constituents, with sugar levels increasing and acidity falling when the grape is ready. A few varieties, such as Gewürztraminer and Sauvignon Blanc, are *flavor-mature* within a narrow range of sugar development; when picked too late or too early, sometimes even within a matter of hours, the grapes lack their distinctive character.

Grapes, even within the same vineyard, may vary in maturity owing to differences in soil type, depth, fertility and water penetration. It is, therefore, crucial that the vintner test the grapes in every part of the vineyard. Using a refractometer, the vintner walks through his vineyard, and measures the sugar content of the grapes on the vine. This sugar, which will ferment into alcohol, is expressed in terms of degrees Brix. Depending on the final product for which the grapes are intended, an acceptable degree of ripeness ranges between 17 and 25 degrees Brix.

STEMS

Stems comprise 2 to 6 percent of the cluster's weight. They are rich in wood tannins but also impart a bitter flavor. For most wines they are removed prior to fermentation but are sometimes used in the vinification of red wines to augment tannins in the grape and add flavor complexity.

SKIN

Skin represents about five to 5 to 16 percent of the grape's weight. When mature, it is covered with a *bloom* of wild yeasts which may sometimes be used for the

THE WINE GRAPE

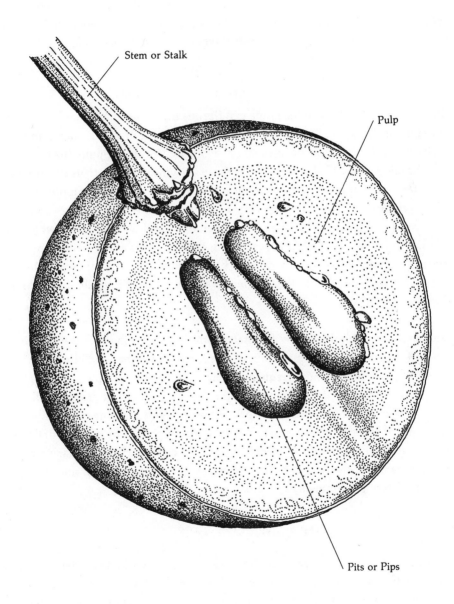

Stem or Stalk

Pulp

Pits or Pips

fermentation. The skin and the layers just below contain most of the of aromatic and flavor constituents of the grape. It also contains *tannins* (also called grape tannins which tend to be softer and less bitter than the tannins found in the stems and pits) which add an essential astringency to red wines meant for aging. Many high-quality white wines begin as unfermented juice left in contact with its skins for a few hours to a day or two to gain additional flavor or tannin. Red wines, which ferment in contact with the skins, ocasionally remain *on the skins* after fermentation is finished to leach out more tannins, color, and flavors. In either case, this is called *skin contact*.

PULP

Pulp contains the juice of the grape in a fibrous membrane and comprises most of the weight of the grape. The juice is a solution consisting of water, sugar, and acids which change their proportion as the grape matures. Within the pulp, the membrane holds the juice and is filled or depleted as the grape vine responds to its environment. The sugar in the grape can drop drastically when it is needed to support the vine under certain conditions. It may also be diluted if the vine receives too much moisture. The pulp also contains a number of complex fruit acids, which also undergo complex chemical changes, along with glycerines, proteins, and other elements which may or not be desired by the winemaker. In the end, the pulp presents a serious concern to the winemaker for he must remove all of it and retain only clear, clean wine.

Advances in technology now facilitate both the harvesting and transporting of grapes to the winery with a minimum of damage to the grapes. Hand-picking is still the rule, but more and more frequently giant machines, resembling preying mantises, work the vineyards through the night and day to harvest grapes at their optimum. These machines sometimes work in tandem with portable crushers, and the juice, crushed in the vineyard, is sent to the winery protected by a blanket of carbon dioxide to avoid premature fermentation and oxidation. However harvested, the key is to transport the grapes to the winery as quickly as possible since the grape begins to deteriorate immediately after leaving the vine.

THE WINE MAKING PROCESS

Once the grape is in his hands, the winemaker gets to work. The diagram on page 34 details the winemaking stages. In simplest terms, the grapes are picked and then dumped into a crusher/stemmer where the stems are removed and, for whites, the skins separated — the juice, called *must*, is pumped into a tank or vat. It then ferments on its wild yeasts or, more likely with modern winemaking, is inoculated with a selected yeast strain. The yeast enzymes react with the sugar, producing alcohol and carbon dioxide and, frequently, minute quantities of highly aromatic compounds which may or may not be pleasing. After fermentation, the transformed juice is called wine. The wine is stored in either casks or tanks; finally, it is clarified, stabilized, and ultimately bottled.

But these are the basic stages oversimplified, and it now remains to focus on the winemaker's involvement as he exercises his options throughout the process. I will confine my discussion to the three basic types of table wine — white, red, and rosé — to indicate how the quality-tiers mentioned earlier are achieved.

CRUSHING AND STEMMING

The juice of most grapes is white, and the wine's color comes from the pigmentation lodged within the skins. This colors the wine only while the juice remains in contact with the skins. Usually, white wine grapes are crushed and the must (juice) is immediately separated from the skins. In addition to contributing flavor, skins can impart bitterness, and sometimes tannins, to white wines. Depending on the type of wine he is making, however, the winemaker may allow some skin contact prior to fermentation.

For some white wines, notably full-bodied Champagnes and still table wines called Blanc de Noirs, dark-skinned grapes are used. The vintner moderates the color by controlling the time the juice remains in contact with the skins; usually the juice is immediately separated from the skins to prevent it from picking up anything other than a slight blush of color.

For red wines the skins remain with the juice and go into the fermentation vessel with it. Both color and tannins are leached from the skins during fermentation. Sometimes the stems also remain with the must, and some winemakers will even add back a percentage of stems which are believed to contribute to the firmness and complexity of some red wines.

Rosé wines remain on the skins just long enough to pick up their required hue and then are vinified in much the same manner as white wines.

FERMENTATION

During fermentation the winemaker is frequently both a scientist and a creative artist. His function may be simply to manufacture wine — such is the case for most jug wines. But for distinctive, quality wine, his role is much like that of a film director whose molding of characters and small scenes results in the creation of an artistic work. The winemaker directs a wine, molds its structure, flavors, nuances, and character to his personal vision, and similarly produces a vinous work of art. The birth of his vision begins with the fermentation. Whether it lasts for a few days or several months, fermentation is replete with chances for success and failure. It is a critical stage, analogous to the first few weeks in the life of a newborn child.

The alcoholic fermentation is described as the reaction between yeast and sugar to create alcohol and carbon dioxide. It is a complex chemical reaction involving numerous stages. The chemcial equation in its simplest form is as follows:

$$C_6H_{12}O_6 \quad = \quad 2C_2H_5OH \quad + \quad 2CO_2 \quad + \quad HEAT$$

natural grape sugar	ethyl alcohol	carbon dioxide gas	

The vintner's biggest concern is to have a healthy fermentation. Only certain yeasts are good for wine. Others can turn a wine right into vinegar or impart unpleasant flavors. The idea is to create a vigorous population of the appropriate yeast before an alien one can take over. The Bordeaux vintners pick some grapes early to develop a "starter vat" which is used to begin fermentation when all grapes have been picked. Once started, fermentation will continue slowly at first, then with increased acceleration. As the yeast cells multiply, fermentation will proceed, usually until all of the sugar is transformed into alcohol or the vintner has stopped, or arrested, the fermentation through one of several techniques. For most table wines, this occurs between 11 and 14 percent. Normally, should the alcohol level reach the 15 to 16 percent level, the fermentation stops automatically since most yeasts can not survive in a high alcohol environment.

The traditional fermentation vessel is a wooden vat or cement-lined tank, but the modern trend is toward using temperature-controlled stainless steel tanks. Stainless steel is neutral in flavor, easy to clean, and easily outfitted with cooling coils and a thermostatic temperature-controlled refrigeration unit.

The temperature of fermentation is an essential consideration in the winemaking process. Each variety of grape or strain of yeast reacts differently at various temperatures affording a kaleidoscopic range of winemaking possibilities. The winemaker's control of temperature to produce individual flavors, nuances of character, and harmony of structure, can be likened to a symphonic conductor's use of his baton to put his own mark on a work. In short, the essence of a wine as inter-preted by the winemaker begins with the control of a wine's fermentation temperature. But fermentations also produce heat as a by-product of transforming sugar into alcohol. In excess this is an enemy of wine. For example, high temperatures can make fermentation proceed at an irregular rate, often too rapidly; oxidize or break down certain aromatic compounds leading to a baked flavor, or spur the growth of undesirable organisms.

The rate and length of fermentation contribute to greater fruity fragrance, or com-plexity, of a wine. At low or cool temperatures, fermentation proceeds slowly, fre-quently for months. For white wines this slow fermentation retains the aromatic flavors of the grape and provides flowery, pleasing wines, particularly with the lesser grape varieties. Cold fermentation has been responsible for the vast improve-ment in most American jug wines. Today, most white wines are fermented within the 45° — 55°F range; reds generally ferment at the 55 — 75°F range. The character of many red wines is determined by the rate of fermentation at particular stages of the fermentation. This can be "fine-tuned" by the winemaker's careful control of his fermentation apparatus. Since the reds are fermented with both skins and seeds, the mass of solids, called the *cap* rises to the surface. To extract maximum flavors and tannins, as well as to allow for the release of heat, the cap must be broken from time to time. It can be manipulated in several different ways: 1) the must is pumped over the cap; 2) the cap is punched down several times a day, or 3) a *false top* is added to force the cap into the must.

The vintner monitors the fermentation frequently by checking the sugar, alcohol, acid, and balance through both tastings and laboratory analyses. Tasting is essential — many winemakers taste each of their wines at least once a day during crucial periods. Thus, he can make any needed adjustments, corrections, and apply new techniques along the way toward his intended goal.

Besides temperature control, there are hundreds of other choices in the winemak-ing process — too many to cover in this book. But what is most significant today is that the application of science to winemaking has allowed the experienced winemaker to produce wines using techniques which prevent many winemaking pit-falls from occurring. Thus, winemakers act rather than react in modern winemak-ing. Even so, ills develop, a fermentation may stop, an off-flavor may develop, or other unwanted condition may crop up. Today, technology allows the perspeca-cious winemaker to act early rather than react later with a severe "cure" to correct a mistake in the final wine. Then too, with modern laboratory techniques, the modern winemaker can sometimes leave a wine to its own devices, while monitoring it to be

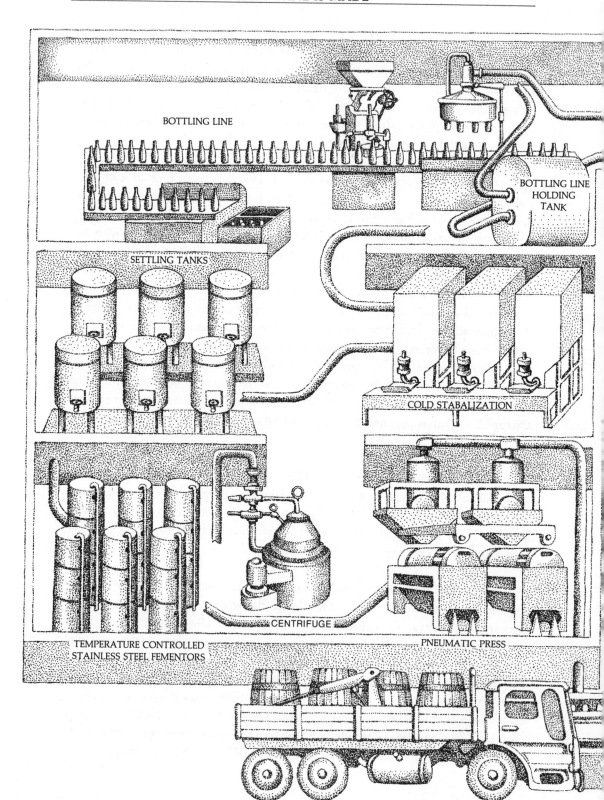

BOTTLING LINE

BOTTLING LINE
HOLDING
TANK

SETTLING TANKS

COLD STABALIZATION

TEMPERATURE CONTROLLED
STAINLESS STEEL FEMENTORS

CENTRIFUGE

PNEUMATIC PRESS

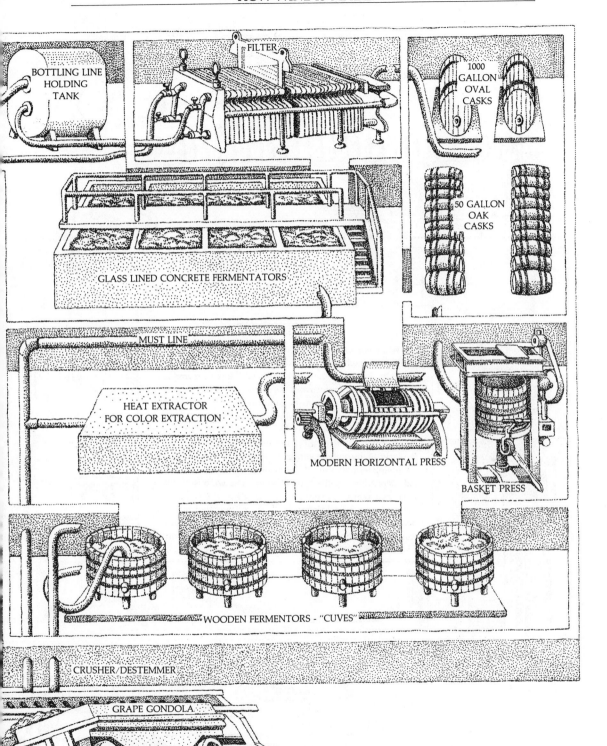

BOTTLING LINE HOLDING TANK

FILTER

1000 GALLON OVAL CASKS

50 GALLON OAK CASKS

GLASS LINED CONCRETE FERMENTATORS

MUST LINE

HEAT EXTRACTOR FOR COLOR EXTRACTION

MODERN HORIZONTAL PRESS

BASKET PRESS

WOODEN FERMENTORS - "CUVES"

CRUSHER/DESTEMMER

GRAPE GONDOLA

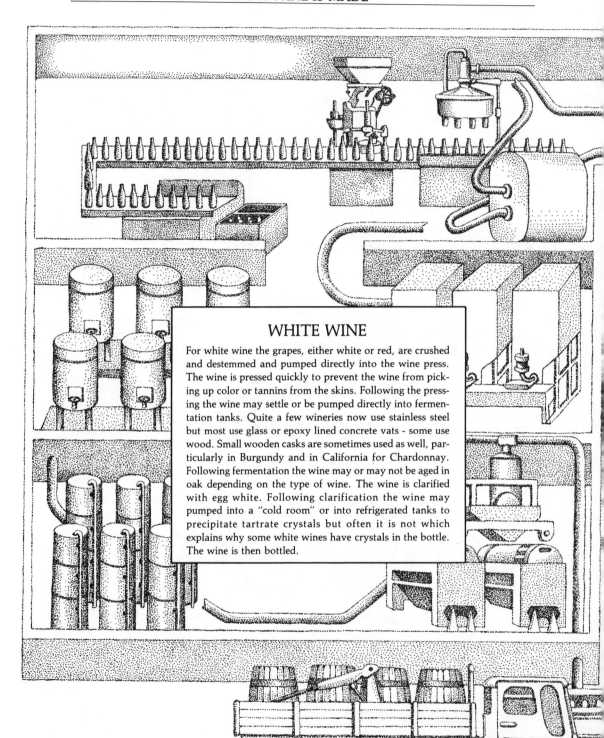

WHITE WINE

For white wine the grapes, either white or red, are crushed and destemmed and pumped directly into the wine press. The wine is pressed quickly to prevent the wine from picking up color or tannins from the skins. Following the pressing the wine may settle or be pumped directly into fermentation tanks. Quite a few wineries now use stainless steel but most use glass or epoxy lined concrete vats - some use wood. Small wooden casks are sometimes used as well, particularly in Burgundy and in California for Chardonnay. Following fermentation the wine may or may not be aged in oak depending on the type of wine. The wine is clarified with egg white. Following clarification the wine may pumped into a "cold room" or into refrigerated tanks to precipitate tartrate crystals but often it is not which explains why some white wines have crystals in the bottle. The wine is then bottled.

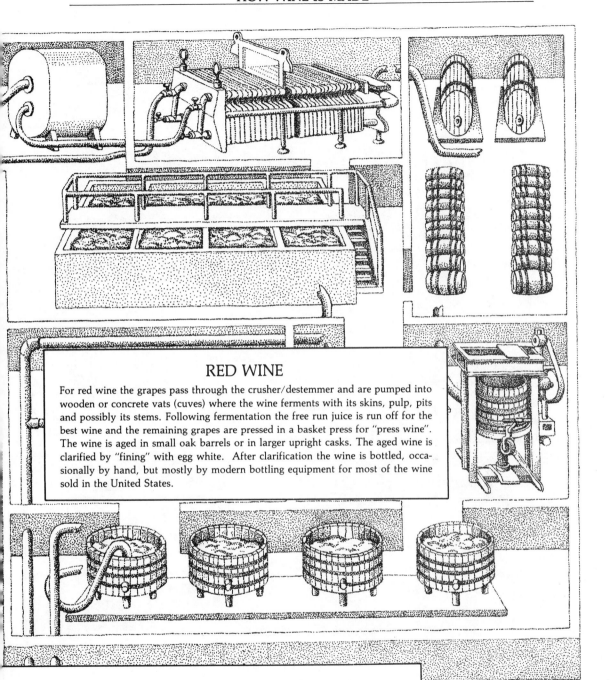

RED WINE

For red wine the grapes pass through the crusher/destemmer and are pumped into wooden or concrete vats (cuves) where the wine ferments with its skins, pulp, pits and possibly its stems. Following fermentation the free run juice is run off for the best wine and the remaining grapes are pressed in a basket press for "press wine". The wine is aged in small oak barrels or in larger upright casks. The aged wine is clarified by "fining" with egg white. After clarification the wine is bottled, occasionally by hand, but mostly by modern bottling equipment for most of the wine sold in the United States.

THE "TRADITIONAL" WINERY

The traditional winery lacks state-of-the-art equipment such as stainless steel fermentation tanks, filtration, centrifuge, and sterile bottling - important inovations essential to modern viniculture. While many of the world's greatest wines are still produced in a a facility such as this one, there has been a movement, particularly in Bordeaux, to utilize modern equipment to avoid the pitfalls of the traditional winery.

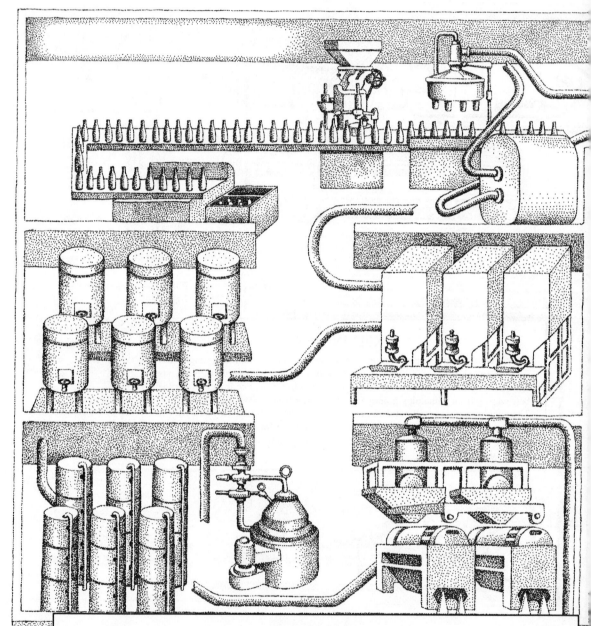

WHITE WINE

For white wine the grapes are brought to the winery in gondolas or special tank trucks blanketed with inert carbon dioxide or nigtrogen to prevent oxidation. State of the art techniques include mechanical harvesting and field crushing. The grapes are gently crushed in a special horizontal press to avoid harsh tannins. The grape juice is often centrifuged prior to fermentation. Or it may be centrifuged after or both. The wine is "cold fermented" to capture the freshness and fruitiness of the grapes. Depending of its type, the wine may or may not be aged in small or large wood casks. If the fermented wine has not been centrifuged it will be filtered. It is then cold stabilized to precipitate tartrate crystas. The wine is bottled in a state-of-the-art sterile bottling line to prevent air and other contaminents from entering the bottle.

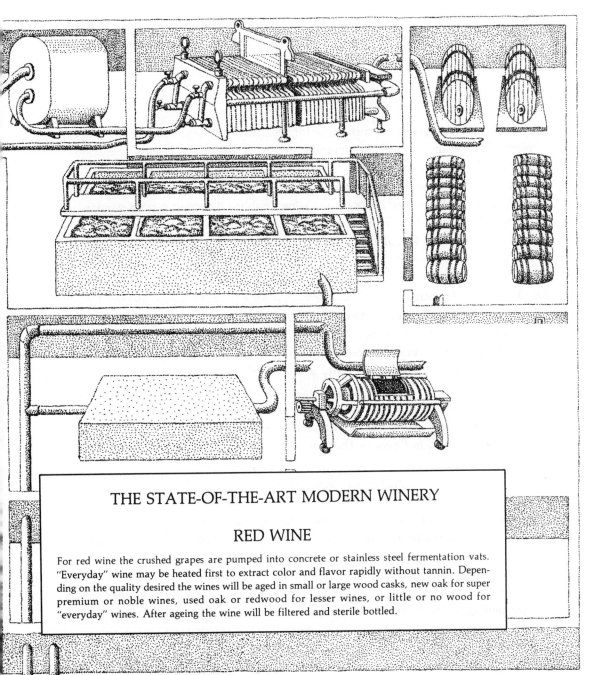

THE STATE-OF-THE-ART MODERN WINERY

RED WINE

For red wine the crushed grapes are pumped into concrete or stainless steel fermentation vats. "Everyday" wine may be heated first to extract color and flavor rapidly without tannin. Depending on the quality desired the wines will be aged in small or large wood casks, new oak for super premium or noble wines, used oak or redwood for lesser wines, or little or no wood for "everyday" wines. After ageing the wine will be filtered and sterile bottled.

sure that it is being a good child. Technology, when *appropriately applied*, benefits wine quality from jug to the finest of wines. Here are a few of the most common techniques.

CHAPTALIZATION

This is the process of compensating for insufficient natural sugar in the grape. Named after Jean Chaptal, one time Minister of Agriculture in France, chaptalization entails the addition of sugar, within certain legal limits, to fermenting wine. Adding sugar compensates for insufficiently ripe grapes of a cool vintage. It increases both the alcohol level and the body of a wine, enabling it to meet certain standards. Permitted in France and Germany, and allowed to happen in most European countries, it is forbidden in California (where it isn't needed anyway) and several other countries. It is allowed in New York, Oregon, and other states in the United States.

When used to increase the alcohol level of a wine by a small amount, say 1 percent, the use of the process when carefully applied is virtually undetectable, even by an expert. The amount of sugar needed is easily calculated — no guessing is required. Many critics decry the technique claiming it affects the quality of the wine, but such need not be the case. Only when the chaptalization process is ineptly employed or used to excess is the character of the wine adversely affected. Carelessly chaptalized (but within acceptable and legal limits) wine could become alcohol-imbalanced, tasting hot or harsh. When used to excess, the resultant wine will taste hot, thin or diluted in flavor or character.

ADJUSTING RESIDUAL SWEETNESS

Many styles of wine require that some of the natural sugar in the grape not be entirely transformed into alcohol. These include the low alcohol, sweet, late harvest wines renowned in Germany, which are produced by arresting the action of the yeasts once the desired level of alcohol or sweetness is achieved. Chilling the fermenting must and removing the yeast cells by filtering to prevent the wine from refermenting is one way to accomplish this. For other styles, fortified sweet wines for example, alcohol added to the fermenting wine kills the yeast and ceases the process.

Many styles of white wines retain a slight sweetness, usually around 2 percent. Chilling frequently does not provide the winemaker with the control to provide the balance needed for these wines. The modern technique is to ferment the wine completely dry and add an appropriate amount of grape juice, which has been set aside to sweeten the wine. The resultant wine can be adjusted with more precision and permits the winemaker to more easily stabilize the wine to prevent it from refermenting in the bottle. This technique is known as sweet reserve or muté and is commonly employed in the United States and Germany where fine, well-balanced, fragrant, slightly sweet, table wines are produced.

THE CENTRIFUGE

The centrifuge can be called God's gift to the winemaker. Those who have one swear by it; those who don't, wish they had. The centrifuge is to the vintner, what the Cuisinart is to the modern homemaker — nirvana! The device, which has a wide and varied usefulness in the winemaking process, simply swirls the wine at high speed taking advantage of the laws of gravity and the fact that certain components of wine weigh more than others. The spinning separates these components according to their molecular weight, thus removing unwanted solids such as yeast cells, pulp, dirt or dust, and the like, and clarifying the liquid passed through it. While the machine sounds simple, in fact it is rather costly and only well-capitalized facilities can afford one. Once installed, it is relatively inexpensive to use.

Many winemakers finding that the centrifuged juice ferments easier and produces a cleaner wine than that which is fermented in the conventional method, use the centrifuge to clean white wine must before fermentation. Fermented wine, both white and simple reds may be centrifuged instead of racking or filtering (see page 44). Wines with certain off-flavors may receive a heavy centrifuging which will strip them of all character but salvage an otherwise unusable wine. It is essential that any wine with residual sugar be entirely free of yeast cells or bacteria when bottled. The centrifuge is widely used to clean jug quality wines just prior to bottling.

ACIDITY CORRECTION

Acidity is the backbone and a key element of a wine's balance. Frequently, the natural acidity is insufficient to provide an appropriate balance to a wine, or, the acidity may decrease during fermentation and may require adjustment. Under these circumstances, acid is added to a wine. This practice is permitted, legal, and universally used even for the finest of wines. Various types of acid are used depending on the style and quality of the wine.

- Tartaric acid, a natural acid in wine, is the most costly to use since it is expensive to produce and difficult to use. Tartaric acid has no distinct flavor of its own, and marries perfectly with wine flavors. Its major disadvantage is that it is unstable in wine and naturally precipitates in the form of potassium bitartrate crystals. It is not unusal for a winemaker to add expensive tartaric acid as a li-

quid, only to discover it transformed into cheap (to buy) crystals shortly thereafter in the bottom of the vat. Its use can add substantially to the cost of a wine.

- Citric acid, the acid of lemons, is relatively inexpensive and is used for many inexpensive wines where the full, less refined flavors mask or marry well with any
flavors imparted by the acid.

- Blending high-acid wines with acid-deficient wines is another commonly
employed method. Careful selection of the blending wines is essential to avoid
clashing flavors in the resultant blend.

A wine too high in acidity can be corrected in several ways:

- Blending is often used as described above. Here low-acid wine is added to the
offender.

- Ion exchange is another method frequently used to adjust excessive acidity. By
passing wine through a bed of sodium ions, the positively charged metal ions
are taken up. Removal of these ions lowers the acidity but also affects the pH of
the wine as well. The pH is a measure of the free hydrogen ions in a liquid,
basically a measure of acidity, but for our purposes, perhaps best described as
the measure of the alkaline quality of a wine. Within a rather narrow range,
and within specific levels of acidity, a low pH tastes acid-like, a high pH tastes
alkaloid. Thus it is not unusual for wines run through an ion exchanger to taste
flat, without life, as a result.

OFF THE LEES

But now, let's return to our winemaking process. Once primary fermentation is
complete, the wine is drawn off the lees and placed in tanks or large casks, usually to
allow the remaining solids suspended in the wine to settle. The wine that flows free-
ly, without pressure, is called *free-run juice*. It is the cleanest and usually most
distinctive wine. For wines fermented on the skins, the remaining pulp, containing
juice is pressed leaving behind a cake-like mass of solids called *pomice*. This wine is
called *press wine*. It varies from *light press* to *heavy press* depending on the pressure
exerted. Frequently the wine is segregated into different vats as the pressing proceeds. The heavier the press, the darker the color, the fuller and coarser the flavor,
and the more bitter and tannic the resulting wine will be. Often each press batch is
handled and aged separately, it may be combined with another wine later on in
some proportion, or not at all.

Certain microorganisms, which may come along with the grape or be present within the winery or the casks, can survive both the fermentation process and the eventual development of alcohol. The two most common bacteria are the *Acetobacter xylinum* and the *Lactobacillus*. The *Acetobacter xylinum* is always present in small amounts in fermenting wine and produces small and acceptable levels of acetic acid (vinegar). It also produces ethyl acetate, a compound which smells slightly of nailpolish remover. Together, and in slight amounts, these compounds add to the complexity of a wine. The *Acetobacter xylinum* thrives on fermented wine, and in the presence of oxygen quickly turns wine completely into vinegar by converting the alcohol into acetic acid. For this reason, air is considered the enemy of wine. As we will see, the spectre of the *Acetobacter xylinum* is the bane of the winemaker. From this point in the winemaking process, he must be on constant guard and exercise utmost care to prevent it from ruining his wine.

Lactobacillus is the most common variety of lactic acid bacteria; it is harmless to humans. In the fermentation process it produces by-products which add to the complexity of a wine. Occassionally *Lactobacilli* run out of control, producing a pungent and offensive odor of geraniums which can only be corrected by stripping a wine of all its flavors.

There are many other dangers, humorously referred to as "bugs" by winemakers, which can interfere in the wine's progress from the vat to the bottle. Modern winemakers are able to control these problems when they occur, and fortunately, the off-characters they produce are rarely encountered in wines offered by modern wine producers.

At this point in the process the jug quality wines are basically finished. They require the final clarifying and stabilizing which will be described later, but little else; but for wines of the premium class and better, the process has just begun. It usually continues for at least one year, and frequently for as many as four or more, and involves many additional steps. From this point our focus is on these better wines.

Once the wine has progressed to a settling vat, it is ready to undergo a bacterial fermentation, commonly called the *second fermentation*, technically known as the *malolactic fermentation*. It may or may not be wanted. A malolactic fermentation transforms the wine's malic acid, which tastes hard or more acidy, into lactic acid which tastes softer or less acidy, but with only a slight decrease in the actual measurable acidity of the wine. It also produces certain by-products which may or may not taste good or be appropriate to a particular kind of wine. At this point it is up to the winemaker to encourage or prevent this malolatic fermentation.

Malolactic fermentation is not desirable for most whites since it reduces the wine's sense of crisp freshness. As mentioned in Chapter Nine, Chardonnay is an exception to this rule. When it undergoes a malolactic fermentation diacetyl is produced and imparts a buttery complexity (diacetyl is the major flavor component of butter) which marries well with the flavors of the Chardonnay.

For many red wines, particularly those made from the Cabernet Sauvignon, Pinot Noir, and similar noble varieties, the malolactic fermentation is desired as it softens the acid taste, and adds considerable complexity, flavor nuances, and suppleness to the wine. Many wines tend to undergo malolactic fermentation spontaneously when temperatures warm up during the spring after the harvest. Winemakers can let this happen naturally by leaving wine in barrels or tanks that will warm with the weather, or they can induce it by introducing a malolactic strain of bacteria. The winemaker must use great care to ascertain that the malolactic fermentation is completed before bottling because the red wines, which benefit from the process, can not be preserved in the same way that many simpler wines can and thus are susceptible to defects which can occur later in the bottle. A malolactic fermentation which continues after the wine is bottled causes the wine to become fizzy, with stinky flavors that will not dissipate after the wine is poured.

RACKING

Once the wine has completed its fermentation it must be clarified. Racking, a natural way to clarify wine based on gravity, has been the traditional method and is still the best one for quality wines. In racking the wine rests in small casks to permit the suspended solids to settle. The clear wine or juice is then pumped or siphoned off the *lees* (sediment — old yeast, grape skins and solids, potassium bitartrate) and into a clean, fresh tank or cask. The racking schedule is frequent within the first year, often five times or more, which requires considerable labor, and includes cleaning the previous casks.

The frequent rackings aerate the wine at important intervals ridding it of natural by-products of the winemaking process which can impair its healthy development. But racking must also be done with care since excessive contact with air can cause the wine to turn to vinegar.

The most dangerous of these by-products is hydrogen sulphide which smells like rotten eggs and occurs naturally during the yeast fermentation (more or less depending on the strain of yeast). It *must* be dissipated early in the clarifying procedure since it rapidly combines with the alcohol to form a compound called mercaptan.

Mercaptan is among the most odorous of all chemicals; its smells range from onions, children's clay, garlic, to skunk! Once it has completely *bound* with the alcohol it will not leave the wine. Careful winemakers make sure that all the hydrogen sulphide has been aired out of the wine. Still, the mercaptan odors are a universal defect in wine — a stigma of sloppy winemaking.

GRAPE VARIETIES

The grapes described below represent the vast majority of varieties that the wine enthusiast will encounter, either in further reading about wine or on the labels of wine bottles. There are many more, but they are not important here. The wine varieties encountered in most wines will generally belong to one of two species, the *Vitis vinifera,* which is the wine grape of European origins and the one which is responsible for all the fine wine of the world, and the *Vitis labrusca*, which is the native North American variety used for inexpensive jug wines produced within the United States, and whose roots are used for rootstock in propagating all *vinifera* vines throughout the world.

ALICANTE-BOUSCHET is a red French *vinifera* cross grown extensively in France for use as a blending wine for its intense, dark color. It is also used for nonfermented grape juice. It is an early-ripening grape and was a favorite among home winemakers during Prohibition.

ALIGOTÉ is a white *vinifera* grape grown in the Burgundy region where it is used as a blending wine with other varieties, though it is sometimes seen as a varietal with a "Bourgogne" appellation. The wine is common and without distinction.

AURORA is a fairly neutral-flavored white French hybrid popular in sparkling wine *cuvées* (blends) in the northeast and midwest regions of the United States. It is sometimes spelled Aurore.

BACO NOIR is a red French hybrid widely cultivated in the eastern United States and often seen as a varietal. Its wines offer good color, a medium body, and flavors that range from vinous to slightly spicy.

BARBERA is a red *vinifera* variety primarily grown in Italy and in California. It is found in many Italian districts where it is usually bottled as a varietal identified by a place name, i.e., "Barbera d'Asti." Depending upon the growing conditions and location, the Italian versions range from pleasantly fruity to slightly rich and tart in flavor. The plantings in California are primarily in warm to hot regions; thus, the wines tend to be fruity and soft, usually blended into jug wines, though an occasional robust, rough, rich wine appears.

CABERNET FRANC is a red *vinifera* and member of the Cabernet family. It is widely planted in France from the Loire Valley to Bordeaux and also in the Midi. It is a minor variety in Bordeaux, and slightly more important in Saint-Émilion. Its wines are rounder and softer than Cabernet Sauvignons with less pronounced personalities. California winemakers are still experimenting with the grape.

CABERNET SAUVIGNON is the red *vinifera* crowned the indisputable king of the noble red grapes. Ideally, its wines can possess great depth of flavor and intensity of color and develop both finesse and breed with bottle aging. It grows well in many wine regions yielding wines ranging from outstanding to mediocre in quality. In France, it is responsible for the high reputation of Bordeaux red wines and represents the predominant element in many of the finest bottlings. In northern Italy it can yield reasonable facsimilies to Bordeaux, and it is also found in many eastern European countries, resulting often in pleasant, light-style wines. Cabernet has achieved remarkable success in California with many bottlings on a par with Bordeaux, and others running the entire quality gamut. South American countries, particularly Chile and Argentina, produce vast quantities, but a few bottlings have been excellent. Cabernet Sauvignon is at its best and long-lived when made close to 100 percent, but it has an affinity to be blended with other wines, such as Cabernet Franc, Merlot, and Petit Verdot in the Médoc; Merlot and sometimes Zinfandel in California, and Shiraz in Australia. Its recognizable varietal character is a spicy, bellpepper aroma and flavor, with high astringency, and deep-color wines made from very ripe grapes are often minty and cedary, with a black currant or cassis character.

CARIGNAN, a red *vinifera* variety, probably of Spanish origin, is the most widely planted grape in all of France. It yields wines with good, deep color, but ordinary vinous flavors and a coarse finish. The vine is prolific, and the grape ripens late in the season. It is used in California mostly as a blend for red jug wines, but a few wines are bottled as varietals.

CASCADE NOIR, a red French hybrid, is grown in parts of the Eastern United States. Usually blended, it is rarely seen as a varietal.

CATAWBA is a red American hybrid with *labrusca* parentage. It is grown widely in the Eastern United States and is used for Champagnes, sweet red and white wines, and many rosé wines. It is distinctly *labrusca* or "foxy," in character.

CHANCELLOR NOIR is a red French hybrid yielding deeply-colored, vinous wines that are occasionally varietally bottled. Most often, though it is used as a blending grape.

CHARBONO is a red *vinifera*, known as such only in California. As of yet, it has never been clearly identified as either Italian or French in origin. Its wines are dark, often inky in color, high in tannins, powerful, without evidencing charm or finesse. They can live for decades, but improvement and development is marginal at best. These wines are usually made in small quantities as the pride of a few wineries.

CHARDONNAY is sometimes mislabeled "Pinot Chardonnay," but is a white *vinifera* yielding the finest white wines with both power and finesse. A French variety, it now grows successfully in many different countries; but it is noted for the fabled white wines from France's Côte d'Or region of Burgundy and primarily identified with such legendary names as Montrachet, Meursault, and Corton-Charlemagne. In northern Burgundy it is responsible for Chablis and plays a role in many wines from Champagne, particularly those called "Blanc de Blancs," which are made entirely from white grapes. In California, the styles of Chardonnay vary widely; some made from ripe grapes are fermented and aged in French oak barrels to yield round, rich wines—flavorful, powerful, and oily in texture. Others approximate that style to lesser degrees, while a few non-oak versions capture the direct fruitiness of the Chardonnay in a crisp style. Most California Chardonnays tend to be fuller in body and higher in alcohol than those from France.

CHELOIS is a red French hybrid that yields a robust, fruity wine on its own. Mostly, it is used as a blended wine for early consumption.

CHENIN BLANC is a white *vinifera*, widely planted in the Loire Valley where it is used for both still wine and *vin mousseux* (sparkling wine). It is also popular in California, Australia, South Africa, and South American wine countries. It is essentially a fruity, barely distinct wine ranging from bone dry (accompanied by a bitter flavor) to slightly and even very sweet. The best sweet versions come from the Coteaux du Layon in France and rise to legendary quality on occasion. Generally, its aroma is reminiscent of fresh peaches; when harvested early, it displays a slightly grassy aroma.

CINSAULT is a red *vinifera* grape rapidly growing in popularity in southern France. It is productive and ripens in the mid-season, yet is capable of yielding soft, fragrant wines in warm to hot climates. It is used as a blending wine in the Rhône Valley and also in South Africa, where it is one of the parents of the South African grape, Pinotage.

FRENCH COLOMBARD is a prolific white *vinifera* grown in several countries. In France, it figures as a Cognac grape for its productivity and high acidity. As a wine, it has a slightly grassy and often tart profile, but is usually finished somewhat sweet. Fruity and simple, it is widely used in jug wines and in sparkling wine *cuvées*.

CONCORD is a native American *labrusca* grape. It is the mainstay of the grape juice and jelly industries as well as the Kosher wine and inexpensive eastern Champagne markets. Its predominant characteristic is its grapy, foxy, aroma and taste which dominates even when the wine is blended. It produces wines which are harsh, acid and overwhelmingly grapy unless treated to remove some of the grapy taste, sweetened with excess sugar, or subjected to other processes to give it a creamy body. It is a prolific producer that survives the northern winters which makes it a popular variety with eastern grape growers. Red, white rosé and Champagne wines made from it are generally inexpensive.

DELAWARE is a white native American variety. Grown in many eastern states, it is produced as a varietal and as a blending grape for jugs and Champagnes. It is quite aromatic with the typical *labrusca* foxiness and is made as dry, semi-sweet and sweet wine.

DIAMOND is a white native American hybrid, which is used as a base wine for eastern Champagne and inexpensive jugs. When bottled as a varietal, it produces wines with the typical *labrusca* grapiness and a spicy fruitiness but is without distinction.

DUTCHESS is a white native American hybrid variety. It produces both relatively neutral, fruity wine used for blending, and varietals. When bottled as a varietal, it usually is quite sweet with muted *labrusca* flavors.

EMERALD RIESLING is a *vinifera* hybrid. It was developed in California by the University of California as a high-quality blending grape ideally suited to the wide range of soils and climates of California's wine growing regions. It is a cross of White Riesling and Muscat which can produce light, stylish, fragrant wines that have the fruity quality of Riesling with the spice of the Muscat grape. It usually produces slightly sweet wine that is fairly low in alcohol and with a tart acidity.

FOCH is a red French hybrid that is popular with small eastern United States and home winemakers as a deep colored, robust varietal. It is used as a blending grape for its fruitiness and deep color.

GAMAY is a red *vinifera* French variety. In California, it is also known as Napa Gamay. In many wine regions this variety produces harsh, acidic wines. Traditionally banned in most of Burgundy, it achieves a special quality in the Beaujolais region where it produces light, delightfully fresh and fruity wines for immediate consumption. In California, it produces a medium-bodied red wine with good fruit, balance and vinosity but without lively character and charm. Produced as a *nouveau* style in Beaujolais it renders a fresh, fruity wine with strawberry and or raspberry flavors; it is imitated in California but less successfully.

GAMAY BEAUJOLAIS is a red *vinifera* variety, which is found mostly in California. For decades, this grape was thought to be the same as the Gamay of Beaujolais but is now believed to be a clone of the Pinot Noir. It is a highly productive variety that is used for blending as well as varietal bottling of a simple, fruity, light-colored, light-bodied wine which is made for immediate consumption.

GEWÜRZTRAMINER, a white *vinifera* variety, is a clone of the Traminer grape and grown in many wine regions of the world. It is best known in the Alsace region of France where it is bottled as a varietal made in a completely dry or slightly-sweet style. It has a distinctive spicy and floral aroma which is easy to recognize. The Gewürztraminer is a difficult-to-grow, pink-skinned grape which is sensitive to its soil, location, and growing techniques. Its spiciness is most intense in the Alsace region and can be elusive in other regions where its flavor is sensitive to its ripeness and other factors. Without its distinctive spiciness, it produces a dull and unexciting wine. In Alsace, the grapes are harvested when still high in acid and produce an austere, intensely dry wine when at its best. It is made slightly sweet there to disguise flaws in quality; in Germany, it is made slightly-sweet and semi-sweet with a more subtle spiciness than in Alsace as a matter of style. Late Harvest Gewürztraminers are occasionally found, usually as a curiosity. In California, they are produced sometimes completely dry where they exhibit a slight bitterness, or slightly sweet and less intensively spicy. A few Late Harvest Gewürztraminers have been made in California in the German style with varying success.

GRENACHE is a red *vinifera* Spanish variety. In France, this grape is known best for its full bodied rosés and simple, fruity reds. In Spain, it is known as the Garnacha and is one of the many varieties blended to produce Rioja. The Grenache is grown throughout the world and produces simple wines, usually used in blends. In California, it is usually blended into generic rosé and red jug wines, although a number of wineries offer it as a varietal rosé. The grape exhibits a distinctive orange color and a fruity, strawberry flavor which makes it ideal for rosés and blending. In the Rhône Valley of France it is used to produce Tavel, a rosé, which at its best is full bodied, assertive, dry and bronze-colored. It is used as a blending variety in Châteauneuf-du-Pape, Gigondas, and Côtes du Rhône, the well known reds of the Rhône. It also produces both full-bodied, fruity reds and stylish rosés in the Languedoc and Provence regions of France. It thrives in hot climates and is found in many hot-climate wine regions throughout the world where it is blended into generic reds and rosés.

GREEN HUNGARIAN is a white *vinifera* variety. This grape produces an ordinary wine and is usually blended into generic whites. In California, a few wineries offer it in varietal versions which range from sweet to dry but none has any distinction. Contrary to its name, the variety is unknown in Hungary.

GREY RIESLING is a white *vinifera* variety known in France as Chauché Gris. It is not a member of the Riesling family and is so named predominantly in California where it produces a simple, fruity, sometimes spicy and slightly sweet, decent wine.

GRIGNOLINO is a red *vinifera* variety of Italian origins. Grown also in California as a varietal, it produces a light, pungent, spicy wine with an orange tinge. Basically it is a light-colored red with the character of an intense rosé. It is best when young.

JOHANNISBERG RIESLING or RHINE RIESLING or WHITE RIESLING is a white *vinifera* German variety. This, the real Riesling for which the noble wines of Germany are so justly famous, is grown throughout the world and made into many styles of wine but attains its distinction when grown in cool climates in inhospitable soil. It is a difficult grape to grow in such locales and frequently fails to ripen in less-than-ideal vintages. It is a shy bearer which also contributes to the relatively high cost of the fine wines made from it. In Germany, where it attains its legendary heights, it produces a variety of qualities and styles depending on the region where it is grown. It is particularly sensitive to soil and vineyard location and produces wines of disparate qualities virtually on the same hillside. At best, it produces wines with depth and intensity, ripe but delicate peachy or apricot flavors, and exquisite balance and finesse; unripe, it produces austere, thin and unpleasantly acidic wines of little merit. When late-harvested, it produces a concentrated wine of great elegance with the ultimate nectar, a luscious, complex and intensely-sweet wine which is low in alcohol. This wine, *Trockenbeerenauslese*, is produced from grapes attacked by the *Botrytis cinerea*, (the noble rot) and picked as late as December. The elegance achieved in the steep, terraced vineyards of the best German regions (Mosel, Rhine, and Palatinate) is rarely replicated elsewhere, although fine examples of Riesling styles are found in France, South Africa, Australia, Austria, South America,

Yugoslovia, and many other countries including the United States. In the Alsace region of France the Riesling is made in a dry, austere style quite different from that of Germany. The wines are refreshing with firm acidity and body. In California, the Rieslings, labeled as Johannisberg Riesling, after the famous Johannisberg vineyards of Germany, are produced in several styles ranging from completely dry to semi-sweet, and from high-alcohol, wood-aged wines to those with moderate alcohol and no cask aging. The recent trend in California is to produce wines with more delicacy, revealing more of the varietal essence and charm of the grape. Recent production of Late Harvest styles, made with *Botrytis*-affected grapes has achieved qualities equal to the finest of Germany. In Chile, the Rieslings resemble the light and austere style of the Franken wines of Germany.

KERNER is a white German *vinifera* cross based on Riesling. With Riesling characteristics, it is a relatively new grape variety for Germany, and is planted to avoid deficiencies of that temperamental variety. It produces a fruity and spicy wine with good acidity and is used for blending in regional wines, although it is frequently the predominant grape and is often so indicated on the label.

MALBEC is a red *vinifera* French variety grown in many wine regions but rarely found as a varietal bottling. It is used in Bordeaux to provide longevity and elsewhere to provide body and substance to blended wines. Small quantities are being produced in California on an experimental basis. Some good varietals come from Argentina.

MERLOT is a red *vinifera* French variety which is grown in many wine regions. This is an early ripening, medium-colored red grape which, when made as a varietal, produces soft and supple yet substantial wines. In France, it is responsible for the renowned wines of Pomerol and produces wines of depth, complexity and longevity. In the Médoc and other regions of Bordeaux it is an essential part of the *cépage*, providing an elegance and mellowing ingredient to the Cabernet Sauvignon. It is grown throughout Italy and produces fine, well-aging wines in the northern parts of that country. In California, an increasing number of wineries are producing varietal bottlings but it is also recognized for its importance as a mellowing agent in blending with Cabernet Sauvignon. Compared to Cabernet Sauvignon, it has a distinctive herbaceous aroma quite different from the bell pepper quality of the Cabernet and is softer in tannins and often lower in acidity, producing a rounder, fatter, wine that generally matures considerably earlier.

MÜLLER-THURGAU is a white *vinifera* which may be a cross between either Riesling and Sylvaner or two clones of Riesling. It ripens earlier than the Riesling and yields a fragrant wine, soft and round. Ripening consistently in cool climates, it has become the most widely grown grape in Germany.

MUSCAT BLANC, MOSCATO, MUSCADELLE, AND MUSCAT OF ALEXANDRIA are all white *vinifera* grape varieties with a unique, easily recognized aroma—pungent, musk-like, and spicy. The Muscat family has many clones and quite a few are associated with regions, i.e., Muscat d'Alsace and Muscat de Frontignan. The Muscat Blanc offers the best potential for winemakers, though all varieties have been made into table, sparkling, and fortified wines. The Muscat character can be subtle or overpowering depending on growing conditions and winemaking. The styles range from dry to very sweet. Unfortunately, the name Muscat was defamed long ago by its association with Muscatel, a cheap, fortified wine consumed for its high alcohol content. The grape is responsible for Italy's sparkling wines, namely Asti Spumante, and many fine fortified wines from southern France. Alsatian Muscat is a light, dry, pleasant wine, and California is enjoying some success with semi-sweet Muscat table wines. The general characteristics are a perfumed, floral aroma ranging from spicy to evergreen, and an inherent bitterness, often countered by sweetness. The wines tend to lack fruity flavors and are low in acidity.

NEBBIOLO is the red *vinifera* and the pride of Italy's Piedmont region. It has many different clones and is sensitive to subtle changes in climate and soil. It is the grape behind the rich, long-lived wines of Barolo and Gattinara, which are sometimes known as Spanna. Some, like the Nebbiolo d'Alba, are bottled as varietals. Most Piedmont versions share a deep color and full body, along with a distinctive fragrance of violets, truffles, earthiness, or even a hint of tar. The grape also grows in the Lombardy region, but has never adapted well to other countries.

NIAGARA is a white American hybrid variety. This grape produces varietal wines of jug wine quality with a pronounced grapy *labrusca* flavor. It is also used as a blending wine.

PALOMINO or GOLDEN CHASSELAS, is a white *vinifera* variety used primarily for Sherry in both Spain and other countries which produce copies. It is a neutral grape which produces high sugar and low acids when grown in hot climates.

PEDRO XIMÉNES, a white *vinifera* variety which produces exceptionally high sugar, is used primarily for sweet wines which are deliberately oxidized to produce wines resembling molasses or syrup. In Spain, it is blended with dry Sherry to produce sweet cream Sherries and bottled as a varietal in Montilla and sometimes in Jerez.

PETITE-SIRAH is a red *vinifera* grape of uncertain origins. Unlike either the Syrah of the Rhône Valley or the Shiraz of Australia, it is grown and varietally-labeled as such only in California where it yields many wines of almost inky, deep color, big body, and high tannins and acidity. The flavor is slightly berry-like, rarely but occasionally peppery. Its depth and alcohol produce hearty, robust wines which are useful for well-seasoned foods.

PINOT BLANC, the white variant of Pinot Noir, is grown in many regions. Some plantings are found in Burgundy, Alsace, Italy, Germany, Austria, California and many other countries. It is called Weissburgunder in Germany; Pinot Bianco or sometimes Pinot d'Alba in Italy. The better versions offer a spicy fruit, hard, high acid, almost tart profile, and demand some cellaring. In California it is used by many wineries for Champagne *cuvées*. As an early-ripener and very shy-bearer, the grape has lost out in competition with Chardonnay.

PINOT GRIS, a white *vinifera* variety related to the Pinot Noir, is known as the Tokay in Alsace and the Rülander in Germany. It produces low-acid, full-bodied white wines without distinction. It is grown in small quantities in the western United States.

PINOT MEUNIER or MEUNIER, is a red *vinifera* variety in the Pinot family which is used primarily in the Champagne region of France as a blending grape. It is rarely seen as a varietal.

PINOT NOIR, is a red *vinifera* variety considered to be one of the noblest of all wine grapes. It is grown throughout the world with varying success due to its sensitivity to soil, climate, and the clonal variant of the vine. In France it is the principal red grape of the Côte d'Or region of Burgundy where it produces some of the most renowned and costly wines in the world. With the exception of the Blanc de Blanc, it is used in the Champagne region of France as a base for all Champagnes and provides body and elegance. It grows best in well-drained chalky or clay soils and cool climates where it produces wines which often require long aging and exhibit complex fragrances resembling violets, roses, truffles, and other scents too subtle to describe. Under less ideal conditions its wines have a distinctive grapiness which is appealing; under poor conditions it produces coarse, undistinguished, frequently thin and acid wines unworthy of varietal bottling. Until recently, it was believed that Pinot Noir could achieve its best only in its traditional regions of France; however, a handful of wineries in the United States (California, Oregon, Washington, and Long Island, New York), Australia, South Africa and Italy have shown that given the proper selection of the vine's clones, exacting care in vineyard and appropriate winemaking techniques, the variety can be grown to rival its French counterparts. In Switzerland it is grown in Valais and produces a wine called Dôle, which is full-bodied and rich, with some aging potential. In Germany it is known as Spätburgunder or Rotclevner and produces thin and acid red wines of little note. In northern Italy it produces flavorful, light-bodied wines with personality and aging potential. In Hungary, Rumania and South America it produces medium- to full-bodied wines with simple direct vinosity of jug wine quality.

PINOT ST. GEORGES is a red *vinifera* variety not related to the Pinot Noir. It produces simple, vinous, medium-bodied, grapy wine with soft tannins and smooth texture. Produced by a handful of California wineries, it commands little interest among serious wine fanciers who consider it a curiosity.

RIESLING is a white *vinifera* variety (see Johannisberg Riesling.) As a wine-label term, "Riesling" is one of the most misused words in the industry and even exceeds "Chablis" for the total quantity of mislabeled wines legally bottled under this catch-all name. While it is used for lesser (other than the noble Johannisberg) Riesling, such as the Grey Riesling, Sylvaner, and others, it is also used to designate a wine type in South Africa and Australia, where vast quantities of simple white wine blends are offered as Riesling and frequently have little resemblance to a Rhine style. In Germany, where the Riesling reigns supreme, the use of the term is restricted to the Johannisberg or true Riesling. In the United States, the word "Riesling" is synonomous with Sylvaner, Grey Riesling, etc. Its use varies with growing regions elsewhere.

RUBY CABERNET is a red *vinifera* cross between the Cabernet Sauvignon and the Carignan developed at the University of California, Davis to produce a high-yielding Cabernet style wine suitable for the hot growing conditions of California's Central Valley. It has not been successful as a varietal bottling and is used primarily for blending jug wines.

SANGIOVESE is a red *vinifera* grape and the predominant variety used to produce Italian Chianti and most other red wines from Tuscany. A large-berry variant is called Brunello and used in Brunello di Montalcino wines. In central Italy the grape yields simple, fruity wines.

SAUVIGNON BLANC is a white *vinifera* which has widely adapted to many winegrowing regions. It is fairly productive and ripens in mid-season. Harvested at full maturity, it provides wines with a characteristic herbaceous, sometimes peppery aroma; picked early, the grape is intensely grassy. In France, it is the important grape of Loire Valley wines from Sancerre to Pouilly-Fumé, and is a major component in Sauternes from south of Bordeaux. White Graves wines are primarily Sauvignon Blanc, ranging in style from dry to semi-sweet and are usually of mediocre quality. The grape provides backbone and flavor to the luscious, sweet wines of Sauternes and Barsac. Most California wines are made dry to slightly sweet, with "Fumé Blanc" a popular varietal designation.

SCUPPERNONG is a native American variety from the Muscadine species grown in the southern states. It figured prominently in early United States efforts to make wines, though its chief virtue is in withstanding high humidity. The wines have a strong musky flavor, distinctive, if not very pleasant, and most are made in a very sweet style.

SEMILLÒN is a white *vinifera* grape important today as a component in the sweet wines from Sauternes, where it is blended with Sauvignon Blanc. It is grown throughout the wine world and usually used as a blending wine. It yields Sauternes-like wines in South Africa and pleasant, dry whites in South American countries. The Australian versions range from dry to semi-sweet and are often labeled "Riesling." Most California wines are finished sweet and blended into generics as the varietals have fallen out of fashion recently.

SEYVAL BLANC is a white French hybrid and ranks among the most widely planted grape varieties in the eastern United States. It ripens in mid-season. Most producers blend Seyval Blanc, but a few solid varietals have appeared in a fruity, crisp style from small eastern wineries. The French grow it to use in *vin ordinaire.*

SOUSAO is a red *vinifera* grown in Portugal to blend with other grapes to produce Port.

SYLVANER (SYLVANER RIESLING, OR FRANKEN RIESLING) is a white *vinifera* grown throughout the world; its wines are often labeled "Riesling." Technically it is not a Riesling variety. In parts of Germany and in Alsace the wines can be light, delicate, and austere with a slight hint of Riesling's flowery aroma. The Alsatians finish it dry and give it a varietal name; in northern Italy, it is made into a dry wine; in Yugoslavia, Austria, and Germany, the wines are light and semi-sweet. In California, Sylvaner is used as a blending wine; the varietal efforts are often given the "Riesling" misnomer and finished sweet.

SYRAH is a red *vinifera* and an informing variety in the finer Rhône Valley wines. Known since Roman days, it is used to make the full-bodied, deeply colored, powerful, long-lived wines from the Côte Rôtie, Châteauneuf-du-Pape, and Hermitage regions. In Australia where it's known as the Shiraz or Hermitage grape, it yields potent wines that are often blended with Cabernet. The Syrah is also responsible for South Africa's finest red wines. California's efforts with this shy-bearing, mid-season ripener are still small and experimental.

THOMPSON SEEDLESS is the highly prolific white *vinifera* used as a three-way grape, for wine, raisins, and eating fresh. It yields a neutral, barely grapy wine, but remains important in the production of jug wines, sparkling wines, and primarily brandy.

TRAMINER is a white *vinifera* once widely planted, but now giving way in the world's vineyards to a clonal selection, the Gewürztraminer. The wine tends to be much less distinctive.

TREBBIANO is a white *vinifera* widely grown in Central Italy. It ripens late, is very productive, and is called Ugni Blanc or Saint-Émilion in France where it is favored for Cognac production. In Italy, it is important in the wines of Soave and Orvieto and is now exported occasionally under the Trebbiano name.

VIDAL BLANC is a white French hybrid that has Ugni Blanc as the *vinifera* parent. Planted in the eastern states, it is very productive and ripens in mid-season. Most wines are blended, and the varietal efforts to date show a lack of distinctive character.

VIOGNIER is a white *vinifera* grown in the Rhône Valley of France. It is a shy-bearer, and the wines are marked by a spicy aroma, similar to melons and apricots. Its fame derives from its use in limited wines from Condrieu and the tiny estate, Château-Grillet.

WHITE RIESLING. See Johannisberg Riesling.

ZINFANDEL is a red *vinifera* grown commercially only in California, though it is related to an Italian grape. Moderately productive and a late-ripener, it is sensitive to climate and location; it tends to raisin in hot climates and over-produce in others. The wines range from thin jug quality to being intensely rich in flavor and heavy-bodied, with heavy tannins and extract. The typical character is berry-like, blackberry or raspberry, with some hint of spiciness as well. The styles vary from light and young to heavy, syrupy and Late Harvest. The trend today favors heady wines that are warm, tannic, and rich in flavor and demand some cellaring.

WINE REGIONS

ARGENTINA

Argentina is the fourth largest wine-producing country with a per capita annual consumption of over twenty-two gallons. This explains why so little is exported! This big wine industry, which dates back to the nineteenth-century influx of European immigrants, is, today, under strict control of the Government. Despite industry growth, however, the wines remain coarse and are usually best enjoyed as rough, heavy-handed *vin ordinaire*, which ranges from powerful and hot to powerful and volatile (turning toward vinegar). Most of the vineyards are concentrated in the hot, arid Mendoza region, shielded from the ocean by the Andes Mountains. Most grapes grow in the flatlands, with the better vineyards situated at higher elevations. Temperatures during the maturation period often exceed 110°F which encourages high sugar development but also adds an unusual baked flavor to the wines. *Vitis vinifera* is almost exclusively grown, and with recent technological improvements, some wines are fresher and better balanced. Their poor image, however, was created a few years ago when cheap Argentinian wines glutted the United States market. As they were duly unrecognized, some of these relics are still around and careful scrutiny of the vintage date is necessary to avoid outdated inventory. The red varietals remain better than the whites.

AUSTRALIA

In Australia, a wine renaissance is on its way. After a poor start lead by cheap, fortified wines, the Australian wine industry, much like California's, has come into its own, producing a wide range of often quite good table wines. Since the 1970s, when the Aussies discovered their own wines, per capita consumption has increased as they enjoy good quality everyday table wines for about the same price as milk. Jug wines are often packed in the popular "Bag-in-a-Box," a collapsible inner pouch which is filled with wine, fitted with a spout and encased in a box.

Australia still makes some of the best Port outside of Portugal. Yet its table wines, particularly some reds, are beginning to rival the best from France and California. The prevailing winemaking attitude is experimental as modern production techniques are still being implemented, and newer plantings of Riesling, Pinot Noir, Cabernet Sauvignon, Chardonnay and Chenin Blanc have yielded impressive results. The trend is toward lighter, better balanced varietal mainstays, like the Shiraz and Semillon.

The main wine regions are geographically and climatically similar to Napa and Sonoma Valleys: dry, not very humid, and ranging in temperature from moderate to rather warm in some parts. The most improved wines are coming from the Barossa Valley, Coonawarra, and the Hunter River Valley, all of which are among the coolest.

Once consumers learn the "language," the labels are easy to understand. The "Riesling" wine, for instance, is actually made from the Semillon grape; Germany's Riesling is labeled "Rhine Riesling", and "Shiraz" may be the same grape as the Rhone Syrah. The ingredients of many blended wines are normally detailed for consumers. A preponderance of German names reflects the contribution of many immigrants from that country.

While the winemaking style is shifting toward finesse and balance, the macho reds and imbalanced, hot-tasting whites can still be found. But there are positive signs for the future. Examples of first-class Chardonnay, small-cask-aged Cabernet Sauvignon and Pinot Noir have garnered international acclaim. After a couple of efforts to sell low-cost, low-quality wines failed, Australians have now begun to export top-quality wines at very reasonable prices. On the West Coast for instance, good Cabernet Sauvignon retails for under $5 a bottle. Shiraz can be found in the $5 - $7 range.

As Australia will almost certainly be making more wine news it behooves us to become somewhat familiar with its regions. The Barossa Valley is the largest area and most highly influenced by Germanic wine styles. Both the Rhine Riesling and the Riesling can be light and delightful; Shiraz and Cabernet Sauvignon solid and consistent.

Coonawarra is well-regarded for its classic red wines, Cabernet and Shiraz, and is now working on some white wines. The climate is cool, but the region experiences wide vintage variations. In fine years, the Cabernets have been standouts.

The Hunter Valley is another fine region. Located in New South Wales, it is shaping up as a premium growing area for a variety of table wines. It has attracted wine-loving investors and lifestyle-seekers recently, making it similar to the Napa Valley in its appeal. The Shiraz and Semillon remain faithful wines, but the breakthroughs are coming from Chardonnay, Riesling, and Pinot Noir. Recent efforts of all three have impressed.

Victoria in the east contains the Great Western sub-region. The region tends to be warmer, and remains known for its commercial quality of white, red, and sparkling wines. It is still a center for fortified wines.

AUSTRIA

Austria, a country rich in history and tradition, predominantly produces white wines which are mostly consumed domestically at a per capita rate of ten gallons annually. The wines, made from German grape varieties, are similar in style to German wines, but reach far fewer heights. Ranging from light and dry to sweet, late-picked, berry selected and dessert styles, they are generally higher in alcohol and less complex.

The best Austrian wines come from Langenlois, Krems, and Wachau, all in the eastern provinces. Baden, near Vienna, yields light, fruity-style wines. The German system of labeling is followed, including linking the varietal name with the place name. The Grüner Veltliner is the most popular white wine, along with Sylvaner, Riesling, Müller-Thurgau, and the Rülander, a local name for Pinot Gris.

BULGARIA

Bulgaria's wine growing regions are located in the Danube and Meritza valleys. All the vineyards are organized as collective enterprises run by "Vinprom," the government's wine organization. They produce varietal-labeled wines of jug-wine quality. The major portion of production is exported, providing a valuable source of foreign currency. This financial aspect has proved to be the prime motivation for increased plantings in this nation. The wines are fairly cheap in England, where they are considered a good form of "plonk". The two most popular grapes are Cabernet Sauvignon and Chardonnay.

CYPRUS

The wines from Cyprus command attention only because of recent, intensive efforts to market them in the United States. Cyprus is among the oldest winemaking countries, but efforts toward improved quality have lagged considerably. Even those wines purported to represent the best examples for export are nondescript in character and often badly made. The worst are utterly unpalatable. The implementation of modern equipment and technology in the hands of better-informed winemakers would enable Cyprus to produce better quality commercial jug wines suitable for the American palate.

CHILE

Chile, like Argentina, owes its winemaking traditions to the arrival of European immigrants in the nineteenth century. In general, Chile's climate is suited to the Bordeaux varieties. Some areas, though, are ideal for the Riesling, which emerges delightfully fresh and dry; austere, and similar in style to German Steinwein. The reds made in a French style are the leading spokesmen, headed by Merlot and Cabernet Sauvignon, which have been singled out internationally. The prices offer good value, but the export efforts are minor and inconsistent.

FRANCE

France produces vast quantities of wine. Among wine connoisseurs, it has always occupied the center stage as the premier wine producing country which has lead to an erroneous assumption that if it is French, the wine must be better than wine from anywhere else. The fact is that some French wines rank as the best in the world, but France also produces immense quantities of ordinary and unpalatable wines which rank among the worst produced in the world. It's a strange irony that the daily wine of the average Frenchman could never find a market in the United States.

France, however, remains unique for its sheer number of wine regions, the amazing variety of wines which are made, and the country's ability to offer so many distinctive wines of world-class status. France ranks first in per capita consumption, yet the finest wines from France represent less than 5 percent of the total production. Strangely, many Frenchmen have not heard of, let alone tasted, their country's finest wines, as most of the best wines are exported.

Of the hundreds of individual wine districts of France, only a dozen are of commercial importance in America. The best of these are Champagne, Alsace, Chablis, Bordeaux, Burgundy, the Loire Valley, the Rhône Valley, Provence, and

Languedoc. The reputation of French wine is based largely on Bordeaux's finest châteaux and several tiny parcels in Burgundy, along with Champagne. These small properties have become so prestigious that worldwide demand for their wines has driven their prices beyond the means of most consumers.

Winemaking techniques in France evolved more by trial and error and intuition than by science, and it is an amazing aspect to learn later on how science has validated many of the traditional procedures and winemaking practices that were codified over a hundred years ago. Science also reinforces the notion that the French have no monopoly on fine wines; French methods combined with American technology will, when adopted in many countries, produce worthy rivals, and sometimes superior wines.

What follows is a very brief overview of French regions whose wines are available in the United States. Further details are contained in Chapters Eight and Nine, but only as they relate to our thematic approach. Other books, mentioned in the review of wine literature in Chapter Twenty-Three, will provide a more detailed in-depth coverage for the interested reader.

ALSACE

Alsace, located near Germany in the northeast corner of France, is set apart from the rest of France by the Vosges Mountains. During the past century the Alsatians have spent at least half their time under German rule which has had a pronounced effect on the character and style of their wines; thus, Alsace produces predominantly white wines. The vineyards are situated on the lower slopes of the Vosges Mountains west of the Rhine River, and are among the most beautiful in the world, dotted with picturesque villages and impressive cathedrals. Alsace is rich both in history and gastronomy. The Alsatian vineyards are largely planted to German grapes — Riesling, Sylvaner, Gewürztraminer — along with some Pinot Blanc, Pinot Noir, and Muscat varieties. The climate and vinification lead to wines with a fuller body, stronger alcohol content and greater austerity and dryness than those of Germany. For dry, spicy Gewürztraminers, Alsace has no equal. Wines are sold by a handful of major shippers, with individual vineyards rarely specified. Alsatian wines carry varietal names. Quality varies, and the reputation of the shipper is of utmost importance.

BORDEAUX

The name Bordeaux refers to both a large industrial city in the southwest corner of France and the wine regions surrounding it. It is, without question, the largest quality wine region in the world and produces more famous wines in greater quantity than any other. Bordeaux is a port city of great commercial importance and the wine trade is but one facet of its activity. However, the city remains the center of the region's wine trade with all the major wine brokers and shippers maintaining their offices along the port's *Quai des Chartrons.*

Bordeaux's fame rests on the strength of several hundred châteaux (vineyards) which produce outstanding wines; but only a handful, of wines such as Château Lafite-Rothschild, Château Mouton-Rothschild, Château Latour, and Château Margaux, which have justifiably achieved reputations as the greatest of wines — the vinous equivalent to a great work of art — are well-known to laymen. These few great names imbue all others with a mystique and make Bordeaux a cachet name at large. The truth is the region produces enormous quantities of mediocre wine, made for local consumption, and unfit for the export trade. Even so, some of this ends up on retail shelves in America.

Bordeaux is an enormous wine region and as such has developed a system of delimited sub-regions tiered according to quality under the regulations of the Appellation d'Origine Controlée (see page 120). The wine districts extend along the plains and slopes of the valley the Garonne and Dordogne Rivers; their vineyards are planted on a variety of soils ranging from gravel to clay.

Bordeaux produces both dry red and white table wines, and sweet white wines. Appellation regulations permit only specified grape varieties; Bordeaux's best wines are its reds produced from the noble Cabernet Sauvignon, Merlot, Cabernet Franc, Malbec and Petit Verdot; the whites are restricted to Sauvigon Blanc and Semillon.

Bordeaux's most famous red wine vineyards are situated in the Médoc and the Graves districts. Their wines,when at their best, can be hard, tannic, intensely vinous when young; with age they can become harmonious, fragrant and scented, and capable of finesse and breed. At their worst they can also be thin, green, acidic and incapable of improving with aging. Quality is dependent on vineyard location, climate, and the integrity of the winemaker.

THE MÉDOC

The most famous and certainly the best red wine vineyards of the Bordeaux district lie within the Médoc, north of the city along the Gironde River. The best vineyards are situated along a narrow strip of gravelly soil, about ten miles long and rarely exceeding seven miles in width. Here, exist the ideal conditions of micro-climate and soil which combined with centuries of winemaking tradition and a devotion to the vine make for quintessential wines. The region is defined into main and sub-regions of legal significance by the Appellation Contrôlée (A.C.). Each sub-region or inner-appellation defines stricter requirements for soil, winemaking techniques and ultimately (and in theory) higher qualities of wine. The principle sub-regions of the Médoc are Margaux, Saint-Julien, Pauillac, and Saint-Éstephe, each of which, in general terms, displays distinct and subtle differences from the other.

GRAVES

Along the southern limits of the city of Bordeaux lie the vineyards of the Graves district which produce both red and white wines. The district is approximately five miles wide and thirty miles long. The best vineyards of the district are situated on gravelly soil, hence its name. Remarkably, the wines of this region also appear to have a gravelly sense on the palate. While Graves boasts several justifiably famous châteaux, most of its production is of relatively ordinary wines which are sold to *négociants* (wine brokers) for their blends.

Within the Graves district, south of Bordeaux, lie the Sauternes and Barsac districts which produce only sweet wines. It is here that some of the most renowned white wines of France are produced thanks to ideal climatic conditions which encourage the growth of a beneficial mold, known as *Botrytis cinerea*, or noble rot. The Botrytis attacks the grapes at their moment of maturity, concentrates their essence and imparts a unique and luscious flavor all its own. While the region produces these expensive and much sought after wines from a handful of famous properties, there are also vast quantities of mediocre Sauternes produced from inferior vineyards within the district.

SAINT-ÉMILION AND POMEROL

To the east of the city of Bordeaux, across the Dordogne River, lie the districts of Saint-Émilion and Pomerol. The town of Saint-Émilion is picturesque, with narrow, stone-cobbled, serpentine streets, tourist craft shops, and many cafés within view of the vineyards which are a stone's throw from the town. There are literally thousands of small châteaux within the district but only a handful can claim the best soil and microclimate necessary to produce great wines.

Adjacent to Saint-Émilion, lies the smaller and less-well-known district of Pomerol which recently has won recognition among connoisseurs. The soil here differs from its Saint-Émilion and Médoc neighbors in that it contains a large amount of clay. The principle grape grown is the Merlot, as opposed to the Cabernet grown in the rest of Bordeaux. This gives the wines of Pomerol a special character all their own.

BURGUNDY

The modern industrial city of Dijon is the hub of the Burgundy region, which consists of several main divisions the best known of which are: Chablis, fifty miles to the northwest; the Côte d'Or immediately to the south spanning a narrow strip roughly thirty-five miles long and rarely more than several miles wide; the vast Mâcon district further south, and finally the Beaujolais. It's possible that this large region has contributed more to France's reputation than Bordeaux; the Côte d'Or, alone, contains more exalted appellations and individual vineyards than any other region of France. These great Burgundies have a nobleness and unique character that defies description; they evoke images of flowers, berries, truffles. Even lesser A.C. wines from the Côte d'Or have distinctive sensory hallmarks.

CÔTE d'OR

The most important district in terms of quality, but least important in terms of commerical availability and affordability to the consumer, is the Côte d'Or, literally the Gold Slope, so named for its many noble wines. It was here that wine legends were made, that individual vineyards were exulted over by the noblemen of France, battles for control of vineyards fought, and history made. The Côte d'Or is divided into two main sub-divisions: the Côte de Nuits known primarily for red wines from the Pinot Noir, and the Côte de Beaune, famed for its renowned whites from the Chardonnay.

The august vineyards of the Côte d'Or are situated on outcroppings of clay and chalk soil amidst gently rolling little hills which provide a kaleidoscope of unique and individual microclimates. Due to the ever-changing composition of mineral content and soil substructure, the vineyards of the Côte d'Or provide hundreds of unique microclimates, called *climats* which impart special, significant, qualities to the wines produced within them. The Pinot Noir is the only permitted grape for red wine. It is particularly sensitive to its environment, and mutates to unique clones ideally suited to each individual vineyard location.

The hills repeat with seemingly-great regularity, and have ideal southern exposure. Yet, slight variations in topography create subtle microclimatic conditions which result in a great diversity of bouquet, taste, structure and quality of the wines produced. The best vineyards are located in the middle of the slopes; grapes grown above and below produce rather ordinary wines. Centuries of natural clonal selection, coupled with ancient vineyard practices have provided each vineyard with its unique *cultivar* adding to the uniqueness of the wine from each property. Nowhere else can the Pinot Noir reach such a magnificent diversity of expression. The fact that wines with dramatically diverse nuances of flavor, yet all bearing a family resemblence, can exist within just a stone's throw of each other is one of the wonders of wine that has perpetuated the fascination of connoisseurs with the wines of Burgundy.

Wines from the Côte d'Or are produced in miniscule amounts. It is not unusual for an individual appellation to consist of one hundred acres; several individual vineyards are so superb and individually distinctive that they have been awarded their own unique appellation. The smallest of these vineyards is a mere two acres. It is no wonder that these wines are in such demand.

CHABLIS

The village of Chablis unfortunately and unjustly shares its name with America's best-known generic wine name. Yet for all its fame, surprisingly little true Chablis is actually produced. The vineyards of Chablis are the northernmost in Burgundy and are situated on the hills of the Serein River valley whose limestone soils impart a special character to the Chardonnay grape from which the wine is made. As in the Côte d'Or, the best wines come from a relatively small vineyard area. Chablis wines are light, austere, and crisp wines with a characteristic bouquet and a steely taste resembling gunflint. The best wines of Chablis, ranked as *Grands Crus*, (Great Growths) develop a degree of elegance and style but are no match to their cousins of the Côte d'Or.

MÂCON

Mâcon, a vast region to the south of Côte de Beaune, produces both red and white wines, and small amounts of rosés. The area is best known today for its whites made from Chardonnay; these are usually blends from many vineyards produced by large cooperative facilities or marketed by *negociants*. The quality varies, and prices are increasing to the point where most no longer offer good value. Within the Mâcon district are two inner appellations which have become popular, Pouilly-Fuissé and Saint-Véran, which are produced on rolling hills with a soil that imparts a unique quality to the wines, that is not unlike Chablis, but is softer and less steely.

CHALONNAIS

The Chalonnais produces pleasant, light red wines and some whites. Its output is small, and its wines are seldom seen in the United States.

BEAUJOLAIS

Beaujolais is a region producing huge amounts of wine, both red and white. Its name is almost as well-known as Chablis. The region is among the most scenic of vineyard areas, with verdant hills and valleys, narrow roads and many vineyards. The production is enormous, as are the number of vineyards and individual growers which number nearly ten thousand.

In the Beaujolais, the Gamay grape produces a quality wine, although it is banned as a quality grape throughout the rest of France where it is ordinary at best. Beaujolais are grown and vinified to be drunk young, with a unique, fresh, fruity, acidic lively character which makes them appealing for quaffing. They are made by a method of whole berry fermentation known as carbonic maceration (see page 33) which captures the flavor and charm of the grape and imparts a strawberry-like, yeasty quality which can be delightful, particularly when the wine is slightly chilled.

Within the Beaujolais are a number of sub-regions, defined by microclimates, that are superior to the rest of the region. Beaujolais from village areas which produce above average quality are permitted to add the village name to the term Beaujolais or label their wine as "Beaujolais Villages." Above this appellation are the nine *crus* of Beaujolais which offer wines of further individuality and distinction. These are Saint-Amour, Juliénas, Chénas, Moulin-à-Vent, Fleurie, Chiroubles, Morgon, Brouilly, and Côte de Brouilly, each of which produces wines uniquely different from each other.

CHAMPAGNE

The word "Champagne" refers to a region, an appellation, and a famous sparkling wine. The Champagne region is located to the northeast of Paris surrounding the cities of Reims and Épernay in the French Department of the Marne. The climate is cool, the soils very chalky, and the predominate permissible grapes are the Chardonnay, the Pinot Noir and Pinot Meunier. The vineyards are located on shallow, low-lying hills, surrounded by farms, forests, and many picturesque villages. The vineyards are situated on outcroppings of a unique soil known as Kimmeridge clay, a limestone-clay mixture which imparts the special character to the Chardonnay and Pinot Noir grapes which, in turn, provide the elegance and style to better Champagnes. The region is rich in history. The Cathedral at Reims is an impressive sight. Many cellars in the massive complex of tunnels carved out of chalk in the Roman times are today actually aging millions of bottles of Champagne. The Champagne houses provide the wine tourist with an excellent opportunity to visit the vineyards and caves — each year hundreds of thousands of tourists are accommodated. The area is less than a one-hour drive from Paris.

Some still (non-effervescent) white wine is made and bears the appellation "Coteaux Champenois." Still red wine is made, the best of which is from the village of Bouzy and made from Pinot Noir. Neither still wine from Champagne is either produced in significant quantities, or outstanding; the tiny amounts seen here tend to be vastly overpriced curiosities.

THE LOIRE VALLEY

The Loire River, extending almost six hundred and fifty miles, nurtures what is the longest viticultural region in the world. The region is rich in vineyards, pleasant and agreeable wines, and magnificent castles and châteaux. It is a fascinating region to visit. The Loire Valley produces a wide variety of wines, many of which have A.C. or V.D.Q.S. (see page 120) status. The best-known wines come from the following districts: Anjou noted for rosés; and Muscadet, Sancerre, Vouvray, Pouilly-Fumé and Coteaux de Layon for pleasant whites; Chinon, Bourgueil, and Champigny for light reds.

Chinon, Bourgueil, and Champigny are appellations seen on the Loire Valley's best red wines. Made from the Cabernet Franc, they are light and pleasant when at their best, intended for early consumption, and without the enduring quality of red Bordeaux.

Anjou offers simple whites and rosés. The latter are produced primarily from the Grenache, a few come from Cabernet. Muscadet in the Upper Loire gives vast quantities of white wines made from the Melon grape; quality varies by producer and vineyard location. Good Muscadet is light, crisp and dry and a good substitute for Chablis. The best vineyards are in the Sèvre et Maine district. "Sur lie" on a Muscadet label means the wine was drawn directly from vat into bottle; these wines retain spritziness and can be refreshing.

Sancerre, Pouilly-Fumé, and Quincy are appellations producing dry white wines from the Sauvignon Blanc variety. A few are outstanding and very distinctive. Most wines from Vouvray are whites, varying from dry to very sweet and made from the Chenin Blanc grape.

THE RHÔNE VALLEY

The Rhône River valley is rich in wine. The region consists of two major divisions, northern and southern, which are separated by an area unsuitable for producing wine. The vast majority of wine produced is simple Appellation Contrôlée Côtes du Rhône or Côtes du Rhône Villages from villages producing somewhat better wine. The important A.C. districts in the north are Côte Rôtie, Hermitage, Crozes-Hermitages, Saint-Joseph, and Cornas. The vineyards of the Côte Rôtie are reputed to produce the best red wines of the Rhône. Consisting of approximately one hundred fifty acres, the vineyards are situated on steep slopes which require terracing to plant the vines. The wines of Hermitage are perhaps better-known than those of Côte Rôtie. The Hermitage vineyards are also situated on steep slopes and produce long-lasting, robust reds and full-bodied whites.

The southern Rhône is best known for Châteauneuf-du-Pape, a robust wine made from as many as thirteen different grape varieties. Its vineyards extend for approximately eight thousand acres and produce about one million cases of wine. Tavel is a close neighbor to Châteauneuf-du-Pape and excells in producing the best and most expensive rosé wines of the world. Close by is Lirac which produces both reds and rosés though not equal to Tavel.

CÔTES DE PROVENCE

Côtes de Provence is located in the south of France, bordering the French Riviera in the hilly region between Marseilles and Nice. It produces vast quantities of refreshing, simple, red, white, and rosé wines, along with tiny amounts of sparkling wine. When well-made, wines from this region can be fruity and refreshing, but are not distinctive. Bandol and Cassis are the better quality A.C. wines, but are seldom exported to the United States. Côtes de Provence is a new appellation, upgraded from V.D.Q.S. status. Its wines can be found here, often at reasonable prices.

LANGUEDOC-ROUSSILLON

The Languedoc-Roussillon Region, commonly referred to as the Midi, is one of the largest wine districts in the world. Situated in the south of France, not far from the Mediterranean Sea, it comprises approximately one million acres of vineyards and produces more than one billion gallons of wine every year. The vast majority of this wine is *vin ordinaire*, officially known as *vin de consommation courante*, the lowest echelon of wines, the price to which is based solely on alcoholic strength rather than place name or distinctive character. Every European country produces these wines but there can be no dispute that France produces the worst. With its hot Mediterranean climate, soil suited to prolific-bearing vines, and regulations that provide economic incentive to overproduce, rather than strive for quality, the district is ideal for producing these inferior wines. However, within this ocean of mediocrity, there are several V.D.Q.S. and A.C. wine districts worthy of note, and some wines from this districts have recently been exported to the United States. Among the best are Corbi`eres, Minervois, Fitou and C`otes de Roussillon-Villages which produce agreeable, fruity, light, well balanced red wines meant to be drunk young.

GERMANY

The vineyards of Germany seem to contradict all laws of nature. Even though they are planted in the northern-most limit, grapes survive the winter and still yield wines despite a relatively short growing season. But it may just be that these adverse conditions are responsible for the outstanding quality wines made in Germany.

Germany's principle wine regions are the Rhine, the Mosel, the Nahe, Franconia, and Baden. The finer wines come from both the area around the Rhine and Mosel Rivers and that of the Saar and Ruwer (tributaries of the Mosel). The large Rhine region is divided into three sub-regions: the Rheinpfalz (known as the Palatinate), the Rheinhessen which yields good, ordinary wines (typified by Liebfraumilch), and the Rheingau, which is known for contributing the most noble and most aristocratic wines of all Germany. The Mosel River joins the Rhine at Koblenz. Mosel wines and those of its tributaries tend to be light in body, due to a lower alcoholic content, and often very flowery and delicate. Nahe is a region for agreeable, pleasant wines of less distinction. Baden is another source of pleasant, uncomplex wines, which are often bargains. The wines of Franconia are unlike other German wines, fuller in body, higher in alcohol, and having an earthy and steely character that replaces the typical flowery, fruity wine profile.

THE RHINE

Let's begin our journey up and down Germany's rivers in the Rheinpfalz which borders the Alsatian district of France. The Rheinpfalz is situated along the main wine road of the Rhein known as the Weinstrasse. Its enchanting and scenic vineyards grow on the high plateau along the Rhine River's western bank. In the finer vineyards the soil contains large amounts of schist (slate) which retains the heat during the cool evening hours. The finest wines are made from the Riesling, but the predominant grapes are the Sylvaner and the Müller-Thurgau. Wines of the Palatinate tend to have more body and an earthier character when compared to wines of the Rheingau. Forst, Deidesheim, Ruppertsberg, and Wachenheim produce the area's best wine.

Further north, along the west bank of the Rhine, is the region of the Rheinhessen, the home of Liebfraumilch. At one time "Liebfraumilch" referred to wine which came from the small valley near Worms. Now, of course, it is a generic term used to describe wine made within the Rhein although the better versions emanate from the Rheinhessen. As the River winds its way north toward the village of Nierstein, we find terraced vineyards located on the upper slopes. Nierstein and its neighboring towns of Oppenheim and Bodenheim are all known for their quality wines.

Our third and northernmost Rhine region, the Rheingau, is the best-known and most famous of all German districts and comes complete with rich history and legends. Its most famous vineyard, Schloss Johannisberg, is said to have been established by the Emperor Charlemagne. Most Rheingau vineyards have topsoils consisting of schist, quartz, and tiny pebbles which reflect and radiate heat throughout the evening. At one time, Schloss Johannisberg Riesling wines were so famous that "Johannisberg" became synonymous with the Riesling grape.

THE MOSEL

Collectively, the Mosel region which lies to the east of the Rhine, beyond the Nahe, refers to vineyards along the Mosel as well as those along the Saar and Ruwer Rivers. Over recent years, many vineyards in this cool locale have been replanted to the Müller-Thurgau which ripens more consistently. The best-known wines come from the village of Bernkastel where the better vineyards face south. The Mosel's primary wines are labeled Piesport, Wehlen, Zeltingen-Rachtig, Graach, Bernkastel, Erden, and Ürzig. The best from the Saar sub-region are those from Scharzhofberg and Scharzberg. From the Ruwer, the names to seek out are Maximin Grünhaus and Eitelsbach.

It is worth repeating, before leaving Germany, that the country offers substantial amounts of outstanding wines. The real surprise is that they are relatively reasonably priced when compared to similar wines from France and the United States. With large acreage available, the supply and demand ratio remain relatively parallel, and prices have not escalated beyond real worth. Another explanation may be that the nomenclature still discourages wide acceptance of German wines, but that only enables the new wine drinker to enjoy some fine wines at prices attractive in today's wine market.

Until 1971, understanding German wine labels was not an easy chore. Some wines were labeled by individual vineyards, others by large groupings of vineyards, and some by larger districts and names of towns. Beyond geography, the wines were labeled according to the level of ripeness achieved by the grapes used, and sometimes specified the wine by mentioning the grape on the label.

So confusing was the German wine labeling situation that the government impos-ed new regulations in 1971 that substantially reduced the number of authorized in-dividual vineyards. Smaller parcels were combined with larger ones, with twelve acres being about the smallest size any one vineyard was allowed to be. At the same time, several arbitrary label terms were prohibited, and the requirements for the grape-ripeness were fine-tuned and made very specific. Though the rules made labeling less confusing, the consumer still had to do his homework, studying areas, growers, and individual properties. As an aside, the difficulty of the German system may explain why the most popular wines in the United States are of the most general type, the Liebfraumilch group.

GREECE

Greece is one of the oldest winegrowing regions in the world. The Greek palate for wine is frequently quite different from ours, and to understand this, one must delve into historical precedents. In ancient times, in order to prevent spoilage of wines produced by primitive methods, the Greeks added preservatives such as herbs and spices, and even goat cheeses. A few vestiges of this practice can still be found; the best example is in the resin flavorings added to the wine to create white Retsina and rosé called Kokkineli.

Retsina is a favorite wine of most inhabitants, but the typical wine lover once sampling such a wine is usually so unnerved that little effort is made again to try another type of Greek wine. Many pleasant, fruity wines are produced in Greece, though little high-quality wine is made. Retsina wines, though, still represent close to half the country's wine output. They are flavored with retsin, a substance also used in the manufacturing of varnish.

Attica, the home of Athens, is one of the principle wine producing areas of Greece and produces most of the Retsina made there. The Peloponnese, the area of Sparta, is the largest wine district producing predominantly sweet wines. Wine is made on many of the Greek islands including Crete, Samos, Rhodes, and Corfu. Little of these wines are found in the United States.

Fortified dessert wines are the second most important Greek wine type. Their reputation is led by a dark-red wine, Mavrodaphne, similar to California Port, though lower in alcohol.

Greece produces some pleasant fruity red and white still table wines which are exported to the United States and are relatively inexpensive. The largest producers are Achaia-Clauss and Andrew Cambas, both of which are nationally distributed.

HUNGARY

Hungary maintains a centuries-old tradition of turning out many good-to-fine wines. Many of the grape varieties cultivated are indigenous to the country. Some other varieties, most notably the Sylvaner and the Wälschriesling, synonymous with the Italian Riesling, have been successfully adapted to the region. A wide variety of good wines, many representing fair value, are produced.

The most important wines of Hungary today are the whites. The region of Transdanubia, near Lake Balaton, yields pleasant white wines. They are usually labeled "Badacsonyi," followed by a grape name, such as Furmint, the widely planted variety. The most distinguished of Hungarian wines, though, are the legendary whites from Tokay, in the Northern Massif region. They are made from the Furmint grape which in this region is often capable of developing a high degree of the noble mold, *Botrytis cinerea.*

Hungarian wines are quite distinct in style, geared toward the local populace. The country's per capita wine consumption, today, is about ten gallons. The State-controlled monopoly, though, produces a fairly consistent quality of wine that is reasonably priced.

Probably the most widely known wine today is the Egri Bikavér. The name literally means "Bull's Blood of Eger," in reference more to the color than to anything else. It is a dependable, full-bodied red wine, with some aging potential. Eger also makes a sweet-style Merlot, given the local name of Médoc Noir but seldom seen outside of the country.

For the wines of Tokay, *aszu* is a descriptor for sweet, and Tokay varies from slightly sweet to the richly concentrated, nether-world wine, Tokay Eszencia, which is made from *Botrytis*-infected grapes in a manner similar to the German Trockenbeerenauslese (see page 172). Rare and always expensive, Eszencia can be close to 50 percent sugar and often contains very low alcohol levels. Over the centuries it was the preferred drink of European nobility and was once considered to have curative, therapeutic powers.

The term *puttonyos* refers to the measure of sweetness as determined by the quantity of *Botrytis*-affected, raisined grapes that were added to the wine. Wines labeled "3 Puttonos" are moderately sweet; those labeled "5 Puttonos" are the highest and the sweetest in the scale sold in America. Unsweet versions of Tokay which are otherwise known as dry to off-dry table wines, are labeled Tokay Szamorodni. They have a slightly nutty, slightly oxidized character, reminiscent to some degree of Fino Sherries.

ITALY

Italy boasts that it produces more wine than any other country in the world and that it exports more wine than France to the United States. While this may be true, it is not to infer that Italy's wines are better or more worthwhile than those of other countries, particularly France. In proportion to its total production, Italy produces fewer truly distinctive wines than do France, the United States or Germany. There are several reasons why.

The first is a lack of a tradition for great wines that has created the kind of hierarchy within wine districts that we have seen in France's Médoc and Germany's Rheingau. Second, was Italy's lack of interest in establishing foreign markets for its wines which were more demanding than its home market in terms of quality. Third, is the fact that most Italian vineyards are just another cash crop for the peasants who intersperse their vines with olive trees and other crops. Thus, the finest vineyards were not discovered over the centuries by the process of "natural selection" as were those of France and Germany. Fourth, continuing use of archaic winemaking techniques, particularly, prolonged barrel aging which robs a wine of those subtle qualities of finesse, delicacy, complexity, and breed, has prevented Italian wine from being a serious contender in the race for international wine supremacy. There are many outstanding Italian wines; there are a few rare producers whose wines rival those of France, but they are few and far between. However, the old traditional ways are slowly disappearing, and new, modern methods of production are replacing them. It is interesting to note that the winemakers who have adopted the certain French techniques are those who are producing the most cosmopolitan wines.

The wine drinking habits of Italians are among the most provincial of the world. Every region of Italy makes wine; and each considers its own the best. Consequently, there are thousands of Italian wines and thousands of Italian wine names, many of which differ little from each other. To intimately know all the wines of Italy is to be an expert in the mundane. Fortunately, there are only a handful of Italian wine regions and Italian grape varieties that produce wines which are above average. Some Italian wines are named for the grape; others are named for the region or village and frequently the better varietals are named for both. Thus, it is relatively easy to sort out the better Italian wines when one realizes that the most are ordinary at best. Only a handful of regions have achieved international acclaim, within which only a few producers shine above the others. Individual vineyards have not gained prominence, thus Italian wine names are much simpler to remember than those of France, Germany, or the United States.

For many years, all Italian wines were equated with that cheap, virtually un-drinkable swill then labeled "Chianti". To correct this impression and to provide a viable structure for the Italian wine industry, in 1963, the Italian government enacted a body of laws called the Denominazione di Origine Controllata (D.O.C.) which was first implemented in 1967. To qualify under the D.O.C., a particular region must be capable of producing wines of a certain merit, must conform to strict regulations (see pages 123 to 124), must meet certain minimum requirements of alcohol, and must employ particular winemaking techniques. Today there are in ex-cess of two hundred individual D.O.C.'s, most of which produce rather ordinary wines by American standards, although they are quite superior to the run-of-the-mill *vin ordinaire* of Italy.

The climate and topography of Italian wine districts span the range of suitable combinations. In the north they are sometimes similar to the Alpine vineyards of Switzerland. To the south they are hot, flat and similar to those of France's Midi. But with few exceptions, all Italian vineyards have as a common denominator: a singular lack of understanding of modern grape-growing technology; improper clonal selection of vines; a casual interest toward attaining the optimum from the grape, and a tradition from which they cannot seem to extricate themselves.

TRENTINO - ALTO ADIGE

This is the northernmost Italian wine region, located in the Tyrolean Alps where the better wines are bottled as varietals. From this region come fine Riesling, Pinot Bianco, Pinot Grigio, Merlot, Cabernet Sauvignon and Pinot Noir. They are plea-sant, agreeable wines, frequently with charm and some distinction.

LOMBARDY

Some delightful red and white wines come from this region. The best white is Lugana, produced from slopes bordering Lake Lugana; the best known reds, Sas-sella, Inferno and Grumello, are made from the Nebbiolo grown in the Valtellina in vineyards resembling those of Switzerland.

PIEDMONT

Situated in the northwest, Piedmont is perhaps Italy's most famous district. It is principally known for its full-bodied red wines made from the Nebbiolo grape; perhaps the best known of these are those which are geographically known as Barolo, Barbaresco and Gattinara, all of which are named for the villages which the vineyards surround, and have relatively small productions which rarely exceed their demand.

The town of Asti is the center of the sparkling wine trade in Piedmont. Its wines, known as Asti Spumante, and familiar to most wine drinkers, are made from the Muscat grape which has an unmistakable pine-like aroma which distinguishes it from sparkling wines made from other grape varieties.

The Barbera grape is also quite popular in the Piedmont, producing light, zesty red wines. The better Barberas are those linked to the village name associated with their vineyards such as Barbera d'Alba, Barbera d'Asti and so forth. A considerable amount of Vermouth is also made in Piedmont, predominantly from inferior grapes not suitable for quality table wines.

VENETO

The next important vineyard area in our vinous travels through the wine districts of Italy is Veneto. The best wines from this region come from vineyards around Verona. It is here that we find Bardolino, Valpolicella and Soave, the best known wines of the district, if not of all Italy. This region yields not only great quantities of premium wine but an enormous volume of well-made, mass consumption vin ordinaire. Wine is a well-organized big business here. The wineries and vineyards are efficient and well-run; many producers specialize in the exacting requirements of the export trade. Modern winemaking technology and grape-growing techniques yield wines that offer some degree of distinction at a relatively low price. The region produces and exports more D.O.C. wine than any other.

Bardolino, a red wine known to most Americans, is named after the charming village situated on Lake Garde. Bardolino also has a Classico zone from which the better wines come. As is the case with Valpolicella, the predominant grape variety is the Corvina.

The Valpolicella district is located on a series of hills, some of which overlook the beautiful city of Verona. The wines are similar in style and taste to those of Bardolino. Soave, undoubtedly the most popular white Italian wine in America, comes from a region located nearby. Soave comes both as Classico and non Classico wine. Most of the better Soaves come from the Classico zone, an area lying to the north and to the east of the charming town of Soave. Soave is made predominantly from the Garganega grape along with some Trebbiano.

TUSCANY

Lying further to the south and to the west is Tuscany, whose best wines come not far from the city of Florence. The best known Tuscan wine is Chianti but the region produces many fine wines. Little known, but among the finest wines of Italy, are Brunello di Montalcino and Vino Nobile di Montepulciano.

Brunello di Montalcino is Italy's most expensive and scarcest wine but not necessarily its best. It is produced in limited, although increasing, quantities as it has become better-known worldwide. It comes from a special clone of the Sangiovese grape known in the district as Brunello. The approved area for Brunello is approximately two thousand five hundred acres.

A rival to Brunello di Montalcino in its claim as Italy's première wine is Vino Nobile di Montepulciano. It is made from a blend of several grapes of which Sangiovese predominates. It produces a noble, robust wine that requires many years of aging.

It has often been said that there was more Chianti sold than could ever be produced in its large growing region. With the advent of the D.O.C. regulations, that situation has fortunately changed for the better. The vineyards of Chianti are situated among olive groves, stone farmhouses, and an occasional castle. The region is bucolic in every sense of the word. Chianti, the largest D.O.C. district in Italy, both in volume of wine produced and in territory, is divided into seven sub-districts. In total, the district consists of more than one million acres, although only approximately one hundred and fifty thousand are planted to vines. There are nearly seven thousand growers entitled to produce Chianti under D.O.C. regulations. The hillside vineyards produce just one of many crops of the individual farmers, with olives, grain and wild game being particularly important. The best Chianti comes from the Classico zone which claims to be the only true Chianti and indisputably produces the best. The other six zones, are Montalbano, Colli Fiorentini, Rufina, Colli Aretini, Colli Senesi, Colli Pisane, all of which turn out good wine. The D.O.C. requirements for each district vary slightly.

UMBRIA

To the southeast of Tuscany, almost in the center of Italy lies Umbria. Its best-known wine is a white called Orvieto, which is said to have been planted since Etruscan times. The vineyards are comprised of volcanic rock providing the wine with a distinctive, earthy character. Orvieto, which also has a Classico zone and is produced both as dry and semi-dry, is made predominantly from the Trebbiano grape.

LATIUM

Next, we come to Latium which lies to the south and west surrounding Rome. This district produces an enormous quantity of wines, the best known of which are Frascati, and Est! Est! Est! di Montefiascone. Frascati is produced in the hills known as Colli Romani which are of volcanic origin and located southwest of Rome. Frascati, named after the town of that name, typically should be light, fresh, charming and fragrant but frequently is not. Both D.O.C. and non-D.O.C. wines are produced.

A lot of ordinary, well-made table wine sold in America labeled simply as "Roman White" or "Roman Red" is produced in this region in modern wineries which provide clean, well-made, agreeable, pleasant jug wines. This is also true of the wines from the D.O.C. district of Marino, not far from Rome.

SARDINIA AND SICILY

As we move south of Rome, virtually all the wine produced is rather ordinary. Wines from Sardinia and Sicily have achieved some popularity in America, but most of the wines produced from these two islands are rather mediocre and are produced primarily for blending with other wines. Some Sicilian wines, though, deserve mention.

The vineyards situated on the slopes of Mt. Etna and within the region of Regaleali produce wines of merit. The white wines of the D.O.C. region of Etna have a volcanic character which makes them particularly attractive. Etna wines are probably the only wines currently made on the slopes of an active volcano. Regaleali produces red, white and rosé. While much of the wine is rather ordinary, I have tasted some extraordinary red examples that rank among Italy's finest wines. Sicily also produces a fortified wine known as Marsala made in styles ranging from dry to very sweet and in qualities from average to quite refined. Marsala is used either as aperitif wine or in cooking, it is further covered in Chapter Twelve.

Other regions whose wines are frequently seen in the United States include:

ABRUZZI

Abruzzi is known in the United States, mostly, for the red Montepulciano d'Abruzzo, which is made from the Trebbiano grape. Both red and white wines are D.O.C.

APULIA

At the heel of Italy's boot, this region is home to the Aleatico di Puglia grape, which makes a red, D.O.C. dessert wine, and the Primitivo, seen here, usually, as the non-D.O.C. Rosso di Sava. Other good wines are made from the Cabernet Franc, Pinot Bianco, Chardonnay, and the Torre Quarto, which is made from Malbec. None of this last group is D.O.C.

BASILICATA

This is an economically backward southern area, distinguished for the production of Aglianico del Vulture, a superb D.O.C. red wine, which improves with age.

CAMPANIA

Located in the region of Naples and Salerno, Compania Taurasi, provides a full-bodied red, made from the Aglianico grape and capable of aging. Lacryma Christi del Vesuvio includes a red and a rosé, made from the Piedirosso and Olivella grapes, and a white, made from the Coda di Volpe.

EMILIA-ROMAGNA

This region is famous for the city of Bologna and the ocean of Lambrusco wine it produces every year.

FRIULI-VENEZIA

There are six geographic zones here, which have been designated D.O.C.: Collio; Colli Orientali del Friuli; Grave del Friuli; Isonzo; Aquilea, and Latisana. Their wines, usually a good value, are often named for the grape variety used. The important exception to this is Picolit, which is an expensive, white dessert wine.

THE MARCHES

Two popular DOC wines are produced here: Verdicchio, a white, and Rosso Conero.

PORTUGAL

Portugal has many wine regions but only several are of significance in terms of quality wine. Portugal is best known outside of the country for its fortified Port wines and its inexpensive rosés, but most Portugese drink white or red table wine.

The country's wine laws are implemented and enforced by two associations — The Instituto do Vinho do Porto (for all Port) and the Junta Nacional do Vinho (for all other wines). Port has an appellation system, called the Denominacao de Origem, which is rigid and stringent in its standards. The areas listed below are the most significant of the six delimited regions.

DAO

Dao is the country's finest table wine region, the best Dao wines are the reds, though there are good quantities of whites produced. Most wines are blends from within the region, and some are vintage-dated. Those aged in wood casks are entitled to Reserva status. Dao wines are usually smooth and full-bodied, but generally are only moderately flavored and not terribly distinct, yet they offer pleasant drinking at more than fair prices.

VINHOS VERDES

This delineated region which lies between the Minho and the Douro Rivers is the country's largest wine producing region and produces both red and white wines. Although *verdes* literally means green, the wines of the Vinhos Verdes are not green in color, but made from green, acidic grapes. They are made for early consumption as fresh and fruity wines and have a definite and intentional degree of carbonation trapped in them. The whites can tend refreshingly toward the fresh, acidic, and somewhat underripe character. The reds are rarely seen outside Portugal and definitely an acquired taste.

BUCELAS

This is a predominantly white wine region located just north of Lisbon. The favored grape, the Arinto, is of little flavor distinction. The wines tend to be light and dry, with an acidic character and a hint of *gôut de terroir*, or earthiness, to them. Few are exported.

COLARES

This small region south of Lisbon, on the sea, is one of the few regions in Europe which has never had to be planted over to grafted vines to discourage the dreaded phylloxera since its predominantly sandy soil has protected the vines from this pest. The red wines from this region are deep red, full-bodied, and somewhat alcoholic. Though assertive and capable of longevity, they lack depth and complexity and can't compete with the world's best wines. Production is small and they are rarely seen outside of Portugal but are priced reasonably when available.

MOSCATEL DE SETÚBAL

The excellent fortified sweet wines of this region still suffer the erroneous association with American-made Muscatel, an inferior fortified wine. Setúbal wines are deeply colored with a strong, complex Muscat character; they improve with long aging. The producers usually offer a six year-old and a twenty-five year-old bottling. They are available in the United States and the price vis a vis quality is often attractive.

THE DURO RIVER

Located in northeastern Portugal, the Duro River region produces Portugal's most renowned wine, Port, along with sturdy red table wines. The terrain is steep and hilly, with hot summers moderated by cool evenings which are ideal for growing the deep colored, full-flavored varieties needed. A detailed account of Port wines appears in Chapter Twelve on Fortified Wines.

RUMANIA

Rumanian wines are almost all ordinary quality. The whites, Riesling, Muscat, and Chardonnay are light, often sweet. The reds are similar. Cabernet Sauvignon and Pinot Noir are often finished slightly sweet.

SOUTH AFRICA

For over three centuries, South Africa has produced wines of various types and in varying quality. It is famous for the dessert-style Muscat wine, Constantia, which was legendary during the early history of South Africa. Great Britain has always imported many of the wines, but few other countries have displayed much interest.

The two major wine regions are Paarl and Stellenbosch, the former northeast of Cape Town, and the latter due east. Production capabilities have been improved through the influence of the Co-operative Wine Growers' Association. Since 1918 it has helped regulate both production and export of the wines. In 1972, the government implemented a new system granting an official "Wines of Origin" seal to certain wines and to certain estates to insure accuracy of label information.

The table wines are made from *vinifera* varieties, and some crosses. The *vinifera* include Cabernet, Riesling, Shiraz (Syrah), Sylvaner, and Cinsault. The best-known cross is the Pinotage, from Pinot Noir and Cinsault. Paarl, the larger region, is better known for white table wines; Stellenbosch for reds. The quality potential is now being recognized, but so far South Africa remains insignificant on the American wine market.

SPAIN

To most American wine drinkers, Spanish wines other than Sherry are seldom thought about, less frequently tried. Even when the intrepid few experiment with the unknown, it is usually with only one type — Cream Sherry, Red Rioja, etc. The important consideration today is that Spain offers a wide range of wine styles and, with proper, careful selection there's a large variety of wines available at bargain-value status.

But the quality ranges ever so widely. Two wines from the same region may often range from good to dismal quality. The labels don't supply any guidelines. The laws are not similar to those of France which provide broad quality distinctions between A.C. and V.D.Q.S. wines. Furthermore, there is no uniform system of regulations for the entire country, and enforcement, where laws exist, is lax. Spanish wine producers, though, are aware of the potential United States market and are trying to improve quality. The following are the more important wine regions. I have mentioned leading brands when relevant.

CATALONIA

Catalonia is a province encompassing two important regions, the appellations of Panadés and Tarragona.

JEREZ DE LA FRONTERA

Jerez is a large wine region in southern Spain noted for the production of Sherry, an English corruption of the word Jerez. The wines from Jerez enjoy the country's highest regulatory system. Sanlúcar and Santa Maria are sub-regions, but the names seldom appear on Sherry labels. For a complete discussion of Sherry, see Chapter Twelve.

MANZANILLA

This is the third sub-district of Jerez, but it also lends its name to a certain style of wine. Located along the seacoast, it yields wines similar to Fino, but with a distinct, salt-like tang.

MONTILLA

Some of the wines made in Montilla are similar to Fino Sherry in general character and style. However, they are not fortified to higher alcohol levels, but derive their strength from the fermentation only. Wines from this region, located near Cordoba, are seldom seen in the United States.

THE PANADÉS

The Panadés can easily be Spain's première region for table wines. Its two leading producers, Torres and Jean Leon, are both known for their outstanding red wines, and the overall quality of the others. A high percentage of Spanish sparkling wine emanates from this region. In the town of San Sadurni to Noya, located in the El Panadés Central, are the leading producers, including Cordorniu, the world's largest producer of sparkling wines by the *methode champenoise*, (champagne method) and Freixenet, growing in production. The region's table and sparkling wines have made recent inroads into the United States market.

RIOJA

Though it has the best reputation and is better known than many other Spanish wine regions, the Rioja, contrary to standard thought, does not offer the best wines. Most are made in large quantities, similar in scale to the big California wineries. The Rioja wines are usually bought throughout the region and blended for consistency, if not for character. A vintage date, even when accompanied by the legal term, *cosecha*, is seldom a guarantee of the wine's real age.

The differences among the wines are more the result of a specific *bodega* (winery) style than of special soil and climate attributes. "Riserva" indicates that the wine was given longer-than-normal cask-aging; but is a statement of aging, not of quality. Most Rioja white wines are of mediocre quality, suffering from overaging, maderization, and poor winemaking. The recent efforts to modernize technology through the use of stainless steel fermenters and better controls have yielded a number of pleasant, but undistinguished white wines.

TARRAGONA

Tarragona, a small region in Catalonia, is better known for its sweet wines and Vermouth. But most of its production disappears elsewhere, often ending up in French-bottled versions.

VALDEPEÑAS

Located in New Castle, this town and its surrounding vineyards offers large quantities of table wine. The red wines are usually the best — smooth, light, and better balanced than other Spanish reds. The whites, though, are generally insipid at best, overaged and oxidized otherwise.

VALENCIA

Known for sweet Muscat flavored wines, Valencia produces red and white table wines that, mercifully, are not well-known in the United States.

SWITZERLAND

This country enjoys wines as evidenced by its high, close-to-twelve-gallon-per-capita consumption. The canton of Vaud is the biggest wine growing region; most of the vineyards are located on slopes surrounding Lake Geneva. A little further south is the other major grape region, the Valais. Most of the Swiss wines carry place names, often with the name of a grape variety, and a town.

VAUD

The two major sub-regions of the Vaud are Lavaux and La Côte. With its southern exposure, Lavaux enjoys the tempering effect of Lake Geneva. The predominant grape planted is the Chasselas, yielding a grapy, if neutral, white wine. On the northern shore, La Côte produces white wines of similar quality.

The canton of Vaud offers more diversity in its wines. The district of Vaudois Chablais is better known for its *pétillant* white wines, low in alcohol and high in acidity. The northern vineyards of Vaud make both red and white, the former from the Pinot Noir grape.

VALAIS

The Valais enjoys a few warmer vineyard sites, particularly on slopes near the Rhône River. The white grape planted is called the Fendant, a local synonym for the Chasselas; it develops full body and offers good balance. Dôle is the local name for red wines, from either Gamay or Pinot Noir, with Petit-Dôle referring to the latter.

In Valais, "Johannisberg" refers to wines from the Müller-Thurgau grape; Malvoisie is a soft, sweet dessert-style wine produced from the Pinot Gris grape. The area still cultivates several vines said to be of local origin, such as Arvine, Amigne, Humagne, and Rèze. The latter grape is of some historical importance since it was used to produce a wine, *vin de glacier*, once made by mountain peasants and reputed to live for decades when kept at high elevation.

NEUCHÂTEL

Among the other vineyard districts, the region of Neuchâtel in the northwest corner is equally adept at producing quality in both the red and white table wines. Here, the Pinot Noir yields a delicate, fruity style of wine, similar to the Oeil de Perdrix rosé. The village of Cortaillod offers some of the better, light Pinot Noirs.

TICINO

In the southern corner, known as Italian Switzerland, has a region known as Ticino. Most of the vineyards are planted to red varieties. Nostrano is the name for a light, blended red. Viti is the name for fuller-bodied reds made from the Merlot grape.

UNITED STATES OF AMERICA

CALIFORNIA

California produces over 80 percent of all wines made in the United States today. Very few wineries grow their own grapes; the usual practice in California is to buy them from growers. Wineries can use grapes grown anywhere within the state, and it is not uncommon for trucks to carry grapes from sources two or even three hundred miles away from the winery. Therefore, the area in which the grapes are grown may have nothing to do with where the winery is located.

Many wineries bottle wines produced from grapes grown in several regions and label the wine as to the source of the grapes. Some regions produce wines superior to those of others. Often this is due to geography, but not always so. Certain districts, such as the Napa Valley, have attracted the best winemakers and substantial capital to build the most modern wineries which contribute as much to the quality of the wine from that district as any other factor.

As of this writing, the United States is in the midst of legally defining certain appellations or viticultural areas. Today, the use of specific place names is more or less unregulated. In 1983, when the new system of nomenclature for regions becomes mandatory, regional place names will guarantee that the wine was made from grapes grown entirely within the stated viticultural area, but will not specify any other standards to insure quality. Details of these regulations appear on page 124.

However, a look at the California wine regions as they now appear on California wine labels will be helpful in determining the general merit of a wine to some extent. There are both large regions, and sub-regions within. For convenience, I will discuss them in alphabetical order.

ALAMEDA COUNTY

This county is of historical importance particularly for its Livermore Valley sub-district which is today, a recognizable regional name in the California wine industry. Alameda and Livermore counties are traditionally associated with white varietals such as Sauvignon Blanc, Semillon, and Chenin Blanc. The soils are rocky in composition, an unusual occurrence in California.

AMADOR COUNTY

Located in the foothills southwest of Sacramento, Amador is largely planted with Zinfandel grapes which reach full ripeness. The Zinfandels are generally warm, ripe in fruit, and very tannic. Small amounts of Cabernet Sauvignon, Sauvignon Blanc, and Mission grapes are also grown and bottled under the Amador County appellation. The Shenandoah Valley is a sub-region located in Amador. Occasionally, Fiddletown, another sub-region, will be used as an appellation by some wineries.

CALIFORNIA

This is the largest regional division permitted by law. Wines so-designated may be made of grapes grown anywhere within the state.

CENTRAL VALLEY

This vast region runs from Sacramento in the north down through the entire state to the Bakersfield area. It is not frequently used as an appellation, but supplies huge quantities of wines that often appear under the "California" appellation. Some of the state's warmest winegrowing areas are found in the Central Valley.

LAKE COUNTY

Currently becoming popular, this county is planted predominantly to red-wine grapes, notably Cabernet Sauvignon and Zinfandel. These wines tend to be lighter bodied, but can be flavorful in a direct appeal. A few strongly-varietal Sauvignon Blancs have been made from Lake County grapes.

MENDOCINO COUNTY

This area has two prevailing sub-districts. Around Ukiah, the vineyards are quite extensive. The Anderson Valley is much smaller and receives the most rain of all winegrowing regions. A full range of varietals is grown, with the region best known today for Zinfandel and Cabernet Sauvignon. Fetzer and Parducci are the two most prominent vintners in the area.

MONTEREY COUNTY

This is a relatively new, but large, vineyard area. Dry, cool, and windy in the northern half, Monterey has two centers — the Salinas Valley near Soledad, and King City in the southern portion. The northern half is dry, cool and windy. Monterey is best-known for white varietals, notably Riesling and Gewürztraminer, and a small quantity of Chardonnay. The red varietals have a strange, strong, vegetative character similar to asparagus which can be offensive. Efforts, which have had some degree of success, are underway to alleviate this problem by control of irrigation and other techniques.

NAPA COUNTY

This county is seldom seen as an appellation because its numerous vintners prefer to use Napa Valley, in which most of the vineyards are located. Few vineyards are located beyond the valley, and those that are relatively unimportant. The county includes part of the Carneros region in the South and runs up to Calistoga, Napa County's warmest sub-region, in the north. The Valley is best-known for Cabernet Sauvignon, particularly from the sub-regions of Rutherford, Oakville, and Stag's Leap. Chardonnay follows a similar pattern, except that it yields better-proportioned wines in areas from Yountville to the Carneros region. Zinfandel is best in the Calistoga vicinity.

SAN BENITO COUNTY

A moderate area that largely belongs to Almadén and a few tiny wineries. It produces wine without any regional distinction.

SAN LUIS OBISPO COUNTY

Another new area which includes two important sub-districts — Paso Robles and the Edna Valley. The former is gaining reputation for Zinfandel, Cabernet, and Pinot Noir, a specialty of Hoffman Mountain Ranch, a local winery. The Edna Valley is attracting attention for the Chardonnay, a grape widely planted there.

SANTA BARBARA COUNTY

An area of beautiful rolling hills, this county is known mainly for the wineries using Santa Ynez Valley as an appellation. A number of small wineries, including Firestone Vineyards, are producing noteworthy Pinot Noir, Rieslings, and Chardonnays. Several interesting Cabernets have been made, though with a definite grassy, herbaceous flavor. The Tepusquet area is a large grape growing center, but seldom used as an appellation. To date it has yielded crisp, often grassy-style Chardonnays.

SANTA CLARA COUNTY

Once widely planted, the area is succumbing to housing developments. It houses several large wineries, such as Almadén, Paul Masson, and Mirassou, which use grapes from other areas, often Monterey. The appellation is occasionally used; it is best-known for Cabernet Sauvignon.

SANTA CRUZ

A mountainous area that runs from San Francisco south to the town of Santa Cruz, this area is home to a dozen small wineries, including Ridge, David Bruce, and Mt. Eden Vineyards. As an appellation, Santa Cruz appears on many big-styled, ripe Pinot Noirs and Chardonnays.

SONOMA COUNTY

Although it is second to Napa in fame, Sonoma County is larger in actual vineyard acreage. Sonoma has two primary regions — the Sonoma Valley inland on Napa's backdoor, and the larger area along the Russian River Valley. The Sonoma Valley is highly regarded today for both Cabernet and Zinfandel. Dry Creek Valley is another Zinfandel haven, noted for producing grapes with ripeness and depth. It is also favorable for Fumé Blanc wines. The Alexander Valley, a sub-region, has yielded some high quality Chardonnays, and certain of its vineyards have excelled with Cabernet Sauvignon and Zinfandel. Some of the finest botrytized Rieslings are grown in the Alexander Valley for Chateau St. Jean.

California is not the only region offering premium-quality wines, nor does the West Coast have a monopoly on the fine wine market; but it does enjoy the economic advantage of suitable soil and ideal climate that makes grape growing more efficient and more viable commercially than it is in other parts of the country.

WASHINGTON STATE.

Washington began growing *vinifera* varieties in the 1960s. The Yakima Valley in the southeast has a cool climate in the summer, and a long growing season. Both Gewürztraimer and Johannisberg Riesling have been the most successful, with excellent varietal character, a less-sweet style than counterparts from California. Chardonnay, Chenin Blanc, and Sauvignon Blanc have been less consistent, but Washington Sauvignon Blancs have been quite strong in character.

OREGON.

This state has two small winegrowing regions, the Umpqua Valley and the Willamette Valley, both of which are extremely cool during the summer and often quite rainy during the harvest. Though vintages vary widely, the Pinot Noirs can resemble good, mid-premium quality Burgundy. The Riesling is the second most successful wine.

NEW YORK STATE.

Several *vinifera* varieties such as Chardonnay and Riesling have yielded superior wines at both the premium, and occasionally, the super-premium levels. But the quantities are small, and the production costs high, due to low yields and labor-intensive means which are necessary to protect the vines from freezing winter weather. The northern fork of Long Island, eighty miles from New York City, has shown great promise with several *vinifera* grapes, notably Pinot Noir, Riesling, and Cabernet Sauvignon.

ARKANSAS.

This state is home to one of the largest wineries in the south, Wiedekehr. It grows a variety of Labrusca, French hybrids, and selected *vinifera* grapes. The production is usually of blended table wines, and large quantities of dessert and sparkling wines. The *vinifera* varietals have yet to reach any noteworthy quality-level.

MICHIGAN.

As a fairly-large grape growing state, Michigan has had a checkered career. It is home to several large producers who concentrate on making dessert wines and blended table wines from *labrusca* and French hybrid grapes. Most of the wineries are centered in Paw Paw. An emerging growing area is situated near the Great Lakes; and the Grand Travers area along with Lake Leelanau are pioneering *vinifera* wines. Though the acreage is small, some areas around the peninsulas in the north-east are climatically suited to making premium wines. In fact, several outstanding wines have been produced from cool climate *vinifera,* including Riesling and Char-donnay, in the area around Grand Travers and Lake Leelanan.

MISSOURI.

This state had a long, fascinating wine history prior to Prohibition. Today it is best known as having the first American viticultural area, Augusta. The grapes are a mix of *labrusca*, hybrids, and a few local species.

MISSISSIPPI.

Just becoming active, this state grows the Muscadine variety, but has yet to define a style of wine for commercial success.

NEW YORK STATE.

As the second largest wine region in the United States, New York is beginning to emphasize the New York appellation. To qualify, at least 75 percent of the wine must be grown within the state. The three leading growing regions are the Finger Lakes, the largest; the Hudson River Valley, and Long Island, the smallest.

The Finger Lakes, in the northern part of the state, grows mainly *labrusca* varieties, used for all types of wine; but wine from *vinifera* grapes, Riesling and Chardonnay, been made successfully on occasion. Most of the wineries are large, led by Taylor, Great Western, and Gold Seal. A few new, small wineries, such as Glenora and Hermann J. Weimer, are paving the way toward high-quality *vinifera* wines.

The Hudson River Valley, a mere forty miles from New York City, is home to Benmarl, Clinton, and several other wineries. They are showing good progress with better quality French hybrids and occasionally succeed with the *vinifera* grapes. The region also grows *labrusca* varieties which are often sold to wineries in the Finger Lakes district.

On the northern tip of Long Island, Hargrave Vineyards has achieved acclaim for a variety of well-made, top-notch *vinifera* wines. Several other small vineyards have planted vines and will be producing wines in the near future.

OHIO.

Once a giant wine state, Ohio never completely recovered from Prohibition. Its reputation today rests on the dessert wines and some sparkling wines from Meiers Wine Cellars.

VIRGINIA.

A few small wineries, headed by Meredyth Vineyards are working hard and well in making a variety of French hybrids. Trials with *vinifera* are underway and so far, are encouraging.

YUGOSLAVIA

Most wines from this country remain within its own borders; only 12 percent of the total is exported. The neighboring countries are the best markets, and only a tiny amount ever reaches the United States. The best Yugoslavian wines are fair in quality; though low-priced, they are only a modest bargain at best.

Yugoslavian winemakers follow varietal labeling for their table wines. The lone major exception is the sweet, white Tigrovo Mljeko (Tiger's Milk). Most of the vineyards are planted to familiar *vinifera* varieties, Merlot, Sauvignon Blanc, Riesling and Sylvaner; a number of indigenous varieties co-exist, with the Plavac being the most popular native red variety.

Four major winegrowing regions are important to Yugoslavia: Serbia, Croatia, Slovenia and Macedonia.

WORLDWIDE WINE ZONES

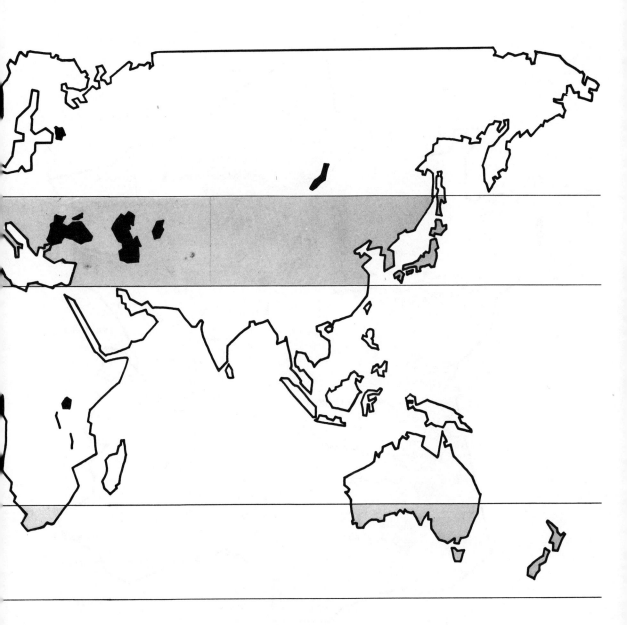

FRANCE

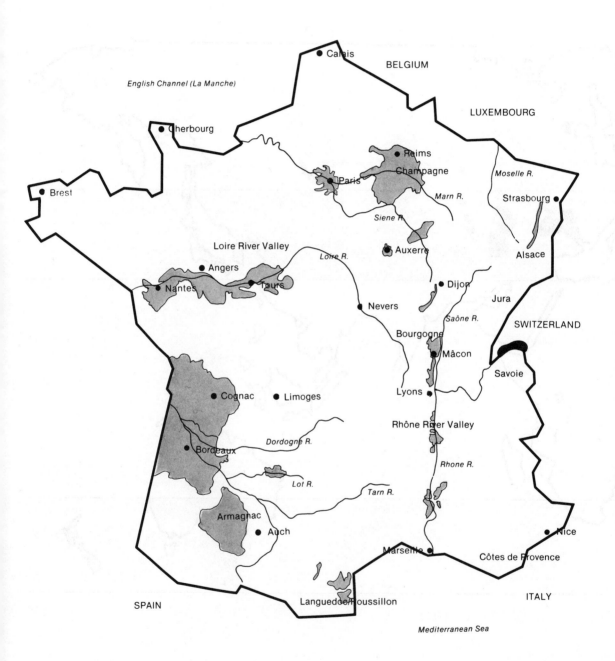

BORDEAUX

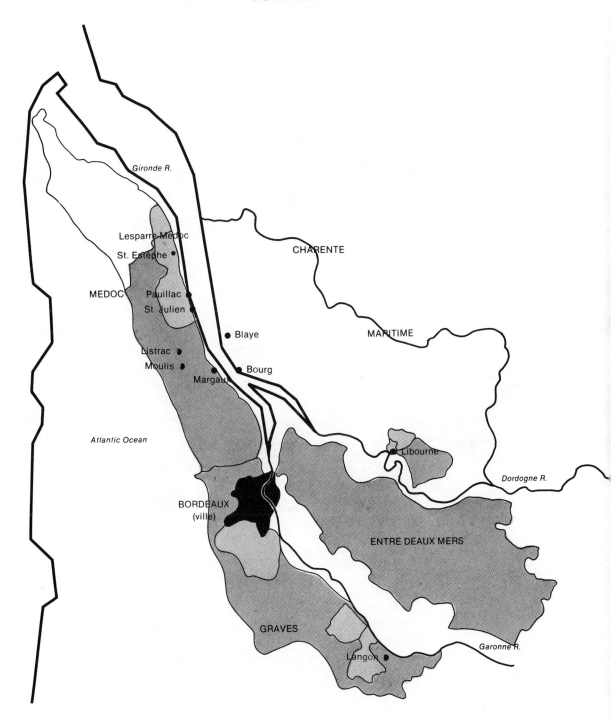

Gironde R.

Lesparre-Medoc

St. Estèphe

CHARENTE

MEDOC   Pauillac
             St. Julien

                         Blaye   MARITIME

Listrac
Moulis
             Margaux   Bourg

Atlantic Ocean

                                                Libourne

                                                           Dordogne R.

BORDEAUX
(ville)

                                        ENTRE DEAUX MERS

GRAVES

                                                        Garonne R.

                    Langon

BURGUNDY — CÔTES D'OR — CÔTES DE NUITS

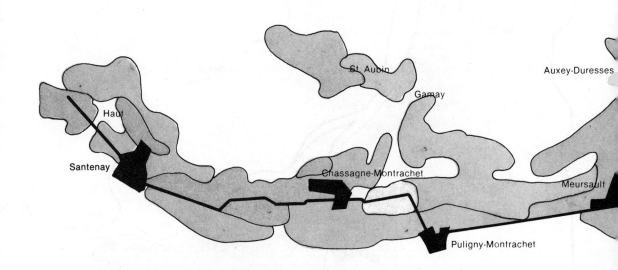

St. Aubin

Auxey-Duresses

Gamay

Haut

Santenay

Chassagne-Montrachet

Meursault

Puligny-Montrachet

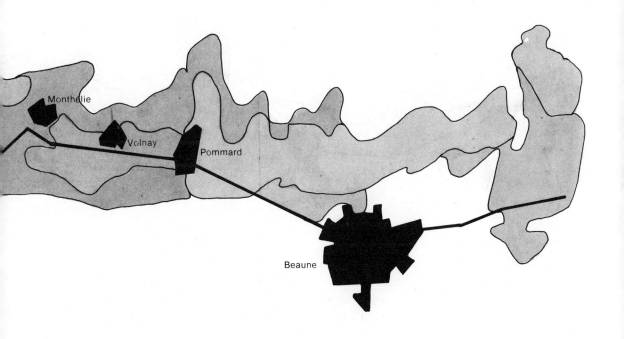

BURGUNDY — CÔTES D'OR — CÔTES DE BEAUNE

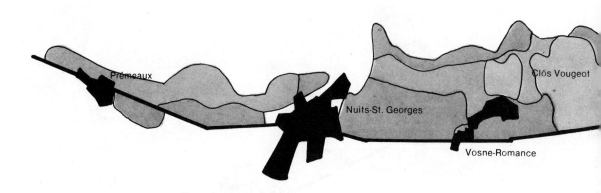

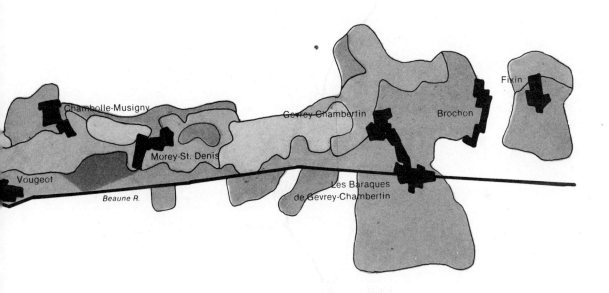

Chambolle-Musigny

Gevrey-Chambertin

Brochon

Fixin

Morey-St. Denis

Vougeot

Beaune R.

Les Baraques
de Gevrey-Chambertin

THE LOIRE RIVER VALLEY

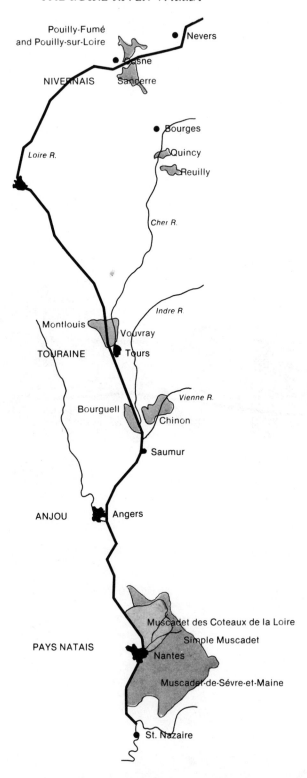

Pouilly-Fumé
and Pouilly-sur-Loire

Nevers

Gasne

NIVERNAIS

Sancerre

Bourges

Quincy

Reuilly

Loire R.

Cher R.

Indre R.

Montlouis

Vouvray

TOURAINE

Tours

Vienne R.

Bourguell

Chinon

Saumur

ANJOU

Angers

Muscadet des Coteaux de la Loire

Simple Muscadet

PAYS NATAIS

Nantes

Muscadet-de-Sévre-et-Maine

St. Nazaire

THE RHÔNE RIVER VALLEY

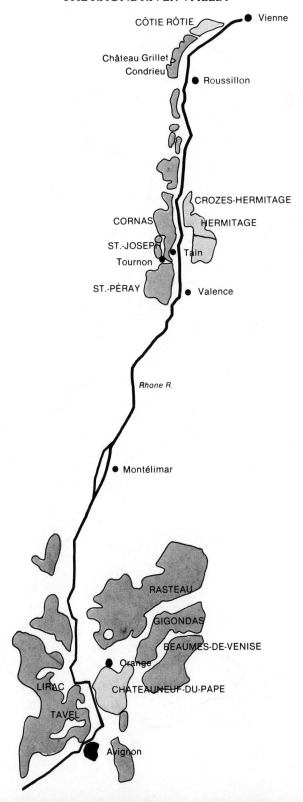

CÔTIE RÔTIE

● Vienne

Château Grillet
Condrieu

● Roussillon

CROZES-HERMITAGE

CORNAS

HERMITAGE

ST.-JOSEPH

● Tain

Tournon

ST.-PÉRAY

● Valence

Rhone R.

● Montélimar

RASTEAU

GIGONDAS

BEAUMES-DE-VENISE

● Orange

LIRAC

CHATEAUNEUF-DU-PAPE

TAVEL

● Avignon

ITALY

Torino

Milano

Verona

Trieste

Venezia

Genova

Bologna

Firenze

Chianti (Classico)

Vino Nobile
di Montepulciano

Brunello
di Montalcino

Rome

Foggia

Napoli

Bari

Potenza

Palermo

Messina

SPAIN AND PORTUGAL

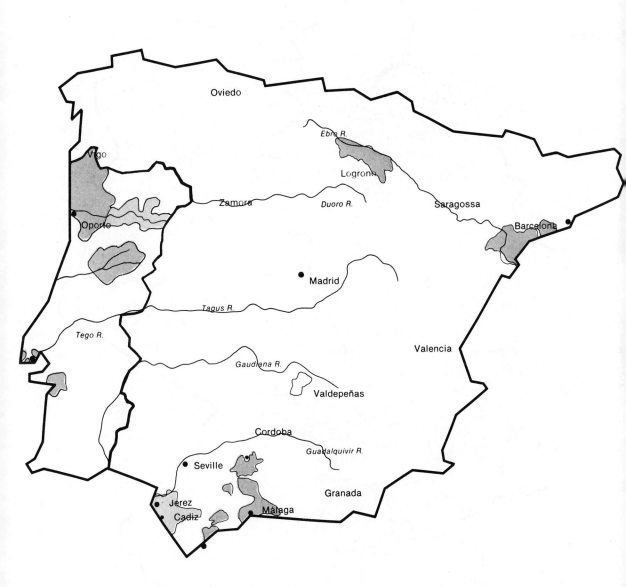

GERMANY

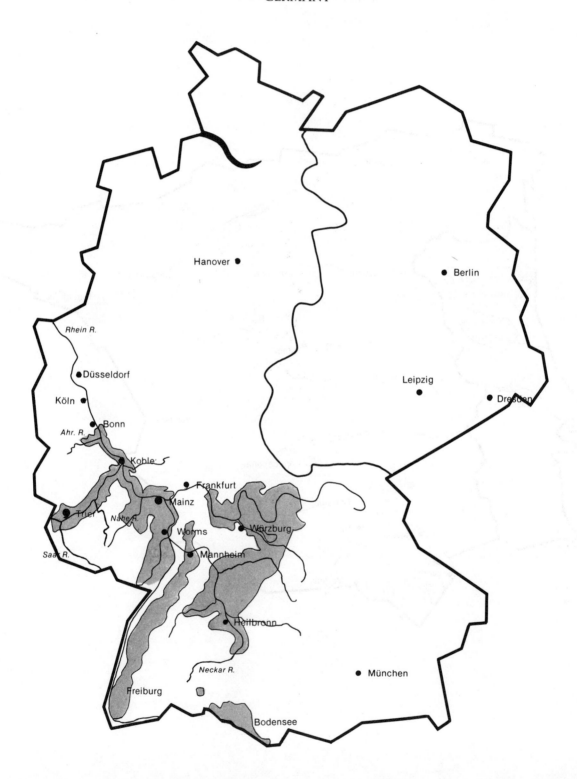

THE MOSEL-SAAR-RUWER

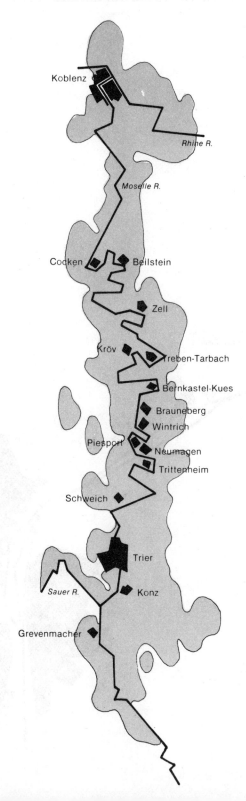

Koblenz

Rhine R.

Moselle R.

Cocken   Beilstein

Zell

Kröv
Treben-Tarbach

Bernkastel-Kues

Brauneberg

Wintrich

Piesport
Neumagen

Trittenheim

Schweich

Trier

Sauer R.   Konz

Grevenmacher

THE RHEINGAU - NAHE - PALATINATE

Rüdesheim
Elbingen
Rauenthal
Johannisberg
Geisenheim
Bingen
Winkel
Östrich
Hattenheim
Erbach
Eltville
Weisbaden
Rhein R.
Mainz
Kastel
Kostheim
Bischofsheim
Gustavsburg

THE RHEINHESSEN

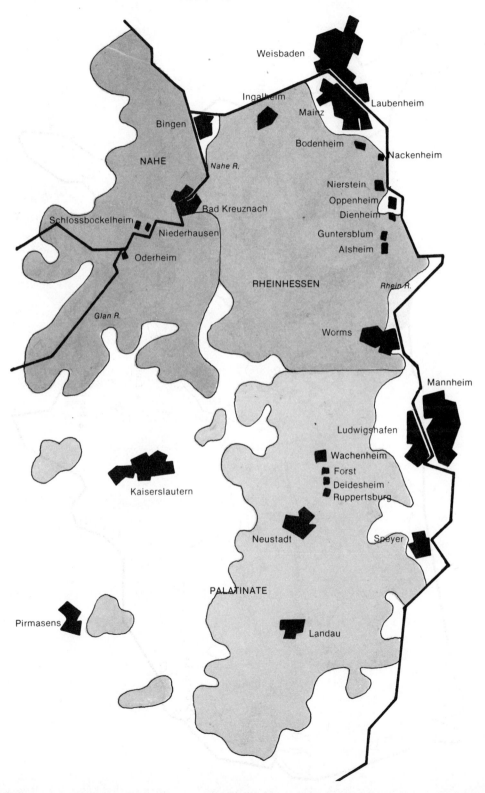

Weisbaden

Ingalheim

Mainz

Laubenheim

Bingen

NAHE

Bodenheim

Nackenheim

Nahe R.

Nierstein

Oppenheim

Dienheim

Bad Kreuznach

Schlossbockelheim

Niederhausen

Guntersblum

Alsheim

Oderheim

RHEINHESSEN

Rhein R.

Glan R.

Worms

Mannheim

Ludwigshafen

Wachenheim

Forst

Deidesheim

Ruppertsburg

Kaiserslautern

Neustadt

Speyer

PALATINATE

Pirmasens

Landau

THE UNITED STATES

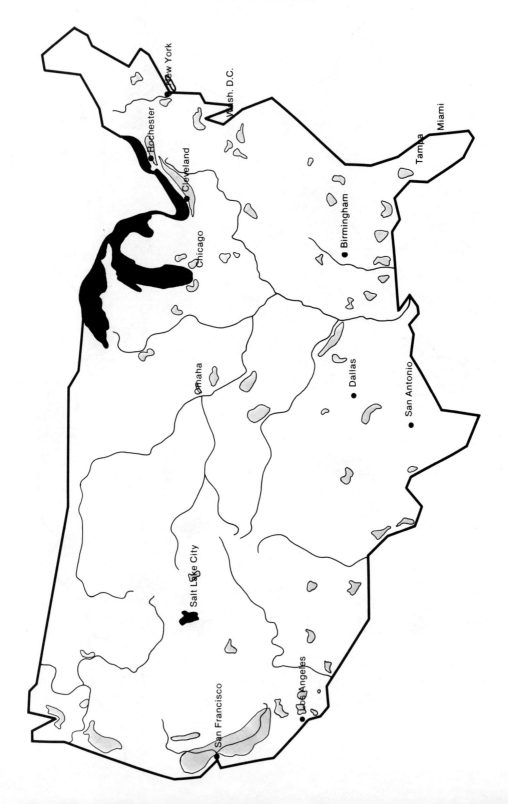

CALIFORNIA

- Eureka
- Sacramento
- San Francisco
- Santa Cruz
- Fresno
- Salinas
- Monterey
- Bakersfield
- Los Angeles
- San Diego

NAPA VALLEY

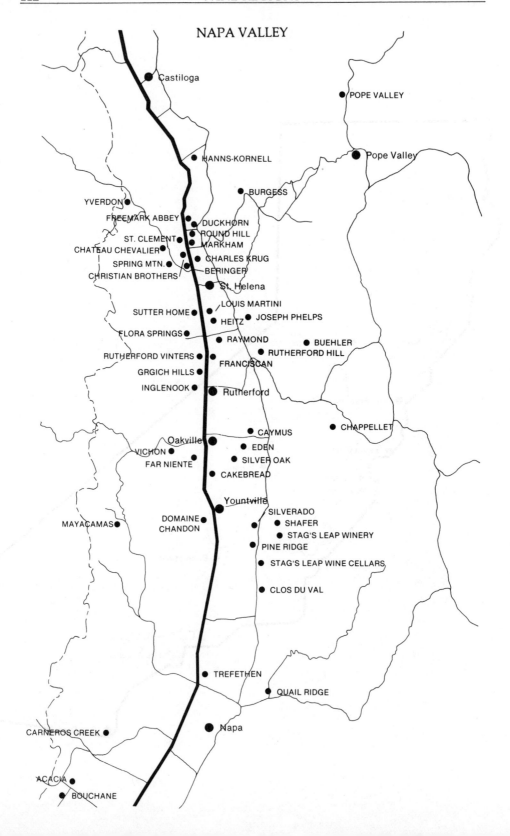

SONOMA VALLEY

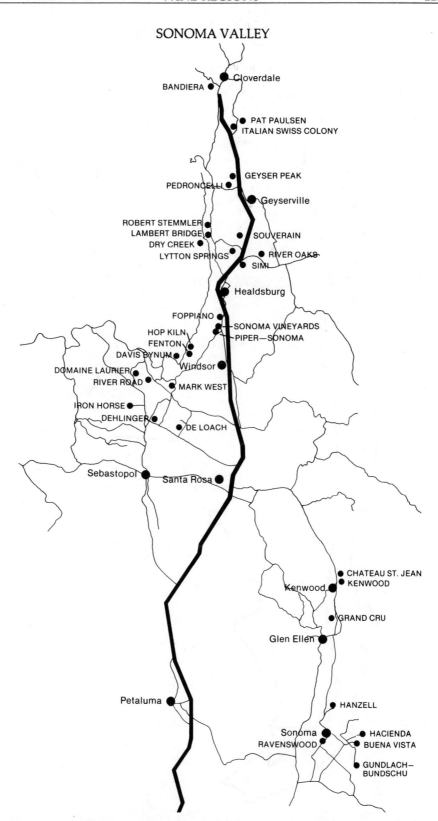

ARGENTINA AND CHILE

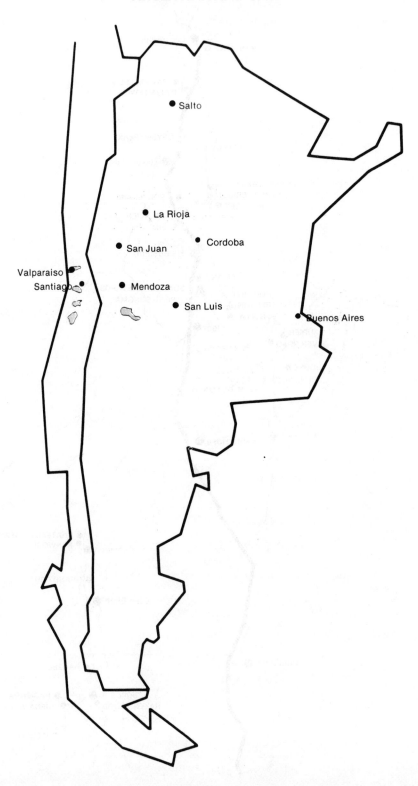

AUSTRALIA

NORTHERN TERRITORY

● Darwin

QUEENSLAND

WESTERN AUSTRALIA

SOUTH AUSTRALIA

NEW SOUTH WALES

● Brisbane

Upper and Lower
Hunter River Valley

● Perth

Barossa Valley

● Sydney

● Adelaide

● Canberra

Coonawarra

Great Western

Victoria

● Melbourne

WINE LAWS

In general, wine regulations relate directly to places, to geographical concepts. Over centuries, some regions produced better wines than others, and certain regions were best-suited for specific grapes. These geographic areas ranged from large regions, to sub-regions contained within the larger area, and even to individual properties. Eventually, these places came to be sorted into quality-tiers or groupings. In an era when supply exceeded demand, there was little need for governmental enforcement of quality standards. But in the late nineteenth century, partly due to the phylloxera epidemic, the supply of wine diminished to a trickle and many wines were mislabeled, misidentified, adulterated, or produced from raisins or other substances. It therefore became necessary for government to take a more active role in regulating wine production.

The basic objective of most wine regulations then, was two-fold: to provide standards for healthful and authentic wines; and to *protect the reputation of regions* renowned for better quality wines by establishing a system that guaranteed the authenticity of place names, frequently with criteria that assured certain minimum standards within such delimited areas. These criteria included: establishing minimum alcohol content; regulating maximum yield per acre, specifying permissible grape varieties and, in some cases, requiring certain minimum aging regimes. In most instances, the regulations established basically codified pre-existent traditional practices and turned standard procedures into laws. The wine laws were intended to maintain the integrity of wine from these places and regions, so that by guaranteeing authenticity, the typical and distinctive taste from each region would be preserved.

Yet, although the wine regulations may be helpful to the consumer, virtually all of them (with the exception of those relating to taxation and distribution) were written to protect segments of the wine trade from each other. In effect, they were enacted to protect the consumer good-will established by wine producing areas, which had garnered a reputation and following, from others who attempted to encroach on their vested interest. The problem is that over the years, many writers have described these wine laws as certain guarantees of quality, in effect, consumer protection laws, which reflect a certain standard of excellence. From this perspective, it is easy to understand why so many people, today, criticize various systems or regulations for failing to guarantee fine taste.

The administration and actual enforcement of wine regulations world-wide has always left much to be desired partly because, in dealing with wine, the legislators must consider the ramifications of regulations which are directed toward not only a business of making and selling, but also toward the livelihood of those who are farmers. Enforcement is made even more difficult because, from a technological point of view, winemaking is still in its infancy, and regulations, often mired in tradition, are unable to keep up with the pace of change. Consequently, they are often outdated by the time they are enforced.

Regulations relating to numbers are relatively easy to check and enforce; but it is more difficult to verify standards which concern taste that require that the wines be taste-tested for are two reasons: On one hand there is usually a lack of competent tasters. On the other, there may be a precedent in which the tasters are members of the trade who may be reluctant to impair their neighbor's livelihood.

Today, regulations relating to methods of production and what can or cannot be added to wines have just about removed all potential health dangers . Wines available in the United States generally meet very high technical standards, and there is usually no need to be concerned about unhealthy winemaking practices.

As wine consumers, we should keep the following caveats in mind.

- The privilege of using a place name on a label does not guarantee that the producers adhered to its regulations.

- One wine from a specific region can't be assumed to taste the same as another wine from the same designation.

- It does not follow that all wines from the same vintage and region or sub-region will be equal in quality.

- Wines from a region, adhering to its regulations, are not, by definition, free from technical flaws or from flavor deficiencies.

- The characteristic taste of a wine described in books may not resemble the wine when you taste it.

The reasons for these caveats relate to the nature of wine, human nature, and the natural difficulty in enforcing regulations. Maximum yield per acre, for example, is controlled by the number of vines planted per acre and by the required method of pruning the vines. To assure control over these matters, vineyards may be inspected once a year to check the number of vines and to verify the viticultural practices being followed, and records must be maintained to monitor the maximum production levels possible for each type of wine.

The bookkeeping is usually extensive, as forms and reports are filled out and filed periodically, and in many cases, certificates of authenticity are issued by the governments involved; but the record-keeping is frequently similar to that used for income taxes in the United States, and the honor system involved in adhering to wine laws is similar to that followed in adhering to tax laws. Not surprisingly, loopholes are also discovered and often taken advantage of in many ways.

The fault of most wine laws is that, try as they may, they can't legislate flavor and character. Most winemakers have a remarkably high degree of integrity and it is on this basis that any body of regulations works at all. This is amazing, since there is tremendous economic pressure today to skirt the law, sometimes ever so slightly, at others, rather blatantly. The penalties for violating wine laws, like a slap on the hand, usually aren't severe. The major exceptions involve the transgressions of famous brands or large shippers who are severely punished to serve as an example to the industry.

Before we turn to the regulations for the major wine regions, I'd like to offer two personal comments. First, since most regulations codify tradition, they may actually discourage creativity and experimentation which could lead to quality improvements. Secondly, the issue of whether governments should become involved in legislating standards of taste as well as in guaranteeing authenticity of origin is a difficult, complex one, and arguments, both pro and con, exist. Now, we will review the regulations of the major wine producing countries found in the United States market: France, Germany, Italy and the United States.

FRANCE

The French regulations provide the most specific guidelines for interpreting the nature and quality of a bottle's contents from its label. The structure is simplistic and easy to understand. However, when applied to France's best wines, it requires a rather comprehensive knowledge of vineyard and place. The French control wine place names under a system known as Appellation d'Origine Contrôlée (Appellation Contrôlée) which comes under the administrative control of the Ministry of Agriculture.

Each wine district has its own organization which enforces the Appellation Contrôlée regulations (which are particular to that region) and determines and implements criteria that may vary from vintage to vintage. Within certain regions, there are also classifications of wines ranked by order of quality within specific appellations. Thus, the Appellation Contrôlée can guarantee a minimum quality and also a system of classification that differentiates the various levels of achievable quality within that Appellation. The French Appellations are divided into three broad categories. The first is called Appellation d'Origine Contrôlée, abbreviated as A.O.C. or A.C. which is the highest tier of French appellations. Below that are regions defined as Vins Délimités de Qualité Supérieure, (abbreviated V.D.Q.S.), below that *vins de pays*, and below that wines which are not classified at all.

In terms of the American taste, the majority of wines entitled to use *vin de pays* would not be marketable in America and are rarely seen. Vins Délimités de Qualité Supérieure wines are relatively ordinary wines with some flavor and distinction, and a number are seen in the United States. The vast majority of French wine marketed in America falls within the A.C. category, which is tiered itself. The first or lowest tier refers to a wide geographic region which is capable of a specific minimum quality wine that has characteristics which merit such recognition. Within the broadest appellations are a series of tiered inner-appellations each of which is geographically specific and relates to a minimum standard of quality. Some regions are entitled to only the broadest appellation; others, to a complex hierarchy of inner appellations. Still others contain vineyards of such caliber that they have their own appellation.

The French appellation system seeks to insure quality first by specifically delineating geographic areas (for example Bordeaux Supérieur is a broad appellation within Bordeaux and Pauillac is a highest-rank inner appellation) and then by establishing certain minimum standards of quality: minimum alcohol requirements, maximum limitations on yield per acre, permissible grape variety, vineyard location or microclimate, and soil composition. However, the French regulations do not require that anything more specific than the designated appellation appear on the label. Thus, judging the quality of wine from the appellation alone requires an intimate knowledge of appellations by the consumer. Within certain appellations the wines are classified into *Crus* (Growths) which have legal standing. The most notable of these classifications is that of the Médoc which was done in 1855 and still maintains reasonably valid today.

Vineyards granted an appellation, theoretically, must be analyzed and tested each year to verify that the wines meet the Appellation Contrôlée standards of quality. However this is frequently omitted or conducted by committees of winemakers who must pass judgment on their peers. Owners whose yields exceed the permissible limits must declassify their wines. Thus, in theory, quality is controlled by discouraging overproduction.

There are many loopholes with regard to these standards. The Appellation Contrôlée specifies the permissible amount of wine from another vintage that may be blended within a vintage wine, defines the term "Château Bottled" and prohibits the blending of wines from other regions with those entitled to a specific appellation.

The V.D.Q.S. appellation has less stringent requirements. It basically controls wines that are just a bit above the ordinary and consequently does not include inner regions or classifications for these wines. When the producers within a V.D.Q.S. region believe the quality of their wines justifies a higher appellation, they may apply for elevation to A.C. status. During the past decade a number of such regions have been elevated.

Wines of the *vins de pays* appellation come under even less-stringent regulations but may seek elevation to V.D.Q.S. status when justified. The specifics of each appellation as it applies to the wines it controls will be discussed in Chapter Nine which deals with Premium and Noble wines.

The French appellation regulations do not control many aspects of wine production or specify any minimum requirements for aging and thus provide a league of creative freedom and innovation.

GERMANY

Today the German regulations claim to be even more stringent than the French, but prior to 1971, German regulations fell into no particular structure. Individual producers were permitted to be the judges of their own wines and to represent that quality assessment on the label. They also ranked their wines by degree of sweetness under a system of nomenclature relevant to Late-Harvested wines. Furthermore, there were tens of thousands of individual vineyards each of which could label wine under its own name regardless of the quality of the wine produced. Thus, the consumer was confronted with literally hundreds of thousands of different wines each of which made different quality claims, often on the merits of the winemaker's own assessments. In 1971, to reduce this confusion, and to provide specific standards of quality for certain types of German wines that were not previously legally defined, the government created a new set of wine regulations.

At this point, the reader should turn to Chapter 9 for an understanding of the various types of German wines which will be discussed below. Under the 1971 laws German wines are differentiated into three basic categories: Tafelwein, the lowest quality of German wines, Qualitätswein (QbA) and Qualitätswein mit Prädikat (QmP).

The regulations also define viticultural regions as follows:

Bereich, an enormous viticultural area, which may be divided into one or more *Grosslage*.

Grosslage, translated from the German, means large site. But for clarity we might want to think of it as a hypothetical vineyard with its own name, which contains smaller vineyards, called *Einzellagen* which, however, must use the *Grosslage* name when labeling their wines. Frequently a *Grosslage* will include several hundred acres and thousands of individual vineyards all of which produce wines of the same relative quality and character.

Einzellage, the smallest defined region, is an individual vineyard, the minimum size of which must be approximately twelve acres. In the 1971 laws smaller-size vineyards were renamed and incorporated with a neighboring vineyard, usually one which had the most notable reputation or produced the highest quality. The drafting of these regulations was highly political, as can well be understood. Proprietors of quality vineyards were not pleased that inferior neighboring vineyards would be permitted to use their name. Vineyards which enjoyed a particular reputation could no longer use their name. Producers who previously used to differentiate the individual quality of each cask of wine by a barrel number or be a particular term such as "finer" "finest" were displeased that such practices were no longer permitted.

Since 1971, the German regulations legally define the Kabinett, Spätlese, Auslese, Beerenauslese and Trockenbeerenauslese (styles of wine) in terms of the Oechsle scale which measures the quantity of sugar in the grape juice prior to fermentation. Similarly, the law sets minimum standards of alcohol with regard to Qualitätswein and Tafelwein and permits sugaring of wines up to Qualitätswein mit Prädikat designation. Above Prädikat, no sugaring is permitted. The regulations permit the use of sweet reserve or concentrated grape juice made from the grapes of the vineyard but these are not permissible in the Auslese level and above. Each bottle of

German wine must bear a control number which specifies the year of production, the year of registration and a code number identifying the producer and the individual lot of wine. Each wine is scientifically analyzed (to determine if it meets its requirements) and is also tasted.

ITALY

In 1963 the Italian government enacted a body of wine regulations called the Denominazione di Origine Controllata, which the Italians claim are the most stringent regulations of any. The D.O.C. laws control quality by legally defining viticultural areas, by controlling the principle yield per acre, grape varieties, and alcohol content, and by setting minimum requirements for cask aging. Legal significance is bestowed on the words "Superiore," "Riserva," and "Classico". The regulations also call for a higher level of appellation entitled Denominazione di Origine Controllata Garantita (D.O.C.G.) which is awarded to those regions that produce superior wines, the quality of which is guaranteed by the Italian government.

As of the beginning of 1981 there are in excess of two hundred and fifty D.O.C. regions. As with French regulations, specific requirements for each D.O.C. vary. An appellation of a Classico region, which has more stringent standards than the broader D.O.C. provides a two-tiered rank order within the basic D.O.C. quality designation.

The D.O.C.G. encompasses all the requirements of the D.O.C. with additional specifications with regard to winemaking practices and tasting-tests of wine. Wines from within the D.O.C.G. region that fail to pass the taste test are declassified as ordinary red wine rather than D.O.C. wine. For producers within a region, failing a taste-test could provide severe economic hardship.

As of May 1983 only four regions, Brunello di Montalcino, Barolo, Barbaresco and Vino Nobile di Montepulciano have been awarded D.O.C.G. status. Several others have applied and are awaiting approval.

The enforcement of regulations is similar to that of France. Vineyards are inspected and maximum production standards set for each winery or vineyard. Record-keeping is by self-reporting with occasional spot checks. There are no tasting requirements with regard to D.O.C. wines. The tasting requirements for D.O.C.G. may or may not guarantee superior quality depending on the qualifications of the taster, the tasting methods and taste standards employed. The first D.O.C.G. wine will not be offered for sale until 1985. Time will tell.

The Italian government is obsessed with its export market. Consequently, all Italian wines exported to the U.S. must be approved by a government wine export authority and receive a control number. Furthermore, the Italian Trade Commission attempts to prevent fraudulent wine from being sold within the United States and makes spot purchases in wine stores in various American states. At the present time, the Italian Trade Commission has no professional tasters or staffers in the United States and wines are sent to Italy for analysis. These systems work well in theory; however, they do not provide the absolute protections that the Italian government would like us to believe they do.

UNITED STATES

The United States wine regulations provide the least quality protection to the consumer of any other major wine producing country. The United States attempts to regulate place names, identification of the producer of the wine, vintage year and varietal content, but there are no regulations with regard to permissible varieties within a place-name designation which, for all intents and purposes, defeats the intent of the regulations — to provide the consumer with wine labels that can be easily interpreted. The regulations which specify bottle size serve only to provide uniformity of bottling to achieve an industry standard of protection, and to provide the consumer with an opportunity to do comparative shopping without having to recalculate volume price ratios with every wine.

Until 1983, when new regulations became mandatory, very few minimum requirements are on the books. A California varietal wine at present need contain only 51% of that named variety to qualify. There was a clause that the varietal should display the varietal characteristics, but that could never be defined or enforced. The vintage-date regulation is, and will remain, a minimum of 95% of the wine's volume must comes from grapes harvested and made in that year. For place names smaller than California, the rule is that 75% of the wine must comes from grapes grown within that region.

The BATF is presently defining viticultural areas, the American version of appellations of origin. The area must have established boundaries, climate, soil, elevation and/or other geographic features to distinguish it from surrounding regions. Furthermore, place names for wine regions with historical significance and with some national recognition meet the federal requirements. As of January 1, 1983, all place names must be approved viticultural areas. The minimal varietal percentage will be 85%, with at least 85% of the wine's volume derived from grapes grown in the named area. The vintage rule of at least 95% from that year remains. Additionally, all varietals without specific place names must be made from at least 75% of the designated grape, beginning in 1983.

The BATF does not attempt to regulate the permissible grape varieties, the yields per acre, nor the minimum alcohol content within any of the definitions of a viticultural area. The BATF sees its definition of viticultural areas as a step toward tighter labeling practices. However, to me, the defining of place names by geography and history without any control over yields and varieties may, in fact, provide greater opportunities for consumer deception than presently exists.

WINES FOR EVERYDAY

Throughout the wine-producing world, every region makes wines intended for everyday enjoyment. These are often called drinking wines, or, by some, quaffing wines. In Europe they may be described as *vin ordinaire* as opposed to *vin grande*, wines meant to be kept and aged. In the United States, the current terminology is to call wines made for immediate consumption "jug" wines. Jug wines may be an unintentional misnomer because the wines in this quality-category can be packaged in any kind of container, size or design. My intention here and in the following chapters is to identify the unifying thread — the viticultural, and vinicultural practices, and the consequent, recognizable characteristics — that bring wines from the various areas of the world together from the perspective of quality.

Ordinary, straightforward wines, often referred to as jug wines, (we will use the terms interchangeably) are wines meant for everyday drinking and should be construed in the same context as the term "ordinary guy." It is not a pejorative designation, but more neutral, like the wines we have in mind. Ordinary wines, like ordinary fellows, are very useful and fairly common in nature. They are nice to have around when you need them.

When marketed, jug wines are as good as they will ever be. They beg for drinking now. The key characteristic of jug wines is that they are made for immediate appeal. Ordinary wines will not develop any beneficial characteristics with aging; they lack this ability. Thus, this category of wine has as its unifying characteristic a lack of complexity — these wines are one-dimensional and that one dimension is a grape-like or simple vinous appeal. They are wine-like, nothing more. Additionally, as a group they tend to lack recognizable distinction, either regional or in grape composition.

The chief characteristic, shared by all ordinary wines, is a vinous nature, which comes directly from the relationship between the grape and climate, and from winemaking procedures. For each country and sub-region, climate is a given factor but grape varieties and winemaking procedures change according to the kind of wine intended. Both Bordeaux and Napa Valley may enjoy a climatic advantage and may bring us some excellent wines, but it would be wrong to assume that each region has a monopoly on fine wines. Every wine region can yield ordinary wines, and this includes France, Germany, Italy, and California. The composition of the wine and the methods of production are crucial factors for ordinary wines.

As I have mentioned earlier, only a dozen or so grapes are capable of yielding complex wines on their own or in concert with other compatible varieties, so we won't belabor that point. These particular varieties do not, happily, lend themselves to commercial quantities of ordinary wines because they are costly to produce and not terribly adaptive to different climates. Ordinary wines, for most consumption, are generally made in volume.

The production methods are the more unifying thread, and they span the globe. The economics of mass production dictate most of the decisions along the way. The vineyards do not contain the shy-bearers, the low-yield varieties, but rather those that love to produce a large crop of plump berries which are rich in sugar but lacking in acidity, tannins and other constitutents which are the essence of high-quality wines. More grapes per vine and more juice per berry are the goals for producers of ordinary wine. Vineyard sites are chosen with these objectives in mind, a hot climate and fertile soil are ideal. If needed and if local laws allow, the vineyards are irrigated, first for foliage development; later for increase in berry size. The Central Valley of California, the Mediterranean climate of the south of France, the hot vineyards of Sicily, Cyprus, or Algeria are examples of areas which are ideally suited for the high yield production required for these wines.

Once they arrive at the production facility, the grapes for ordinary wines are usually rushed through the most efficient procedure in terms of both time and equipment usage. Economics dictates procedure in the winery as well. Crushing is followed immediately by fermentation; no effort is made to sort out the good batches of grapes from the mediocre. The must is all channeled into the same, and usually large, fermenter. No skin contact for white prior to fermentation, or for red afterward is desired. The juice is converted into wine, and those components of the grape which contribute to complexity or aging potential are deliberately excluded since these are usually bitter and harsh when the wine is young.

The fermentation process is often as rapid as possible. The yeast used is generally an all-purpose, heavy-duty yeast strain. If off-odors or off-characteristics develop from grapes or fermentation, they will be blended out with neutral wine or filtered out (usually with a centrifuge) later on. As quickly and as efficiently as possible after fermentation, the wines are clarified and stabilized. They are stabilized with preservatives such as potassium sorbate or by flash pasteurization or millipore filtration to insure consistent quality during a normal shelf life of one to two years after bottling.

Pasteurization was once the only tried-and-true method of stabilizing jug wines. It often left the wines with a burned, or cooked, character which led to their poor reputation. But with modern technology at hand, most ordinary wines can be flash pasteurized which kills any microorganisms in the wine without producing a baked taste. Flash pasteurized wines can be relatively clean, vinous wines with pleasant, fresh, fruity flavors. After fermentation and clarification, the wines are held in large temperature-controlled tanks, frequently as large as one hundred thousand gallons (there are even a few of one-million gallons capacity), until needed for bottling. This is simply "holding" as opposed to "aging" since the wines do not improve or change while in these tanks; ordinary wines seldom spend any time in small barrels or casks, which add additional flavor or character.

Once made into wine, they are blended or corrected for any deficiencies. The corrections often relate to acidity, and the usual procedure is to add acid afterward for balance. Sometimes the sweetness is adjusted, usually by adding some grape concentrate or sweet blending wine. Another option is to blend batches to compensate for weaknesses in terms of acidity, sweetness, structure and balance. Just prior to bottling, the wines are filtered to safeguard against any changes which might occur in the bottle that might harm the wine.

This general scenario has many variations, but all jug wines follow it to some degree. The final products are fruity and clean with enough flavor and balance to be easily drinkable. Even when the techniques vary signficantly, the end result is a wine that is characterized by simplicity, directness, little or no complexity, and what is called "vinosity." Being widely appealing is the desired virtue.

Jug, or ordinary wines, as we have defined them can, indeed, be brought together as an entity from an international wine perspective. Each country or major region produces jug wines, and their vinous character can be described within certain parameters. What follows is just such a survey from this quality-perspective. Each general wine-type mentioned is available in the United States. Some of the wine-types mentioned are *always* ordinary in quality, while others may range across the three-tier quality-system — Jug, Premium, or Noble — that I have laid out in Chapter One. These ranges, along with the general characteristics, will be noted.

AUSTRIA

Almost all Austrian white wines fall into the ordinary wine tier, and vast amounts of simple, quaffing wine called *heurige*, are consumed in local bars and taverns. Varietal wines such as the Grüner Veltliner range from jug to premium quality, are light and refreshing in a spicy character, and best when young. The Rieslings are light and soft, while the Rheinerisling is more aromatic; both are jug quality, except when the Rheinriesling is made from *Botrytis*-infected grapes.

GERMANY

The ordinary quality wine of Germany, *Tafelwein*, is mostly consumed on the spot and seldom exported. Wine labeled "*Qualitätswein*" is usually premium quality but sometimes falls into my jug category. Price can be a helpful guide to these wines but should be considered with caution since many jug quality wines with names of premium wine reputations are sold at inflated prices — Bereich Bernkastle or Liebfraumilch are prime examples. Most German jug wines are soft and slightly sweet in style. The best-known is Liebfraumilch, which ranges in quality from a bland, semi-sweet jug wine to a premium quality wine with style and distinction. It is often give a proprietary name, such as Blue Nun, for example.

Some Mosel bottlings tend to be modest in fruit, sharp and thin in style, and unlikely to improve with age. The regions offering many ordinary quality wines are Franconia, for Franken wines, and Baden where the wines are generally soft, full-bodied, but a trifle dull. Some of the Piesporter versions are best when young, and among varietal names, those labeled Rülander, Kerner, and Scheurebe yield simple, slightly fruity, round, soft wines.

FRANCE

France produces vast quantities of mediocre wines. Fortunately the worst are rarely exported to America but a lot of what is offered in the jug quality category is quite inferior to its California counterparts and considerably more expensive. In this category, the wines of France rarely provide good quality or value. An understanding of French wine regulations and label nomenclature is essential in differentiating these wines from the "better" wines of France. It would be helpful to turn to page 120 before reading further.

Most French jug wines will not bear either Appellation Contrôlée or V.D.Q.S. (see pages 120-121), instead. they will be labeled as "Rouge", "Blanc" or "Rose" with no reference to a specific region or place name. Frequently, they will bear a brand name as a trademark and, as such, are known in France as *Vin de Marque*. While they may come in either a Bordeaux or Burgundy-shaped bottle (see page 234) inferring a regional origin, the bottle style has no relationship to the quality of the wine. These are not "declassified" wines from these regions as some retail establishments are prone to represent. Under recent French laws regulating these wines, a bottler may not list a legally delimited region as part of his address. This is to prevent the consumer from assuming that the wines came from a quality wine region such as Bordeaux, Burgundy, etc. Instead a code number, such as *Negociant à 1245789*, is used. Furthermore, wines from A.C. designated districts may not be declassified to non-appellation wine but rather must be distilled into industrial alcohol. In order to avoid further deception, French *Vin de Marque* may not bear a vintage date either, although to the consumer, this would be a helpful way of determining the freshness of the wine.

The fact that a French wine bears an Appellation Contrôlée or a V.D.Q.S. designation does not preclude it from falling within the jug wine category. Simply stated, many Frenchmen drink wines that are quite inferior to even the most ordinary wine produced in America; our taste standards for even these wines frequently exceed those of certain controlled wines of France. Thus, a legal designation on a French wine may, in some instances, indicate no better quality than an inexpensive, well made, California Chablis or Burgundy. Also, since wines within certain regions of France, and even within the same appellation, may fall within three of our categories, it is essential not to assume that you are buying a high quality wine on place designation alone. Good quality jug wines are produced in many A.C. districts, although most of them are not exported. The regions discussed below all produce wines of better than jug quality; in the chapter that follows, these regions will be covered in terms of premium and noble quality wines.

ALSACE

Good quantities of ordinary wines are produced here, but only a small percentage is exported. The Sylvaner, slightly fruity, highly acidic, is the leader, followed by the Tokay d'Alsace (made from Pinot Gris) and the Muscat d'Alsace, a slightly bitter, often dry white.

BORDEAUX

All wines labeled "Bordeaux Blanc" or "Bordeaux Rouge" are generally on the order of jug wines; the red wines tend to offer more vinosity than the Bordeaux Blancs. Bordeaux Blanc may be semi-sweet or dry; the dry wines are bottled in light green bottles, the semi-sweet in white. These whites are frequently over-sulphered to the point of being unpleasant. Those labled "Bordeaux Blanc" are whites that can be light and fruity, often slightly sweet in finish. Those simply labeled as "Graves" are little more than slightly fruity, somewhat acidic wines with differing degrees of sweetness and cleanliness. Wines bearing the "Bordeaux Supérieur" appellation, regardless of type, are usually ordinary in quality although the reds occasionally offer exceptions to the rule.

BURGUNDY

Red and white wines with the "Bourgogne" appellation are generally fruity in aroma and light in body and flavor. Beaujolais is light, very fruity, short in the finish, and best if consumed within a few months to a year of bottling. Beaujolais Blanc, Mâcon, and Petit-Chablis are all dry, early maturing white wines, fruity and medium- to light-bodied.

THE LOIRE VALLEY

Muscadet and wines labeled "Gros Plant" are both ordinary, light, slightly fruity, wines that are intended for early consumption. Muscadet is meant to be light, dry and crisp, but frequently is not when it falls into the jug quality category. Gros Plant is heavy, coarse, and acidic and not often found in the United States. Anjou rosés are fruity, sweet, and occasionally, slightly spritzy, while the whites made from Chenin Blanc are fruity and light-bodied. Loire Valley reds, Bourgueil, Chinon, and Champigny are vinified for medium color, fruitiness, and light tannins. Bourgueil will sometimes improve in bottle. Sancerre white wines are slightly fruity with a hint of grassiness, high in acidity and without much depth. Pouilly-Fumés range from slightly thin, ordinary wines to more aromatic and slightly complex premium wines.

THE RHÔNE VALLEY

The Côtes du Rhône and Côtes du Rhône-Villages appellations cover a wide range of simple, straightforward red and white wines. The regional reds have good color and a ripe fruity character, but lack complexity. The whites are modestly fruity, and light- to medium-bodied.

ITALY

Italy now exports vast amounts of ordinary wines. As with the French wine regulations, Italy's legal appellations, known as D.O.C., do not implicitly imply that the wines are better than ordinary, although certain D.O.C. regions do produce only premium quality wines. Presently, there are well over two hundred D.O.C. areas, the vast majority of which produce wines that fall within the jug quality category. Even so, the bulk of Italian wines exported to the United States are non-D.O.C. wines sold as simple "Bianco," "Rosso," or "Rosatto," and usually hailing from a large winegrowing region. These are usually neutral or straightforward in vinosity, sometimes identifiable as being of Italian origin by taste, and can provide good value when they are well-made.

Also contributing to the impressive Italian export statistics are low-alcohol, soft, fruity, and slightly carbonated wines known as Lambrusco and sold under brand names such as Riunite. Lambrusco wines, made as white, red and rosé are produced in the Emilia-Romagna region, from the Lambrusca grape as both D.O.C. or non-D.O.C. wines. In Italy they are usually less grapy and sweet than those exported to the United States, the bulk of which is non-D.O.C. Lambruscos vary from slightly to cloyingly sweet. The reds have a distinctive "jammy" flavor and appealing fruitiness which is enhanced by a slight carbonation making it ideal for quaffing slightly chilled. They are usually sold under a proprietary name and vary in sweetness and style with each brand. They offer wide appeal and are easy to drink.

These whites enjoy wide distribution in America; some are also produced in premium quality under the same name and will be discussed in greater detail in the chapter that follows:

EST! EST!! EST!!! is soft, bland, ranges from slightly sweet to sweet, and comes from the Latium region near Rome.

FRASCATI, from the region of that name near Rome, is fruity, soft, often spritzy, and ranges from dry to slightly sweet.

LACRYMA CHRISTI, is barely grapy, usually light and sweet.

ORVIETO and some ORVIETO CLASSICO are fragrant with a medium texture; smooth and on the dry side.

PINOT BIANCO is fairly neutral, slightly vinous and usually dry.

SOAVE offers fresh vinosity, medium texture, and is dry to varying degrees of sweetness. The better ones can be quite distinctive.

TREBBIANO is a wine characterized by a fruity aroma with slightly bitter flavors.

The red wines which follow span the quality spectrum; they are offered in premium quality as well.

BARBERA can be finished slightly sweet and intentionally spritzy.

BARDOLINO is light in color, and has sharp, rough, vinous flavors.

CHIANTI is a fruity, sometimes spritzy, and often warm wine. Chianti spans the ordinary and premium quality tiers.

GRIGNOLINO is a light colored, rough, acidic wine.

NEBBIOLO D'ALBAS have an earthy fruit, medium-body, and short finish; some are capable of aging into simple premium quality.

VALPOLICELLA is a wine with medium color with an almond-like fruitiness and a light body.

THE UNITED STATES OF AMERICA

Among American jug wines, you will find wines with "generic" names such as Chablis, Rhine, or Burgundy which imply emulation of the traditional European styles but as a rule do not bear any resemblance to the wines from the regions from which they have borrowed their name. Use of these names, which is legally "controlled" in the countries of their origin, is a trade abuse that has withstood the exigencies of time. Imported wines may not bear these geographical place names unless they actually come from the specified regions — American producers are permitted to continue to use this deceptive nomenclature over the objections of the foreign governments involved. However, responsible producers are beginning to forsake this practice and label their wines as Red or White "Table Wine," for example, or with a propriety brand name. All these wines are meant to be of ordinary quality. They are grown in relatively warm regions, such as the Central Valley of California, and are conducive to high yields with good vinosity. Frequently wines from cooler regions are blended in for character. Viticultural regions (appellations) are required of American wines (see page 120), most California jug wines bear the designation California, North Coast Counties, etc. Most New York State jugs are blended with neutral California bulk wine to tone down the strong flavors of native eastern varieties and are thus labeled as American Chablis or Burgundy, etc. Many California jugs display the term "Mountain" which has no legal meaning nor any requirement that wines so designated are mountain grown. The term is often found on a producer's lesser grade of wines.

California's jug quality whites are often fruity in aroma, less so in flavor, and vary from slightly sweet to very sweet. This applies, as well, to those few called Blanc de Blancs, and most proprietary whites.

CHABLIS spans the spectrum of flavors, styles and degrees of sweetness. It rarely resembles French Chablis which is usually dry, crisp and flinty in flavor.

GREY RIESLING, FRENCH COLOMBARD, GREEN HUNGARIAN are major white varietals that seldom exceed ordinary status. They offer fresh fruitiness in aroma and flavor, with a normal degree of sweetness for immediate appeal.

CHENIN BLANC offers a vinous, fruity character and is made for early consumption.

SAUVIGNON BLANC, GEWÜRZTRAMINER, and some JOHANNISBERG RIESLING straddle the jug/premium line. When the grapes are in an inappropriate location or picked at the wrong time, their character is lost or muted.

Red wines follow a similar pattern. Most generics, BURGUNDY, CLARET, CHIANTI, and RED TABLE WINE offer vinosity, and tend to be rather full-bodied from the hot climate in which they are grown. They have a characteristic roughness and robust character that is surprisingly consistent.

GAMAY and GAMAY BEAUJOLAIS are best when young; this is truer for the latter which is often fruity and light-bodied.

BARBERA and PETITE SIRAH, especially those with "California" as the appellation are in the fruity, full-bodied, robust mold.

The dessert wines from California can be almost entirely labeled as ordinary wines. All Sherries and Ports within this quality-tier offer little resemblance to their European counterparts. Premium quality Sherries and outstanding California Ports are beginning to emerge and are discussed in Chapter Twelve.

OTHER AREAS

PORTUGAL

Portugal's best known ordinary wines are its rosés marketed under proprietary names, Lancers and Mateus being the best known. In Portugal the most popular are the Vinhos Verdes, or types of green wine, characterized by a tart and sharp acidity. They are either red or white, and retain a degree of carbon dioxide. They are traditionally consumed a few months after the harvest. A number of light red and white wines come from the Dao region, with the whites being light and simple. The reds are soft and mellow from time in barrel.

ROMANIA

Romanian wines are almost all ordinary quality. The whites, Riesling, Muscat, and Chardonnay are light, often sweet. The reds are similar. Cabernet Sauvignon and Pinot Noir are often finished slightly sweet.

SPAIN

Spain offers ordinary wines from many regions, including the Rioja and the Panades regions which also produce better quality wines. Most Spanish white wines are dull and unexciting; those from Panades are lighter and fresher, though still intended for early drinking. Only a few Rioja red wines are above ordinary quality; most inexpensive Riojas are soft, mellow and vinous.

GREECE

Most Greek wine found in the United States is ordinary in quality and is generally sold under proprietary names for red, white, rose and retsina. Best known producers are Achaia Clauss and Cambas.

PREMIUM & NOBLE WINES

Premium is a word that has been rather loosely used by the wine industry. It has no legal definition and each winery that labels its wines as "Premium" defines the word for itself. For the purpose of this book, I have used the word "Premium" to define wines which have style and distinction. By this I mean they offer more than the direct vinosity, simplicity, and immediacy of drinkability, found in jug wines. They are more than wine-like. They have a certain distinctiveness that comes from the grape variety or from a specific region and sometimes both. The quality factors may come from cultivation practices, vinification methods, or the winemaker's intent, and is usually a combination of all three.

This general definition of premium spans a broad spectrum of quality. Therefore, I have further delimited the word into three, more precisely defined quality-categories: "Simple-Premium," "Mid-Premium" and "Super-Premium" dependent on certain qualities which I will define in a moment. In determining whether a wine is or is not within a particular category, the decisive factor is the structure and character of a wine, not its price or prestige. One you become familiar with the concept, identifying wines within each quality-category will be relatively easy, it is firmly based on taste. All of these wines have a pedigree above the ordinary.

Premium wines contain numerous aromatic and flavor compounds. These compounds provide such wines, first of all, with an ability to change over time creating new flavors, for better or worse, with age. They do not "hold" or change just by becoming old. These compounds are usually not present in jug, or ordinary, wines — they contribute to a wine's character by providing an aromatic or perfumed aroma or bouquet, a complexity of flavors and tactile sensations in the mouth, usually with a degree of tannins for red wines, and always with an aftertaste that continues the flavor and sensation of the wine after it is swallowed. A wine without this aftertaste rarely falls within my premium-quality categories. Premium wines always offer a balance of components, called style, which is appropriate to the type of wine.

Now let's return to the subtle distinctions within my tier-structure of premium wines. In this framework, simple-premium wines are those which offer more than jug wines, but not very much more. Their aroma will frequently be simple or straightforward, and their finish will lack complexity or length. They are premium because they have a degree of distinction which places them above jug wines, and frequently offer enough clues for an experienced taster to identify the grape variety or origin of the wine. Mid-premium wines offer complexity, but lack the supple structure that permits a wine to be assertive, yet display subtle nuances of flavor and tactile sensation. Super-premium wines do just that. Noble wines, which will be discussed later, bring the quality of Super-premium wines to their ultimate conclusion.

To better understand these distinctions, let us return to winemaking and grape growing for a moment to see what factors make these distinctions possible. The following is more important for mid-premium and above than it is for simple-premium wines. The production of premium wines begins in the vineyards with good viticultural practices. The grapes are matched to a favorable climate and soil, and the yields are controlled to obtain high-quality, rather than high quantity, fruit. At the harvest, the grapes must be picked within very narrow parameters of sugar and acidity, along with the proper level of pH and the flavor maturity of the fruit. The reason is that the appropriate raw materials must be available to produce a wine that requires a minimum of adjustments in the winemaking process.

Once the ideal sugar-acid ratio is reached, the grapes must be harvested quickly and carefully. They must reach the winery as soon as possible to avoid any oxidation from broken skins, or changes in sugar or acid after the grapes have been picked. The grapes must have been picked carefully to avoid any rotten clusters or berries.

Vinification must take place under closely-regulated conditions. The temperature must be controlled and the rate of fermentation also kept within a particular flavor-producing range appropriate for the specific grape varieties. The fermenting vats are usually small, since the huge ones used for jug wines do not permit juice to be cooled adequately to maintain the temperature within the appropriate limits throughout the entire tank. While fermenting, the juice must be periodically monitored, both by tasting and by laboratory analysis so that no off-flavors develop.

Many crucial decisions are made from the beginning to the completion of fermentation. For white wines, the winemaker must decide if and how long to allow the juice to remain in contact with the skins, whether to centrifuge the juice, and how heavy to press the grapes. For reds, the decisions are whether to include stems, and whether to ferment warm or cold. There is also the selection of the yeast, if cultured yeasts are used. Most such decisions relate to avoiding problems as well as determining quality. An unwise decision can't be easily reversed later on, if at all.

The complexity of flavors and aromas results not only from both grape growing and vinification, but also from working with the wine after fermentation. The choice of cooperage by type, size, kind of wood, and age is an important factor. How one combines the free-run and press wine, (if combined at all) will influence the wine's character and is an element of winemaking artistry. Wines are assembled, by and large, from small lots; the winemaker combines the same wine from several different tanks, batches, or barrels as a fine saucier works his sauces in a great restaurant. The potential combinations are numerous, as each barrel or tank offers discernable differences even for wines made from grapes from the same vineyard.

In making premium-quality wines, technical acumen is even more essential than when producing technically sound jug wines, but it must be applied in concert with some degree of artistic vision so that technology and artistry work toward one goal. It is in the realm of technology, applied in conjunction with an individual artistic concept, constrained by business economics, that wines fall into simple, mid or super quality levels. Winemakers are aware that what they produce is intended to be sold for a profit amid vast competition. Premium wines still remain commercial products and production costs are a vital consideration in the winemaking process. The costs of the equipment, farming, interest rates, labor, and holding a wine for aging, whether in cask or bottle are all constraints which separate premium wines from those rare noble wines which have a ready market, regardless of demanded price.

From this perspective, it should be evident that the winemaker is frequently not permitted to produce the best wine possible. Given grapes that are grown in the finest locale and brought to a peak-perfect maturity, the vintner will often use them to improve a blend of average-quality, mid-premium wine rather than create a wine of rare beauty.

The three levels of premium quality wine must all begin with grapes that are at least conducive to quality. A great vintner in a posh, fully-equipped winery can't turn poor grapes into premium or noble wines. But a vintner lacking in skill, experience, or artistic vision can turn the most noble of grapes into rather ordinary wine.

The final tier in my quality scheme is the tiniest of all, the noble quality wines that represent the quintessence of the grape and the winemaker's artistic vision. These are individually hand-crafted wines. They transcend commercial considerations — cost is no object in producing them — they are made for the connoisseur who is willing to pay the price of perfection. They are wines many producers of super-premiums hope to achieve, but rarely can. Natural conditions, artistic decisions, and, perhaps, even luck must all fall into place in order for noble wines to result. I sometimes refer to such wines as collector's or museum wines. Coincidently, noble wines (with rare exception) can only be produced from the noble grape varieties.

Many of the techniques applied to making noble wines are the same as those for making premium wines, except for greater care and fewer considerations for commercial exigencies. There's more personal involvement behind noble wines. There's a matter of luck involved mainly because many chances must be taken along the winemaking path with the risk of potential disaster omnipresent there. It all begins with an artistic vision of perfection; at no point does the vintner back away or begin making compromises.

As usual, the quality begins in the vineyard. And it begins long before Mother Nature either smiles or frowns upon the human vision. The grape varieties (known as cultivars) must be planted in a location which is ideal in terms of microclimate, appropriate soil and exposure to the sun. The first risk is taken by pruning for a small crop to maximize grape quality, for a small crop can also be entirely wiped out by frost or hail. During the season, some clusters may be thinned out to maintain a low yield. But, of course, the elements have to be close to perfect, free from excessive heat waves, cold spells, and other climatic problems. Then, as the harvest approaches, the vintner weighs a decision to delay harvest for perfect ripeness and character against the risk of unexpected storms. Noble wines require such risky waiting games. The requirements for sugar and acid in the grapes are the most exacting, and may require, perhaps, just a 5 percent improvement in sugar content, or just a little extra time on the vine for flavor improvement.

Picking is another matter handled with the utmost care and with the single goal of selecting only the best clusters from each vine, which sometimes entails several pickings. The grapes are crushed, and vatted separately, apart from lesser-quality grapes. Frequently, the grapes are hand–sorted to further weed out inferior clusters which should have been passed over during picking. Normally, fermentation procedures, pushing for that extra quality, involve a few unconventional techniques.

Fermenting on the wild yeasts for additional complexity is one example; others are fermenting red wines at slightly warmer temperatures and pushing down the cap, by hand, regularly, for maximum color, flavor, and tannin extraction. The inclusion of stems or the use of prolonged contact with the skins are other techniques used depending, always, on the vintner's vision. Many possibilities exist, but the paramount feature is the choice and the execution of them.

Afterward, the free-run juice and press wine are usually kept separate, but sometimes are allowed to age before being combined later on. The press wine may not be used at all. At this point, some producers of noble wines will select the best of each component wine, the *crème de la crème*, and assemble the blend prior to the barrel-aging regimen. Whatever the particular course taken, noble wines are aged in small casks, the most expensive, best coopered versions available. The wine is handled as little as possible, only when required. Clarification is accomplished often by racking, transferring the wine from one cask to another to leave the sediment behind. This is costly, labor-intensive, and risky, since it exposes the wine to air. Fining is achieved quite often by using fresh egg whites; a costly procedure which requires skilled labor and great care.

Then the wine must be bottled and bottle-aged. Much too often these wines are bottled with hand-operated machinery described at best as primitive. Such is the case when wines are produced at small wineries. Despite this exception to the "cost is not object" rule, tragic disasters from bottling procedures have rarely occurred.

Harmony, symmetry, complexity, finesse, and elegance define that rare quality, breed, which is the hallmark of noble wines. These wines represent an artistic concept, a standard of excellence which has evolved with time. They have evolved from centuries of winemaking, experimentation, and pursuing the ultimate. Their existence is possible only because there have been connoisseurs who have demanded perfection and were willing to pay the price.

A noble wine realizes an image of perfection by an individual artist — it represents a singular creative achievement that is rarely encountered. The vintner, as an artist, uses grapes as his palette. He tempers them with other elements such as rare oak, to add nuances. He has a special talent and a unique instinct that sets him apart from the ordinary winemaker. At the great châteaux and vineyards of France, it is not unusual for the job of *maître de chai*, the winemaker, to pass from father to son, with each generation.

There is no wine region that produces only noble wines; their existence requires a rare combination of topography, soil and climate which occurs only in small pockets, or *climats* in larger wine regions. Some regions have a greater incidence of these *climats* than others. These special conditions do not occur in the vast majority of vineyards of the world; and where they might exist, there has not been a winemaking tradition which has sought them out.

France has a virtual monopoly on the reds in this tier, with truly quintessential wines coming from both Bordeaux and the Côte d'Or of Burgundy. The noble dry whites of France come from the southern portion of the Côte d'Or known as the Côte de Beaune. A mere handful of outstanding white wines in this class comes from the Graves commune of Bordeaux. For sweet whites, the majority come from Sauternes with others from small areas of the Loire. Rosés do not fit into our noble quality wine scheme. All in all, there are less than two hundred individual French Châteaux or vineyards which produce wine within this class. Only Germany rivals France for consistently producing wines within this grade, and only for white wines predominately from the Riesling. Within Germany, there are less than fifty vineyards that qualify.

France and Germany are not the only nations to produce this class of wines, but they are the only ones which produce them with consistency. France does not have a monopoly on soil or microclimates but it does have a few centuries headstart in the selection of the best vineyards and the development of winemaking techniques. There have been truly outstanding noble wines produced in California, Australia, Italy and Spain, but never with the consistency achieved by the French. That wines which rival the best of France are possible, represents a promise for these other regions — the opening of a new vinous era as ideal vineyard/cultivar combinations are discovered and as the winemakers modify their techinques. As the price of France's noble wines rises beyond reach and demand for wines of this quality continues to grow, winemakers throughout the world will strive to compete in producing noble wines. A single and significant factor in the achievement of noble wines in other regions has been the adoption of the techniques responsible for their prototypes in France and Germany. As vintners recognize this, we can expect more great wines from elsewhere throughout the world.

Noble wines are open to criticism because they are different, incomparable by ordinary standards. Like those few truly great artists in other creative disciplines, producers of noble wines face the ultimate risk — of being critically examined, surveyed for departures from a nearly-perfect ideal, damned for the slightest flaw. Yet, rarely do they receive personal recognition. Rarely do they become celebrities among wine connoisseurs. Nor do they want to be. Their rewards are in realizing their visions; they are anachronisms, perhaps as rare today as the wines they produce.

Throughout the balance of this chapter I will describe, in detail, the premium and noble wines which are widely distributed within the United States or are of such importance that they should be mentioned in passing. These come mainly from six countries: the United States, France, Italy, Germany, Spain and Portugal. Wines of this quality are produced in many other wine producing nations, but are not widely available. The list of recommended books in Chapter Twenty-Three will provide coverage of these other regions for the reader interested in widening his vinous horizons.

At this juncture, remember that "premium" in its three manifestations refers to quality. The references to value within each section that follows are based on the earlier description given for each tier of premium wine.

SIMPLE-PREMIUM

In terms of aesthetics, these wines display some personality that can, with experience, be recognized and described in meaningful language. These distinguishable, individualized characteristics separate simple-premium wines from jug wines. Simple-premium wines are a step above jug quality wines. Their flavors are distinct, and they have ample alcohol, acidity and (for the reds), tannins, to supply a structural framework, or backbone, for support. What they lack is a finish or aftertaste beyond the brief and fleeting.

MID—PREMIUM

These wines offer an even more distinct personality which may be varietal (coming from the grape) or regional (of a specific wine-growing region). Often, they offer both.

SUPER-PREMIUM

These wines, however, transcend even these traits, and include a notable refinement, a sense of style . . . qualities connoisseurs refer to as "finesse" or "breed". Thus, super-premium wines are multi-faceted. They may be light and ethereal in nature, or they may be warm, rich and very sensitive. They stand out from the crowd.

Super-premium wines are also unified. All their different facets work together as nuances and build toward a complex, yet harmonious, overall impression. Light and elegant super-premium wines offer a refinement that is ethereal; fuller-bodied wines have more polish than power, a subtle complexity rather than blatant contradictions. But whether they are light or full-bodied, super-premium wines share an important attribute—an ability to linger on the palate long after they are swallowed. The super-premium and noble wines of the world make you think and contemplate. They demand and command attention and reflection, and, by their very nature, transcend the immediate occasion and mundane world. Rare, and justifiably expensive, the super-premium wines, along with those in the noble category, reward the painstaking methods of production and the costs to consumers.

One fallacy about wines that is carried over from our experience as cost-conscious consumers is that price is directly related to quality. Although this kind of thinking may very well apply to some commodities, it is not necessarily true when buying wine. Nonetheless, as a point of reference, I will present broad price structures which can be used as a rule of thumb; but please remember that in this discussion, I am talking not only about a price range of wine, but also about quality within that range.

Most wines in the premium quality category range from $3 — $15 a bottle. These are broken down into: simple-premium wines ranging $3 — $5 a bottle; Mid-premium wines from $5 — $8 a bottle, and super-premium wines from $6 — $15 a bottle.

Can any rules of thumb be applied to specific countries? There are, but take them as generalizations only. French wines are "in," and thus often priced beyond real merit. So-called hand-crafted wines from small California wineries are also fashionable and are often priced on the basis of mystique rather than value. Wines from Italy are more difficult to pigeonhole; when considered in terms of both quality and quantity, they tend to be priced too high. From the same perspective, however, the wines from Germany can offer a good value.

These comments apply specifically to our three grades of premium wines. When dealing with wines of noble stature, we are playing a different game. Noble wines are for enjoying on rare occasions, and to some consumers, price for these wines presents no object.

FRANCE

ALSACE

There are some wines from Alsace that are of simple-premium quality, lacking the character of premium wines. Among the varietals, prime candidates include the Tokay d'Alsace (made from the Pinot Gris, not the Tokay grape) and some Muscat d'Alsace bottlings. If you find Muscat, Sylvaner, and Riesling wines labeled with the simple "A.C. Alsace" but without the name of a producer mentioned in this book, and sold at low prices, beware. The wines are likely to be simple-premium quality. Unlike those with a specific district name, they are lighter in body, less distinct, somewhat imbalanced and, often with sweetness that detracts from their appeal.

Other than the name of the producer, Alsatian wines offer no real clues to help differentiate between the inferior and higher-quality gradations. In my experience, I've seldom encountered Alsatian Gewürztraminers in the simple-premium range; they are usually higher ranked.

BORDEAUX

In Bordeaux we have to navigate a vast sea of inferior-quality wine — both red and white. One dead give-away to inferior Bordeaux is the absence of an A.C. designation. Wines without it are likely to be mediocre. Within the simple-premium range, most Bordeaux wines are simply labeled "Bordeaux Rouge" or "Bordeaux Blanc," along with either the words "Bordeaux" or "Bordeaux Supérieur." (Bordeaux Supérieur merely signifies a higher alochol content). These wines may come from anywhere within the large Bordeaux district, but are not likely to be from the better sub-districts. Most Bordeaux Rouge tends to be light and thin, weak in flavor, with either harsh astringency, poor balance, or both.

The white wines in this category may be labeled "Bordeaux Blanc," "Bordeaux Supérieur," or "White Graves". Simple-premium white Bordeaux tends to be coarse and flabby in body, sometimes too sweet, and sometimes overly-sulfured, rendering the flavor unappealing. It is impossible to distinguish quality between the Bordeaux or Bordeaux Supérieur appellations. The name of the shipper should be an important determinant, but even well-known, advertised brands or trademarks cover White Bordeaux that lack character. Finally, since any piece of property in Bordeaux can be called a *château*, labels with handsome-looking castles and hyphenated names often simply try to disguise inferior Bordeaux wines.

BURGUNDY

As a catchall appellation, Red Burgundy and White Burgundy under the "Vin de Bourgogne" designation also covers a considerable amount of inferior wine. The most common phrases seen under the "Vin de Bourgogne" umbrellas are "Bourgogne," "Bourgogne Passe-Tout-Grains," "Bourgogne Aligote," and "Bourgogne Blanc."

Wines labeled "Bourgogne Passe-Tout-Grains are now being seen in the United States. Made from a blend of 65 percent Gamay and 35 percent Pinot Noir, they bear a slight resemblance to medium-quality red Burgundy, but are sold at higher prices than the quality merits. Red wines with the original "Bourgogne" appellation, the catchall designation, are submitted to more stringent standards than their Bordeaux counterparts. However, what comes to the United States under this name tends to be somewhat coarse, awkward in balance, and excessively priced. The average California Pinot Noir provides similar taste experiences at lower prices.

"Bourgogne Blanc" and "Bourgogne Aligoté" refer to simple-premium white Burgundies. The Aligoté, a grape variety, may not be used in white wines with higher appellations in which may use only the noble Chardonnay. Aligoté wines are second-rate, often quite acidic and sharp and lacking distinctive flavors. When offered in the United States, their prices tend to be higher than quality warrants. Bourgogne Blanc varies from flat, thin and insipid to crisp, and moderately fruity.

BEAUJOLAIS

The red Beaujolais wines range from simple-premium quality through mid and on up to, occasionally, super-premium status. The quality of wines simply labeled "Beaujolais" or "Beaujolais–Villages" may range from light-bodied with simple, fruity character, to well-balanced. A few are full-bodied and flavorful, resembling better Burgundies in style and structure. Inexpensive Beaujolais is usually that — cheap, and with a nasty, sharp acidity, sometimes accompanied by a dirty character which is usually the result of poor winemaking techniques.

Though the labels provide few clues, specifying only vintage and producer and/or shipper, we can say that Beaujolais Primeur generally falls into the simple-premium ranks. It offers strong vinosity, youthful fruit, a hint of yeastiness, and high acidity. Within six months or so, it tends to lose its vivacity and freshness, becoming dull, lackluster, ordinary wine at best.

CHABLIS

From this district, we find large amounts of simple-premium quality wines. Invariably, wines labeled "Petit–Chablis" fall into this quality-tier or, even into the jug wine category. Either way, they are expensive for what they offer. Petit–Chablis is usually thin, somewhat sharp and acidic or overly green, and quite ordinary.

But, let me digress for a moment. Some well-known producers who call Chablis home, and mention the name on labels of white wines, often market blended wines under a proprietary name. You should not assume that all wines marketed by shippers located in Chablis are authentic Chablis. Nor, for that matter, should you believe the wine must be declassified wines from Chablis. Neither assumption necessarily applies.

CÔTES DE PROVENCE

There are numerous white wines labeled either "Côtes de Provence" or "Cassis" which are offered in the United States at relatively inexpensive prices. These are simple, direct wines with some degree of distinction. They are usually relatively dry and pleasingly refreshing when well-made. They are simple wines, ideal for the casual life style indigenous to the south of France, but rarely anything to be excited about. White wines from the Appellation Contrôlée Cassis tend to be more austere and richer in flavor; but rarely is the quality above the simple-premium class. Numerous simple rosés, sometimes slightly sweet, are available from this district. The red wine from Bandol made from the Cabernet Franc, is tasty, pleasant and occasionally available at a reasonable price, but most is usually overpriced.

THE LOIRE VALLEY

The Loire Valley produces vast quantities of serviceable simple-premium quality wines that are frequently attractively priced. The white wine most commonly available in the United States is Muscadet, a light–bodied, simple, crisp white wine that, generally, is bone dry. It is an excellent accompaniment to shellfish, a good alternative to the considerably more expensive, authentic Chablis of France. The best Muscadet comes from the district of Sèvres-et-Maine and it would be wise to look for that district on the label. The most refreshing and flavorful Muscadet is bottled *Sur Lie*, which means right out of the cask. At its best, it will retain a zesty effervescence and piquant vinosity for approximately one year from the vintage date. Sur Lie Muscadet must be bottled in the spring following the vintage; its vinification does not sustain bottle aging. Unfortunately, many Muscadets tend to be over-sulfured and may become totally flat or coarse in flavor. The key, again, is the shipper's name on the label.

Wines from Sancerre, Quincy, Pouilly-Fumé, and Vouvray generally tend to fall into the mid-premium quality range, but some are simple-premium wines. Poorly made versions, often the least expensive ones in the United States, from Sancerre, Quincy and Pouilly-Fumé, will often be dry, but lacking in character. Vouvray, often over-sweetened to conceal its defects, will be correspondingly cloying, and thus of simple-premium quality.

Red wines from Bourgueil, Chinon, and Champigny tend to be of simple-premium quality. All are made from the Cabernet Franc in a light, fruity style that is intended to be consumed when young. Light in tannins, they can be tasty, if un-complex.

The Loire Valley also produces huge quantities of rosé wines, particularly from Anjou. These popular rosés are orange-pink in color, low in acidity, but appealingly fruity, ranging from slightly to quite sweet in finish. They are of simple-premium quality.

MÂCON

The Saint-Véran and "Appellations Pinot Chardonnay, Mâcon Contrôlée" are two newer appellations offering white wines that are seen in fair numbers in the United States. Wines from the Mâcon, made from Chardonnay, range from simple- to mid-premium quality. However, they may carry different label informtion. Some are highlighted as varietals — either Chardonnay or Pinot Chardonnay are used. Some may bear a "Mâcon A.C." designation, with some of the better versions label-ed "Mâcon-Villages, A.C." So far though, no meaningful quality designations are presented on labels from Mâcon. Consumers have to be familiar with the individual shippers or else assume that when low-priced, the Mâcon whites are likely to be of low quality. Wines from Saint-Véran tend to be light in character, round, sometimes soft, and ranging from simple- to mid-premium quality.

THE RHÔNE

Wines labeled "Côtes du Rhône" or "Côtes du Rhône-Villages" are either red or white. The reds are generally fruity, light-bodied wines similar to inexpensive Beau-jolais. Simple in character, they can withstand a slight chilling to provide fruity vinosity, accompanied by low acidity, light tannins, and pleasant drinking. Occasionally seen in the United States, white Rhône or Côtes du Rhône bottlings are mildly fruity, somewhat coarse and rough, and represent pleasant drinking at best.

GERMANY

The vast majority of simple-premium quality German wine remains in that country. These include the *Tafelwein* category which is always so–labeled. The German people consume most of the best simple-premium wines much the way they consume beer. Thus, a great deal of what is left over for the United States market in the lower-price range is often inferior to what remains at home.

Simple-premium exported wine usually falls into the *Qualitätswein* category, minus the *"mit Prädikat,"* or special attribute, designation. In approaching these wines, consumers might rely on price; the cheaper versions are likely to be lacking in flavor and low in acid — with none of the floral charm and elegance German wines are noted for. Liebfraumilch, for example, must legally be a *Qualitätswein*, but most of what we see on our shores is simple-premium in quality, either poorly made or lacking in character. Zeller Schwarze Katz, the Mosel's equivalent of Liebfraumilch, is usually of simple-premium quality. A variety of wines bearing only the Bernkastel designation or carrying the Bereich Johannisberg name are blended wines from their respective districts and are normally simple-premium quality as well.

ITALY

When viewed from the simple-premium quality perspective, Italy provides a marvelous array of flavorful, interesting wines. Just about every wine district offers a contribution or two, except for Barolo and parts of Barbaresco, that is. The best known of all Italian wines, Chianti, crosses every range of premium-quality. Many varietal Barberas, along with Lambrusco, Soave, Orvieto, and Frascati wines are easily placed in the simple- or occasionally, mid-premium brackets.

Chianti is the most variable. Those still sold in the straw bottle, the *fiasco*, are without question of simple-premium quality. Most of the Chianti sold in the non-Bordeaux botles or at low prices are quite likely to be simple-premiums as well. At their best, they are mellow, fruity, light-bodied and, so long as they aren't overly acidic, pleasant and agreeable enough.

Lambrusco is another popular Italian wine sold in the United States. The reds we receive come from the area of Emilia-Romagna, though whites and rosés are exported as well. The reds tend to be full-flavored, jammy in fruitiness, with both obvious carbonation and detectable sweetness.

Wines from Barbera are usually medium-bodied reds with a fruity profile and good acidity, though the quality range is wide. Normally, Barberas in the simple-premium quality range are not labeled with a village or district name. Grignolino wines are similar, though much lighter in body and more tart in flavor.

With few exceptions, most Italian wines imported to the United States which are labeled "Soave," "Verdicchio," "Est, Est, Est," "Orvieto," and "Frascati," tend to fall into the simple-premium range. Better versions of Soave and Orvieto can approach mid-premium quality.

In this realm, those Italian wines mentioned offer a consistent, recognizable character that places them above jug quality. They have regional or varietal identities, but still display a character that is fundamentally Italian. Among the whites, Frascati ranges from light and ethereal to dull, heavy-handed, and occasionally over-sweetened. At its best, it is of simple-premium quality.

THE UNITED STATES OF AMERICA

CALIFORNIA

Most of the simple-premium quality wines from California carry varietal names, but there are exceptions. One exception is the jug quality varietals which were referenced in the previous chapter; and although some blended wines from a few wineries are made more complex by using two or more grapes, the concentration of all California premium wines lies in those which are varietally labeled. The quality achievements come from the growing region, winemaking procedures, and specific style the producer sees as his end-product.

CHARDONNAY ranges from fruity, simple simple-premium quality on up to super-premium, and bordering occasionally on noble quality. Many of the Chardonnays with California appellations and without a vintage date fall within my simple-premium category. They can offer a clean, fruity, slightly apple-like aroma and flavor, but lack depth, rich texture, and the complexity of aging in small oak casks. Most are made in a crisp, high-acid style, often with lemony overtones like some French Chablis. They can sometimes improve in bottle but basically are meant for immediate consumption.

Among the appellations for simple-premium quality Chardonnays, Mendocino, Monterey, and North Coast are the more consistent areas. Those from Mendocino are generally lemony and crisp, made in firm, lean style. The North Coast bottlings are usually fuller-bodied because of the use of Napa and/or Sonoma grapes which develop higher sugars. Many Monterey-grown Chardonnays have a unique, green or grassy character, medium-body, and a sharp, crisp finish. Some of Napa's and Sonoma's larger wineries style Chardonnays to be medium in style, with an apple-like aroma, lemony notes, and moderate alcohol without wood character.

CHENIN BLANCS are generally ordinary quality. But some wineries allow the grapes to develop 24° sugar or so, ferment to dryness, and then age the wine in small oak. Several dry finished Chenins from Napa Valley have enough varietal intensity, a ripe peach and melon character, and depth of flavor to be called simple-premium wines; but they seldom attain a higher quality status. Chenins normally have a slightly bitter aftertaste as well.

GEWÜRZTRAMINERS from California normally fall into the ordinary or simple-premium quality range, except for a few which achieve the style of wines from the Alsace in France. Gewürztraminers from Napa and Sonoma can be very spicy in fragrance and fruity in flavor, but a little low in acidity. Most are finished slightly sweet to avoid high-alcohol "hotness." Most Napa Valley Gewürztraminers are of simple-premium quality.

Gewürztraminers from the Central Coast counties, Monterey, Santa Barbara, and San Luis Obispo, are less emphatic in aroma, but often better structured for longevity. Some retain a slight degree of Muscat-character which adds complexity.

PINOT BLANC, though not plentiful, is becoming more popular with California producers. Those with California appellations are moderately distinct, round, and slightly above ordinary with a spicy, apple-like character.

SAUVIGNON BLANC or FUMÉ BLANC, synonymous names, range in style widely. Most are in my simple-premium or mid-premium quality range. Only those Sauvignon Blancs sold in jug bottles at ordinary wine prices lack the characteristic varietal personality. Most bottlings offer sufficient varietal character — a grassy, weedy, or black pepper flavor — to earn premium wine status. Napa, Sonoma, Monterey, and Santa Barbara have been the best regions so far. The emerging region of San Diego County, overlapping into Temecula is also part of the simple-premium quality.

The grassy varietal, moderately complex, but early-maturing Sauvignon Blanc style is typical of those which come from Mendocino County. Its versions are muted in personality, soft, and the lightest of all. The Livermore Valley Sauvignon Blancs tend to be more open, fruity and varietal, medium-bodied and are slightly grassy and crisp. Napa and Sonoma are known for higher quality versions but several from larger wineries are straightforward, varietal, but lacking in real depth and oak complexity. As with many California varietals, the label nomenclature will not offer any clue as to quality in an instance such as this.

RIESLINGS, whether labeled JOHANNISBERG or WHITE RIESLING, are predominantly premium quality wines, with many falling within the simple-premium quality category. They are usually made with a low acid, and in a slightly sweet style. Many from Napa, Sonoma, Mendocino, and Lake Counties are simple-premium wines, when made from grapes of normal ripeness.

For dry-styled, or only slightly-sweet Rieslings, Monterey and Santa Barbara Counties offer more flowery, yet firm and stylish versions which are are similar to German Rieslings in a *Kabinett* style. These so-called "Soft Rieslings" to date are simple-quality premiums. They are often opulently fruity and flowery, but are sweet, low in alcohol, and meant for simple sipping.

BARBERA — Only two or three producers in California offer premium quality Barberas. They come from Sonoma County or bear a California appellation. The best display a rich, berry fragrance and flavor, a tannic composition, and a high-acid tartness. With aging, they soften in tannins, develop a few nuances.

CABERNET SAUVIGNON falls into all three premium quality categories, although a select few fit into the noble class. Most that are labeled "California" can offer straightforward varietal character, herbaceous aroma and flavor and improve slightly with aging for two or three years. The majority of simple-premium Cabernets come from the Central Coast Counties, and from those labeled "California" in origin. Actually, few with the state-wide appellation exceed ordinary quality, but those that do offer a berry, herbaceous fruit character, moderate tannins, and medium depth of flavors. Though Napa and Sonoma produce predominantly higher echelon Cabernets, many simple-premium versions carry that appellation.

Lake County, to date, falls into a simple-premium range for Cabernets, though I've had a couple that have been better. The Lake County wines are fragrant with a herbaceous, green-olive flavor, but for the most part have lacked the substance and the tannic spine to reward aging.

MERLOT could someday evolve into a high-quality California varietal. At the moment, it ranges in the simple- to mid-premium quality group, with a potential of reaching super-premium status as evidenced by a few wineries. Simple-premium Merlots come from Monterey, Sonoma, and Santa Barbara; they are often deep-colored, and aromatic in a weedy, coffee-bean tone, but, at least to date, lack richness and structure.

PINOT NOIR has not fared well in California until relatively recently. Most fall within the simple- to mid-premium quality categories though many producers are striving to emulate the noble stature of those from the Côte d'Or of Burgundy. Sonoma County and Mendocino make Pinot Noirs with some character above the stale, weak colored wine quality. They offer varietal fruitiness; a cherry, smoky character and medium-bodied, slightly tannic styles. Most labeled "Napa Valley" are warm, but light in color, and rather dull in flavors, except for those made from cool-climate areas.

ZINFANDEL is characteristically fruity and berry-like, but the degree of its character and intensity vary with climate and winemaking techniques. Zinfandel is unique to California, though it is a *vinifera* variety. Prior to the 1960s, most Zinfandels were light, fruity "picnic" wines but now span the range from jug to super-premium quality. Most Napa Valley and inexpensive Sonoma County Zinfandels are simple- to mid-premium. They are berry-like, medium-bodied with moderate tannins and often a tart aftertaste. Mendocino-grown Zinfandels vary from simple and berry-like, to riper, and excessively tannic, depending on climate.

So far, I have talked about wines of the world, which offer good quality for everyday enjoyment, and range from the ordinary to those with some distinction in their agreeable flavors. Now we enter a much different realm, one that excites connoisseurs, inspires poets, and embroiders the many mystiques which surround wine lore: Wines which are much more than merely compatible companions to a meal; wines that convert wine drinkers into wine connoisseurs; wines that make wine an avocation not just a hobby.

The wines in the category that will be discussed here satisfy more than a wish for a good wine with some character. They adhere to a traditional style of excellence, with a time-honored, aesthetically-pleasing character and style. They are readily identifiable to the experienced wine buff, and they require greater knowledge of specifics — châteaux, small vineyards, and vintages — than the previously-mentioned quality categories. While entire books have been devoted to the smaller regions and even to individual producers within these areas, my intention is to highlight only what is essential to encourage an understanding of these wines.

As I've done before, I'll follow the same sequence introduced in Chapter Eight with the hope that the reader will become involved in cross-referencing for a complete picture.

FRANCE

At this juncture in your wine education, it is necessary to study and memorize, to taste and associate those tastes with individual labels and properties; regions and vintages. This is a normal requirement for greater enjoyment of fine wines. This curious quest for greater knowledge that links taste with specific information, is what separates wine lovers from ordinary drinkers. When it comes to wines, one doesn't stop the learning process just because one particularly exciting brand or type is encountered. In the better-premium and noble wine categories, France provides fairly detailed, useful label information to help the consumer in selecting wines of quality. However, each major region has also adopted its own set of regulations. Learning is made somewhat easier by the fact that for a certain quality of wines, there are rules germane to specific regions that proceed by fairly well-defined hierarchies. An adequate understanding of the French system of wine classifications provides a solid foundation for comprehending those of other regions, which, to some extent, parallel the French approach.

The common denominator of all fine French wines is the appellation system which legally defines wine regions, specifies certain viticultural practices relating to quality and sets minimum standards for certain measures of quality. A detailed explanation of appellation regulations appears beginning on page 120. It is axiomatic that non-A.C. wines are incapable of achieving mid- to super-premium quality. But the converse is not always necessarily true — not all A.C. French wines are automatically of high quality. The most complex set of appellation laws are applied to both Bordeaux and Burgundy which maintain a multiple-tier hierarchy of quality gradations. To further complicate matters, each follows its own system of classifications and regulations.

BORDEAUX

In terms of quality and the sheer number of châteaux, Bordeaux, without question, is France's, and possibly the world's, premiere wine region. Over the decades, the style of wines evolved through a close historical tie to England whose wine lovers have determined the style and quality of Bordeaux wines. The history of the Bordeaux wines is a fascinating subject, but beyond the scope of this book. Chapter Twenty-Three lists several outstanding works on the subject.

Within the general appellation of Bordeaux lie the following inner appellations which are of significance to use. The Médoc, actually consists of the Médoc and the Haut-Médoc. The better wines are those with Haut-Médoc as an appellation. (Haut, incidentally refers only to location in the Médoc, not quality.)

Wines bearing the Médoc or Haut-Médoc appellations may be either regional blends or wines produced by a specific château. They are recognizable as Bordeaux in origin based on a well-defined structure, harmony, some complexity of flavor, ample tannins and alcohol, and an ability to age in the bottle. The aroma is usually peppery or spicy, with some oak component as well.

Throughout Bordeaux, some of the regional wines or even the château-bottled wines under these appellations may be the responsibility of what is known as a *négociant*. These *négociants*, or shippers, traditionally are involved in buying wines from different producers and blending them, balancing one against another for flavor and style, and bottling them under thier own control and names. Many of the *négociants* are so adept at blending and aging that their whites are often better than those from lesser, individual châteaux. The *négociant* has the added advantage of knowing the stylistic preferences of his intended markets far better than the small château owners.

For many decades the *négociants* handles most of the Bordeaux wine trade. Only within recent times have the proprietors moved toward bottling their own wines. By keeping the bottling "at home," these Bordeaux winemakers found a common way to avoid having others stretch the quality of their wine with wines from other regions. At one time, when all wines were sold in casks, the "Bottled at the Château" concept implied control from grape to bottle; but today it is commonplace, and no longer, if ever, associated with quality standards. Actually, the bottling operation may take place on a portable bottling line which is rented and delivered to the château premise for the bottling. My point, here, is that a label reading "Château Bottled" should no longer be construed as being better than other wines. The name of the producer and the piece of property involved are much more significant.

THE MÉDOC

Within the Médoc, the highest level of inner appellations are linked to townships—Saint-Julien, Margaux, Pauillac, and Saint-Estèphe. From these communes emanate the finest super-premium and noble wines of Bordeaux.

But there are regional blends from each commune (that should be distinguished from the châteaux) which are allowed to use the communal appellation. The blends are labeled "A.C. Pauillac," etc., and are usually shipper's wines or wines assembled by *négociants* from within the named borders. Blended for the consistency, some of these regional wines can be quite good, priced in the range of lesser châteaux; sometimes higher. Regional blends from an established, well-known shipper are often reliable choices in the mid-premium ranks.

These four townships of the Médoc all share the best-possible soils and microclimates within their respective boundaries. The soils are generally slightly rocky or pebbly with excellent drainage and exposure to the sunlight. Within each appellation, the conditions are as close to ideal as possible. Unlike other regions of France where classification is solely by place, the wines of Bordeaux (and some of the tiny parcels of Burgundy) are further classified into quality-rankings, or Growths, by châteaux names. The Médoc estates made up a large part of the official classification of 1855, which still remains the most useful guide to the best of Bordeaux.

The 1855 classification was based on the reputation of each châteaux during the previous years; and by reputation, the guideline was the price commanded in 1855. This ranking, officially called the Classification des Grands Crus Rouges de Bordeaux, remains the "bible" to this day, although over the last one hundred years enough changes have occurred to raise more than a few questions about validity. Authorities such as Alexis Lichine, myself, and others have modified the 1855 classification by updating it according to present quality-performances.

With this disclaimer aside, it should be useful to explain the 1855 classification. It consists of five fairly-close levels of Growths, all of which, it is fair to say, yield wines falling within the super-premium to noble ranks. Today, some sixty one châteaux are among those classified; a few have disappeared, having been absorbed by other properties. Those châteaux still among the five top Growths are labeled Grand Crus Classés. Below them are a group of estates, numbering about twelve, known as Crus Exceptionnels, followed by about one hundred twenty-five châteaux ranked as Crus Bourgeois.

But within the Grands Crus Classés we have the five top-ranked growths, or crus. They are ranked from first or Premiere down to the Fifth, or Cinquième. Sometimes it is possible to differentiate between two Growths, say a Fourth or Third Growth. Quality performances over the last decade or more are such that some are ranked higher than they now merit; others are under-ranked on their present records. This has to do with ownership changes, vineyard restructuring, financial situations, and successes with many vintages.

For the most part, the classified Growths consists of estates which are distinguished by the signature of the proprietors. The style varies with the location, the cépage, and the aging and vinification methods. Each component of the cépage, or blend, provides a certain character. Cabernet Sauvignon is hard, tannic, and redolent of bell-peppers and black currants; Merlot adds softness and suppleness, along with an herbaceous flavor. Cabernet Franc is dark, soft, flavorful, and ripens earliest. How they are combined, how the blend is assembled, accounts for differences in character and style. In the Médoc, Cabernet Sauvignon may represent either 90 or 60 percent of the blend depending on the producer and on vintage.

Some châteaux in the Médoc use new, small oak barrels each vintage; others mix old, seasoned barrels with the new ones. Most of the casks come from the Nevers Forest outside of Bordeaux which imparts a definite oak character and some complexity to the wine. Additionally, the differences can be attributed to the vintage itself—when the harvest began and what the climate was during that time. The Cabernet ripens the latest and is, thus, vulnerable to late rains. Merlot ripens early, but spring frosts often hinder both the quantity and the quality of Merlot grapes in the Médoc.

Although each vintage produces wines that are different in character, the classed growths provide their own signatures. In making the best wine, not every ounce or barrel is used. The winemaker selects the best casks for the label of the château, and places others aside for use either under a second label of the châteaux, or for sale to *negociants*, or other estates.

The lesser ranked growths of the Médoc often provide fine wines worthy of consideration. Since they are unable to command the highest prices, winemakers often take some short cuts in both vineyard practice and in the winemaking procedures. They may bottle every drop produced, rather than make cask selections or may not purchase new casks each year. These wines lack complexity and finesse as a result, but are still distinguished as better-quality Bordeaux. As such, they are roughly analogous to a good California Cabernet Sauvignon for quality, but different in style.

Of non-Médoc appellations in Bordeaux, the Graves region can offer red wines ranking as peers of some great Médoc wines. No inner, or township, appellations exist for Graves, though the wines were generally classified in 1953. Graves red wines have structure and flavor quite distinct from other Bordeaux wines. They tend to be more austere in character with a gravelly or earthy taste, hard to describe but easy to remember from experience. Some regional blends are labeled "A.C. Graves," and many tiny châteaux use the Graves appellation as well. In Graves, only Château Haut-Brion was admitted to the 1855 Classification, and it ranked among the First Growths. Though Château Haut-Brion remains deserving of this singular award, its neighbor, Château La Mission-Haut-Brion, has recently rivaled it in quality, a further testimony to some of the weaknesses inherent in the 1855 ranking. Despite the attempted classification of 1953 and the update in 1959, the Graves region was not submitted to the same rigorous, meaningful quality approach taken in 1855. Thus, when buying Graves wines, the consumer is better served by being familiar with specific names, rather than relying on these classifications.

SAUTERNES

The Sauternes district south of the city of Bordeaux has specialized in the production of sweet, white wines for centuries. Its best were classified in 1855, and only one, Château d'Yquem, was granted top rank and special, singular status. The region is prone to the appearance of the noble mold, *Botrytis cinerea*, which accounts for the typical unctuous, lush, honeyed character of the best wines from Sauternes. The predominant grapes are the Sauvignon Blanc (adding flavor and firmness) and the Semillon (adding softness, flesh, and roundness).

Sauternes is an expensive, risky wine to make. Not every vintage brings the right conditions to encourage *Botrytis* grapes which are usually harvested late in the season. Furthermore, the vineyards must be picked by hand on a berry-by-berry basis, usually, over several separate occasions. The cost of labor is staggering, and not every producer, today, can afford to follow the traditional practices unless he is compensated by demand and a fair return via the price of a bottle.

Sauternes vary widely in quality. The key factors are the composition of the vineyards and the methods of harvesting. If the vineyards are picked in one fell swoop, then not every berry will be infected by the desired *Botrytis;* the wines will be less flavorful, less concentrated and honeyed as a result. Too much Semillon and the wines become too soft, without enough structure to support the alcohol, and often too low in acid to carry the desired sweetness. Fermentation of the highly concentrated juice is difficult from initial pressing to completion. In lesser-quality wines, massive amounts of sulfur are often used to stabilize the wine and to conceal winemaking flaws.

Therefore, Sauternes can be divided into two broad quality categories. On one hand, there are those that are overly sweet and lacking balance or are simply poorly made. On the other hand, we have those that are honeyed and harmonious, balancing richness, complexity, and sweetness. Most of today's offering of regional, blended Sauternes fall into the first category and are best avoided. The finest are those ranked in the 1855 classification.

THE APPELLATION STRUCTURE OF FRENCH WINES

NON - APPELLATION

"Everyday" or Jug quality wines blended from grapes grown or wines produced from anywhere in France. Most of the wine is mediocre at best, however some proprietary brands from the better shippers can be pleasant drinking.

V.D.Q.S. - *Vins Délimités de Qualité Supérieure*

Wines from a V.D.Q.S. delimited area rank one step in quality below *Appellation Contrôlée*. The majority of the wines in this category are Simple-Premium — some may be better.

APPELLATION CONTRÔLÉ — A.O.C. or A.C.

Within this category there is a hierarchy of appellations. Wines within a specific appellation may also be "classified" i.e. included within a "classification" of wines of particular merit.

FIRST TIER — REGIONAL APPELLATION
ex: Bordeaux Superior

These wines range from simple to mid-premium quality

SECOND TIER — SUB - REGION APPELLATION
ex: Haut-Médoc (Bordeaux)

Somewhat higher in quality than the first tier but still range from simple to mid-premium quality with some wines occasionally better

THIRD TIER — COMMUNE - DISTRICT - PARISH
ex: St. Julian (Bordeaux) - Gevrey Chambertin (Burgundy)

These wines can be considerably better than the previous appellations depending on the producer. When the wines are blended from several or more vineyards within the commune or district they are known as Regional or Village wines depending on the custom of the locality. These wines range from mid to super-premium quality

FOURTH TIER — CLASSIFIED WINES
SINGLE VINEYARD AND RANKED APPELLATIONS
ex: classified - Ch. Lafite-Rothschild (Bordeaux - Pauillac) Ch. d'Yquem (Sauternes)
ex: single vineyard - Clos de Vougout (Burgundy) - Château Grillet (Rhone Valley)
ex: ranked appellation - Chablis Grand Cru or Chablis Premier Cru

These wines are the very best wines although they may not always live up to their expected quality depending on the climate and human factors. In off vintages these wines range from mid to super-premium and can reach noble quality in great years.

THE APPELLATIONS CONTRÔLÉES OF BORDEAUX

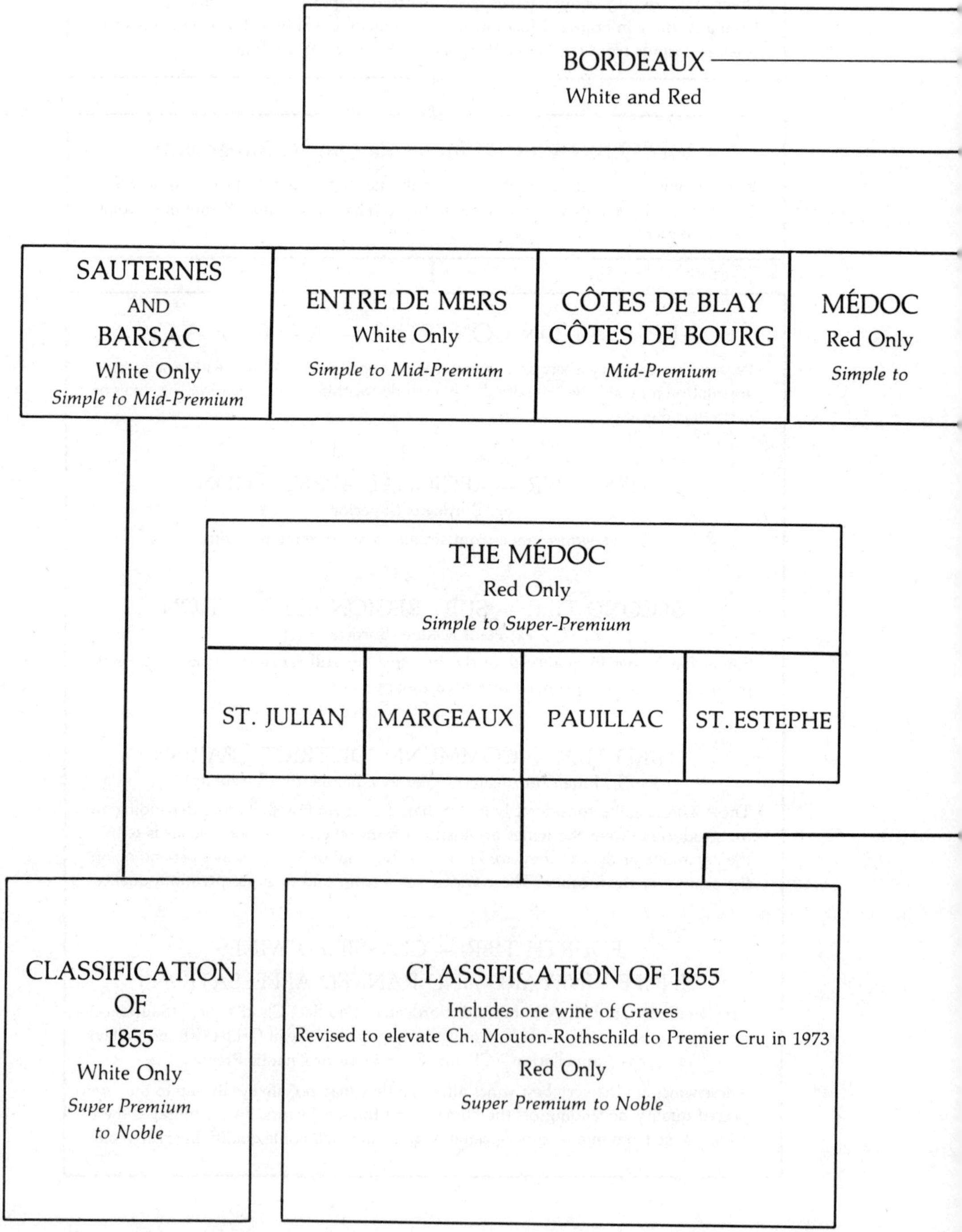

BORDEAUX ——————————
White and Red

SAUTERNES
AND
BARSAC
White Only
Simple to Mid-Premium

ENTRE DE MERS
White Only
Simple to Mid-Premium

CÔTES DE BLAY
CÔTES DE BOURG
Mid-Premium

MÉDOC
Red Only
Simple to

THE MÉDOC
Red Only
Simple to Super-Premium

| ST. JULIAN | MARGEAUX | PAUILLAC | ST. ESTEPHE |

CLASSIFICATION
OF
1855
White Only
Super Premium
to Noble

CLASSIFICATION OF 1855
Includes one wine of Graves
Revised to elevate Ch. Mouton-Rothschild to Premier Cru in 1973
Red Only
Super Premium to Noble

THE APPELLATIONS OF BORDEAUX

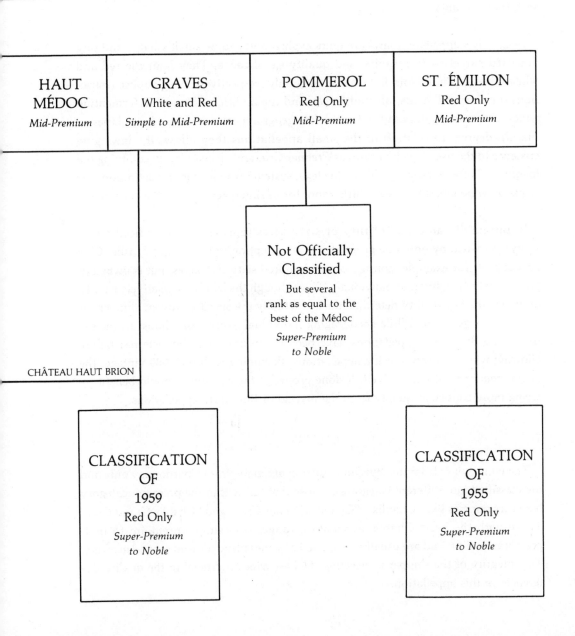

BORDEAUX SUPERIOR
"Everyday" to "Simple-Premium"

HAUT MÉDOC	GRAVES	POMMEROL	ST. ÉMILION
Mid-Premium	White and Red	Red Only	Red Only
	Simple to Mid-Premium	*Mid-Premium*	*Mid-Premium*

Not Officially Classified
But several rank as equal to the best of the Médoc
Super-Premium to Noble

CHÂTEAU HAUT BRION

CLASSIFICATION OF 1959
Red Only
Super-Premium to Noble

CLASSIFICATION OF 1955
Red Only
Super-Premium to Noble

BURGUNDY

The best wines from Burgundy are among the most fascinating and interesting of all. It has been so for many decades, but only in the 1960s did the wines of Burgundy begin to attract international attention, resulting in a steady increase in prices. Given the limitations of output among the finest, they are virtually unobtainable since they are now stratospherically priced. To the average, well-informed American, Burgundy is becoming a less significant factor in the wine market because many importers and merchants refuse to handle such expensive wines allocated in such tiny amounts.

Burgundy's appellation laws are quite explicit and endow small villages and tiny vineyard parcels with meaning and quality significance. They limit the red and white wines to Pinot Noir and Chardonnay only, respectively; they impose restrictions on vineyard yields, alcohol levels, and the addition of sugar to fermenting wines. But mainly, Burgundy's laws define geographical names and boundaries to the *nth* degree. In relation to the small appellations they allow, the laws give credence to the use of such phrases as *Premier Cru,* and *Grand Cru* by codifying the longtime unofficial rankings. Thus, the legal system provides specific definitions for terms on wine labels that leave little room for misinterpretation by the consumer.

In Burgundy, an estate of fifty or sixty acres represents a large holding. A vineyard owned by only one proprietor is an exception to the Burgundy rule. Clos de Vougeot, for example, consists of one hundred sixty-five acres, but is owned in part by sixty-five different individuals. Thus, though the labels are relatively easy to decipher, the key quality determinants are actually the specific grower, shipper, or vineyard in question. While encouraging individual expression almost to the extreme, the Burgundy appellations have been lax in imposing the taste test before allowing wines to carry specific appellations. Beginning with the 1980 vintage, the tasting requirement was revived. If done properly, the consumer should benefit by seeing more consistent quality from the myriad of Burgundy appellations.

CHABLIS

The white wines from this Burgundy district are made from Chardonnay only and are classified into different categories. Those that fall within the premium category here carry names like "Chablis," "Chablis *Premier Cru,*" and "Chablis *Grand Cru.*" Those with the basic Chablis appellation range from simple-premium to mid-premium quality, and are usually comprised of wines blended from several growers. The integrity of the shipper in selecting the best wines is crucial to the quality differences in this appellation.

The higher appellations for Chablis — A.C. *Premier Cru* and A.C. *Grand Cru* — are based upon higher minimum alcohol levels, location of the vineyards, and lower yields per acre. The names of individual vineyards may appear if all requirements are satisfied; wines bearing the simple A.C. Chablis by itself are forbidden from using vineyard names. Over the years, various vineyards have established reputations for quality. Many of the producers prefer to blend wines from different vineyards rather than offer wines from one vineyard. Thus, you may see wines labeled *"Premier Cru"* or *"Grand Cru Chablis,"* without a vineyard name attached. With or without a vineyard name, they are generally better quality than A.C. Chablis — rounder, firmer, and more typically Chablis in a steely, hard, but fruity, earthy way. Differentiation among the higher appellations of Chablis becomes more a matter of style than of quality.

Chablis, typically, is said to have a green-apple, austere, hard character often linked to a chalky flavor. Indeed, while the soils are chalky in composition, the uniqueness of Chablis may derive from the particular microclimate and quite possibly, at least in my opinion, from the selected strain of yeast used in fermentation. In recent years, the use of stainless steel tanks in Chablis has become standard and the small oak barrel has all but disappeared from view. Despite any changes, Chablis remains austere and steely, quite unlike white Burgundies grown in other regions.

The *Grands-Crus* bearing one of the seven permitted vineyard names can, in good years, achieve super-premium quality. The hallmarks of premium Chablis are a green-gold color, a fresh, sharp fruitiness, a flinty flavor, and crisp aftertaste. Chablis will improve in bottle for several years.

CÔTE d'OR

Wines from this region are unquestionably the most costly today; alas, they are also the most overpriced as well. When they are on target, they are superb; when they miss, they can be dreadful, suffering from poor winemaking or overly-ambitious vineyard practices for big production. They should be subtle, replete with nuances, supple in texture, and unique in style. They are not intended for everyday drinking.

The final quality depends on both the skill and the integrity of the grower. Forced to deal with the Pinot Noir grape, the world's most temperamental variety, growers who make one mistake will end up with disappointing quality. The consumer, therefore, must become more familiar with small growers and producers, and my best advice is to seek some reliable, informed outside source of information before spending a fortune on one bottle. Look to books, guides, magazines, and good wine merchants before taking a chance.

Today, Burgundy still offers wines of superior quality, mainly from those owners and shippers who follow stringent personal standards. In just about all of my price breakdowns correlated with wine-quality, Burgundy at least doubles the normal range. For example, mid-premium Burgundies today sell for $10 to $12 a bottle; the super-premiums are going for upwards of $20 to $25. And the noble quality wines are now in the $75 a bottle range. They are asking prices for wines when released, without bottle aging. But the best require at least five years or more before developing the characteristics one pays for. While possible, today, to purchase older, aged, bottles of Bordeaux, the consumer is unlikely to ever see mature Burgundy offered at retail. It is almost a "can't win" situation.

The mid-premium Burgundies come from two general appellations. First, there are the larger place names, called Côte de Nuits or Côte de Nuits-Villages, in the northern half of the Côte d'Or and those labeled Côte de Beaune or Côte-de-Beaune-Villages in the southern half. These are normally blended from the individual vineyards or communes within the areas of the northern Côte d'Or and the southern half. Wines with village names are usually slightly better in quality, though they fall within the general range of mid-premiums quality. They have a recognizably fruity, vinous aroma of Pinot Noir, with the regional character of red Burgundies. This is to say an experienced taster will know he is tasting red Burgundy from the aroma. Such wines are straightforward, uncomplex, reasonably well-balanced, with soft tannins and a lingering aftertaste. Though possibly coarse and lacking in finesse, they exhibit the character of the large appellation used.

The red wines from the Côte de Nuits tend to be fuller-bodied, firmer and more sharply defined than those from the Côte de Beaune. The generally–tendered description is that the former are masculine in style, and the Côte de Beaune wines are more feminine. Furthermore, to continue the broad distinctions, those from the northern part of the Côte de Beaune, around Aloxe-Corton, are softer, fuller-bodied, and richer in flavor. Red wines from the south and Côte de Beaune, such as Santenay, are lighter, more delicate, and have less aging potential in the bottle.

CÔTE de NUITS

It is within the Côte de Nuits that each individual commune or sub-district offers wines that are much more distinctive and that exhibit more traditional flavors characteristic of the place-name. Fixin, for example is the name of a village (or commune) in the north. Its wines are entitled to be labeled either as "Fixin" or as "Côte de Nuit-Villages." They are mid-premium quality, with some distinct character. But just a few miles south, in the village of Gevrey-Chambertin, the quality range improves considerably.

Gevrey-Chambertin, located in Burgundy's Côte de Nuits is a rightfully-famous wine village. Some wines are sold under the village name only, while others have a vineyard name attached. The difference is that the Gevrey-Chambertin bottlings are slightly less rich and fall into the mid-premium quality range. Here, those labeled *"Premier Cru"* offer greater intensity of flavor and balance, and usually rank as super-premiums. The *Grands Crus*, outstanding growths, are those labeled either "Chambertin" or as Chambertin hyphenated as part of a vineyard name.

The best known noble wines of Chambertin are Chambertin and Chambertin-Clos de Bèze, its neighbor. Complex, rich, harmonious, and beautifully structured, they combine power with finesse as they age. The other *Grands Crus* vineyards of Chambertin possess a little less complexity, but are generally of super-premium quality.

Further south lies Chambolle-Musigny whose wines tend to be delicate and to possess considerable finesse. The area is typified by the *Grand Cru* vineyard, Les Musigny, a noble wine of uncommon breed. Other *Grands Crus* tend toward the delicate side, and are considered to be super-premiums.

Vougeot is another village name containing the large *Grand Cru* vineyards of Clos de Vougeot. The vineyards, however, have numerous owners, close to one hundred, each of whom offers a bottling. Though the quality varies widely, Clos de Vougeot wines are enormously aromatic, sturdy and complex, though not quite as muscular as those of Chambertin. The quality is usually super-premium with the finest efforts from Vougeot belonging to noble stature.

Flagey-Échezeaux is the name of a commune, but is not used as an appellation. It contains two *Grands Crus* wines, Grand Échezeaux and Échezeaux, each of which has several owners. These are super-premium quality wines, aromatic, with a slightly more refined style than those from Vougeot.

Vosne-Romanée is a village associated with many of Burgundy's finest red wines. Its *Grands Crus* — La Romanée-Conti, La Romanée, La Tâche, Richebourg, and Romanée-Saint-Vivant — often reach legendary quality heights. They combine a depth and complexity of flavor from truffles, herbs, and berries in a style that is the epitome of finesse and rare breed in a wine. All of the *Grands Crus* with the exception of Saint-Vivant, which is slightly lighter, usually achieve noble quality status. The aging potential is tremendous and, with bottle age, the harmonious character and the aftertaste are accentuated.

Though it contains no *Grands Crus* vineyards, Nuits-Saint-Georges has many *Premiers Crus*. Stylistically, they are strongly aromatic, often more tannic than other communes' wines, with a full-bodied, very vinous flavor, that comes into harmony with long aging. They are in the super-premium bracket, lacking, perhaps, the finesse and breed of the noble wines already mentioned.

CÔTE de BEAUNE

In the Côte de Beaune, fewer *Grands Crus* and noble wines are found, but there are numerous *Premiers Crus* and super-premium red wines. From the village of Aloxe-Corton, the mid-premiums are labeled under the simple "Corton" appellation. The better, super-premiums are Le Corton, Corton-Clos du Roi, and Corton-Bressandes.

Wines from Savigny-les-Beaunes are entitled to use that village appellation, with five of them each using the vineyard name of one of the five *Premiers Crus*. The wines of the Savigny-les-Beaune appellation are mid-premium quality, while the *Premiers Crus* offer delicacy and finesse that place them in the super-premium category.

Wines from the Village of Beaune are entitled to use one of three appellations — Beaune, Côte de Beaune, or Côte de Beaune-Villages. The latter wines are generally mid-premium in quality with some finesse and moderate aging ability. The *Premiers Crus* are often super-premiums, combining greater depth with a distinctive aroma, lightness of body with a firm structure.

The village of Pommard produces many mid-premium wines, under its appellation. The *Premiers Crus* are fairly rich in aroma and body and have a typical, earthy characteristic in the aftertaste. They age fairly well, and can achieve super-premium status.

Of all the wines of the Côte de Beaune, those of Volnay are the lightest in style, almost to the point of being fragile. Delicate and early maturing, the Volnay *Premiers Crus* offer delicacy and finesse that places them in the super-premium division. A similar style is shared by the red wines from Auxey-Duresses. The reds from Chassagne-Montrachet are often on the same trajectory, but the *Premiers Crus* are fuller and firmer in structure, with a distinct earthy flavor and character. They are often super-premium wines.

The village of Santenay is entitled to use that appellation or else add Côte de Beaune as a place name. Usually of mid- to super-premium quality, they are light, silky in texture, and subtle in character. They improve with aging, are capable of finesse, but don't display unusual breeding.

The Côte de Beaune is home to several noble and many super-premium white wines from the Chardonnay. The two *Grands Crus* vineyards from Aloxe-Corton — Corton-Charlemagne and Charlemagne — are of noble quality. Stylistically, they offer a rich perfumed aroma of complex fruit and butter with classically proportioned components. The texture is oily, like butterscotch, but with fine acid balance for structure and longevity.

The white wines from A.C. Beaune, the *Premiers Crus,* are super-premium wines. They are lighter in body, but distinctively aromatic, firm in structure, and more subtle in character.

As a place name, Meursault offers white wines ranging from mid- to super-premium. The general rule is that those labeled simply "A.C. Meursault" are the mid-premiums — floral in character and streamlined in body with high, crisp acidity. The *Premiers Crus* of Meursault are the super-premiums, which retain a silky texture, but offer a more assertive aroma and more complex flavors.

In the village of Puligny-Montrachet, white Burgundies are wrought to perfection. The *Grands Crus* — Montrachet, Bâtard-Montrachet, Chevalier-Montrachet, and Bienvenue-Bâtard-Montrachet — are capable of achieving noble quality. Some of the vineyards, namely Montrachet and Bâtard-Montrachet, cross over into Chassagne-Montrachet, and reach similar quality heights. They have a rich, complex fruity aroma, often buttery in character, and combine depth of flavor with a hard veneer, that is intense, yet austere. They achieve unusual power for white wines and require many years of cellaring.

The *Premiers Crus* of both Puligny and Chassagne tend to be super-premium wines. Some, such as Les Combettes and Les Pucelles have on occasion rivaled the *Grands Crus* in noble quality. However, the vineyards are owned by so many different proprietors and the appellations used by so many shippers that the names of owners and shippers become crucial quality determinants.

THE MÂCON

On rare occasions, a well-made wine with a Mâcon-Villages appellation can achieve mid-premium quality. Soft and generally round and fruity, Mâcon-Villages lack the complexity and distinction of Pouilly-Fuissé.

The wines of Pouilly-Fuissé, despite currently being priced far beyond their worth, are nonetheless mid-premium quality. They are distinctly Chardonnay in a crisp-apple aroma, with a smooth texture, and slight depth of flavor. The best quality wines come from the villages of Solutré-Pouilly, Davaye and Fuissé. They have more fruitiness and depth than Chablis, and in the aftertaste reveal a clean, earthy flavor. With three or four years of aging, Pouilly-Fuissé develop a subtle degree of finesse.

BEAUJOLAIS

The mid-premium wines from the Beaujolais are those with the appellation, Beaujolais-Villages. They are fruity, but with more depth of flavor, body and better structure than the simple Beaujolais wines. Light in tannins, they can improve in bottle for two years or so.

The wine communes of Beaujolais yield potential super-premium quailty wines. The *Crus* are as follows: Moulin-à-Vent, Fleurie, Brouilly, Côte de Brouilly, Morgon, Saint-Amour, Chénas, Juliénas, and Chiroubles. Those from Fleurie and Brouilly tend to be elegant in style, but very fragrant. Moulin-à-Vent and Morgon offer richer flavor and body, are capable of aging longer and, with time, resembling red Burgundy to some degree.

THE RHONE VALLEY

The red wines with the appellation Chateauneuf-de-Pape vary from mid-premium to occasional super-premium versions. The latter follow the more traditional production methods and are slow-maturing, hard, sturdy, tannic wines. Some producers now make a fruitier wine, less complex and rounder. The quality varies from brand to brand, with changes continuing through the present.

Côte Rotie wines vary less and many reach super-premium levels. They are firm and long lasting, develop a berry and truffle with aging, and have a smooth texture that gives them a little finesse when mature.

Hermitage reds are mid-to super premiums with richer flavors, but less potential for finesse. They are also long lived, high in alcohol and develop complexity and vigor when fully aged.

GERMANY

As an introduction to this section on Germany's premium and noble wines, it will be helpful to once again review the classifications applied to viticultural areas and quality.

Germany has eleven separate quality wine growing regions called *Anbaugebiete* , but only six produce wines of any commercial importance to the American market. These are the Rheinpfalz also known as the Palatinate, the Rheingau, the Rhein-hessen, the Mosel-Saar-Ruwer, Franconia and the Nahe. Each of these areas is divided into one or more *Bereiche* which are composed of several *Grosslagen*, an assemblage of several individual vineyards (equivalent to regional or commune wine in the French nomenclature). Wines may be labeled as being from either the Bereich, Grosslage, or a particular vineyard, *Einzellage* which under the new regulations must be a minimum size of approximately twelve acres. It may be divided among several owners, however. *Einzellage* represents the highest degree of individuality and, in theory, quality. Wines from a Grosslage take their name from the nearby village and the name of the Grosslage, which may have been an actual vineyard name prior to the 1971 reforms. An Einzellage wine takes its name in the same manner — a system of identification which leads to ambiguity since the fact that a wine comes from a Grosslage need not be indicated on the label. Thus an encyclopedic knowledge of individual village and site names is required to decipher labels of premium and noble wines. Mastering the German wine regions takes considerable practice and patience.

The hierarchy of quality is determined by the ripeness of the grapes when they are picked, the grape variety used, the origin of the grape, and, all other things being equal, how the wine is made. Depending upon the ripeness of the grape at harvest, the wine will fall into one of three broad categories: Tafelwein, pleasant and uncomplicated wines, none of which will achieve premium status; Qualitätswein Bestimmten Anbaugebiete (QbA), which must come from one of the eleven quality wine regions; and Qualitätswein mit Prädikat, which is produced only from fully ripe grapes from a specified Bereich. Those wines which fall into the Qualitätswein mit Prädikat category are further divided into wines labeled Kabinett, Spätlese, Auslese, Beerenauslese, and Trockenbeerenauslese.

Tafelweins and those of QbA stature are often made from grapes which have not reached their full maturity, and are consequently enhanced with sugar to raise the level of alcohol. This is the same process as chaptalization discussed in Chapter Four. Any wine designated Qualitätswein mit Prädikat (QmP), however, may not be sugared but must gain its alcohol from the sugar naturally present in the grape.

This leads the vintner who wishes to make more than one style of wine to pick his vineyard several times over in order to have the appropriately ripe grapes.

Wines qualifying as Qualitätswein mit Prädikat range from Kabinett to Trocken-beerenauslese quality. The finest at any level are those made from the Riesling grape, although the quality of all the wines made from other grape varieties improves as riper grapes are used. Kabinett wines, at the lowest end of the QmP category are generally relatively dry, fruity and well balanced. Wines labeled from Spätlese on indicate some special degree of selection. Spätelese wines are made from grapes ranging from fairly ripe, to greatly mature, and can span the spectrum from relatively dry to slightly sweet.

Wines in the Auslese category are made from over-ripe grapes that provide the wine with a fuller body and a higher concentration of flavor. They are easily percep-tible as sweet and are usually balanced with sufficient acidity so as not to be cloying. Wines of Beerenauslese stature have over-ripened to the point of being shriveled or raisined, and have almost always been attacked by the noble rot *Botrytis cinerea*, which provides them with a honeyed and luscious oppulence. In choosing to make a Beerenauslese, the winemaker takes the considerable risk of losing his crop to frost as he must leave the grapes on the vine to ripen. Because of this risk, only a small quantity of Beerenauslese is produced and it is quite expensive.

Trockenbeerenauslese are the most exotic wines in the hierarchy. They are indivi-dually berry-selected, and are generally attacked by the Botrytis, though this is not a legal requirement. These wines have flavor akin to nectar, a concentrated luscious-ness which comes from the essence of the grape and the flavor of Botrytis, and owes much to a high level of residual sugar which may approach 20 percent. Trockenbeerenauslese are expensive wines to make. In addition to the risk of crop loss, it is a difficult wine to vinify and requires great skill and care throughout the entire winemaking process.

These three levels of wine, Auslese, Beerenauslese and Trockenbeerenauslese, depending on the vineyard, range from super-premium to noble in quality, with the grape variety the final determinant. While wines made from the Riesling have the potential to gain noble stature, those from the Kerner, Muller-Thurgau and Sylvaner are frequently without the nuances and breed indigenous to the Riesling.

One nice thing about the German winemaking industry is that it is full of specific cases of esoteric wines which are made out of love and tradition that goes beyond commercial considerations. These wines include Eiswein, made from grapes left on the vine to freeze. Once harvested, the grapes are gently pressed to retain the grape juice but not the frozen water which imparts a high concentration of sugar and acidity to the wine. Depending upon the skill of the producer, these wines can equal some of the finest Auslese, Beerenauslese or Trockenbeerenauslese.

Other wine styles which defy traditional winemaking include St. Nicholas wine, made from grapes harvested on December 25, St. Nicholas day.

Traditionallly, German wines were made almost exclusively from the Riesling and Sylvaner grapes. However, both are difficult to grow and bring to maturity in the cruel and fickle northern climate. Consequently, over the last decade, scientists have worked to develop new hybrids that have a more generous yield and ripen earlier. These include the Muller-Thurgau, Kerner and Scheurebe, all of which can yield the high quality wines equal to or approximating the Sylvaner. Wines made from the Muller-Thurgau, for instance, are light and fruity with a slightly muscat quality and less acidity than those made from the Riesling. When limited in production, they can produce wines with an elegance and charm reminiscent of the Riesling, although they will never attain the suppleness or subtleness of Riesling wine. Even the character of the Riesling will vary from region to region, depending predominantly on the soil. It is nonetheless the undisputed king of German wine grapes.

Because the maturity of the grape is so crucial due to the marginal nature of the climate there is great concern about where the grape were grown. In reality there is not one generalized climate as known in other winegrowing areas but rather a vast series of microclimates that vary with every turn of the serpentine rivers which the vineyards border. The best vineyard sections face south rather than west or east. Every element of topography affects the wine: the steepness of the hill on which are the plantings; the amount of reflection of sun from adjoining rivers; the nearness of a sheltering forest (and its density) or a mountain peak, either of which could protect the site from strong, cold wind; the altitude; let alone the soil variation that controls the retention of moisture and the minute quantities of minerals which the vines will transmit to the grapes and eventually to the character of the wine.

It is for these reasons that the growing areas have been so carefully delineated. While it is true that one plot of land will produce noble wines, that the adjoining one may come forth only with low-premium and a few feet from that the land is left untilled — there is no guarantee that the site alone will define how good the wine in the bottle will be. But it is the first definition of quality, the conditions from which grape maturity will come. So in Germany it is the most important. Not only because of the climate in general but also because the microclimate will dictate what grapes are to be grown. And as each site becomes more or less famous, so varies the price the wine will bring and this, in turn also has an effect on how much money there is to spend on cultivating the land and on winery equipment.

THE APPELLATION STRUCTURE OF TRADITIONAL GERMAN WINES

GEOGRAPHIC APPELLATIONS

German wine districts are ranked by potential quality in a very complicated manner. In terms of label nomenclature, they are divided into large regions (*Anbaugebiet*), large districts within (*Bereich*), collective vineyards (*Grosslagen*) and individual vineyard sites (*Einzellagen*). Each is strictly delimited and only superior sites are granted an *Einzellage* designation.

QUALITY DESIGNATION BY GRAPE MATURITY

German wines are also ranked by quality based on grape maturity.

TAFELWEIN

"Everyday" or Jug quality Wines blended from grapes grown, or wines produced from anywhere in Germany. Most of these wines are mediocre as most of them are usually made from grapes that have not ripened fully or from varieties which are not capable of producing quality wine.

QUALITÄTSWEIN BESTIMMTER ANBAUGEBIETE - Qba

QbA wines must be submitted to the government authority for analysis. Upon approval they are given a code number which must appear on the label. These wines must have a minimum alcohol of 8 percent and may be *chaptalized* within certain limits. Liefbraumilch and Zeller Swartze Katz wines must be at least of this quality. The majority of the wines in this catagory are simple-premium-some may be better.

QUALITÄTSWEIN MIT PREDIKAT - QmP

Within this catagory there is a hierarchy of catagories - depending on *must* weight measured in *oechsle* which is a function of ripeness. QmP wines may not be *chaptalized.* In ascending order of sweetness QmP wines are called: *Kabinett* (ex: Piesporter Michelberg Kabinett) the majority of the grapes must be ripe; *Spätlese* (ex: *Whelener Sonneneur Spätlese*) wines are made entirely from fully mature grapes - these are high quality wines which can attain splendid balance, finesse and dreed, they will be somewhat sweeter than the kabinett wines although when perfectly balanced may taste dry; *Auslese* wines are made from late-picked overripe grapes and produce a wine which has greater concentration of flavor, fuller body as well as sweeter than *Spätlese*; *Beerenauslese* wines are made from very late picked overripe grapes and *Trockenbeerenauslese* from shriveled or raisined overripe grapes - both are wines which are very concentrated, rich in flavor, full bodied and low in alcohol. In years when the grapes are infected with noble rot, called *Edelfaule* in German, the wine will have a high counterbalancing acidity and a rich honied, uncious taste.

With this background let's proceed through the German vineyards district by district realizing that the subject is so complex that it is best left to the specialized volumes listed in Chapter Twenty-three.

MOSEL

The two most important wine producing areas of the Mosel (the area which actually includes the land surrounding three rivers, the Mosel and its tributaries, the Saar and Ruwer), are the Mittlemosel (Central Mose) which produces the greatest wines of the region, and the Saar-Ruwer, from which we find good, but not distinctive wines.

Mosel wines are commonly referred to as feminine wines. Those made from the Riesling are light in body, delicate in flavor and refined in a way that defies description. They are often described as "floral" and evoke images of fresh flowers in spring meadows. They have a lively and refreshing taste, are light-bodied and low in alcohol, and are meant to be drunk young. The wines of the Mosel, usually found in green bottles range from simple to super premium quality. They are among the lightest of the great wines in the world, as they seldom exceed 10 percent of alcohol by volume and they often contain a slight effervescence.

In the Mittlemosel, Bereich Bernkastel is the best known and wines in the premium and noble categories can be found in four of its six Grosslagen: Michelsberg, Kurfurstlay, Munzlay, and Schwarzlay. Two others, Probstberg and St. Michael rarely produce wines better than simple-premium.

The villages of the Grosslage Michelsberg produces some of the Mittlemosel's more distinctive wines. The fresh, light wines of Trittenheim may reach mid-premium quality. Those of Neumagen bear a somewhat more intense aroma, but rarely exceed simple premium quality. The best and most famous village in this Grosslage is Piesport. Piesporter Michelsberg is the name of the districts Grosslage wine and is easily confused with *Einzellage* wines. Although the Kabinett wines are at best mid-premium quality, with typical Mosel delicacy, those of Auslese and above, from the better vineyards can achieve super-premium quality — richly sweet, complex and flavorful.

In the Grosslage Kurfurstlay, the two villages producing the best wines are Brauneberg and Bernkastel. Wine from Brauneberg are very full-bodied, rich in flavor and long-lived. Those from the best vineyards, such as Juffer, can attain super-premium class.

Noted for their elegance, wines from Bernkastel are just as good or perhaps better. The most famous vineyard is the world-famous Dokter (also Doctor) property which rarely falls below super-premium stature and in great vintages produces outstanding noble wine out extraordinary breed and finesse. The Grosslage wine is Bernkastler Kurfurstlay which relies on that village's fame for its popularity. It is a simple-premium wine at best.

The three villages of Graach, Wehlen and Zeltingen in the Grosslage of Munzlay can produce wines capable of reaching super-premium or noble status. These wines are well-balanced and fragrant, although the style can vary from vineyard to vineyard and range from fine, fragrant and delicate to full-bodied and big. Wehlen is the home of some of the Mosel's finest wines and the renowned Prums estate, which wines often reach super-premium to noble quality heights. The fuller-bodied wines of Zeltingen range from ordinary quality wines to those in the super-premium category which rank along side of those from Graach and Wehlen.

The wines of the Saar, located in the Grosslage of Scharzberg, can, depending upon the year and nature's inclination, range from barely jug quality to, in the case of Scharzhofberger, a wine of noble proportions.

These wines are often described as having a "steely" character and a hardness and austerity which can often contribute to great character and breed. The wines from the towns of Menning, Wawer, Nazem Saar Bur and Serrig, are of simple-premium quality. Those from Ockfen, Oberemmel and Ayl range from mid to super-premium quality. Although these wines are, in many ways typical, those from Ockfen are somewhat more full-bodied; while those from Ayl are softer and fruitier.

The tiny Ruwer valley gives us the lightest and most delicate of the Mosel wines. These wines will almost never reach super-premium quality status, but several do in great years, notably from Maximin Grunhaus and Eitelsbach. Usually they fall into the mid-premium range.

RHEINGAU

This tiny wine region, only one-quarter the size of the Mosel, is divided into ten Grosslagen and 120 lagen (vineyards) over twenty-eight communities. Its wines range from simple-premium to noble quality. The best, made of course, from the Riesling, are rounder, softer and deeper in color than the wines of the Mosel.

The wines of Hochheim are full-bodied and fruity, often with a trace of earthiness. Wines from the best vineyards, which include Domdechaney, Hölle and Sommerheil fall within the mid-premium quality range, and are comparable in quality to those from Johannisberg. Wines from its lesser vineyards rarely exceed simple-premium quality. The finest estate is that of Schloss Eltz, followed by the vineyards of Taubenberg and Sonneberg. Somewhat better are the similar wines of Kiedrich, which show more character than those of Eltville. Wines from the vineyards of Grafenberg and Wasseros can almost attain noble status. The wines of Hallgarten, can in good vintages attain mid- to super-premium status. In poorer vintages, they barely rank as ordinary quality wine.

The reputation of Erbach's sturdy wines rests mostly on the reputation of the wines of the Marcobrunn estate, which in their best years can rank with the world's noble quality wines. The wines of Erbach are noted for their fine, full-bodied flavors and long life.

Similarly, the estate Steinberg, located in Hattenheim, produces wines superior to those of its neighbors. The mid- to super-premium wines of Hattenheim are somewhat more delicate and less firm than those of the noble class Steinberger vineyard.

In Winkel once again, one vineyard, Schloss Vollrads, eclipses all others. Its wines are characterized by their ripeness and great fruit, can without question, attain noble rank. However, those labeled Kabinett, and Spätlese are most often found in the mid- to super-premium categories.

More so than for any other wine of the Rheingau, a sense of fruit and an almost spicy quality characterize the wines of Rauenthaler. Although the wines generally fall into the mid-premium quality range, some of the better vineyards, which include Baiken, Wulfen, Langenstruck and Nonneburg are quite capable of producing wines of noble status.

Eltville produces wines that are pleasing, fine, soft and with a good bouquet. Although these wines are less distinguished than those of the Rauenthaler, they represent drinkable simple to mid-premium quality wines.

Lastly, we come to the most famous name of the Rheingau — the village Johannisberg. The vines of this village range from simple to super-premium quality with noble status achievable only by the wines of Schloss Johannisberg. Johannisberger wines are distinguished for their finesse and fine bouquet; those of Schloss Johannisberg may have an extra dimension of breed which places them with the world's great wines.

RHEINHESSEN

The Rheinhessen produces a greater variety of wines, ranging from small table wines to *spritzenwein* or "peak" wine, than any other German wine district. Its most famous export is Liebfraumilch, which is produced by nearly 99 percent of the region's 167 villages. The wines of the Rheinhessen, which account for 50 percent of all German wine exports range in quality from jug to super-premium. They are soft wines with a pronounced character that is the easiest of any German wine to iden-tify. But due to the temperate climate, the wines lack the character they might have had if they had to fight for their lives. The popularity of Rheinhessen wines is pro-bably based on their intense bouquet and straightforward sweetness.

Most Rheinhessen wine comes from the Muller-Thurgau variety which produces juicy, soft, fruity wines. Those from the Sylvaner, the second most widely used vine, produce full, round wines. Recently, viticulturists have been experimenting with various hybrids, including the Scheurebe, Kerner and Bacchus and the Huexl which is used in the best vineyards to make Prädikat Auslese, Beerenauslese and Trockenbeerenauslese wines.

The Rheinhessen is composed of three Bereiche: Bingen, Nierstein and Wonnegau. The most important of these, contributing the most high quality wine is Nierstein (and its towns of Oppenheim and Nierstein), followed by Bingen, Wonnegau, which contains the city of Worms, produces wines which can only be called full-bodied and clumsy. Alzey, the center of the inland area, and its surrounding towns produce good, clean tasting wines that form the backbone of many Liebfraumilch.

A word about Liebfraumilch. Until 1971, and dating back to 1562, the word Lieb-fraumilch had been used as a blank term applied to any Rhine wine of good quality. Unfortunately, while this generic application has created wide recognition of the wine, most of its reputation has been bad. But contrary to popular thinking, there are many fine Liebfraumilch that rank in the mid-premium levels. Today, the term is still rather broadly applied, referring to Qualitätswein from the Rheinhessen, Nahe, Palatinate and the Rheingau, but the production of Liebfraumilch is limited to wine made from the Riesling, Sylvaner or Müller -Thurgau.

In the Bereich of Bingen, the village of Bingen produces wines similar to those of the Nahe which are fuller, heavier, and almost more concentrated than the average Rhine wine. These wines profit from a warm microclimate that gives them a special fullness and ripeness. Wines from the Riesling develop elegance and style, and those from the Sylvaner can also develop some distinction.

But the greatest Bereich in the Rheinhessen is Nierstein which produces long lived wines, especially those from the Riesling, which are unquestionably the best Rheinhessen wines. They are soft, full-bodied, and elegant. Those of the Riesling have an easily identifiable, marvelous bouquet.

Some Niersteins resemble wines of the Rheingau, others are quite different and resemble the great wines of the Rheinpfalz, but the reputation of Nierstein wines rests on the reputaion of about only 20 percent of the areas production.

Wines from Oppenheim in the Bereich of Nierstein rival, and in hot, dry years often surpass those of Nierstein, although on the whole, Niersteiners have more elegance.

The wines of Nachenheim, from the finest vineyards, have great bouquet and are remarkable for their elegance, finesse and class. The best wines combine depth, fire, spiciness and delicacy in marvelous and noble harmony, qualities which have only come to the forefront in recent years.

From Mainz to Guntersblum, the wines show substance, fullness and elegance. Elegant and fine wines are made from the Müller-Thurgau and Sylvaner. Small amounts of wine are produced from Gewurtztraminer, Sylvaner and Pinot Gris.

The Rheinhessen is composed of three Bereiche: Binge, Nierstein and Wonnegau. The most important of these, contributing the most high quality wine is Nierstein (and its towns of Oppenheim and Nierstein), followed by Binge. Wonnegau, which contains the city of Worms, produces wines which can only be called full-bodied and clumsy. Alzey, the center of the inland area, and its surrounding towns produce good, clean tasting wines that form the backbone of many Liebfraumilch.

A word about Liebfraumilch. Until 1971, and dating back to 1562, the word Liebfraumilch had been used as a blank term applied to any Rhine wine of good quality. Unfortunately, while this generic application has created wide recognition of the wine, most of its reputation has been bad. But contrary to popular thinking, there are many fine Liebfraumilch that rank in the mid-premium levels. Today, the term is still rather broadly applied, referring to Qualitätswein from the Rheinhessen, Nahe, Palatinate and the Rheingau, but the production of Liebfraumilch is limited to wine made from the Riesling, Sylvaner or Müller-Thurgau.

In the Bereich of Bingen, the village of Bingen produces wines similar to those of the Nahe which are fuller, heavier, and almost more concentrated than the average Rhine wine. These wines profit from a warm microclimate that gives them a special fullness and ripeness. Wines from the Riesling develop elegance and style, and those from the Sylvaner can also develop some distinction.

But the greatest Bereich in the Rheinhessen is Nierstein which produces long lived wines, especially those from the Riesling, which are unquestionably the best Rheinhessen wines. They are soft, full-bodied, and elegant. Those of the Riesling have an easily identifiable, marvelous bouquet.

Some Nierstein wines resemble those of the Rheingau, others are quite different and resemble the great wines of the Rheinpfalz. But the fame of Nierstein wines rests on the reputaion of about only 20 percent of the district's production.

PALATINATE

The Palatinate, the largest of the German wine districts, produces 1/5 of Germany's total wine production, although most of it never sees export. Much of the wine is pleasant but undistinguished. However, thanks to a long, warm fall, which fosters grape maturity, the area produces a great deal of intense sweet wines which range from Spätlese to Trockenbeerenauslese. Some of these reach super-premium or noble levels.

The Palatinate is divided into three areas geographically, taking their names from the Haardt mountains: The Upper Haardt, The Middle Haardt and the Lower Haardt. However as a result of the 1971 reorganization, legally it is divided into two areas: the Bereich Mittlehaardt Deutsch Weinstrasse, consisting of the upper and middle Haardt from Herxheim to Neustadt, and the Bereich Sudliche Weinstrasse, which produces wines in quantity rather than of quality, although on occasion, wines of super-premium quality have been produced in Maikammerre and Edenkbener. Over all, the best wines are produced from the Middle Haardt, an eighteen mile span between Herxheim and Neustadt.

The great wines of the Palatinate come from the Riesling, although only 14 percent of the area is planted to that noble vine. The Palatinate Rieslings offer an attractive and remarkable balance. They are fuller than those of the Mosel, less mild and soft than those of the Rheinhessen, and less overwhelming in bouquet than those of the Rheingau. Some of the world's finest Auslese and Beerenauslese are produced from Palatinate Rieslings.

Müller-Thurgau is the dominate grape, producing pale fresh wines. The Sylvaner, which accounts for 20 percent of the vineyard's production, yields wines ranging in quality from simple premium to mid-premium. A small amount of spicy wine is produced from the Gerwürtztraminer.

Six villages produce wines ranging from mid- to super-premium: Kellstadt, Ungstein, Bad Durkheim, Gimmeldingen, Königsbach, Neustadt. But without a doubt, the finest wines come from the towns of Forst, Deidesheim, Ruppertsberg, and Wachenheim. The 4,000 acres comprising this area are divided into forty vineyards. One parcel can have as many as twenty owners, producing twenty different wines.

The wines of Forst are produced from the Riesling and have an unusual quality and bouquet due to an outcropping of black basalt. The heavier soil stores water in dry years, making them greater in dry year than those of Deidesheim. This soil also retains the sun's heat, releasing it at night helping the grapes to ripen more completely. The soil of Deidesheim is lighter than that of Forst and produces wines with more finesse and elegance. Ruppertsberg gives strong fruity wines with a great deal of breed. Its soil is volcanic rock, shingle, sand and lime. Wachenheim has six vineyards which have acquired international fame. These wines are the most sought after as they combine substance and bouquet with finesse and light body.

In the northern part of this Bereich, towns of Zell and Herxheim produce a wine from Gewürtztraminer, called Schwarzer Heergott, which is robust, steely, and unlike any other Palitanate wine.

Wines from the southern district, the Südliche Weinstrasse do not merit discussion in the quality category.

NOTE

Before the stringent 1971 wine regulations went into effect, winemakers could arbitrarily select certain lots of wine of a vintage and add the words "feine" or "feinst" or a fass or fuder (cask) number which indicated a superior wine. But as this practice was not regulated and depended upon the integrity of the producer there was no guarantee that the wines were indeed any better or indeed even from different casks. Because of many abuses this practice was prohibited under the 1971 regulations.

Today, some winemakers circumvent this prohibition by using color-coded capsules for selected lots. For instance, they might use pink capsules on the wines from one cask, gold ones on wines from another to indicate the "preferred" batch. Cognoscenti recognize the difference and pay accordingly.

TROCKEN WINES

Recently, German vintners introduced dry German wines suitable for the connoisseur. Two wine styles, Trocken and Halbtrocken have emerged. Trocken wines have virtually no residual sugar and range in taste from austere to tart. Halbtrocken wines contain a certain amount of residual sugar and taste fairly dry. They are more mellow than Trocken wines, and are somewhat higher in alcohol than Kabinett or Spätlese wines. These wines are decidedly different in character than the German wines which have traditionally been available in the United States.

In the last several years, German vintners have been working to develop a dry German wine. As a result, two wine styles, Trocken and Halbtrocken have emerged. Trocken wines have virtually no residual sugar and range in taste from austere to tart. Halbtrocken wines contain a certain amount of residual sugar and taste fairly dry. They are more mellow than Trocken wines, and are somewhat higher in alcohol than Kabinett or Spätlese wines. These wines are decidedly different in character than the German wines which have traditionally been available in the United States.

ITALY

Until recently the majority of premium and noble wine of Italy were virtually unknown outside of Italy. With good reason, the provincial Italians preferred to keep their best to themselves. Since they historically were not involved with a export trade for quality wines as was France and Germany, their best known wine was the Chianti bottled in *fiaschi*, the majority of which was of the lowest quality and frequently produced outside of the Chianti district. For a long time the wines of Italy were almost without legally regulated quality standards. Since there was little incentive to counterfeit wines which were relatively inexpensive and that rarely left their district, there was little need to establish a structure of regulations similar to those which were established in France beginning in the 1900's. The best districts had local producer's consortiums whose seals on a bottle insured a guarantee of authenticity and quality. As wine became increasingly important as an export commodity and as the wines from better districts were more in demand nationally, the Italian wine industry realized the need for strict and comprehensive government wine regulations and controls. What emerged was what is known as the Denominazione di Origine Controllata (D.O.C. see page 123) and a multitude of premium and noble wines that have permitted Italy to rival France in the international market.

Beacuse of the late start even the best of Italian wines have yet to become as chic as their French counterparts. Thus they are still good values. In fact, it is still possible to get wines from the sixties that are almost twenty years old for under fifteen dollars.

The regulations for the D.O.C. were established for each growing region and differ from region to region, much as the Appellation Contrôlée of France, but with the important difference that the appellation structure for Italian wines does not provide for the detailed differentiation in quality in the the ranked manner of the French A.O.C. Thus, within the D.O.C. there are wines that range from simple premium to

THE D.O.C STRUCTURE OF ITALIAN WINES

NON - D.O.C. WINES

The vast majority of Italian wines fall into this catagory — there are literally thousands of them. Most are never exported to the United States, however those that are must meet stringent export standards, as do all Italian wines.

D.O.C.

Denominazione di Origine Controllata

These wines come from delimited areas and must meet strict production and quality standards. There are several hundred D.O.C. districts, each of which has its own standards which vary widely from district to district. Within the D.O.C. there is no official hiararchy of quality standards. Hence the term is of little use as a quality guide. It does, however, guarantee authenticy as to geographical origin and the particular standards therein.

D.O.C.G.

Denominazione di Origine Controllata e Garantita

Wines with this designation are guaranteed as to both geographical origin and a high standard of quality. There are presently only four districts that qualify — Borolo, Brunello di Montalcino, Barbaresco and Vino Nobile di Montepulciano — others are awaiting approval which is not easily granted. Wines from districts granted the D.O.C.G. must pass stringent laboratory arialyis and taste tests to qualify for D.O.C.G. If they fail, they are declassified to Non-D.O.C. status. This is quite unjust for wines that just miss the mark. There may be a change in the regulations in the near future to permit such wines to use the D.O.C. or some other designation to indicate that they are indeed still a quality wine from a delimited district.

noble wines that are designated simply D.O.C. Furthermore, there are many premium and noble wines that are made outside of the D.O.C. system. Recently the next higher level of quality designation, D.O.C.G. in which the authenticity is guaranteed has been awarded to a few wines with more to come. Even within this highest of grades, there can be quality variation from mid-premium to noble.

Some wine types, particularly Chianti, will cross every quality grade from vin ordinaire to Noble, making the consumer easy prey for impressive labels that do not deliver the expected quality.

As has been our practice, we will cover each important region district by district. We'll go from north to south and generally from west to east as we work our way down the peninsula. You will find that we have covered many of these districts in our previous discussions as we examined their lesser wines.

AOSTA

The vineyards are located in the higher altitudes of the Pre-Alps. Most of the wines come from Aosta Valley which leads northward to the St. Bernard Pass into France. While clearly Italian, French is the dominant language. The soil is sparse and rocky, the altitude between two to six thousand feet. The battle here is against the cold and often the harvest is completed with snow already on the ground.

There are two commercially important wines on the export scene. *Donnaz*, coming from a local variety of the Nebbiolo grape, is a wine of high fixed acidity and therefore ages well. It will range from simple to mid-premium. The other wine seen here is *Carema* which comes from the border between Aosta Valley and Piedmont, where the vineyards are from two to three thousand feet high. It tends to be somewhat austere and is produced in small quantities, probably less than 15,000 cases a year. It is a wine that has its devoted followers and often ranks as a mid-premium.

PIEDMONT

Some of the very best of the Italian red wines come from Piedmont, many arguing, the most noble. Of these the finest come from the Nebbiolo grape. This is a variety that can be found under a variety of names, often simply that of the township or district preceded by or followed by the varietal name, for example Nebbiolo d'Alba. The best are known by their district name without mention of the grape variety, such as Barolo, Gattinara, Lessona, Ghemme, Boca, and Sissano. The Nebbiolo grape mutates easily to adapt to its environment, and its various clones produce remarkably different wines from district to district.

There is a hierarchy of reputation of these wines in which Barolo is the king and Gattinara the queen. After that there is great controversy about which comes next. The nature of the wines of this region made from this grape is often fascinating in that the wines can present a continually changing face after being poured in the bottle. I have tasted an aged wine from a good bottle, over a period of several hours, in which it seemed as if I was presented with four or five or even more different wines -the changes were so profound. So, too, there is a tremendous quality difference between producers and from vintage to vintage. The history of winemaking in this region, as is true in much of the nation, has been that the best wines often have been the result of a fortutious escape from accident as many are made without great care and/or skill. Often the level of volatile acidity may be unpleasantly high; mercaptans and other flaws are frequently encountered. The varied complexity and depth of these wines, are frequently the result of flaws which would otherwise be sensed as " defects" but for the miraculous counterbalance of the multiplicity of elements in these wines. Ironically, technical ignorance gives these wines their great complexity and appeal.

Barolo comes from the central part of the Piedmont region as does Barbaresco and Nebbiolo d'Alba. Barbaresco tends to be less austere a wine than Barolo, little lower in alcoholic content, more delicate, softer and can be consumed earlier. Neb-iolo from the hills north of the Cuneo will be up to about 13 ° alcohol which is the minimum for Barolo. It often has a sort of fruity sweet undertone.

About half of the production of Piedmont is from the Barbera grape. It is similar to the wines of the varietal from the California but the range of quality is wider. It is the jug wine of northern Italy and it can be, on occasion, a mid-premium. Usually consumed young, it can, when carefully grown and from a good vintage, age well. The problem stems from the fact that the vine is a strong one, heavy bearing unless it is drastically pruned. It is often the restaurant house wine. The best areas for quality are Asti and Alba and the wine name will reflect it, such as Barbera d'Alba. Most of the Barbera produced is non-D.O.C. Another wine of the region is Dolcetto which is less expensive, shorter lived, is easy to drink even with a slight bitter undertone. While the name means sweet, the wines are dry.

Quite a ways to the north, up above the city of Turin in the lake country is the Gattinara area. The wine is one that ages well and often deserves its reputation but frequently wines called Spanna, another local name for the Nebbiolo are a better value and sometimes even better wines. They are non-D.O.C. Gottinara ages well although it is not as long-lived as Barolo.

LOMBARDY

The name of Lombardy is not well known in the United States wine although huge amounts of wine do come from the region. Those that have made a reputation here, as mid-premiums, are from the Valltellina region, high up in the pre-Alps, just below the Swiss border. Once again the Nebbiolo grape is prominent but here is known as Chiavennasca. The nature of the wines are more like the Donnaz and Carema from the similar area to the west in Aosta. While there are a number of wines, four are the best known D.O.C. wines here: Sassella, Inferno, Grumello and Valgella.

TRENTINO - ALTO ADIGE

Just below the Austrian border is the Alto Adige. The language and the winemaking are largely Germanic and both Italian and German are spoken. Adjoining the Adige (from the name of the south flowing river that runs sdown the middle towards the city of Verona) is Trentino, Italian speaking but allied in climate to Germany. In this area the wines are known by their varietal names. Cabernet (mainly Cabernet Franc), Merlot, Pinot Nero (Pinot Noir) and Lagrein are the main producers of red wines. The village of Tramen on the west hillside of the Adige Valley is reputed to be the original source of the Tramen or Gewurztraminer vine. Other whites are Sauvignon (bianco or blanc), Sylvaner, Müller-Thurgau (having come down from Germany to the north), Pinot Bianco (blanc) and Riesling. A caution is in order for those ordering a bottle of Riesling from Italy may well be disappointed if there they get Riesling Italico or, sometimes just labeled Riesling, for the Italian Riesling taste much more like a Traminer and lacks the perfumey, light quality that we are accustomed to or expect from Germany or Austria.

Most of the wines from both regions are exported north to Austria, Germany and Switzerland. While there are interesting wines here none seem to be in the noble range although a few reach mid-premium.

FRIULI - VENEZIA GIULIA

Better known in our country simply as Fruili, this prolific wine producing region that is nestled up against Austria and Yugoslavia is becoming increasingly important as more and more of their white wines are being brought to our shores. (About four times more white wines are produced than reds.) What we see here are Riesling (both Rhein and Italico), Muller-Thurgau, Pinot Bianco and quite a bit of Pinot Grigio.

D.O.C. is widespread and covers most of the bottles coming here. Once again we have premium wines of various degrees of quality that don't reach the noble state.

The cooler northern climate produces grapes that are now being made into wine through the extensive introduction of modern winemaking technology. As a result, there is a much higher level of quality than there was only a few years ago. The lovely white wines are now crisp and clean though often bland.

VENETO

Geographically the main portion of the Veneto is just under the Trentino-Alto Adige and below Friuli even though a finger of the region does run north between the two up to the Austrian border. Certainly this is true of the vineyard portion of the region. The name Veneto, however, is rarely seen on the wines we know for they are apt to be identified as coming from the Veneto district of Verona. The names of Bardolino, Soave and Valpolicella are the best known, being world famous.

In general, much of the vineyard area is hilly and the grapes from these upper elevations produce wines which are much superior to those from the valley floors and plains. From the latter come quite ordinary wines whose main merit is often their low price. Good producers process their hill grapes separately in order to achieve a higher level of acidity, more depth of flavor and get a better potential for aging. This is a region of large production, most of which is for the national consumption or sold in bulk to the nations to the north. About 12 to 15 percent is accorded D.O.C. status.

Of the wines of the Verona district, Bardolino comes from the western portion, a north-south rectangle that lies along Lake Garda. This is a light, fruity wine that is pleasant in its youth and which parallels in many respects Beaujolais as to its usage with food and its quaffing character. It is not made with carbonic maceration and so it is not like a Primeur or Nouveaux style of Beaujolais. It quality ranges from simple to mid-premium and should be consumed within three years of its vintage.

Although Valpolicella is made from the same grape varieties as is Bardolino (in somewhat different percentages and from different areas) it has a little more color, alcohol, durability, complexity and depth. Those desigated as Classico come from the best growing area (except for Valpantena which is from a valley to the east that doesn't have the Classico level but whose quality is as good as and sometimes better). Superiore on the label means a minimum of a year's aging and 12° alcohol at minimum. These are fine wines which can sometimes attain the mid-premium level and can improve in quality for several years.

There is another classification of Valpolicella called *Recioto*. Usually from high up on the hillside some clusters will have a portion of the grapes sticking up like ears and they receive more sunlight for maturing. These are, for this designation, picked separately and semi-dried in lofts or attics to concentrate the sugars and fruit before being vinified. Three different Recioto wines are made: a sparkling which is rarely seen in the U.S.; one simply labeled Recioto which will be sweet because the fermentation stopped or "stuck" before all the sugar was fermented; and lastly Recioto Amarone (or Amarone) which has fermented completely. The latter is one of the special red wines of Italy that merits top premium and even nudges the noble category. Velvety, round, soft, well-balanced and full of character are the adjectives it merits. Ten to fifteen years of life are possible for good Amarone although they are usually delightful after five years of age.

TUSCANY

The history of winemaking in Tuscany is the oldest in Italy starting as it did with the Estruscan some three millenia ago. The name of its most famous wine, Chianti, was recorded as early as 1260 A.D. but then it referred to a white wine. The anomaly is that today white wine from the area cannot be called Chianti.

For decades the only Italian wine known in this country was that rather thin, acidic wine that was brought to these shores in round bottles protected by straw. Nowadays the cost of weaving these fiaschi that they are becomming a relic of the past. Besides, the better Chianti benefit from aging and are best bottled into a Bordeaux type capable of resting on its side. . This wine comes from the largest D.O.C. district of Italy with more than one million acres, seven thousand registered growers and about 25,000,000 gallons of wine.

Quality in Chianti, particularly in the Classico district in its center, was the work of the consortium of growers whose insignia has been the *gallo nero* or black rooster on the neck of the bottle. This league of producers set minimum standards. Particularly in recent years a second *consorzio* for the area outside of the inner Classico zone has grown to be the largest producer oganization in the country. Any distinction between Classico and non-Classico, as far as quality is concerned, are really non-exsistent.

The cépage (blending of several grape varieties) in Chianti is to a certain degree at the discretion of the producer although only certain varieties are permited and certain ones required. Sangiovese is set at from 50 to 80 percent and the other red Canaiolo at from 10 to 30 percent. The prescibed mixture must contain 10 to 30percent of the white grapes, Trebbiano or Malvasia. In addition a "15 percent correction" of wines from outside the area, the best do not make use of this provision. Indeed, while claiming to adhere to the legal blending, it is strongly suspected that some producers omit some or all of the white grapes required and there is a move to change the requirements. They claim that they don't need them to make their wine more supple, easier and quicker to mature and that, instead, they cause an excessive lightness to the wine.

There are basically three types of Chianti found on the market. The first, in the lowest price range, is usually found in a flask, and is a prickly, fruity wine to be drunk young. . . .an ordinary wine, no matter how delightful (or dreadful) it may be. The second is that great mass of bottlings, Classico or otherwise, that are in the simple to mid-premium category and these wines repay several years of bottle age although they can usually be enjoyed when you buy them. Finally comes the *reservas*, the product of special selection of vineyardsor of the harvest, of greater care in making and longer aging before released. These wines are, at a minimum ten year wines and many will double and triple that time.

But Chianti is not the only wine of Tuscany, it just seems like it is. There are two other important red wines that cannot be overlooked. South of Florence in the Sienna hills around the town of Montalcino there is grown a "clone" or variant of the Sangiovese known as the Brunello or large Sangiovese. This wine, Brunello Di Montalcino, brings the highest prices of any wines of Italy. Currently the regular bottling of Biondi-Santi of the year 1975 retails in the U.S. for over $33 while the 1971 reserve bottling fetches over $130 and both of them are considered extremely young and in no way ready to drink. The regulations prevent marketing until it has four years in wood and another in bottle. Often the wines will last, and in most cases improve, decade after decade. Even so this is a controversial wine because a lot of Brunello that came to market wasn't very good despite its high price

The third part of the Tuscan triumvirate, and, in many respects, close to a good Chianti is Vino Nobile di Montepulciano from vineyards surrounding the hill town of Montepulciani. Its minimum age is two years (Chianti five months), a *riserva* must have three years and with four can be designated *reserva speciale*. It sells at a premium with respect to Chianti and responds better to aging.

There are a couple of other wines in Tuscany that should be noted even though they are in very limited supply but all three do come to this country in limited quantities and all three owe a good part of their high quality to the presence of Cabernet Sauvignon: Carmignano in the Montalbano Chianti zone west of Florence, Tignatello in Chianti Classico by Marchesi Antinori, and Sassicaia which is almost entirely Cabernet from the coastal region.

THE MARCHES

Out of the usual travel routes and without any great historical attractions, its white wine Verdicchio has given fame to this region, even when the drinkers knew nothing of the land of origin. The most famous is the Verdicchio dei Castelli di Jesi, a large zone. The grapes are the Verdicchio with up to 20 percent of Trebbiano Toscano and Malvasia Toscano permitted. It is a wine to be enjoyed young, within about two years at most. The firm of Titulus (Fazi-Battaglia) is the dominant producer and exporter. A simple to mid-premium wine.

LATIUM

Latium (or also Lazio) is the area around Rome. Castelli wine comes from the hills to the southwest of Rome and Frascatti is the best known of the Castelli. Labeled *asciutto* or *secco* it is generally dry with no more than one percent residual sugar allowed. There are also the sweeter versions of *cannellino, dolce* or *amabile.* There has been heavy investment into the wineries and vineyards of this region and the general level of the wines are consistent and good. Since, however, it is a wine to be consumed very young, it is not one for greatness. Some Frascati are being brought here in refrigerated containers and arrive in our wine shops within a year of the harvest or less. These are generally clean, bright wines with often a not unpleasant back-bite of bitterness and fall within the mid-premium category.

CAMPANA

This is the area around Naples, the land of Mt. Vesuvius. To the northeast of the city come some outstanding wines, ranging from mid-premium to, at times, noble which are the work of Antonio Mastroberardino. If his name is difficult to pronounce, the wines are worth it. Greco du Tufo and Fiano di Avellino are the whites. The Greco is quite strong in bouquet and flavor, sometimes also in alcohol, but always well balanced. Its flavors have a bitter almond edge which increases with bottle age. Fiano has greater elegance of body and texture and a sort of toasty bouquet. Both are good as accompaniments to seafood simply prepared. The best of this wine is a red, Taurasi. It comes from the Aglianico grape grown at 1,000' and higher. In great years such as '58, '61, '68 this wine maintains itself well for ten or twenty years and can attain noble wine status.

APULIA, BASILICATA, CALABRIA

These three regions of the "boot" of the Italian peninsula are full of vineyards and wines — literally a sea of wine. Until recently Apulia was practically nothing but a vineyard and much of what was grown was table grapes of which the region still furnishes more than half the nation's total. Until the last decade most of the wines were sunbaked, heavy in alcohol that sold in other parts of Italy at the lowest of prices. Then a serious overhaul began to achieve wines that are fruitier, fresher, lighter. There are new trends, new vines, new varietals which are stirring but which have yet to reach full production in commercial levels, enough for export. Such varietals as Cabernet, Merlot, Pinot Noir and even Chardonnay are showing some promise. So the premium story of Apulia is one for the near future to tell.

In Basilicata Fratelli D'Angelo exports a small amount of aged Aglianico to our shores that is quite good. This is a mid-premium that is quite smooth and has a carmel background and lots of fruit. Except for slight stirrings such as this, both Basilicata and Calabria have yet to produce premium wines.

SICILY

Sicily is also a place of great vinous change. While always a heavy producer its wines were not very attractive. Most of its wine was shipped north in bulk — the bland, neutral whites to Turin for making vermouth; the alcoholic, heavy reds to France, Switzerland or northern Italy for blending with weaker wines.

It used to be difficult to get a decent, let alone outstanding, bottle of Sicilian wine. A viticultural and vinicultural revolution within the last two decades now is showing results with some excellent wines even though there is still a lot of progress to be made. But there are many bottlings that the Sicilians can offer without apologies — and at reasonable prices. Among the reds ten year old Etna Rossos grown at 1200'-3000' elevation and selling for less than $10 are impressive since they still have a life expectancy of another decade. Whites are also showing a different nature by being lighter, fruitier, fresher, with more varietal character.

From the island's western coast still comes Marsala but now there are available quality bottlings that are far above those desecrations of wine and berry concoctions that have been so prominent on shop shelves for so long. Look for the *vergine* wines, those rich, dry, complex wines that stand apart much as do dry Olorosos in Jerez or single malt scotches. There are also a few sparkling wines of note ranging from the Corvo Brut to the sweet, muscat flavored spumantes from the Island of Pantellaria.

THE UNITED STATES OF AMERICA

The United States is unquestionably the most exciting emerging premium and noble wine producing region in the world. Of the two hundred or so new wineries that have entered the industry within the last decade in California, Michigan, New York, Oregon, Washington and elsewhere, virtually all of them strive to produce mid-premium or better wines. The smaller wineries, known in the trade as "boutiques" concentrate on producing a limited number of varietal wines. Many, particularly in California have achieved an enthusiastic and loyal following. Frequently, the demand for wines from these "boutiques," even new ones following their first vintage (called "first release"), is such that they command prices equal to or exceeding those of their European counterparts.

As I have already mentioned, virtually all the mid-premium and better class wines produced in America are called by a varietal name. Requirements differ from state to state as to the minimum proportion of the stated grape variety in a varietal, although all must meet minimum Federal requirements. Several states prohibit generic names such as Chablis, Burgundy, etc.

CALIFORNIA

Once again we will approach the wines of California from a varietal perspective as has been our practice.

CHARDONNAY, along with Cabernet Sauvignon, ranks as California's finest wine. Many excellent wines are made spanning the range to noble quality, with several California Chardonnays ranking above some of the finest of those from the Burgundy region of France during international competitions. What differentiates mid-premium and higher quality rankings from the simple-premium Chardonnay is the character that comes from aging in small oak casks, and the buttery taste and texture which come from the malolactic fermentation. Chardonnay frequently undergoes wood aging and cellaring similar to that of red wines, and as a consequence can have great depth of flavor, full body, and potential for prolonged bottle aging. The best do not show well when young and require several years in the bottle to develop their complexity and style.

Mid-premium quality Chardonnays have increased in number as many new vineyards in Monterey, Santa Barbara, and Sonoma and Napa Counties come into maturity, usually with vines five years or older. Also, the use of techniques borrowed from the Burgundy region of France has permitted California Chardonnay to

THE APPELLATION STRUCTURE OF AMERICAN WINES

U.S.A. or AMERICAN

Wines blended from grapes grown or wines produced in more than one state may only specify "American" as the place of origin. Many jug wines, particularly those made in the eastern United States, are blended with neutral (flavorless) California wine and so fall into this category.

STATE

Wines blended from various area within a state, with the exception of those made from grapes within certain approved appellations (see below), are limited to indicating only the state of origin. Hence many jug wines are labeled as "Califiornia" or "New York", etc.

SPECIFIC VITICULTURAL REGION

Wine producers may, under present regulations, petition to have a district designated as a "Viticultural Area" if the district has particular merit as a quality wine producing area. Unfortunately the procedures and the criteria used to determine this merit are overly simplistic based on the history of the region and its geographical continuity, rather than on specific quality standards. An appellation may be granted to a large district which may only be suitable for growing one or two grape varieties. Wines produced from other locally grown grapes are inappropriately entitled to carry the appellation on the label. Furthermore, there are no requirements as to the yield of the vines nor wine making procedures as exist in other countries, thus permitting wines of lesser character, produced within the district, to carry the appellation. Despite this caveat, certain areas have achieved acclaim over others. Napa and Sonoma Valleys are examples. As a general rule wines labeled with an appellation referring to a small geographical district have more individuality of character and a higher level of quality. Wines that are blended from several approved Viticultural Districts may state those districts as an appellation, i.e. Napa/Sonoma Chardonnay. Understanding the nuances of the hundreds of variety/viticultural/producer relationships makes "being an expert" on American wines infinitely more difficult than gaining expertise on any foreign wine producing region.

develop its full potential. The mid-premiums from Monterey are more taste more of the grape varietal character in aroma and flavor than those produced further north, have some depth and texture, along with high acidity. The accent is on fresh, varietal fruitiness. Several producers use small-barrel oak aging to soften this wines sharp edges.

Chardonnays from Santa Barbara and San Luis Obispo counties reach mid-premium status, though they tend to be relatively early maturing. They possess a unique grassiness and, depending on sugar development which determines the alcoholic content, range from very firm and hard in style, to rounder and softer, though without the rich texture that earmarks Napa Chardonnays. They have excellent acidity, and a slightly silky texture.

Parts of Sonoma County yield both mid- and super-premium Chardonnays. The areas of Dry Creek and Alexander Valley tend to accentuate a very fruity varietal aroma with a lemony flavor, and have a medium-bodied, slightly oily texture. The principle difference between Napa and Sonoma Chardonnays is that the latter are fruitier and leaner, but are improved by long bottle aging. Sonoma Chardonnays sometimes resemble the style of French Meursault or high-quality French Chablis. The major exceptions are some Chardonnays from hillside vineyards in the Alexander Valley which are extremely fruity, strongly varietal, and richer in body and flavor than most others from Sonoma.

Napa Valley Chardonnays represent the highest quality group. The finest have a ripeness of aroma and flavor that is often spicy, with a melange of apricot, pineapple, and citrus flavors. The texture is often thick and oily, and the alcohol levels are high, 13 percent or more, giving the wines a headiness when young. Some are either fermented in barrels in the true Burgundian manner or aged in small French oak casks. This regimen gives the Chardonnays a vanilla character that harmonizes with the varietal personality, along with a little bitterness from the oak tannins. Mid-premium Napa Chadonnays are made from less-ripe grapes and/or spend less time aging in small barrels. They are fruity, appley, and less complex.

SAUVIGNON BLANC or FUMÉ BLANC, frequently attains mid-premium quality with a style which resembles that of Fumé Blanc of France. Rarely does this variety rival the finest Sauvignon Blanc of the Graves or the Medoc;but neither do most of the Sauvignon grown in France as well.

Mid- to super-premium Sauvignon Blancs regularly come from the Napa Valley, the Dry Creek sub-region of Sonoma. A few may come from Monterey and Santa Ynez, along with one or two from San Diego. These regions yield Sauvignon Blancs with an aggressive, pronounced aroma of grassiness, black pepper and fruit that need to be tamed and rounded by cask aging, bottle aging, or blending with a small percentage of Sémillon. Depending on developments in winemaking techniques, Sauvignon Blancs from these areas could improve to super-premium quality over the next few years.

Napa Valley Sauvignon Blancs range from subtle, light, and moderately oaked to heavy, powerful, warm, and very oaked, depending on the style of the winery. In most cases, the wines are mid-premium quality. The Napa Valley style leans toward full ripeness in the grapes, producing wines with high alcohol, which are counter-balanced with assertive oak flavors that modulate with the varietal personality. They can be attractive when young, and are capable of rewarding bottle aging.

RIESLING, usually labeled JOHANNISBERG RIESLING, when produced within the mid-premium and higher quality categories, rank among California's finest achieve-ments. Few dry or slightly sweet versions can match the unique style and charm of those from the better districts of the Rhine and Mosel of Germany, but they can stand up to Rieslings produced anywhere else in the world. They tend to be fuller in body, particularly in middle body, and more fruity than the German versions. California Late Harvest Riesling, the equivalent of the QmP catagory of Germany, has demonstrated outstanding promise. In professional tastings, several of these wines have outclassed some of the most noble of Germany.

Some vineyards in Napa, Sonoma, and Monterey Counties will regularly develop *Botrytis* which permits the production of Late Harvest wines in the German tradi-tion. The nomenclature for these wines often proves inadequate, since the tradi-tional German terms may not be used on American wine labels. However, many Rieslings labled "Late Harvest" and finished with, say more than 3 percent residual sugar, can fall into the super-premium ranks. They offer varietal character, the Riesling floweriness, along with *Botrytis* complexity — honeyed aroma, and a hint of almonds, with corresponding balancing acid to parallel the sweetness.

CABERNET SAUVIGNON produces mid-premiun and higher quality wines from many areas in California. In the better growing areas, the Cabernet Sauvignon is capable of producing wines with intense varietal character, good structure and potential for developing considerable complexity with bottle age. The best Cabernets compete favorably with those from the Médoc district of Bordeaux and can withstand many years of cellaring.

Sonoma County is the home of many mid-premium Cabernet Sauvignons. Most are straightforward in their vinosity, medium-bodied, moderately tannic, early maturing, with a slightly weedy, peppery character. These traits are especially evident in wines from Dry Creek, the Alexander Valley, and the Sonoma Valley.

Mendocino Cabernet Sauvignons have more tannic astringency, and often more weight than those from Sonoma. The area often yields Cabernets with an appealing ripe fruit aroma, redolent with berries and herbs, but also with more tannins, more drying astringency. Those achieving mid-premium rank have a fresh violets and plum-like character, and moderate (under 13 percent) alcohol. Amador County-grown Cabernet is similar in its high tannins, but is often dry, dusty-weedy in aroma, aggressive to a fault in its tannins, and also too-high in alcohol to be considered well balanced.

Cabernet Sauvignons from Santa Barbara and San Luis Obispo Counties occasionally approach mid-premium standing. They have moderate, Bordeaux-like alcohol levels (under 13 percent), and a rich, herbal, berry-like aroma and flavor made complex by a weedy overtone and, in some cases, by wood character imparted by long aging in small casks. As of yet, they don't show the regal lingering aftertaste and depth of flavor found in Napa Valley and in the middle Médoc of Bordeaux.

Cabernet Sauvignons from Monterey County have been controversial. In the late 1960s and early 1970s, they were overwhelmingly vegetative to a fault. They tasted like uncooked asparagus, and smelled like bell-peppers. Since about 1977, some Monterey Cabernets have improved as winemakers have learned to cope with their unusual characteristics. The vegetative character is less apparent and the wines have an herbal, spicy flavor, a moderate, peppery overtone, and good varietal flavor.

Napa Valley Cabernet Sauvignon ranks among the best in California. Those made from grapes grown from north of Yountville, a cool area south of St. Helena, generally fall into the mid- or super-premium range. Some from a few selected sites in Rutherford, Oakville, and the Stag's Leap areas can yield noble wines. Napa Cabernets in this quality-tier offer a berryish, herbal aroma, fairly full body, ample tannins and some warmth. The supper-premiums possess a riper character, reminiscent of cassis, dried sage, and black currants that frequently develops cedary, "cigar-box" characteristics with bottle age.

California Cabernets differ from the wines of Bordeaux in several ways. First, they usually have a higher alcohol content, tend to have more body and a "fleshy" texture, less volatile acidity and less complexity. They rarely achieve the distinction of a Bordeaux, whether in a supple style, or in a subtle style. Most tend to be straightforward in vinosity as opposed to refined and elegant. Few California Cabernets can be said to have finesse. Those that do are outstanding and are difficult to distinguish from the *grands crus classés* of Bordeaux. They are few and far between but prove that such wines are possible in California. Among those wineries that consistantly produce Cabernets in the noble class are Stag's Leap Wine Cellars, and Joseph Heitz.

Noble Cabernet Sauvignon wines are not strictly a matter of soil and climate, although such is a requisite for these wines. Winemaking technique must be geared to subtlety. This requires selecting particular strains of yeast which produce complexity, making the proper choice of oak and finish for barrels, providing just the right amount of skin contact during fermentation, and oak extract during aging, and so forth — basically not being heavy handed. Many California winemakers fail to realize that strong, tannic character is not what makes for an outstanding wine. Too often they attempt to extract every bit of the grape when working with Cabernet. There is also too much emphasis on using one hundred percent Cabernet Sauvignon. The winemakers of Bordeaux have understood the necessity of moderating the assertive character of the Cabernet with less severe varieties such as the Merlot and the Cabernet Franc. California Cabernet benefits as well from the addition of these varieties. Many of the finest California Cabernets I have tasted have been blended with Merlot or other varieties, though still labeled as Cabernet Sauvignon. Once this becomes a general trend, California will undoubtedly produce many more wines that will rival the best of France.

MERLOT might evolve into a high quality varietal someday. At the moment, only a handfull of wineries produce it as a varietal with a few making wines within the mid- to super-premium class. Napa Valley has the edge for quality. The best are very ripe and herbaceous in aroma and flavor. They have a round, soft, and very fleshy character, often with a "sweet" aftertaste from the ripeness. The tannins are less harsh, less astringent in Merlot than in Cabernet.

MERLOT might evolve into a high quality varietal someday. At the moment, only a handfull of wineries produce it as a varietal with a few making wines within the mid- to super-premium class. Napa Valley has the edge for quality. The best are very ripe and herbaceous in aroma and flavor. They have a round, soft, and very fleshy character, often with a "sweet" aftertaste from the ripeness. The tannins are less harsh, less astringent in Merlot than in Cabernet.

PINOT NOIR has yet to become a popular variety among California producers as it is a difficult grape to grow and vinify. There is no question that it is the most difficult varietal wine to make. Soil and a precise micro-climate are essential to produce delicate varietal flavor. Winemaking expertise plays a vital role as well. What works in one district may prove disasterous in another. The major difference between California's best Pinot Noir and those from France's Burgundy is in the heavy-handed hotness or roughness of the California versions. Yet a small number of California wineries have produced some outstanding Pinot Noir, several virtually indistinguishable from the noble wines of Burgundy.

Pinot Noir generally produces wines with an attractive cherry-like fruity vinosity. Throughout the world it is grown as a mid-premium wine at its best. Yet, the pro-totype all winemakers seek to emulate is that from the Côte d'Or of Burgundy which produces noble wines of exquisite character and finesseyet with a total production that can be measured in quantities less than the production of one of the larger California wineries. The Côte d'Or has a near monopoly on the soil, climate, and other conditions required to achieve such excellence. Here and there in California, small microclimates have been discovered that yield wines of this character and uni-que taste. With the enthusiasm of wine buffs for anything new, and prices for the limited quantities of French Burgundies approaching the stratosphere, outstanding California Pinots sell out quickly.

So far, no California winery has been consistent in producing super-premium or noble class Pinot Noir. This variability in quality and style is a result of continuing experimentation on the part of the winemakers as well as climate. The most com-patible growing regions are in the southern part of Napa Valley in the Carneros district, in the Santa Cruz Mountains, and in both Upper Monterey County and in the Santa Ynez Valley. However there are many other regions offering mid-premium Pinot Noirs that lack finesse or substance, but which improve with moderate aging.

Sonoma County and Mendocino make Pinot Noirs with some character, above the stale, weak colored Pinots frequently encountered. They offer varietal fruitiness, a slightly cherry, smoky character, medium-body, and slight tannins. Most "Napa Valley" Pinot is warm alcohol, light in color, but rather dull in flavors.

However, from the Carneros region of the Napa Valley, Monterey County, and Santa Ynez and Santa Cruz, the potential for mid to super-premium Pinot Noirs has been encouraging. The Pinots are often deep colored, with herbal, cherry-ish, and slightly roasted aroma and flavors, a velvet-like texture, some depth, and a long finish. Monterey County Pinot Noirs are similar in style to the top-ranked French Beaujolais, with a well defined, sharp aroma that develops into an earthy, cherry-like complexity with bottle aging.

ZINFANDEL, as a varietal wine is difficult to define in simple terms due to the wide spectrum of style and quality. Some are light, soft and fruity; others deeply colored, harshly tannic and so intense in extract that they defy drinking. Their style and intensity vary with climate and winemaking techniques and the marketing objectives of the winery.

Zinfandel does best in the Napa Valley when grown on hillside sites and allowed to ripen to high sugar levels. It does less well on valley floors in Napa and other counties.

Super-premium Zinfandels come from the hillsides or from very old vineyards. Parts of Napa, a big block in Sonoma County's Dry Creek and Alexander Valley, along with Amador County, and the Paso Robles are in San Luis Obispo are the favorable regions. The wines produced there are intensely fruity, warm from alcohol that often exceeds 14 percent, rather thick in texture and quite tannic. The best from Dry Creek offer an earthy, peppery character. Amador's are usually intensely fruity, almost jam-like, and very powerful in both alcohol and tannin. The Alexander Valley Zinfandels, range from super to mid-premium and offer a distinct, ripe cherry, blackberry character, along with depth and richness.

Most Napa Valley and inexpensive Sonoma County Zinfandels are lesser to mid-premium. They are berry-like, medium-bodied with moderate tannins and often a tart aftertaste. Mendocino-grown Zinfandels vary from simple berry-like to riper, and excessively tannic, depending on climate. Mendocino's high alcohol Zinfandels tend to be brawny and lack real harmony.

Reliable California Producers

The following is a brief listing of established California producers which have demonstrated consistency in producing wine in each varietal catagory below.

CABERNET SAUVIGNON

Beaulieu Vineyard (Private Reserve)
Burgess Cellars
Caymus Vineyards
Chappelet Vineyards
Charles Krug Winery (Vintage Select)
Chateau Montelena
Clos du Val
Conn Creek Vineyard
Durney Vineyards (Private Reserve)
Heitz Cellars (Martha Vineyards)
Inglenook Vineyards (Cask Bottling)
Jordan Vineyards

Joseph Phelps Vineyards (Insignia)
Louis M. Martini Winery (Special Selection)
Mount Eden Vineyards
Raymond Vineyards
Ridge Vineyards (Montebello)
Robert Mondavi Winery (Reserve)
Sonoma Vineyards (Alexander's Crown)
Stag's Leap Wine Cellars
Sterling Vineyards (Regular and Reserve)
Villa Mt. Eden Vineyards

CHARDONNAY

Beaulieu Vineyard
Burgess Cellars
Chalone Vineyard
Chateau Monteleña - Napa Valley Bottling
Chateau St. Jean
Conn Creek Vineyard
Cuvaison
David Bruce Winery
Dry Creek Vineyards
Firestone Vineyard
Freemark Abbey Winery
Grgich Hill Cellars
Hanzell Vineyards
Jekel Vineyards
Mayacamas Vineyard
Mt. Eden Vineyards
Robert Mondavi Winery- Reserve and regular bottlings
Santa Ynez Valley Vineyards
Sonoma Vineyards -River West and Chalk Hill bottlings
Sterling Vineyards
Trefethen Vineyards
Ventana Vineyards

GEWÜRTZTRAMINER

Buena Vista Winery
Almaden Vineyard — Charles Lefranc
Chateau St. Jean
Grand Cru Vineyards
Hacienda Wine Cellars
Joseph Phelps Vineyards
Louis M. Martini Winery (dry style)
Parducci Vineyards
Pedroncelli Vineyards
Wente Bros.

MERLOT

Clos du Val
Lawrence Winery
Rutherford Hill Winery
Stag's Leap Wine Cellars
Sterling Vineyards

PINOT NOIR

Acacia Winery
Beaulieu Vineyard
Buena Vista Winery (Cask)
Carneros Creek Winery
Caymus Vineyards (Special Selection)
Chalone Vineyards
David Bruce Vineyards
Davis Bynum Vineyards
Hacienda Wine Cellars
Hanzell Vineyards
Parducci Wine Cellars (Cellarmaster)
Joseph Swan Vineyard
Kenwood Vineyards (Jack London)
Mount Eden Vineyards
Rutherford Hills Winery
Santa Cruz Mountain Vineyards
Villa Mt. Eden Vineyards
Zaca Mesa Vineyards

LATE HARVEST RIESLINGS

Almaden Vineyards — Charles Lefranc
Chateau St. Jean
Estrella River Winery
Freemark Abbey Winery
Hacienda Wine Cellars
Hoffman Mountain Ranch
J. Lohr Vineyards
Joseph Phelps Vineyards
Monterey Peninsula Winery
Veedercrest Vineyards

WHITE RIESLING

Chateau St. Jean
Concannon Vineyards
Felton - Empire Vineyards
Grgich - Hills Cellars

Joseph Phelps Vineyards
Robert Mondavi Winery
Monterey Vineyards
Rutherford Hills Winery

SAUVIGNON BLANC

Almaden Vineyards
Beringer Vineyards
Cakebread Cellars
Charles KrugWinery
Concannon Vineyards
Dry Creek Vineyards
E. & J. Gallo Winery
Joseph Phelps Vineyards
Kenwood Vineyards
Montevina Vineyards
Parducci Wine Cellars
Preston Vineyards
Robert Mondavi Winery
San Martin Winery
Sterling Vineyards

ZINFANDEL

Caymus Vineyards
Clos du Val
Dehlinger Vineyards
Dry Creek Vineyards
Edmeades Vineyards
Fetzer Vineyards
Grgich-Hills Vineyards
Kenwood Vineyards
Monterey Peninsula Winery
Mount Veeder Winery
Montevina Vineyards
A. Rafinelli
Ridge Vineyards
Roudin-Smith Vineyards
Rutherford Ranch Cellars
Simi Winery
Sonoma Vineyards (old Vines)
Souverain Cellars
Sutter Home Winery

WHAT MAKES A VINTAGE?

Many wines sold in the United States bear a vintage date. American consumers have been led to believe that a vintage date indicates quality; that only inferior or inexpensive wines are not "vintaged." Frequently, a vintage date on a wine has very little bearing on the quality of the wine, and the general lack of familiarity on the part of consumers as to vintages often increases the merchant's potential to sell mediocre wines at excessive prices. To be a savvy wine buyer, it is essential to understand just what a vintage date on a wine signifies and what makes a great vintage. How to react to a vintage date on wine is a source of confusion among many wine buyers. I would like to begin by explaining what a vintage date means and then go on to discuss certain key elements related to interpreting vintages.

A declaration of a vintage on a label merely indicates when the grapes were harvested and the wine made. In California the requirement is that at least 95 percent of the grapes be picked that year. In France, the minimum is generally 80 percent, and in Germany, it is 75 percent. Each country, and often each wine region within that country, establishes its own minimum requirements. Some regions have no requirements at all and producers may use any date they desire.

A vintage date declares when the wine was made, but not how and under what conditions. As such, and lacking information as to the reputation of the vintage or the individual producer, only the wine's relative age or freshness can be determined with certainty. As I have said elsewhere, most wines, perhaps at least 80 percent of all wines made, are best when consumed young, and do not improve with cellaring (prolonged aging). On average, most wines should be consumed within two years, three at the most, after the vintage date. In other words, for most wines, the vintage, if indicated, is of interest only as a guide to freshness. Just about every rosé wine, most white wines and, yes, a high percentage of red wines should be drunk early on.

Now let's consider the factors that make one vintage better or worse than another. Grapes, climate, and the winemaker are all important. They always interrelate, but the crucial factor ultimately always comes down to climate. An ideal vintage would meet certain requirements during the entire year. In the winter it needs ample rainfall and enough cold to send the vines into dormancy. The spring should be mild, free from frosts, rains, and other severe weather patterns. A mid-season that begins cool and then builds up heat in increments, without wide fluctuations should be followed by a ripening period that is not excessively hot or rainy. Gradual heat toward the late mid-ripening period increases sugar development; the incremental warming with cool evenings allows grapes to retain high acidity. The absence of rain in the mid or late season enables the berries to avoid becoming swollen or diluted with water.

The grower or winemaker has a vital role in a vintage, and for most growers it is a genuine gamble. In mid-winter, the vines can be pruned for a small crop which would assure high quality fruit, or the vineyardist could hope the vintage will bring warm (but not hot), and dry conditions so a slightly larger crop would still yield high quality. The better growers/vineyardists understand the capabilities of each grape variety they work with. If they hope for a crop which is good or excellent in both quantity and quality, they could lose out to the vagaries of climate on both counts. If they play it conservatively and prune severely for a small crop, a bad weather spell could wipe them out completely.

When to harvest the grapes is a crucial decision. In general, vineyardists would rather pick too early than too late. Picking too late runs the risks of rains, hail, or unwanted molds from high humidity. Sometimes the decision to harvest is a wise, "gut" or instinctive reaction; sometimes it is a fearful reaction made without justification. Another factor in vintage quality is whether a vineyard, a variety, or the whole crop is picked at one swoop or over several dates based on optimum ripeness of the vineyard, row, or individual vine. We know, for example, that young vines normally produce a light "small" crop and thus ripen rather early; really old vines also yield small crops, but ripen very late, with average-age vines (seven to twenty-five years of age) yielding average-size crops.

This is just the beginning of the series of complex variables behind a vintage date. It encompasses the general climate for a region, the grape varieties grown, and the winemaker's sense of how those specific grapes are faring in a particular region for a particular style of wine.

Evaluating a vintage then, is more than compiling weather reports, though that's a good beginning. The other variables are the precise moment of harvesting with regard to sugar and acid and how the winemakers coped with the quality of the grapes picked that year. Even in so-called "great vintages" some producers make a mistake or two, and the quality is below that of the vintage. Conversely, in an off-year, there are usually a few exceptions who beat the odds by better farming, better winemaking, or better luck.

SPARKLING WINES

Ever since its discovery in Champagne, in the eighteenth century by the Benedictine monk and cellarmaster, Dom Pérignon, sparkling wine and Champagne have been symbols of elegant lifestyles, celebration, and festivity. We have all seen the Champagne themes played out many times, among them, proper butlers serving shimmering glasses from silver trays or mink-clad starlets celebrating conquest with a Champagne toast in a classic movie. But no one has captured the essence of Champagne more eloquently than Dom Pérignon who, upon seeing the bubbles, remarked, "I am drinking stars."

Ironically, the exacting standards and costly procedures surrounding the production of Champagne from the French Province east of Paris, created an image of the wine as "highbrow" and best reserved for special occasions. Indeed, with its precisely delimited growing region, Champagne is limited in its production today and the rising prices only tend to reinforce its image as a luxury wine. The irony is the way our associations carry over to encompass just about all sparkling wines, from all regions, over a range of prices. By the way, though I do not approve of the way other countries, particularly the United States, have borrowed and converted the name to generic use, I will use "Champagne" for all sparkling wines and "French Champagne," however redundant, to distinguish the authentic wine in this discussion.

Good quality Champagnes can be purchased today at reasonable prices, similar to those for good quality table wines. Champagne is an ideal prelude to dinner, a fine accompaniment to most meals, and an excellent way to enhance any occasion. Such versatility inevitably leads us to ask: "Why isn't it enjoyed more frequently in our day-to-day life?" The answer is that it is surrounded by too many misconceptions and too large a mystique. Does it have to come from Champagne or, at least, from France? Is serving a domestic Champagne gauche? A sign of an unsophisticated palate? Are there real differences in taste? And what about Champagnes labeled "Extra Dry" and "Demi-Sec" or "Brut"? Some of the confusion is understandably related to terminology and definitions that either vary or are contradictory.

For instance, in France, by law, Champagne is a sparkling wine produced within the defined geographic boundaries of that district and made under the strict guidelines of the Appellation Contrôlée laws. Only certain grape varieties may be used, and only one technical procedure, the *méthode champenoise*, is allowed. Sparkling wines from elsewhere in France are called *vin mousseux*, never Champagne, even if the same grapes and same methods are used.

In the United States, Champagne and sparkling wine are synonymous terms and, by definition, are made effervescent by undergoing a second fermentation in a closed container. The bubbles must be produced naturally, not as a result of artificial carbonation, and that's the only limiting point. The choice of grape varieties is up to the producer, and Champagne can be made by several methods with no restrictions on growing conditions. The only unifying factor for all United States wines called Champagne is the presence of bubbles, trapped carbon dioxide, created *during* the Champagne making process.

What Dom Pérignon described as stars was nothing more than carbon dioxide retained in the bottle following a refermentation of residual sugar and live yeast cells which had remained after the original fermentation. The same discovery, though now less dramatic, is probably made by every home winemaker. To him, refermentation in a bottle is a disaster, but the early Champagne pioneers quickly parlayed a mistake into one of man's finest beverages. The bubbles added sparkle to wine, but what was needed was a strong closure and a special bottle to withstand the pressure. Shortly thereafter, the first was devised by Madame Clicquot, and the Champagne industry was born.

Essentially, Champagne is table wine made to ferment a second time so that the bubbles are trapped in the wine; but this mistakenly implies that Champagne is simple to make and easy to duplicate. French Champagne derives its quality from a series of time-proven methods within exacting restrictions. The permissible grape varieties are the noble Chardonnay and Pinot Noir, plus minor blending grapes which, even in Champagne's characteristically cool climate, develop character when picked at low sugar levels ranging from 15°—19° Brix (normal is 20°—23°). The grapes are conventionally fermented into wine, then assembled by the Champagnemaker into a base wine or blend, known as the *vin de cuvée*. That blend may be entirely from one vintage, but usually consists of wines from two or more years.

quired for each of the firm's markets. It may be different for different countries — drier for England, a bit more sweet for America, but generally within an established house style.

Now, to reinforce my point, we should stop here and deal with a hypothetical model. Let's divide our *cuvée* into three batches, and convert each one into Champagne using one of the three prevailing methods. They are as follows — the *méthode champenoise*, the transfer method, and the bulk, or Charmat Process. Let's follow each batch through one of the three possible techniques to see the different results.

After assembling the *cuvée*, the Champagnemaker, adhering to the *méthode champenoise* bottles the wine in the same bottle the consumer will purchase later on. A sugar and yeast solution, which will ferment in the bottle, is added to the wine. The bottles are sealed, either with a temporary cork or metal crown cap, and then placed on their sides. This second fermentation requires three to four months to complete. By law the wine must remain in contact with the dead yeast cells for a minimum of one year, though some spend as many as five years. Time "on the yeast" adds flavor complexity through a process of *yeast autolysis*, which contributes both richness and a desired yeasty character. Virtually all the top-line French Champagnes spend several years on the yeast.

Once the bubbles are created and the flavors developed, the problem is to remove the dead yeast cells from each bottle. The method, called *dégorgement* (disgorgement), distinguishes the *méthode champenoise* from a less costly shortcut method called the transfer process. Prior to *dégorgement*, the Champagne must be prepared by going through a laborious and time-consuming process called *remuage* or riddling. In this technique, each bottle is placed neck-down in special A-frame racks. Each day, cellar workers riddle (slightly shake and rotate) each bottle so that the sediment gradually moves from the side of the bottle to the neck area. After about six weeks, the sediment is lodged in the neck, up against the closure, at which point the bottles are carefully removed neck down, and taken to the *dégorgement* room.

Whether done totally by hand or by automated machines, the principle behind *dégorgement* remains the same. The neck of the bottle is immersed in a freezing brine solution, trapping the sediment in a plug of ice. The bottle is opened, the plug is expelled by the pressure, and the Champagne is thus free from the sediment. Some liquid is lost from each bottle and is therefore replaced, according to house style, with either Champagne or a solution of Cognac and a sugar syrup. Champagnes range widely in sweetness from this small dollop, known as the *dosage*, which contains some degree of added sugar.

Following *dégorgement*, a special, multi-layered cork is inserted, the protective wire hood attached, and the Champagne set aside for further aging in bottle to allow the *dosage* to marry with the wine. When sold, French Champagne is ready to drink; it will change a little in bottle, but improvement is not likely in the consumer's cellar.

The second method of making Champagne is the transfer method, a shortcut to bottle-fermented wine, which saves labor and time. The transfer process differs from the *méthode champenoise* in two ways. First, although the wine undergoes its second fermentation in a bottle, it is not the bottle ultimately purchased by the consumer. Secondly, both riddling and disgorging are eliminated as steps in favor of filtration. During the transfer process, the wine is transferred from its bottles, by a special machine which prevents the loss of pressure, into a large, pressurized tank. It is then filtered to remove the yeast cells and all other sediment and, finally, bottled. You can understand how this method cuts the cost of the Champagne by eliminating many hand operations. The Champagne is assured of being free from its sediment but may lack some of the character it developed as a result of its filtration.

Actually, it can be difficult to distinguish between two bottle-fermented Champagnes even when different processes are used. If the *cuvées* are similar, as we have assumed, then the important considerations are the length of time the Champagne spends on the yeast and the degree of filtration used. Both influence flavor. However, the transfer method can still give us Champagnes with the sought-after tiny bead and persistent effervescence which are hallmarks of a fine sparkling wine.

With our third batch of *cuvée* we can discuss the Charmat, or bulk process. Here, the *cuvée*, after its initial fermentation, is poured directly into a closed tank and a solution of yeast and sugar added. The size of the tank can vary, but is often several thousand gallons. The second fermentation takes three to four weeks, at which point it is filtered and bottled. Bulk process Champagnes normally have large bubbles that dissipate quickly and also lack much of a yeasty character because they spend little time, if any, in contact with the yeast. All we have here is good still wine made bubbly, and not always pleasantly so. Charmat lends itself to large volume and an efficient use of time, labor, and equipment. Thus, it is the process used to make inexpensive Champagne, often from neutral or even poor quality grapes.

At this juncture, let us return to our discussion of various Champagnes available in the United States. The labels will tell you which technique was followed. The French Champagne method will be declared by one of two phrases: "*Méthode Champenoise*" or "Fermented in this Bottle". The transfer process is usually identified by the phrase, "Fermented in the Bottle." Note the subtle wording. For domestic Champagnes, either "Charmat" or "Bulk" must be declared.

The style and level of sweetness of a Champagne is not quite as easy to discern from the label because of rather vague definitions. The term "Brut" is widely seen, suggesting a general style that is fairly dry; in actual commercial practice, this word describes sweetness ranging from "nonexistent" to up to 2 percent.

"Extra Dry" in Champagne usage commonly refers to medium-sweet style Champagnes, sweeter than Brut for sure. "Sec" may literally mean dry, but Champagnes so-labeled are definitely sweet. "Demi-Sec" is often twice as sweet, not half as sweet as it might imply. This lack of precision and consensus is unfortunate. Sweetness in Champagnes can easily mask defects — either a weak *cuvée* or winemaking flaws. By the same logic, the drier a Champagne is, the more perfect it has to be rendered as its weaknesses and flaws can't be concealed. The most delicate Champagnes, particularly those called Tete de Cuvee by the producer to signify the best, must be flawless — the epitome of perfection. Since the going rate for such treasures is $50—$60 a bottle, they have to be.

Our review of the Champagne and sparkling wine regions begins, appropriately, in France. Vast amounts of sparkling wines are made in France; however this is no guarantee that all of it will taste like fine Champagne. In addition to the region of Champagne, sparkling wine is made in the Loire Valley, particularly Vouvray, in Provence, and to some degree, in Burgundy and Bordeaux. Outside Champagne, the transfer and Charmat processes are permitted and are the most prevalent. The quality of French sparkling wines ranges from perfection to below average in Champagne, and from above average to awful in the other regions.

In France, the Champagne appellation is rigidly enforced and guarantees a certain style, if not always superior quality, regardless of brand name. Both the grape varieties and their yields are closely regulated with quality in mind; the main varieties are Chardonnay, Pinot Noir, and Pinot Meunier. The Pinot Noir adds fullness and body, and the Chardonnay offers finesse and backbone; but the combination depends on the Champagnemaker's preferred style. The highest quality comes from the free-run juice. Pressing is an art in Champagne because it is essential to avoid tainting the juice of the dark-skinned grapes with anything more than the slightest hint of color and/or any bitterness in flavor. Approximately sixty thousand acres are planted to vines in Champagne, and the vineyards are graded on a quality basis, which is used to determine prices paid each vineyardist. Incidentally, the prices for Champagne grapes are set by a committee of growers, producers, and government officials who determine the going rate for each vintage. The highest ranked vineyards are sought after by the prestigious houses, especially for their top of the line Tete de Cuvee. Certain vineyards are esteemed for Pinot Noir, with others cherished for Chardonnay. Except for the Blanc de Blancs, both grapes are usually blended together in some proportion, usually two-thirds Pinot Noir to one-third Chardonnay. Any Champagne labeled "Blanc de Blancs" is made solely from white grapes. Blanc de Noirs connotes a Champagne made from black grapes only.

Making Champagne is more of an art than a science. The selection of the *cuvée* is made by tasting and retasting potential components. Monitoring the time of the yeast, carefully riddling the bottles, and later disgorging the sediment are all acts requiring more than simple manual labor. But the final product with its small, delicate bead, persistence, subtle yeastiness, and balance of the parts justifies the extraordinary time and labor involved in the *méthode champenoise.*

Most sparkling wine made in France outside of the Champagne region is called *Vin Mousseux.* The most popular comes from the Loire Valley, with some appearing from the Rhône and Midi regions. The Loire Valley sparklers can be quite good and relatively inexpensive. The difference, however, is that they are made from different grape varieties and spend less time on the yeast than does Champagne. Vouvray is the Loire Valley's biggest appellation for *vin mousseux.* Some is made by the *méthode champenoise,* but recently the style has been decidedly sweet and the quality rather mediocre. Sparkling Vouvray enjoyed some success in America a few years back as a cheap substitute for Champagne but is less popular today. The small amount of sparkling wine from Burgundy is rarely of good quality only because the best grapes are used for the still table wines and the discards rendered sparkling. In Bordeaux, sparkling wines are made in limited quantity and mainly for local consumption.

Italy is one of the leading volume producers of sparkling wines, most of which are called *spumante.* These wines range from bone dry to very sweet in taste and from excellent to very mediocre in quality. The big production center is in the Piedmont which gives the world Asti Spumante. Most of this best-known Italian sparkling wine is made from the Muscat grape which has a musk-like, or pine-like aroma that is attractive when not overpowering and when the wine is well-balanced. *Spumante* is made in other regions, and in these cases the regional names precede the word Spumante. The Italians enjoy their sparkling wines sweet, so as a rule, even those labeled "Brut" are on the sweet side. Some high quality *spumante* has been produced in relatively small quantities using the *méthode champenoise,* and the quality is good. However, little of that has been exported.

Despite the fact Germany is known for producing some of the finest white table wines known to man, most of the sparkling wines it makes, labeled "Sekt," are derived from wines deemed unworthy to be drunk. The reason for this is that Sekt is made either from grapes that fail to fully ripen sufficiently to be produced as table wine or from common blending wines produced in other EEC countries. Very little Sekt is made from the Riesling grape, but those that are provide an interesting taste experience. Generally, Sekt tends to be thin, high-acid, coarsely bubbly, and often sweetened to disguise its poor flavor or lack thereof. Only a handful of brands make quality Sekt. The vast majority is, frankly, awful in quality. Fortunately, very little is shipped to the United States. It is that bad.

Spain is a real comer in the world of sparkling wines. The best are found in the Panadés region of northeast Spain, and those made by the *méthode champenoise* can be well-balanced, with a fine, steady bead. However, the grapes used in the *cuvées* have traditionally been more neutral in character and, thus, these wines lack complexity even though they are light and delicate. Spain offers relatively inexpensive sparkling wines in the United States, primarily from the two or three best producers.

Most of the Champagne sold in the United States is made there, primarily in California and New York State. Until recently, most domestic Champagne was mass produced by the Charmat process and intended for the low end of the Champagne market. New York Champagnes tend to be grapy, with the Labrusca flavor quite evident. Often they are very sweet with large, short-lived bubbles. California Champagnes, until very recently, were neutral or even off-flavored, heavy handed, and so high in alcohol that the bubbles had virtually no life expectancy.

Happily, both regions have improved the quality of their Champagne over the last few years. For both, the improvements come from the use of better wines in the *cuvées*, more expertise in the technical arena, and an overall better regard toward American Champagne as a wine deserving of serious attention. Coincidentally, the quality has improved throughout the three methods of production, all of which are used in both states.

The vast upturn in quality from California certainly owes much to a handful of trend-setters, most of whom are Champagne specialists. At first, Korbel and later Kornell specialized in sparkling wine. They were joined later on by Schramsberg which introduced *méthode champenoise* to the Napa Valley and produced a wine which set the standard for quality with a style approaching that of authentic Champagne. Recently, several French Champagne firms have turned their attention to California. The first of these is Moët et Chandon, the Champagne house which produces Dom Pérignon. Their Champagne, named Domain Chandon and made by the *méthode champenoise*, is among the finest produced in California and carefully avoids the use of the term "Champagne" on its label. More recently, other California producers have turned to *méthode champenoise* or have sought to produce more stylish wines from the transfer process, and have, thus, produced wines which provide a viable substitute for the more expensive French Champagne.

Other countries produce sparkling wines to some degree. The wines of Australia and the South American countries have fairly substantial production, but most of the sparkling wines never leave their respective homes.

FORTIFIED WINES

The chief distinctions between table and fortified wines are the style and alcohol content. By definition, a fortified wine is one whose alcohol content has been increased by the addition of brandy or neutral spirits. While table wines are legally limited to 14 percent alcohol by volume; fortified wines usually range between 17—21 percent. The simplicity of the definition owes much to the fact the wines are taxed on the basis of alcoholic strength. The higher the alcohol, the higher the tax rate assessed in the United States by the Bureau of Alcohol, Tobacco, and Firearms, a division of the Treasury Department.

Historically, wines were fortified to make them stable — to prevent unwanted fermentations and to strengthen them for long transport. At about 15 percent alcohol or higher, normal yeast populations are killed and fermentation ceases.

Fortified wines can be produced in two basic ways. In the first, the must, from grapes chosen for their ability to develop high sugar content and potential to ferment to high-alcohol levels, is inoculated with special, powerful yeasts capable of working in high alcohol ranges. Under such conditions, the alcohol level will naturally reach 17 or 18 percent and automatically inhibit fermentation. Sweetness can be adjusted afterwards.

In the second and much more common traditional procedure, a fortifying agent is used to raise the level of alcohol, and where necessary, halt fermentation. For most Ports, Sherries, Marsalas and Madeiras, grapes with high natural sugars are used. They may be fermented dry, or when sweetness is desired, be fortified to stop fermentation at a particular point and still retain some sweetness. The selection of the brandy or neutral spirits used in fortification is a crucial quality factor; some may have been aged in wood for smoothness, others may be raw and rough. Some countries insist that the fortifying material originate within their borders, often within a delineated region and from specified grape varieties.

PORT

It would be simply presumptuous to try to explain Port without first quoting H. Warner Allen, the finest authority. He wrote: "Vintage Port...has a lushness, unctuousness, delicacy and refinement that make Port unparalleled by any wine of its type in the world." The quality of Port ranges from the Vintage Port just described to the cheap, poor quality, baked-tasting dessert wines produced by the early California wine industry. True Port comes from Oporto, the seaport city of Portugal and is made in a variety of styles which are dictated by the market's preference. A Port producer may make as many as five or six different kinds of Port depending on the taste preferences of the market to which he is shipping.

Port has long been a favorite English beverage and is possibly a British invention. Until 1968, most of the Port exported to the United States was bottled in England after being shipped in cask from Portugal. To counter the widespread use of the name "Port" by other countries, the Portuguese government insists its product be bottled only in Portugal and labeled "Porto" when sent to the United States. The generic name, Port, is used in just about every wine-producing country, with California and New York State the most active parties in the United States. Most Americans, however, may be familiar with the name through domestic versions, an unfortunate circumstance as until recently most California Port was cheap and had little resemblance to the authentic style of Porto.

Port is made from a blend of grapes grown on the steep slopes within Portugal's Douro region, where the soils are generally gravelly-schist in composition and the climate is warm, practically hot. Anywhere from twelve to fifteen different grape varieties, the most prevalent of which include the Touiga, Sousao, Bastardo, and the Tinta versions — Tinta Cao, Tinta Madeira, and Tinta Francisca — which are chosen for their ability to develop high sugars, good color, and when used in concert, character and finesse. Once gathered from the terraced hillsides, the grapes are fermented and brought to Oporto for prolonged aging, blending and bottling. The quality of Port is derived from the vintage, the aging, and the blending; variations in these factors account for differences in style.

VINTAGE PORT

Vintage Port, the "crème de la crème," is only produced in exceptional vintages which are declared by each individual shipper according to his own standards. Usually made from selected lots, Vintage Port is capable of aging and developing complexity for many, many years. Once it has been fermented, fortified and adjusted for sweetness, Vintage Port must be aged for two years in wood before it is bottled. At that time, it is concentrated and rich, to the point of being undrinkable.

In bottle aging, the spirits and flavors "marry," and the wine throws a heavy deposit, or sedimentation. Ten years in bottle usually yields a mere infant as most Vintage Port will not be ready for consumption until it has bottle-aged for twenty or thirty years. It is almost criminal to open and consume Vintage Port before its maturation. As the normal deposit from bottle-aging forms a crust on the bottom and along the sides of the bottle, Vintage Port must be carefully opened and decanted to avoid having the sediment ruin the drinking pleasure.

In the Port trade, no legal requirements exist for declaring a vintage. Some shippers are very conscientious and abide by high standards while others declare a vintage virtually every year. For example, 1972 was a mediocre vintage, yet two shippers declared a Vintage Port; 1977 was well-above average and was declared a vintage by most houses except for three rather prominent ones. Declaring a vintage in Port is really a matter of one's reputation and standards, and the integrity, confidence, and expertise of the shipper.

CRUSTED PORT

Crusted Port is usually a blend of vintages which the producer thinks approximates the richness of Vintage Port. Because it is bottled when young, after cask aging, it will throw a deposit, or form a crust, which necessitates careful handling and decanting by the consumer. Crusted Port will develop in the bottle for six to eight years, but seldom reaches the heights possible for Vintage Port.

LATE BOTTLED VINTAGE PORT

Late Bottled Vintage Port comes from one vintage that is aged in cask for at least four, often five years, before being bottled. Most of the sediment falls during cask aging and, as such, Late Bottled Vintage Port is a compromise between Vintage and non-Vintage varieties. It is less expensive, less complex, and sometimes made from young vines or less traditional grape varieties.

RUBY AND TAWNY PORTS

Ruby and Tawny Ports represent two different styles, though each spends many years aging in cask. Both are blends of vintages which probably lacked the intense purple colors and flavors of a better-quality Port to begin with. Tawny Port lies in cask for many years, until the color becomes light or tawny through oxidation. Ruby Ports are blended for consistent color and style and are usually the least expensive because they are the youngest and are rougher and less harmonious than a Tawny. On the other hand, they have better color. Some well-aged Tawny Ports can be marvelous and subtle.

Occasionally, a Tawny Port will be so outstanding that it is not blended with Ports of other vintages but aged individually. When bottled, these wines are fre-

THE QUALITY CATEGORIES OF PORT

WOOD AGED PORT	BOTTLE AGED PORT

RUBY PORT

Young wood aged port, generally bottled after seven years in cask. It is ruby in color, fruity, sweet and easy to drink.

LATE BOTTLED PORT

Bottle aged port which has been aged in wood for three or four years, as opposed to only two years for true vintage port. Late Bottled port has the character of Vintage port but matures earlier an is not capable of attaining the heights of Vintage port in an outstanding year.

TWANY PORT

Port aged in wood ten years or longer. Inferior versions are made by blending ruby port with white port. Twany port developes a twany color, hence its name, and a nutty and pleasing bitter taste. Many houses make very old twany ports, twenty years old or older, in small quanities as a matter of pride and prestige.

CRUSTED PORT

Bottle aged port made from a blend of two or more vintages. Generally the wine is not aged in wood more than three years. It matures more quickly than true Vintage port but retains most of its character and finesse. It develops a hard crust of sediment along the sides of the bottle as does Vintage port, hence its name. Seldom seen these days.

PORT OF THE VINTAGE

Twany port made only from the wine of one vintage. Most twany ports are "refreshed" with younger wines and are a blend of several years. Port of the Vintage will generally be more nutty, austere and bitter. It is best only when made from wine from an outstanding year.

VINTAGE PORT

Vintage Port is the quintesence of fortified wines. It is made only from the highest quality wines which meet strict criteria. It is bottled after two years in wood retaining most of its extract. It requires a minimum of ten years before it can be enjoyed. An outstanding vintage may require twenty or more years to peak - some have survived a century or more.

quently labeled "Port of the Vintage" as opposed to "Vintage Port." While they can be quite distinctive and outstanding examples of an aged Port, frequently nurtured for decades in cask, they bear no resemblance to true Vintage Port, nor is the labeling meant to imply that they do. When buying Vintage dated Port, it is essential to understand this distinction and read the label carefully. "Ports of the Vintage" frequently fetch prices equal to true Vintage Ports.

WHITE PORT

White Port is rarely seen outside of Portugal and France. Made from white grape varieties, most is finished dry, bottled young, and drunk as an aperitif. The sweet-finished version are usually inferior in quality.

"PORTS" FROM OTHER COUNTRIES

Non-Oporto Ports are generic dessert wines made in many countries. Those from New Zealand, Tunisia, and Cyprus are decidedly of poor quality by any standard. Historically, Ports from South Africa and California have been dull and ordinary, tainted by baked qualities which come from inappropriate grapes grown in a hot climate. Recently, both regions have evidenced a renewed interest in better-quality Ports and have planted the traditional grape varieties and searched for finer fortifying spirits.

In California, several very interesting Ports have been made either from blended grapes or from blends in which Zinfandel predominates. Among the Port revivalists, Amador County and parts of Sonoma County are gaining attention as respected Port wine regions. South Africa, a country rich in tradition when it comes to making fortified wines, is coming alive with finer Port wines. Some South African versions of late are virtually indistinguishable from the Oporto models.

SHERRY

Sherry, from the Jerez region of southern Spain, is said to be an Anglicized pronunciation of Jerez. It is a fortified wine, but its methods of production are quite unlike those of Port. The predominant grape variety is the Palomino, a prolific vine whose fruit is delicious to eat, but which normally yields thin, neutral, and sometimes harsh table wines. The chief liability of Sherry is converted into an asset; the wine oxidizes easily during aging and yields a characteristic and desirable nutty aroma and flavor, which are its hallmarks. Pedro Ximénex is a secondary grape for Sherry, yielding very sweet wine which is often used as a blending or sweetening agent.

Sherry makes a critical, possibly irrefutable, statement about the importance of not only climate, but also soil. As a viticultural area, Jerez is divided into three sections, all based on soil type. The most prized and least productive regions have soils characterized by *albariza* a soil that is predominantly chalk, with limestone and magnesium. These areas, easy to detect by their white topsoils, bear the best Sherry grapes, and by law, at least 40 percent of the grapes used in Sherry must come from the famed *albariza* soils. *Barro,* another soil division literally meaning "clay," is more productive; *arena,* the third region meaning "sand," bears grapes which are immensely productive, but weak in character.

Sherry is made in large volume and most producers follow modern, efficient methods of crushing and vinification. It begins as wine which, today, is fermented in stainless steel tanks. The first year wine is then aged in the *bodega* (winery) in butts (oak barrels, which are made in the United States, with a capacity of one hundred fifty eight gallons) filled to about one-third of capacity. What ensues over the next year or two is a drama of self-fulfillment. Some butts will reveal a propensity toward developing the unique, thick, white film yeast, called *flor* in Jerez, while others won't. The appearance of the *flor* yeast, technically known as *Saccharomyces fermenti,* is unpredictable, discerned only by frequent tastings, and also found nowhere else in the world. It may result from location within the *bodega,* from the butt, from the climatic changes — or a combination of all three. Call it manifest destiny, or whatever. During the aging, the *bodega* master (vintner) tastes wine from each butt, and rates it on the basis of its propensity to develop the *flor* on the wine's surface. This is an example of the aging wine telling the experienced vintner where it wants to go.

The wine's progress in each *butt* is chronicled in chalk. Based on the intrinsic character and development of the *flor,* the wine is channeled into one of three directions.

- Those wines without any *flor* character and with weak flavors will either be distilled into spirits or made into vinegar.

- Those that develop only a small degree of *flor,* but have good body and flavors are marked as Olorosos and introduced into a *solera.*

- Those light in color with a thick layer of *flor* yeast are marked as Finos and sent to another *solera.*

Within the bodegas, butts marked Fino will be made into three different styles of Sherry: Fino, Manzanilla, Amontillado. The Olorosos will be made into Oloroso, Cream Sherry or Brown Sherry.

The crucial determinant in achieving quality in a Sherry lies in the aging process. Most Sherries are non-vintage wines, and almost all are the product of the *solera* system of blending and aging in butts. The *solera*, itself, is a configuration, usually triangular in shape, of barrels containing Sherry of various age, from which the producer blends the final product. This procedure, called "fractional blending" marries old wine with newer wine from the different tiers of the *solera*. The word *solera*, incidentally, is not derived from the word *sol*, or sun, but rather from *suelo*, the word for bottom or ground, which refers to the bottom tier of the *solera*.

A solera is usually composed of three tiers, or rows, and each successive tier represents a younger wine. The major premise operating behind the system is that older wines blended with newer wines combine a host of flavors, as newer wines "refresh" the older ones. While the bottom tier contains the oldest Sherry, those above it, called *criadera*, are a sort of nursery in which the Sherry matures. In an established *solera*, the butts remain; the wine moves first diagonally and then down from one tier to the next. When the Sherry master bottles wine, he will drain off part (no more than one-third from each butt) from the bottom tier, and replace it with wine from the tier above. As Sherry moves throughout the solera, it is in the process of being blended fractionally.

FINO

Fino, the finest Sherry, is always produced and aged within Jerez. It has a pale color, a yeasty, slightly nutty aroma, delicate flavors, and is usually dry, sometimes slightly bitter. A Fino averages about three to five years in *solera* before bottling, does not develop in the bottle, and once opened, loses freshness within a week or so.

MANZANILLA

Manzanilla is best described as Fino produced in Sanlucár de Barrameda, ten miles from Jerez and close to the sea. Some say the wine's slightly bitter, tangy, and pungent character is due to the salty flavors picked up from the sea air. Wines made in Sanlucár but sent to Jerez for aging in *solera* do not develop the typical character of Manzanilla, so there seems to be some merit in the traditional explanation.

AMONTILLADO

This is simply aged Fino which spends a longer time in the *solera*. It is medium-bodied with a more pronounced, nutty flavor than a Fino.

OLOROSO

Oloroso is a rich, full-bodied style of Sherry, aged for a considerable time in butts and lacking the *flor* yeast character. These are dry wines, often sweetened to satisfy the demand of most markets.

THE QUALITY CATEGORIES OF SHERRY — FINO

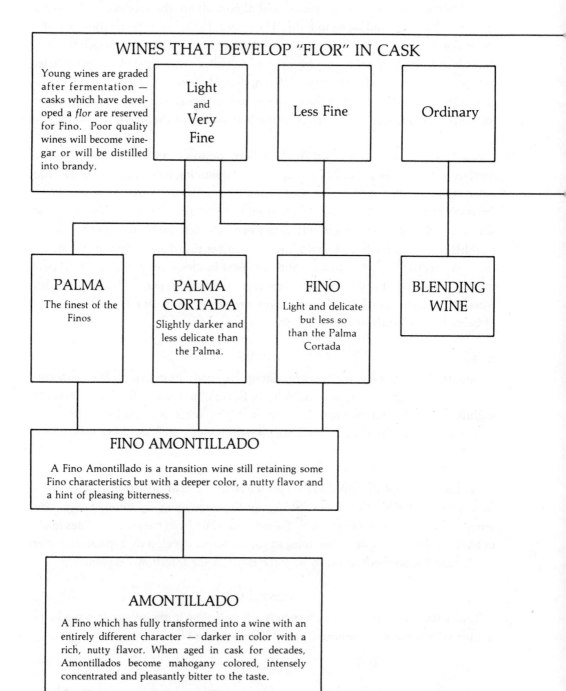

WINES THAT DEVELOP "FLOR" IN CASK

Young wines are graded after fermentation — casks which have developed a *flor* are reserved for Fino. Poor quality wines will become vinegar or will be distilled into brandy.

Light and Very Fine

Less Fine

Ordinary

PALMA

The finest of the Finos

PALMA CORTADA

Slightly darker and less delicate than the Palma.

FINO

Light and delicate but less so than the Palma Cortada

BLENDING WINE

FINO AMONTILLADO

A Fino Amontillado is a transition wine still retaining some Fino characteristics but with a deeper color, a nutty flavor and a hint of pleasing bitterness.

AMONTILLADO

A Fino which has fully transformed into a wine with an entirely different character — darker in color with a rich, nutty flavor. When aged in cask for decades, Amontillados become mahogany colored, intensely concentrated and pleasantly bitter to the taste.

THE QUALITY CATEGORIES OF SHERRY — OLOROSOS

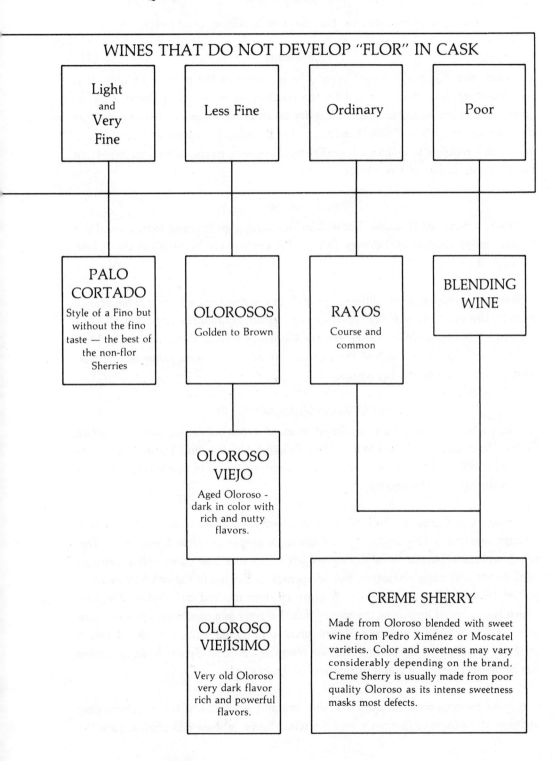

WINES THAT DO NOT DEVELOP "FLOR" IN CASK

Light and Very Fine

Less Fine

Ordinary

Poor

PALO CORTADO

Style of a Fino but without the fino taste — the best of the non-flor Sherries

OLOROSOS

Golden to Brown

RAYOS

Course and common

BLENDING WINE

OLOROSO VIEJO

Aged Oloroso - dark in color with rich and nutty flavors.

OLOROSO VIEJÍSIMO

Very old Oloroso very dark flavor rich and powerful flavors.

CREME SHERRY

Made from Oloroso blended with sweet wine from Pedro Ximénez or Moscatel varieties. Color and sweetness may vary considerably depending on the brand. Creme Sherry is usually made from poor quality Oloroso as its intense sweetness masks most defects.

AMOROSO

This is a style of sweet Oloroso, but the term is seldom used today.

CREAM SHERRY

Cream sherry is made from Oloroso wine, often of the poorest quality. It is sweetened and its color darkened by the addition of wines from Pedro Ximénez grapes, which are picked and left to sun-dry on trays for a week to ten days for further sugar development. Pedro Ximénez , a thick, concentrated wine is very sweet; not much is required to make a Cream Sherry. However, its character is an important factor in the quality of Cream Sherry.

BROWN SHERRY

This is a blend of Oloroso, Pedro Ximénez, and a sweetening agent, usually a syrupy, grape concentrate. Brown Sherry will most likely be found in the British markets, if at all.

Sherry is marketed under different proprietary names for each style. These range from totally dry to very sweet, and have an alcohol content ranging from 17 to 21 percent. The best-known producers are Gonzales Byass, Pedro Domecq, Duff Gordon, and Harvey's. Each of these producers markets a wide range of Sherries, which span style and quality vistas.

"SHERRY" FROM OTHER COUNTRIES

Wines labeled "Sherry" are produced in many other countries, including South Africa, Australia, the United States, New Zealand, Cyprus, and Tunisia. Some are of good quality; most are ordinary. Few countries outside of Spain use the *solera* system for aging and blending.

Producers in California and other states attempt to achieve the taste of Sherry through two unusual methods. In one, high-sugar grapes are picked, fermented, fortified, and then "baked" in casks that are left in the sun. The wines will acquire an aged flavor and nutty character, but are generally lacking in the delicacy or complexity found in Spanish Sherries. A more modern method is to induce the *flor*, which is capable of imparting the Sherry *flor* character in a continuous process, into large tanks. Several California Sherry producers emulate the traditional *solera* method. The best of California Sherries resemble those of Spain; however, none has achieved the delicacy and distinction of Spain's best.

A more modern method, used in California and Australia, involves submerging and mixing cultures of *flor* yeast into the wine. Some of these can approximate the aroma, but not quite the flavor complexities and texture of Fino. A few Sherry *soleras* are found in California, and the results are often much improved quality. When priced below Spanish Sherry, some of these others can be a good value.

MADEIRA

Madeira, an island off the coast of North Africa, and under the control of Portugal, lent its name to the once-famous drink of Colonial America, Madeira. The grapes for this wine are grown on very steep hillsides which ring the perimeter of the island. Madeira still clings to old-fashioned techniques that rely on hand labor for picking and carrying the grapes down on the backs of men. Some producers still use bare-footed men to tread on the grapes before fermentation. The wines of Madeira are often identified by the grape variety from which they are made. These include, principally, Verdelho, Sercial, Bual (or Boal), and Malvasia.

The juice of the grapes, or *mosto* is fermented in large vats. Again, wines destined for a dry style will complete fermentation, while the sweeter versions will be arrested through the addition of brandy to retain sugar. Madeira follows one unusual production technique that accounts for its unique character: a system of baking or heating the wine that started accidentally when the wine was en route to the East Indies. Stored in the warm ships while passing through tropical heat, the wine changed character and was so much appreciated that winemakers began to duplicate these conditions by aging the wine in large casks in the sun for gentle baking. Today, the slightly roasted or smoky tang is achieved by aging in heat controlled vats, a process known as *estufagem*, taken from the word *estufas*, or ovens. In the *estufas*, the temperature increases gradually until it reaches about 110°F where it remains for several months. Then the Madeira is allowed to cool and recover for the same period of time. It is then fortified and aged in wood cask before being bottled.

Appreciating high quality Madeira is an acquired taste. It is characteristically dark in color, with a rich, nutty aroma and a sharp tang to the flavors. Most Madeira is sold under proprietary names; authentic vintage Madeira is rare and usually comes from a single cask. Many Madeiras are aged in *solera* and those with dates refer to when the *solera* was established, not the entire contents of the bottle.

There are about seven styles of Madeira, which are differentiated by both the grape and level of sweetness; these names reflect either the grape variety or style.

SERCIAL

Sercial, the finest dry Madeira, has a lightness and delicacy that lends itself nicely to enjoyment as an aperitif. The grape is one of the latest to ripen in Madeira and offers the most distinctive aroma.

VERDELHO

Verdelho is slightly sweeter and rounder on the palate than Sercial. It has a more typical Madeira nose that can best be described as a toasted, nutty character.

BUAL

This is, again, sweeter and also much fuller in body and deeper in color. It is commonly served with dessert.

MALMSEY

Malmsey is the sweetest of all, dark in color and with a smooth, almost unctuous texture. It is made from the Malvasia grape variety, and is probably the most famous Madeira name today.

RAINWATER

Rainwater, also well-known in the United States, is variable in its range of sweetness; but, as its name implies, should be rather pale in color. The name, incidentally, was coined by a well-known Madeira collector in Savannah, Georgia.

MARSALA

Marsala, a fortified wine from Italy, bears some resemblance to Madeira. Its production is centered in Sicily, in the town of Marsala. In vogue in the late eighteenth century, the wine was in vogue; today, it is used primarily as an inexpensive cooking or dessert wine. It is dark in color with a caramel aroma and often very high sweetness. The sugar comes either from allowing the grapes to dry in the sun prior to fermentation or, more commonly, from the addition of grape concentrate after fermentation. Dry Marsala is often blended in a *solera* system; but dates on Marsala bottles refer to the founding of the *solera*, not a particular vintage.

VERMOUTH

This flavored, fortified wine which derives its name from the German word *wermut* (wormswood) is made in many wine regions of the world. The flavoring agents are a concoction of herbs, juniper, coriander, and wormwood to name but a few. Vermouth normally begins as inexpensive, bland white wine. The herb infusion, which was steeped in alcohol, is then added, and the whole quickly blended together to marry. The herb formula varies from brand to brand, and Vermouth varies from fairly dry to quite sweet. It is inexpensive and used as an aperitif or mixer.

A word of caution: with the exception of Vintage Port, most other fortified wines do not improve in bottle; they will change by losing freshness, but won't develop any nuances. Nor can they be left opened for weeks without loss of quality, for after a week the wines become oxidized and go flat.

WINE BOTTLES

The bottles used for wines come in several different shapes, each providing, to some extent, a clue to what is in the bottle. At one time, the shape of a wine bottle provided a relatively good indication as to its contents. Today, as bottles become more and more standardized, this has become less true. There are several predominant shapes, each of which has variants. Most popular are the Bordeaux, or Claret bottle with straight, slightly tapered sides, and the Burgundy bottle with its wider, gracefully curved sides and squatter appearance. Tall and elegant are the Hock and Mosel bottles of Germany. Each wine region has its own variation; several have shapes uniquely their own. The explanation for the existing bottle shapes is tradition and reputation.

The Bordeaux bottle, with its straight sides and sharp shoulders, is used for wines approximating a style of Bordeaux wines as well as for wines made in Bordeaux. Red Bordeaux, Sauternes, and Graves wines are all packaged in this bottle. Wines made elsewhere with some resemblance in type or grape composition are often so-bottled. These include California varietals such as Cabernet Sauvignon, Merlot, Sauvignon Blanc, Sémillon (all Bordeaux grape varieties) and Zinfandel, because the latter is said to resemble a Bordeaux in style.

The same system, largely based on tradition and exercised as an individual option by wine producers, applies to the other bottle shapes. Generally, wines fuller in body or richer in perfume than Claret-styled wines are bottled in the narrow-shoulder, rounder Burgundy bottle. California Chardonnay and Pinot Noir, Burgundy varietals, for instance, are sold in the Burgundy bottle. Fuller bodied Spanish wines and the sturdier Italian wines, such as Barolo and Barbaresco, find their way into variants of this shape.

The German Hock bottle is tall, slender and brown in color. A variant is the Mosel bottle which is green in color. In Germany, the general rule is Rhine wine in brown bottles, Mosel in green. Today this is no longer strictly adhered to, but is still

"Magnum"   "Claret" or   "Vintage Port"
              "Red Bordeaux"

"Burgundy"   "Loire"   "Champagne"

"Alsace"   'Provence"   "German"

"Sherry"   "Sherry"   "Chianti Fiasco"

a good guide. Most wines from Alsace are bottled in a shape similar to the German bottle. California Rieslings, Gewürztraminers, and Sylvaner varietals frequently come in the Hock bottle. The shape is used throughout the world; frequently it signifies nothing about the wine within.

The one-time popular Chianti *fiasco* with its straw wrapping was used only for inexpensive Chianti and is still occasionly seen; but it has largely been dropped due to the increasing cost of hand labor in Italy. Therefore, most Chianti, particularly the better versions, today comes in a Bordeaux bottle. Another bottle shape is the Bocksbeutel, once used only in Franconia, but now used for several Portuguese rosé wines and a few made in Chile.

The Champagne bottle is a slight modification of the Burgundy bottle. It usually has an indentation or "punt" at the bottom, and thick walls to withstand the pressure. The most expensive Champagnes generally are bottled in special shapes unique to the brand.

Most wine bottles have a deep green or brown color because the color protects the wine from sunlight. Although most bottles are dark green, some, usually in a Hock shape, may be found in brown as many believe it provides even better protection from the sun's harmful rays. Thus, brown bottles are used for many low-alcohol, sweet-finished white wines. With advances in winemaking and better methods of stabilizing wines for bottle aging, clear glass, which allows the consumer to view the actual color of the wine, is becoming increasingly popular.

In 1980, many California vintners worked together with some bottle manufacturers and designed what is called the "California bottle," which comes in both the 750 ml and the 1.5 litre magnum sizes. It was a slightly redesigned Burgundy bottle, but similar enough so that wineries would feel comfortable and not terribly anti-traditional if they wanted to use it for all kinds of wines — Riesling, Cabernet, Zinfandel, and Chardonnay. Economic efficiency has much to do with the use of the California bottle, since wineries order one shape which they use for all types of wine.

The really traditional Bordeaux bottle which was slightly tapered from top to bottom and made with a deep punt has all but disappeared. Bottle manufacturers found it an unprofitable item to maintain, and retailers often found it difficult to place in their shelves or racks. Many small wineries loved this particular bottle shape because it set the wine apart from others and often used the bottle for their special selection, or Reserve-type wines.

CORKS & CLOSURES

More than bottle types and sizes, the presence of a cork more likely influences people to make quality inference than any other element. Most corks used throughout the wine world come from either Portugal or Spain which together provide close to 90 percent of the world's total supply. The tree used for cork is the cork oak, *Quercus suber*, which grows in warm climates.

Cork contains millions of tiny cells and is light in weight; each cell is separated by a strong, impermeable membrane. A cork can be compressed for insertion into a bottle but will also expand within it to create a tight fit. Most producers prefer a straight cork, untapered, of at least one and one-half inches in length; the two-inch cork is used for special wines requiring long aging. Corks vary in quality; the lowest quality of which is very porous. Because of limited availability and increased costs, many corks used in inexpensive wines are one-inch in length and not of top-quality.

The cork closure for Champagne is a laminated seven-piece closure, said to be first-used in 1895. It is constructed to be, first of all, compressed by the corker and then to flair out for a tight seal with plenty of strength once in the bottle neck.

ALTERNATIVES

Plastic and metal screw caps are the two most widely-used alternative closures for wine. The screw cap unfortunately bears a negative image mainly from those who link cork to high quality. The screw cap can provide a fairly tight seal and the only area of controversy is that the cap is not as permanent a seal as the cork for long-term aging. In their favor, screw caps do not leak as corks might and do not carry fungi as some corks could. For most wines which will not be cellared, the screw cap has many advantages over the cork. It costs less, is consistent in quality, does not require a corkscrew, and can easily be replaced if the wine is not completely consumed.

There's a popular plastic closure used for inexpensive Champagne bottles; like the wine it protects, it is relatively cheap. However, it has many disadvantages, primarily that it is not capable of providing the kind of seal required to hold the gas pressure for prolonged periods of time. The use of such a closure is a certain sign of a cheap product. But if such is what you want, be certain that the wine has been recently bottled to avoid a "flat" bottle.

HOW TO READ A WINE LABEL

Wine labels are more than pretty decorations designed to entice you into buying the wine they are affixed to. Of course, their design, fancy or plain, creates a certain cachet which is intended to lure you into selecting them. But, they also provide useful information about the type of wine and where it came from. Information runs from sparse, where only the bare essentials and mandatory requirements are included to a detailed mini-lesson in winemaking. The issue for the wine buyer is separating the useful from the window-dressing, the wheat from the chaff, to help make an intelligent purchase.

All labels on wines sold in the United States must first be approved by an agency of the federal government, the Bureau of Alcohol, Tobacco and Firearms (BATF), a division of the Treasury Department, which, in addition to collecting alcohol taxes, is charged with insuring that the information on a wine bottle is truthful, accurate, and not misleading. All wines must conform both to the mandatory label requirements of the United States and to the regulations of the country of origin. Each state may impose its own regulations individually, but these must also conform to the federal standards.

The philosophy of the United States wine labels seems to be to keep them simple. One primary requirement is a declaration of the alcohol content, expressed usually, in terms of alcohol by volume. Table wines contain between 7 to 14 percent alcohol by volume; fortified wines at least 17 to 21 percent. Secondly, the label must indicate where the wine was produced, either by country or by state; imported wines must read "Product of Spain," "Product of France," etc. Finally, there must be some indication of the brand or business responsible for the wine, whether that be a trademark, shipper, *negociant*, or corporate name.

Otherwise, the key points largely depend on the reigning philosophy of the producing country. Most wines carry either a varietal (grape), geographic, or generic name. In some countries, the choice is more a matter of marketing decisions; a wine may be labeled either Mâcon or Chardonnay, or White Graves or Sauvignon, as examples. Because most geographic names are closely regulated as to permitted grape varieties, I tend to equate the two to some degree. White Burgundies must be made from the Chardonnay; Bordeaux red from the family of Cabernet grape varieties, and so on.

As a general guideline, the more specific the information is on a wine label, the more likely the quality will be higher. Or, to put it another way, assuming some familiarity with the details on the label, the greater information provided, the better off you will be to make a more meaningful decision. To help point you in this direction, I will summarize some of the more significant label terms likely to be encountered from different wine regions. Again, this is not intended to be an exhaustive listing, but more of a guide to the essentials of wine label terminology. For the wine consumer, it comes down to knowing whether that country's regulations are rooted in geography or in wine composition.

THE UNITED STATES

In terms of mandatory information, there is very little on an American wine label that is useful in differentiating a quality from an ordinary wine. Mandatory label information can be useful; however, it must be understood that with regard to America's best wines, American wine regulations do not lend themselves to providing labeling requirements that parallel those of France or Germany. Many producers provide precise information as to the technical aspects of the wine, such as harvest date, sugar and acid content of the grape, etc. which can be useful. The law requires that such information be accurate and truthful. But don't be surprised if it translates to rather ordinary wines. Truth in labeling is fine; but understanding this truth is left up to the public. That, unfortunately permits the American wine industry to easily prey on an uninformed, and gullible public.

American wines are only required to state bare essentials. Geography is just beginning to emerge as an important aspect, but present regulations in this regard will not provide any assurance of quality since no standards have been codified as to viticultural or vinification practices. Label terms are as follows:

Wine Type. The name of a grape on a label means that at least 51 percent of the wine's volume was derived from that grape. The minimum percentage is to increase to 75 percent by 1983.

Places. The state designation "California" means that 100 percent of the grapes used were grown within California. Other states require only 75 percent.

Viticultural Area. A name like "Napa Valley" or "Sonoma Valley" means that at least 75 percent of the wine was made from grapes grown within that designated area.

Procedures. "Produced and Bottled By" means the named winery made and bottled at least 75 percent of the wine in the bottle. "Made and Bottled By" only means that the named winery made at least 10 percent of the wine in the bottle.

Vintage Date. 1978 or any vintage date means at least 95 percent of the wine was made from grapes grown in and fermented during that year.

FRANCE

The French wine label provides exacting information as to certain quality standards through its system of Appellation Contrôlée regulations which are linked to carefully defined geography. The smaller the piece of property named, the more stringent the regulations are for methods of cultivation and production. Other than names of properties and estates, it is worthwhile to bear in mind that the name of the shipper or importer must appear on the label (often as a strip attached to the bottle) so it is worthwhile to study and record the importer's name for future reference.

Of all French wines, "Champagne" is a name that guarantees much more than geographic authenticity. It goes beyond to guarantee that only one production method, the *méthode champenoise*, was used. Any other place name, from "Bordeaux" to "Pauillac" simply guarantees that the wine originated within that clearly delimited region. Wines with village names meet more stringent requirements than those with only regional names.

A.O.C. (A.C.) This is the abbreviated form of Appellation d'Origin Contrôlée, and now includes some two hundred fifty French wine regions. However, that covers no more than 20 percent of all French wines.

V.D.Q.S. This abbreviation stands for a category below that of A.C. wines and means Vins Délimités de Qualité Supérieure.

Vins de Pays. This is another category of wines that falls below V.D.Q.S.

Vin de France or Vin de Table. These terms signify wines made anywhere in France. Usually nationwide blends, they represent the lowest category. Such wines may not use any name that has been granted A.C. status as part of their address and must indicate their location by the French equivalent of a zip-code.

Mis en Bouteilles au Château. This means the wine was estate-bottled at the named château, which is now a fairly common practice and does not, by itself, signify anything special.

Mis en Bouteilles au Domaine. Much the same is meant here. This is seen on wines from Burgundy.

Mis en Bouteilles dans nos Caves. This is not a legally defined term and is meaningless. You can assume that its use is intended to deceive the purchaser into believing that he is buying an estate-bottled wine.

Mis en Bouteilles dans la Region de Production. This is an even more ambiguous statement.

Cru Classe. Literally meaning a "classified growth," or property, this is more significant for wines from the Médoc and Burgundy. Some prestigious regions were never classified.

Premier Cru. This term, meaning first or top growth, is relative to the region's classification; in Bordeaux, it is the top, in Burgundy, it follows after Grand Cru.

Grand Cru. In Burgundy this represents the top classified growths. In the Bordeaux classification scheme, it is the second.

Negociant. A negociant is a merchant who buys wines from producers and estates and blends them for sale under his own label. He may also buy wines, bottle them, and sell them under the producer's name and add his as *"negociant-eleveur."*

GERMANY

The German wine label nomenclature is exceedingly precise as to quality specifications; it is linked closely to growing regions, large and tiny; to a designation of quality; and also to the degree of ripeness achieved by the grapes that went into the wine. The labels often appear more complicated than they are, but are less forbidding once the system is learned.

The region in which they are grown and ripeness of the grapes are the two main concerns, and both play important roles on the labels. Though blended wines are made from grapes grown either entirely within Germany or even with some grapes from outside the boundaries, those imported into the United States are usually above this low level of table wine, designated as Tafelwein.

In terms of quality, the largest category is the Q.B.A. wines (Qualitätswein bestimmten Anbaugebiet) mercifully shortened to Qualitätswein. These wines are permitted to have sugar added to increase the alcohol content because the grape ripeness was insufficient. They are usually shipped with the name of a large region, such as Rheingau or Baden, declared.

Second, and more important to the United States wine buyer, is the category Qualitätswein mit Prädikat, QmP, Quality Wine with Special Attributes. This phrase indicates that no sugar was added to the grape juice as the ripeness was sufficient. Several levels of Prädikat wines, all based on an ascending order of grape ripeness, exist. Correspondingly, there is a usual ascending order in the relative sweetness of the wine.

The QmP step-ladder begins with Kabinett wines, the least sweet. Next is Spätlese, followed by Auslese. Then come the larger wines, Beerenauslese, (selected harvest) and Trockenbeerenauslese (individually berry picked) wines. From Auslese on up, the higher sugar levels owe something to the development of the noble mold, *Botrytis cinerea*, though there's no official requirement. However, usually from Auslese on up, *Botrytis* played an increasingly important role. This categorical approach applies to wines from all approved grape varieties and regions.

As for the place names, the German labels adhere to a standard convention. The first name to appear refers to the town and ends with an "er" suffix; the second name refers to either a particular vineyard, called an *Einzellage*, or to a group of adjacent vineyards, called a *Grosslage*. Wines from an even larger area, including several villages and many individual vineyards are labeled as coming from a *Bereich*. In general, the more specific the geography, the better the quality and more distinctive the wine. Unfortunately, the name of a *Grosslage* often appears as the same as that of an individual *Einzellage*, or vineyard, easily confusing a consumer unfamiliar with all the *Grosslage* names into believing that the wine is from an actual vineyard. There is no easy solution; memorizing the major *Grosslage* is the only way to avoid buying what is, in essence, a village wine when a higher quality vineyard is desired. Knowledge about some of the finer German vineyards is essential, all the rest of the information needed to determine the worth of a particular German wine is required to appear on the label.

Some German producers specify the grape variety on the label, but this is optional. The word "Riesling," on a German wine label means that only the true Johannisberg Riesling was used. Following the vineyard and, if any, the grape, the label states the category, Kabinett, Auslese, etc. The word "Erzeugerabfüllung" indicates who bottled the wine. It is followed by the location where the wine was bottled.

Today German wine labels must bear a ten digit code known as the "Prufung-snummer," which is the official government code recorded for identifying each batch of wine tested and analyzed. Samples of each coded wine, along with its laboratory analysis are maintained to verify that the wine bearing the code is actually the wine approved for it.

ITALY

Italian wine labels provide a fair amount of meaningful information regarding what is in the bottle. Nomenclature for certain wines is regulated under laws enacted in 1967. These laws followed the French concept but were without the refinement of official classifications. The Italian wine-regulating system, the Denominazione di Origine Controllata (D.O.C.), is government approved and defines growing regions. For several types of wine, the D.O.C. laws basically guarantee the authenticity of the growing region and certain minimum standards of production.

Italian quality wines indicate the place name, either as the name of the wine itself, (Chianti, for example), linked to a grape variety, such as Barbera d'Asti, or through a D.O.C. designation. Not all places have earned D.O.C. status, but most better Italian wines sold within the United States will be so-designated.

Wine named after a grape variety will usually be referenced by a place, i.e., Nebbiolo d'Alba. If it is not, then chances are that the wine will lack distinction. "Classico" refers to special inner zones with approved special merits within larger D.O.C. regions. "Riserva" seen on labels means that the wine was aged for an additional period over those without the designation. More than two hundred Italian wines have been granted D.O.C. status so far.

An even higher denomination, Denominazione di Origine Controllata e Garantita (D.O.C.G.) was recently instituted. To earn this stamp, wines must be sampled throughout the winemaking process by a special committee and meet the standards or else be declassified. Wines with D.O.C.G. status are sealed with a special seal by government inspectors.

THE IMPORTED WINE LABEL
Example of a Lable Meeting Mandatory Federal Labeling Requirements

1. QUALITY DESCRIPTORS

None are indicated — none are required

2. STYLE DESCRIPTORS

None are indicated — none are required

3. PROMOTIONAL MATTER

Neck tags, booklets, and descriptive back labels are permitted as long as they are truthful and accurate. No health or nutritional claims may be made.

7. VINTAGE

May be stated on the main label or on a separate label such as the neck label depicted here.

8. **WINE TYPE**

The catagory of wine must be indicated — i.e. Table wine, Desert Wine, Sparkling Wine, etc.

9. TRADE MARK

4. **ALCOHOLIC CONTENT**

Must be stated within 1 1/2% by volume

5. IMPORTER

The name and address of the importer is required

6. CAPSUL

This is a protective cover over the cork generally made of lead or plastic. It may bear a name or trademark.

10. WINE NAME

11. PRODUCER

12. **COUNTRY OF ORIGIN**

13. **CONTENTS**

Must be indicated by volume in standard metric measure and conform to approved size. The most common sizes are 35 cl, 75 cl (standard size, approx. 4/5 qt), 150 cl (magnum), and 300 cl (double magnum).

NOTE: The Mandatory descriptors printed in bold face are required on all wine labels. They will not be included in the examples that follow in order to simplify the diagrams.

THE FRENCH WINE LABEL

Vieux Château Certan
Grand Cru
POMEROL
1967

Appellation Pomerol contrôlée
SOCIÉTÉ CIVILE DU VIEUX CHATEAU CERTAN
(Héritière de Georges Thienpont)
PROPRIÉTAIRE A POMEROL (GIRONDE)
MIS EN BOUTEILLE AU CHÂTEAU

1. WINE NAME

Wine Type - Red, White, Rosé
Trade or Proprietary Name
A.O.C. name
V.D.Q.S. name
Regional or Commune name
Individual Vineyard

2. VINTAGE

Specific year only or none

3. PRODUCER

Name and address of producer
is required. If the wine comes
from an A.C. district different
from that of the négociant then
the address is indicated by a
code number similar to a "ZIP"
code to prevent consumer deception. However if the wine is
bottled outside of an A.C.
district then a real address may
be used. To circumvent the
code address regulation some
producers from well known
A.C. districts have acquired
additional facilities outside
A.C. districts.

4. ORIGIN

The delimited area in which the
grapes were grown and the
wine produced. These areas
may be regulated (by A.C. or
V.D.Q.S., etc.) or may be unregulated. When blended from
several regulated districts the
wine must be identified only by
the larger appellation which encompasses all the districts i.e.
multiple appellation designations are not permitted. For example, a wine blended from
wine from the Médoc and St.
Emilion must use the broader
appellation, i.e., Bordeaux.

5. SHIPPER

The name and address of the
négociant or party involved in
exporting the wine must be
stated on the label. Frequently
this is the producer or négociant involved in bottling the
wine but is not always the case.

BASIC FRENCH WINE LABEL LANGUAGE

VINTAGE

Anné—year

Récolte—crop or harvest

Vendange—grape harvest

BOTTLING TERMS

Caves—the French word for cellar

Château-bottled—estate-bottled

Mis(e) au Château—estate-bottled

Mis(e) en bouteilles au Château—estate-bottled

Mis(e) au (du) Domaine—estate-bottled

Mis(e) en bouteilles au (du) Domaine—estate-bottled.

Mis dans nos caves—bottled in our cellars

Mis par le propriétaire—bottled by the grower or négociant. This and the above term are easily confused with the legitimate terms for "estate-bottled."

Eleveur—literally "improver" - a négociant who buys young wine from the grower and matures it in his own cellars.

Négociant—a businessman who purchases wine from growers and bottles it under his own brand or for resale under the individual Château name.

Propriétaire-Récoltant—Owner and Manager

ORIGIN DESCRIPTORS

Appelation Controlee (A.C. or A.O.C.)—on a label this term refers to a wine which has met with the viticultural, geographic and quality standards of France's highest level of wine regulation.

Monopole—single vineyard site

V.D.Q.S.—stands for Vins Délimites de Qualité Supérieure a second rank (below A.C.) of delimited wine areas.

QUALITY DESCRIPTORS

Appellation Contrôlée—see above

Château-bottled—estate-bottled

Cru Bourgeois—in Bordeaux, one of the many good vineyards just below the classified growths in quality.

Cru Classé—a classified growth of Bordeaux from the 1855 classification - the highest ranks of Bordeaux wines.

Cru Exceptionnel—a Bordeaux classification between cru Bourgeois and Cru Classé.

Grand Cru—great growth; in Burgundy the highest level of classified vineyards; in Bordeaux any of the five levels of classified growths.

Grand Vin—no legal definition; means great wine.

Methode champenoise—the champagne method of sparkling wine production; synonomous with fermented in this bottle.

Premier Cru—first growth; in Burgundy, the second level of classified growth; in Bordeaux, the very highest vineyard classification.

Supérieur—indicates the the wine is at least one degree of alcohol above the minimum allowed for a particular A.C. It does not mean "better" or "superior".

V.D.Q.S.— see above

GENERAL TERMS

Chai—an above ground building where wine is stored in cask.

Chambre—a French word for bringing a red wine from cellar temperature to room temperature.

Château—castle; in Bordeau a single estate

Clos—French term for a walled vineyard

Côte—a French term which refers to a slope with vineyards as opposed to graves or flatter land.

Cru—growth; refers to legally defined vineyard

Cuvée—a vat or batch of wine

Domaine—French word meaning wine estate

Servi Chambre—serve at room temperature

Servi Frais—serve chilled

STYLE DESCRIPTORS

Blanc de Blanc—a white wine made made entirely from white grapes.

Brut—Dry (actually almost dry)

Demi Sec—semi-sweet

Doux—sweet

Mousseux—sparkling wine other than Champagne.

Pétillant—slightly sparkling or crackling

Sec—dry

Sur lie—bottled off the lees without racking or filtering.

Vin Blanc—white wine

Vin Rouge—red wine

Vine Rosé—rosé wine

NOTE: Label terms with important legally controlled definitions are indicated in bold face.

THE GERMAN WINE LABEL

1. WINE NAME

Proprietary name

Trade name

Bereich

> Ex. Bereich Nierstein

> Grosslage in this format:
> Village name + er +
> Grosslage name
> Ex. Piesporter Michelsberg

Einzellage in this format:

> Village name + er +
> Einzellage name
> Ex. Piesporter Treppchen

Grape variety (which may be appended to any of the above)

Note: A *Grosslage* is a collective vineyard name, i.e. there is no specific site with that name and all the vineyards, including even the best *Einzellage*, may label their wine with this designation if they choose to do so. In general, most wines with a *Grosslage* site name will be simple regional wines of simple-premium status. An *Einzellage* must be a minimum of approximately 12 acres which may be divided among several owners. Generally, an *Einzellage* site name indicates a wine of significantly greater merit than that from a *Grosslage*. All the great wines of Germany bear a *Einzellage* name on their label. Often a *Grosslage* has taken its name from that of a vineyard that did not receive *Einzellage* status under the 1971 German wine laws. It is also the custom for the *Grosslage* to attach the name of its most famous wine town to its *Grosslage* name. Therefore it can be quite difficult to tell which is which as there is no requirement to disclose that the site name is a *Grosslage* as is required for a *Bereich*. The best known and most popular *Grosslage* and *Einzellage* wines are listed in Appendix III.

2. VINTAGE

Specific year or none

3. PRODUCER

The name and address of the producer is required. In addition the label must bear an A.P. code number which identifies each individual lot of wine submitted for analysis as required under the German wine laws.

4. ORIGIN

The label must indicate which of the eleven major wine districts it came from. In addition, if labeled as a *Bereich* it must state which one along with the term "Bereich." A vineyard less than 12 acres may only indicate the *Grosslage* as a site name. An *Einzelage may use either its actual site name or its Grosslage name.*

5. SHIPPER

The name and address of the exporter must be stated on the label. With the exception of the major estates, the shipper did not produce the wine bottled but purchased finished wine for blending and bottling.

BASIC GERMAN WINE LABEL LANGUAGE

VINTAGE

BOTTLING TERMS

Abfüller—Bottler

Abfüllung—from the producers own estate

Aus Eigenem Lesegut—estate-bottled

Eigene Abfüllung—bottled by the producer

Erzeuger Abfüllung—estate-bottled

Keller—cellar

Weingut—wine estate

Weinhändler—Wine shipper or merchant

Weinkellerei—wine cellar

Winzergenossenschaft—winegrower's cooperative

Winzerverein—same as above

ORIGIN DESCRIPTORS

A.P.(Amtliche Prüfungsnummer)—official testing number found on all better German wines -the code indicates the place of origin as well as the producers individual number.

Bereich—a large subregion of a Gebiet

Gebiet—one of the eleven major German wine regions

Grosslage—a subdivision of a Bereich consisting of numerous adjoining vineyards which may span the boundries of many individual villages

Einzellage—individual vineyard site (name) of a minimum size of approximately 12 acres

QUALITY DESCRIPTORS

A.P.(Amtliche Prüfungsnummer)—in addition to the location codes this number consists of an individual "lot" number and the year (not necessarily the vintage) that lot was submitted for testing.

QbA Qualitätswein bestimmte Anbauge biete—quality wine from a specified origin, the middle level of German wine quality.

QmP Qualitätswein mit Prädikat—quality wine with special attributes, the top level of wine quality consisting of five degrees of ripeness. No chaptalization is permitted forthese wines.

Tafelwein—table wine, the lowest level of quality. Tafelwein may not bear a vineyard site name.

STYLE DESCRIPTORS

Auslese—wine made from very ripe grapes render ing a fairly sweet and luscious dessert wine.

Beerenauslese—very sweet wine made from over ripe grapes some of which have been shrivelled by botrytis ("noble rot").

Eiswein—made from frozen grapes

Halbtrocken—half-dry or off-dry

Kabinet—the basic grade for QmP wine which must be made from grapes with sufficient natural sugar to produce a wine with a minimum of 9 1/2% alcohol.

Perlwein—slightly sparkling wine

Sekt—sparkling wine

Spätlese—late picked— a wine made from fully ripened grapes.

Trocken—completely dry wine

Trockenbeerenauslese—wine made entirely from grapes shriveled by botrytis. During the harvest the pickers keep these grapes seperate from the others. Frequently, a vineyard will be picked several times to secure grapes suitable for this catagory of wine.

GENERAL TERMS

Bocksbeutel—the flat sided squat bottle used for Franken wines.

Botrytis cinerea—noble mold which shrivels grapes giving it extra concentration and a honeyed flavor.

Fass—cask

Fuder—cask

Moselblümchen—the generic wine (Tafelwein (class) from the Mosel.

Liebfraumilch—the generic wine (QbA class) from the Rhein region.

Rotwein—Red wine

Schloss—Castle

Stätswein—wine from the government owned vineyards.

Steinwein—wine from Franconia

Weisswein—white wine

NOTE: Label terms with important legally controlled definitions are indicated in bold face.

THE ITALIAN WINE LABEL

1. WINE NAME

Proprietary Name
Wine Type — Red, White,
    Rosé, Spumante, etc.
Grape Variety
Grape Variety + Village
Grape Variety + Region
Village + Grape Variety
Region + Grape Variety
D.O.C. Area

2. VINTAGE

Specific year only or none

3. PRODUCER

Name and Address required

4. ORIGIN

This defines the delimited area in which the grapes were grown and the wine produced. The areas may be regulated (by D.O.C. or D.O.C.G.) or may be unregulated. When blended from several small regulated districts the wine must be identified only by the larger appellation which encompasses all the districts, i.e. multiple D.O.C. designations are not permitted. For example, a wine blended from Bardolino and Valpolicella must use a broader appellation, (Verona might be suitable in this instance) and may not state that the wine is from the two D.O.C areas of origin.

5. SHIPPER

The name and address of the party involved in exporting the wine must be stated on the label. The export license number must also be present. Frequently the shipper is also the producer involved in making or bottling the wine but this is not always the case

BASIC ITALIAN WINE LABEL LANGUAGE

VINTAGE

Vendemmia

BOTTLING TERMS

Cantina—winery or cellars

Cantina sociale—winegrowers co-operative

Casa Vinicola—wine company

Consorzio—local winegrowers association with legal recognition

Fiasco—flask

Infiascato alla fattoria—bottled in flask at the winery

Imbottigliato nel'origine—Estate-bottled

Imbottigliato del produttore—Estate-bottled

Imbottigliato nello stabilimento della ditta—bottled on the premises of the company - not estate-bottled.

Messo in bottiglia nel'origine—Estate-bottled.

Tenuta—farm or agricultural holding

ORIGIN DESCRIPTORS

Classico—from a legally defined, inner section of the district; ostensibly denotes higher quality

Denominazione di Origine Controllata—produced in accordance with the D.O.C. wine laws

Denominazione di Origine Controllata e Garantita—quality as well as origin of the wine is guaranteed by the Italian government

QUALITY DESCRIPTORS

Denominazione di Origine Controllata e Garantita— see above

Riserva—aged in wood for a specified time

Riserva Speciale—aged one year longer than Riserva

Stravecchio—very old; rarely used

STYLE DESCRIPTORS

Abboccato—semi-dry or semi-sweet

Amabile—off-dry; semi-sweet

Amaro—very dry

Cotto—concentrated wine

Dolce—sweet

Frizzante—semi-sparkling

Vino Liquoroso—dessert wine, fortified with alcohol

Passito—made from semi-dried grapes

Secco—dry

Spumante—general term for sparkling wine

Vino santo—made from grapes dried indoors

GENERAL TERMS

Bianco—white wine

Rosato—rosé wine

Rosso—red wine

Nero—very dark red

Vino da Tavola—table wine

NOTE: Label terms with important legally controlled definitions are indicated in bold face.

BASIC AMERICAN WINE LABEL LANGUAGE

1. WINE NAME

Wine Type - Red, White, Rosé
Trade or Proprietary Name
Generic Name - Chablis, Rhine
 Burgundy, etc.

Varietal name— Cabernet Sauvignon, Chardonnay, Riesling,
 Pinot Noir etc.

Geographic name - California,
 New York, Napa Valley, etc.

Individual Vineyard

2. VINTAGE

Specific year only or none

3. PRODUCER

Name and address of producer
is required.

4. ORIGIN

The delimited area in which the
grapes were grown and the
wine produced. This area may
be a State or County or a legally recognized Viticultural Area.
The terms valley, district,
region may only be used on the
label if that area is an officially
recognized Viticultural Area.
Generally 75% of the wine
must be from the named appellation.

5. BOTTLER

The name and address of the
party bottling the wine must be
stated on the label. Usually this
is the producer but not always
the case.

BASIC AMERICAN WINE LABEL LANGUAGE

VINTAGE

Vintage

BOTTLING TERMS

B.W. No. 0000—Bonded Winery's license number

Grown by— the grapes were grown by winery.

Selected by—the wine was purchased by the named winery.

Made and Bottled by—the named winery fermented a least 10% of the wine and bottled all the wine.

Cellared and Bottled by—the named party blended and/or aged or otherwise treated and bottled all the wine.

Produced and Bottled by—the named party fermented at least 75% and bottled all the wine.

Proprietor or Vintner Grown and Bottled by— the same as Produced and Bottled by.

Estate Bottled—the named party fermented all the wine from grapes 100% from the named Viticultural Area. The grapes came from his own vineyards or from vineyards in which he controls the viticultural practices. The wine was bottled on the same premises where the wine was made.

ORIGIN DESCRIPTORS

State—75% of the wine must be from the named state. California regulations require 100%.

County—75% of the wine must be from the name county.

Valley—must be a B.A.T.F approved viticultural Area to be used on the label and at least 75% of the wine must come from the named area.

District—same as above.

Region—same as above.

Individual vineyard or ranch.

NOTE: No appellation of origin may be used unless it has been officially approved by the B.A.T.F. Generally the smaller the geographical area specified the better the reputed quality. Viticultural Areas as defined by the B.A.T.F. are granted based on geographical merit based on prior reputation of the area, however no production criteria are imposed as with other countries so this geographical guarantee does not assure any minimum level of quality.

QUALITY DESCRIPTORS

Botrytis—affected with botrytis

Brix—a measure of potential alcohol based on the sugar content of the grape.

Classic—meaningless puffery - wines so labeled are rarely "classic."

Fermented in the bottle—sparkling wine made by the transfer method.

Fermented in this bottle—sparkling wine made by *method champagnoise.*

Late Harvest—made from overripe grapes - may or may not be affected with botrytis.

Mountain—seen on jug wine - no legal definition.

Nouveau—quickly fermented young wine usually made by carbonic maceration and usually bottled immediately after fermentation.

Rare—usually seen on jug wine - no legal definition and the wine so labeled is rarely "rare."

Residual sugar—the amount of remaining natural sugar in the wine after the fermentation is completed - more than one percent tastes sweet.

STYLE DESCRIPTORS

Dry—no residual sugar

Off-dry—slighty or semi-sweet

Soft—low alcohol, low acidity

Light—low alcohol, low sugar

Late Harvest—Concentrated flavor and sweet

Selected Late Harvest—as above but more so

Individual Berry Selected Late Harvest—very concentrated and sweet, usually with botrytis.

Botrytis—favorably affected with "noble rot," concentrated, honnied and sweet similar to a German Bereenauslese.

Residual sugar -%—a measure of sweetness

Essence—Very concentrated and sweet late harvest wine - frequently red wine.

GENERAL TERMS

White —white wine

Rose—rosé wine

Red—red wine

Champagne— sparkling wine

Table Wine—wine made without the addition of alcohol, usually less than 15%.

Dessert Wine—sweet wine fortified with additional alcohol, usually between 17 to 20%.

NOTE: Label terms with important legally controlled definitions are indicated in bold face.

The labels on the left are classic examples of understatement - great wines that provide minimal clues as to their pedigree on the label. Each is entitled to state "premiere grand cru classé" of the famous 1855 Bordeaux Classification. Château d'Yquem is undisputedly the finest of the sweet white wines of Sauternes. Château Lafite Rothschild has been considered as the finest of the wines of the 1855 Bordeaux Classification (but has slipped in recent vintages). As labeled each could be a minor "petite château." Similarly the label on the right, with all its embellishment, could also be used by a minor wine. It too is entitled to use term "cru classé" ("premier cru classé for vintages after 1972). Great wines are often labeled without any clues as to their stature. Conversely, many mediocre wines are expensively and elaborately labeled to give the appearance of a wine with a better pedigree than what is in the bottle.

Gouache de Marc Chagall réalisée pour le Mouton Rothschild 1970

1970   1970

Cette récolte a produit :
315.000 Bordelaises et 1/2 B^ses de 1 à 315.000
7.000 Magnums de M 1 à M 7.000
615 Grands Formats de G F 1 à G F 615
double-magnums, jéroboams, impériales
5000 "Réserve du Château" marquées R.C.
Ci, № 137979

Philippe de Rothschild

Château
Mouton Rothschild

BARON PHILIPPE DE ROTHSCHILD PROPRIÉTAIRE A PAUILLAC

APPELLATION PAUILLAC CONTRÔLÉE

PRODUCE OF FRANCE

TOUTE LA RÉCOLTE MISE EN BOUTEILLES AU CHÂTEAU

OTTO DÜNWEG
1979
Piesporter Michelsberg Riesling
KABINETT
Qualitätswein mit Prädikat
Erzeuger-Abfüllung Weingut Otto Dünweg
Amtliche Prüfungs-Nr. 2 594 323 045 80   e750ml
Alcohol 7.3 % by Volume   Produce of Germany
MOSEL·SAAR·RUWER

VERBAND DEUTSCHER PRÄDIKATS-WEINGÜTER E.V.

Unsere Mitglieder besitzen Lagen von Weltruf!

V D P

Qualitätswein mit Prädikat aus eigener Erzeugung eines unserer Mitgliedsbetriebe

GROSSER RING DER PRÄDIKATSWEIN-VERSTEIGERER VON MOSEL, SAAR UND RUWER

PRODUCE OF GERMANY

MOSEL — SAAR — RUWER
QUALITÄTSWEIN MIT PRÄDIKAT
1979
Piesporter Goldtröpfchen
Riesling - Spätlese
Alcohol 7.7 % by Volume
A. P. Nr. 2 596 287 / 001 / 80
Erzeugerabfüllung Weingut Tobias - Piesport/Mosel
Lintz, Trier

German wine labeling requirements provide for terms indicating ripeness as well as geographic appellation. However, determining whether a wine is from an individual vineyard or not requires an intimate knowledge of *einzellage* and *grosslage* names. The example above is from the *grosslage* Piesporter Michelsberg, an area surrounding the town of Piesporter encompassing many vineyards, many of which are not permitted to use any other name on the label. Below is Piesporter Goldgropfchen, one of the finest vineyards of the area.

There is often a direct correlation between sweetness and quality in sparkling wine as sugar masks many defects. Terms for residual sugar in sparkling wine are stringently regulated. Thus a wine labeled as "brut" or "nature" must be of a high quality to stand on its own. Wines made outside the French Champagne region made by *method champenoise* will most likely be of a high quality to justify the extra cost of the process. While the French Champagne regulations are among the most exacting in the world, there are no requirements governing "tete de cuvee" brand names. Most houses will cater to the connoisseur, reserving the quintescence of style, balance and elegance for their tete de cuvee, such as the Tattinger Blanc de Blanc above. Others, like Dom Perignon, are made for mass appeal and are too bland and sweet for the discriminating palate.

SENSORY EVALUATION

In our earlier chapters, we discussed the principles of both viticulture and vinification within the context of wine quality. Now that we have a feel for what can go right or wrong in winemaking, by accident or intent, we can begin to look at tasting wines. The fun and fascination of wines lies in their variety and diversity of flavors and aromas, and their subtleties of styles. Learning how to taste wine and distinguish the characteristics that give each its own quality is the first step in developing an experienced wine palate.

The notion that good wine tasters are born with a unique ability is utter hokum. Learning to taste wines can be as easy as learning to ride a bicycle or drive a car. The physical requirements are minimal and just about universal. Anyone can become a good wine taster and therefore enjoy wines fully; all it takes is practice, practice, practice and concentration throughout. The thinking that goes with wine tasting sets it apart from sheer drinking.

In this chapter I would like to present some information that will help you tune your senses and develop a palate. As a starting point we will begin with a look at the major senses, sight, smell, and taste. By knowing how these senses function, we can begin to appreciate what we smell and taste.

SENSORY ELEMENTS

Except for hearing, wine tasting relies on all of our major senses. Generally, we look at a wine, checking for clarity and appearance. We smell it for fragrance and cleanliness. We rely on our tactile sense to feel the wine in our mouth. Then, of course, we taste the wine before, during, and after swallowing. Professionals refer to this as "organoleptic examination". Of these, the least important aspect is the appearance because it can mislead you. Flaws apparent to the eye are almost always apparent when the wine is smelled and tasted.

THE OLFACTORY SYSTEM

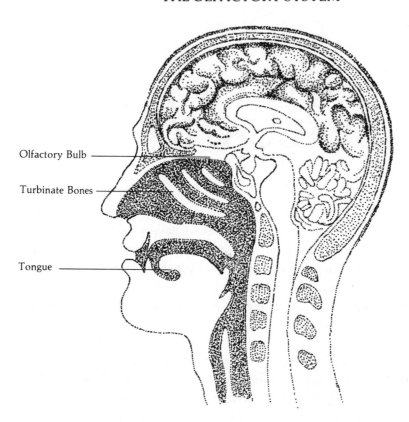

Olfactory Bulb

Turbinate Bones

Tongue

Cross Section
of the Olfactory Epithelium

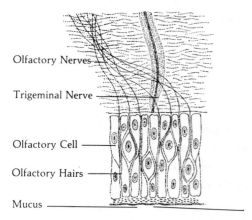

Olfactory Nerves

Trigeminal Nerve

Olfactory Cell

Olfactory Hairs

Mucus

Cross Section of a Taste Bud

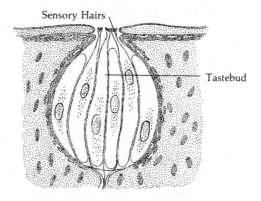

Sensory Hairs

Tastebud

SMELL

Often what we consider "taste" is actually a perception of a scent which enters the olfactory canal through the mouth. Most flavors are experienced by the sense of smell. So far, over three hundred different constituents of wine have been identified, and scientists indicate at least two hundred of these may be odor-producing.

Smells are detected by a complex of nerve endings called the olfactory bulb which is located in the upper part of the nose. It is a very acute sensor. Odors are better-noticed when air is inhaled, stimulating the olfactory nerves, which explains why wine must be sniffed. Most of the air inhaled is trapped by mucous membranes before they reach the olfactory bulb, and what is not, passes through a tiny aperture. Scientists have yet to learn what mechanism allows us to experience the multiplicity of scents and aromas that we can sense. We do know that certain weak flavors can be detected despite the presence of a dominant one, or that certain substances can mask the smell of others. The olfactory sense also becomes acclimated to a scent after it is experienced, and after a short period that scent can no longer be perceived. You will see this as you begin to learn to discern subtle aromas.

TASTE

On the tongue there are specific areas which correlate to our four basic tastes: sweet, salt, bitter, sour. The sweet sensation is best experienced on the tip of the tongue; saltiness and sourness on the sides, and bitterness on the back. These tastes are conveyed to the brain through cells within the taste buds. The taste buds, themselves, are contained within the papillae, the tiny cell-like structures that seem to pave our tongues. Sensations pass through the pores of the papillae to the taste cells in the taste buds and travel via nerve endings to the cortex of the brain. Interestingly, these nerves end very near to where "smelling" nerves end, and although taste is conveyed in this process, it is easy to see how any discussion or comparison of food or flavor involves an understanding of the sense of smell.

THRESHOLDS

To fully understand why and how we taste and smell what we do, we must go beyond a simple, clinical look at the senses, and expand our understanding to the concept of thresholds. For although the physical receptors may be universally similar, the ability to actually perceive a flavor or aroma varies first within the flavor and aroma itself, and secondly within the person's individual ability to perceive it. This is called a *threshold*, or more clearly defined, the point at which one experiences an aroma, flavor, or taste sensation.

It is important to understand the concept of thresholds for two reasons: 1) it clearly shows that our responses to wine may not always be the same 2)once you recognize the concept, you can learn where your own thresholds lie, understand when those limits are not up to par, and finally, improve on them. As you become more knowledgeable about your thresholds, you will clearly see that it is possible to have a "bad tasting-day."

The first point that we must remember in talking about thresholds is that each smell or taste has a particular level at which it can be detected and another at which it can be recognized. Of course, these thresholds are based on averages, nonetheless, this concept explains why some substances can be perceived (tasted or smelled) more readily than others. For instance, among the four basic tastes, bitterness is said to be detected at much lower concentrations than the others, but can be masked by sweetness or other flavors. Sugar, or sweetness, is said to have an average threshold of about fifty-four parts sugar to one hundred parts solution. Ethanol (the predominant alcohol in wine) can be detected at about four and two-tenths percent in solution. Individual thresholds vary, not only from person to person, but within one person as well. The reasons are many.

Health is an important factor. We can't smell if we have a cold or an allergy. Mood and psychological state are others. Even slight fatigue or mild depression, for instance, can affect our ability to discriminate between tastes or smells. External factors play another role, frequently raising or lowering our thresholds according to the temperature of the room or even the company we are with.

Still another factor is age. As we age our ability to detect sweet, bitter or salty flavors becomes impaired. This loss of sensitivity, however, may be offset by greater experience. Young children have a lower threshold (greater sensitivity) to flavors simply because their palate contains taste buds, whereas adults have taste buds only along their tongues, not the roof of the mouth.

People with low blood sugar levels have a generally higher threshold to sugar than those with normal levels. Others are simply very sensitive to ethanol due to either biological or environmental reasons.

Being sick or tired will easily raise one's threshold to most components of both aroma and flavor. A cold obstructs the air passages and negates the olfactory sense. As of now, there are no hard-core facts about the relationship between smoking and threshold experiences. Though it is generally agreed that smoking must impair the taste buds, we don't know what compensatory factors are at work. Smokers who abstain often claim they are unable to detect any flavors in wine, but that may come from being psychologically off-kilter or from simple rationalization. The real issue is whether the presence of a smoker, with the smell trapped in clothing, significantly alters the threshold of the others.

The time of the day also influences thresholds. After a meal, most of us are less sensitive to smells and flavors than right before. It is a matter of sensory over-load, I presume. Most professionals prefer to taste in the morning hours, sometime before lunch. This tends to avoid the influence of food and also the fatigue factor which appears in afternoon hours.

GETTING INTO THE SWIRL OF THINGS

Before you actually get down to tasting wines, you should practice swirling just to become comfortable with the act. Swirling wine in your glass helps bring the aroma and flavors up to the surface where they are captured by the curved design of the glass. Fill the glass to about one-third, but no more than one-half of its capacity. To begin with, try swirling with water. Keep the glass parallel to the floor and use the wrist to make a subtle, circular motion. Small circular motions made without tilting the glass are the trick. One way to practice is to first keep the glass on the table while you swirl. When you feel secure, try it at waist level. By the way, white wine or club soda will prevent a red wine spill from becoming a permanent stain.

The goal in swirling is to vaporize the wine within the envelope of the glass. It defeats the purpose to swirl, pause, and then sniff into the glass. Give the glass a few swirls, then bring it to your nose. Once you have gained confidence in swirling and sniffing with water, you can move on to using wines.

It's customary to check the color and appearance of a wine, but let's remember that appearance is more of an aesthetic feature, not always a qualitative one. In fact, the custom of checking the appearance stems from the old days when wines were not often made clean and clear. Given the improved winemaking techniques today, the appearance is often over-emphasized in evaluating wine. The main points to look for are clarity and color. The wine should be free from a hazy or cloudy look; haziness usually indicates a biological instability or a bacterial or chemical contamination resulting, probably, from faulty winemaking. When a wine is flawed, though, you will always smell and taste the defects.

The color and appearance should not be neglected, however. Color will sometimes provide clues to both overall quality and relative age. A colorless white wine is usually light in body and flavor, whereas an opaque, or deeply colored red wine is heavy in body and often powerful and assertive.

You should always examine wines in natural or incandescent lighting. A soft light bulb is fine. Fluorescent lights should be avoided as they give off a bluish cast which makes red wines appear brown. A few guidelines about color should be helpful.

White wines are seldom white, but range in color from a pale straw, to a light green-yellow, on through yellow to varying degrees of gold. A young wine with a deep color that is somewhat turgid in appearance can be prematurely old or oxidized. Oxidation causes wines to turn brown — the same thing that happens to an apple after you bite into it and allow the air to contact it. Even a hint of brown in a white wine is a sure sign of defective wine.

Red wines, by and large, range from light red or varying degrees of deep red coloration down to purple and almost inky. By tilting the glass, you can examine the edge of the wine, known as the rim. Young red wines retain some color on the rim; with aging, the rim will become lighter, moving from the color of onion-skin, to orange, to amber, and eventually to brown. Those with the brown edges are often well over-the-hill.

All of the critical tasting procedures center on matters of smell and taste. Wine is the only natural beverage capable of offering a multiplicity of complex smells and flavors. Orange juice, fresh or frozen, always smells like orange juice; milk, in all its forms, still smells like milk. Gin and Scotch are both one-dimensional. But wines are different — offering a mélange of flavors and aromas, sometimes very similar, sometimes very opposite. The best analogy is to a musical symphony or arrangement. You can pick out the different melodies, counterpoint, and even individual instruments as they work toward the whole effect. Similarly, you can taste the individual components and flavors that contribute to the structure of a wine.

You might call wine a sensory symphony, pieces perceived as part of a whole. The range of smells and fragrances is almost unlimited. They can be just vinous, wine-like and grapy, or multi-faceted, with layers upon layers. Wines can offer complex fragrances that can be identified; truly great wines can be characterized by complexities and facets that are beyond the capabilities of descriptive language.

What do you look for when you place your nose in a glass? First of all, because unpleasant sensations are immediate, you look for off-odors — from vinegar, to mold, to stale and then to non-wine-like smells, such as raisins and cooked or baked qualities. The most frequently encountered faults are:

- the smell of sulphur dioxide which resembles the scent of a just-struck match
- hydrogen sulphide, the smell of rotten eggs
- rancid corn chips — the smell of dekkera

- volatile acidity, i.e. acetic acid, the smell of vinegar
- ethyl acetate, like acetone, accompanies acetic acid
- mercaptans, ranging in smell from garlic and onion to skunk
- smells of decay, like wilted lettuce, dead leaves, mucus, manure, vomit
- petro-chemical scents like diesel fuel, vaseline, or a refinery
- geraniums, from bacterial spoilage
- potassium sorbate, a preservative that tastes slightly sweet with the flavor of bubble gum
- cork, actually the scent of a particular mold that grows in corks; wines so impaired are said to be "corked."

Sulphur dioxide, a harmless preservative, is found in many white wines. It should dissipate with airing, but if the wine was overdosed, airing won't help. The other flaws are permanent and justify returning the wine to the place of purchase.

If clean and free from faults, the wine is now ready for your studied evaluation. Most scents or fragrances in wine are described through analogy, with the most common, popular analogies coming from the worlds of fruits, berries, and flowers. Food analogies are also common since wine is made from a fruit or berry and is part of a vegetative process. Herbs and spices are frequently used descriptors for wines.

ORGANOLEPTIC EXAMINATION

Wine tasting is not, totally, a free-association process; though a fresh, unencumbered mind which offers spontaneous associations of fragrances and flavors is often as good as an experienced palate for discovering descriptions of wines. The nomenclature of wine tasting is vague; tasting terms mean different things to different tasters. Tasting experience, coupled with an expert's description of the wine under examination is the best way to develop a tasting vocabulary of your own. Wine tasting clubs provide a good way to develop your palate. But for now, remember that when a wine smells fruity, it is a positive attribute, but not a distinctive quality. Wines that remind you directly of raspberries, ripe cherries, cinnamon, sage, fresh leaves, roses, and wild flowers are more distinct. Their impression can either be very direct or blatant, as in "one-dimensional" or else, combined in a "complex" structure.

The scent of a wine is referred to as its "nose," which may be described as having aroma, the scent of young, undeveloped wine, or "bouquet," the complex, difficult to describe perfume of a wine which has had time for its components to interact, creating soft and supple fragrances technically known as esters. To fully appreciate the scent of a wine, you should put your nose into the glass after swirling. It is for this reason that a large, half-filled glass is recommended. Too small a glass, or a too full one can result in a wet nose.

The nose of a wine can be "non-existent," "weak," "moderate," or "intense." A weak nose may be simply weak, or "closed-in," referring to a wine that has not yet developed. The other taste components provide the clue. Interpreting the clues requires experience. Beside intensity, the nose is examined for its "structure," the relationship of flavor, alcohol, and acidity. A young acidic white wine can be "refreshing," a positive attribute. An equally acidic red will be "unpleasant" and "flawed." Some wines are simple in their flavor, described as "straightforward," or "one-dimensional." Others display an array of flavors, frequently with subtle and supple overtones; this is described as "complex." When the various elements of the nose appear to be harmonious, the wine is said to be "balanced." When one element sticks out over the rest, the wine is "unbalanced." The balance is described in relative terms, from "harmonious," "excellent" and "perfect," to "good," "normal" and "average," to "poor," "acidic," "heady," or "unbalanced." Each expert has his own favorite way of expressing the same thing.

Many wine scents may seem strange to you at first. The scent of a fine Burgundy frequently resembles wild violets, tar, or truffles. An aged Bordeaux smells "roasted." A Late Harvest Riesling smells nutty and honeyed. A young Riesling or a Muscat resembles pine oil. American *labrusca* varieties, referred to as "foxy," have a pungent odor all their own. Many wine smells require getting used to; some wines just smell strange.

The next step is to take a sip. You should fill your mouth with wine. Roll the wine over your tongue and palate to get the feel of the wine, called "body." Body is determined by the alcohol, glycerine, and extract of a wine. It is either light, moderate, or full, and may or may not be in balance with the flavor and other components of a wine. The body may appear to be firm when accompanied by sufficient acidity, or it may be "flabby,"when low in acidity. It may feel "heavy" from residual sugar, or may feel "harsh," "rough," "coarse," "silky," "velvety," "smooth" or "creamy," depending on its structure. Red wines frequently contain tannins which add a necessary and pleasing astringency to fine wines. At first, this puckering quality may seem strange or unpleasant, but as your wine experience progresses, certain wines will appear to be flat or dull without it.

With the wine in your mouth, you should purse your lips and draw air into your mouth, slightly gurgling the wine to vaporize it. This "whooshing" sound identifies experienced wine tasters; it isn't bad mannered, though I would not suggest it for formal gatherings. This procedure permits the full flavor of the wine, warmed by the mouth, to flow through the nasal canal, to the olfactory bulb, thus enabling you to fully experience every nuance of flavor. It's a simple motion: purse your lips as if you are going to whistle, then suck in the air over the wine.

The flavors in your mouth should confirm what you smelled. Continuity is the sign of a well-structured wine. After the wine is swallowed, there is usually a lingering aftertaste, known as the "finish" of a wine. It can be "long," "lingering," "fleeting," "non-existent," along with, " complex," "acidic," "sharp" or "dull." Frequently, the finish of a wine will add new facets to the taste of the wine, new flavors that were not apparent when the wine was in the mouth. Professionals evaluate the finish of a wine in terms of the time, usually in seconds, that the flavor lingers. Wines beginning to pass their peak of maturity reveal their passing first with defects in their finish; there may be hints of dead leaves, or a lack of vinosity which is called "dried-out."

The flavors, along with the body, alcohol, acidity, and astringency provide the total "impression" of a wine, known as its "structure." A wine may be "well-defined," "tightly knit," "firm," or with "good backbone"; "broad," "one-dimensional," "multi-faceted," and the like. The harmony of a fine wine, when all elements of structure, flavor and complexity attain an indescribable perfection, is called "breed" or "finesse." These terms are frequently used to describe classic wines but are virtually impossible to define. When you experience such a wine you will immediately recognize it for this elusive quality.

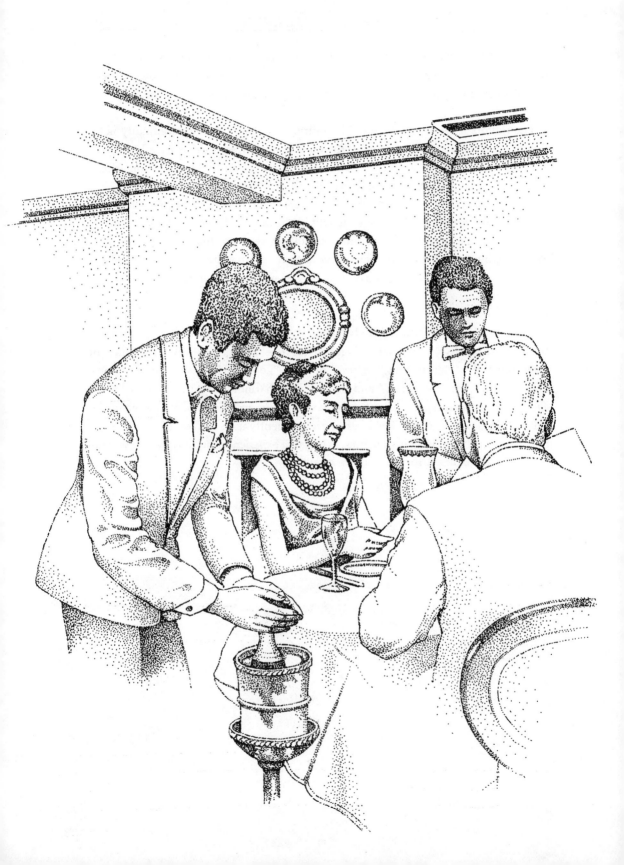

WINE IN RESTAURANTS

No fine dining experience is truly complete without wine; but trying to complement a restaurant's menu can often be a frustrating, sometimes futile experience.
Our displeasure is usually roused by one of three occurences: 1) Exorbitant prices
which are the result of an unjustified markup; 2) A wine list that is small and limited
to a choice of run-of-the-mill wines which offer only varying degrees of mediocrity;
3) The appearance of a key-jangling "sommelier" who is overtly condescending, and
frequently not familiar with his wines, their vintages, and availability. When all
three factors are in evidence, they make a good case for ordering the coldest beer.

To be fair, there are restaurants which offer a wide variety of carefully selected
wines matched to the cuisine; a few even afford an opportunity to try wines unobtainable elsewhere. When the wines are fairly priced (and some restaurants have
realized that well-priced wines often encourage people to enjoy more than one bottle) dining with wine can be a most pleasurable experience.

It is hard to say, precisely, what a "fair" restaurant price is; but as a rule of thumb
I would say that for wines which need neither aging nor special handling, twice the
retail price or less is probably fair enough. Generally, most restaurants mark up
wine to twice the retail, which is three times their cost. In other words, you can expect to pay ten dollars for a bottle of wine retailing for four or five dollars at your
local wine shop. However, when they think they can get away with it, some places
will go four or five times above cost. For the prestigious and, often scarce bottles,
you will be required to pay more.

I am happy to say, though, that in certain wine-aware parts of the United States
the pricing policies are more appealing. In San Francisco and both Napa and
Sonoma Counties, for examples, wines are often priced at retail or one dollar above
it. Of course, such restaurants sell considerable amounts of wine and deal with
customers aware of current prices. As wine increases in popularity and as consumers

become better informed, such delightful pricing practices could spread far beyond the wine country borders. Consumers can make it happen faster.

To the unknowing, older wines, in general, represent a potentially nasty pitfall as many restaurants tend to insist their old wine is always better and therefore worthy of an exorbitant price. Old is not necessarily better; nor is it always good. Poor or "past their prime" vintages of wines with prestige labels like Châteaux Lafite-Rothschild or La Romanée-Conti, for example, can be offered at astronomical prices. Recently, I found a 1965 Lafite-Rothschild, one of the worst vintages in many years, listed at seventy dollars a bottle. At this particular resort hotel, it was selling rather briskly!

As a rule, most mid-priced wines listed for one or two dollars above the lowest group on the list often represent the better value. Many restaurants today seem determined to earn a minimum profit for every bottle of wine and, therefore, impose a higher markup on inexpensive wines. Consequently, three-dollar bottles of California Chablis are bumped up to eight or nine dollars, while, for example, a seven-dollar Sauvignon Blanc is listed at eleven or twelve dollars. Wine prices are often clustered closer together than they ought to be which makes discovering good value more difficult.

This practice becomes scandalous, often enough, when applied to the glass or carafe of "house wine." House wines are usually your ordinary California or Italian generic wines, purchased in large containers, and then marked up to, frequently, *ten times* over cost. If you dislike being ripped off, I urge you to study the wine list carefully rather than order a glass or carafe of house wine thinking you "can't go wrong."

The real prestigious names in the world of wine (the Château Lafites and Château Latours from Bordeaux; Robert Mondavi and Heitz Cellars from California) also suffer from a similar kind of price gouging. They are often priced for the world's unlimited-expense-account-types, celebrated label-buyers, or uninformed wine snobs who take the "name" bait and pay exorbitant prices for what may frequently be wines not yet ready to drink or well past their prime.

Being fairly treated over a bottle of wine contributes to the ambiance, and a well-matched wine surely increases the total dining experience. The first step, of course, is the wine selection and the wine list itself. Good wine lists, which we will expand upon in a moment, rarely present problems. But some lists can seem deceptively good, although they have some built-in flaws you may not detect. Here are a few tips on how to recognize typically-thoughtless wine lists.

THE BRAND LIST

Suspect any wine list with a preponderance of major, nationally distributed brands. B&G, Mouton Cadet, Bolla, Paul Masson, Wente Bros., for example. The wines are not necessarily bad, but a list dominated by a brand or two is much too restrictive. In addition to offering wines that are commonly available and all too familiar to you, a list like this suggests the restaurateur prefers to allow a sales representative to prepare his wine list and makes no effort to match wines with his cuisine. There's neither imagination nor creativity in such a wine list, and chances are both are missing in what comes out of the kitchen as well. Check to see if most California wines come from one producer or if most imported wines are from one shipper/importer. If so, you have a brand-dictated list.

THE SHORT LIST

A long-standing joke among wine lovers is a wine list with the following three wines: 1) Chablis, 2) Burgundy and 3) Rosé followed by the note, "Please Order Wine by Number." It really is no joking matter, however, since such lists are all too common, even today. A list with a popular rosé from Portugal, a Liebfraumilch, an unknown Bordeaux château, and one or two California wines is simply another manifestation of a restaurant simply going through the motions without any sensitivity to its customers or desire to attract wine lovers.

THE FAMILIAR LIST

Have you seen this list before at another restaurant? Does the red leatherette cover look familiar? Do you know what the wines will be even before you get to the first page? Are the vintages once again not specified alongside the same names? Such a feeling of déjà vu usually means that the list was developed, printed, and supplied by a wholesaler or distributor who understandably has his own interests in mind. He offers his company's services and provides the binder and a general sweep of his most profitable wines. You might see such a list in an Italian restaurant one weekend; in a small French establishment the next. Familiarity in this case easily breeds contempt. The restaurateur using such a wine list opts for economy, convenience, and minimal personal effort. Watch out for his food!

THE FAT WINE LIST

Although it is always nice to find a restaurant with a really extensive wine list, one which reads like a doctoral thesis or a Henry James novel can often bog you down when you are trying to make a simple selection to go with dinner. The well-run restaurant provides such a list for the patron who doesn't mind losing himself, and a "short list" for the person who simply wants to match a wine with his meal.

Whenever I decide not to order wine in a restaurant, I make my reasons and objections clear to the owner, manager, or maître D. Whether my complaint is about the selection or prices, I feel he ought to know. Then again, there are many restaurants that have a poor wine policy but attract me frequently, anyway, simply because the ambiance is excellent, the cuisine superior, or both. When price is outrageous, I try to strike a bargain by ordering two bottles at a price which is somewhere between the retail and the wine-list price. Sometimes this works because a small profit on each of two bottles of wine is better than none at all, and the restaurateur is liable to get a loyal customer out of the deal.

Bringing your own bottle is a time-honored alternative to a weak wine list. Some good small places can't afford a wine license or even to stock a good supply of wines. Where permitted by law, you might even want to bring a bottle of wine to a licensed restaurant which has an adequate list. This is all possible so long as you follow a sensible protocol and are prepared to pay a corkage fee. I suggest it would be appropriate under the following conditions:

- That the wine you are bringing is something special and *not* on the list.

- That you consider ordering another bottle from the list to maintain good will.

- That you call ahead to ask for approval, and what the corkage fee is.

- That you are a fairly regular client.

- That you include a reasonable value for the wine you bring when calculating the tip you leave.

A reasonable corkage fee, by the way, is anywhere from two to five dollars. Some restaurants try to discourage the practice by charging an exorbitant fee.

THE GOOD WINE LIST

I love wine lists which offer variety and a wide selection of wines from the major wine regions of the world providing there's an indication that the owner exercised a modicum of caution in the wine selection. Bordeaux from different châteaux; different vintages of the same wine; wines in a wide price range; wines from a local producer, wines chosen to complement the restaurant's menu: this is the beginning of a good wine list. Such a list usually shows that the owner or one of his staff is quite knowledgeable about wines; he or she will be generally enthusiastic in suggesting wines within your price range. Incidentally, well-assembled wine lists and an informed staff usually go hand-in-hand with a properly run kitchen and fine cuisine.

The key to obtaining the best value from a restaurant wine list is, first of all, a familiarity with the prices, vintages, châteaux and producers, and importers and shippers. If the wine list omits specific information about vintages, importers, etc., the wines may not be worth ordering. It never hurts to ask questions of the waiter/waitress or wine steward.

In many often high priced restaurants, the wine list and your order are handled by a sommelier. By definition, a sommelier, or wine steward, is knowledgeable and familiar with the wines listed. Better yet, he may have bought, stored, and cared for them, and even trained the rest of the staff in wine protocol. In France, Italy, and a few other countries, professional schools exist to train sommeliers. With only a few universities offering courses on restaurant and sommelier training, the United States has yet to catch up with the Old World in this regard.

Thus, for us, it is important to distinguish between well-informed, full-fledged sommeliers and the imposters, who strut around with pomp, ceremony and haughtiness, whose sole purpose is to intimidate and ultimately coerce people into buying wines with high markups and/or those purchased in great quantities. Worse yet, these characters survive because customers, unsure in their own knowledge, are afraid to speak up.

A good sommelier is supposed to taste the wine to determine its quality *before* it's brought to you. The practice of tasting wine at your table is generally a bit of a performance and a charade.

In my opinion, a restaurateur is just as responsible for his wines as he is for his food. By placing a wine on the list he assumes responsibility just as he assumes responsibility for his meat, fish and vegetables. After all, you are being charged for his expertise via the markup route. If he made a mistake, let him absorb the cost.

Perhaps the biggest concern of all in the minds of restaurant-goers is when and under what conditions a wine should be refused and returned. It is an option either exercised too often by a very few or not at all by most people. It comes down to this: defective or flawed wines should not be accepted. The confusion in some minds results over whether a wine's smell and taste are defective or whether they are just unfamiliar and unusual.

Certainly, a wine past its peak should be refused. If a white wine is dark yellow in color and smells like Sherry, it is over-the-hill and likely maderized. Red wines become somewhat brown in color, often orange around the rim, and, when accompanied by a flat, dull flavor, like dead leaves, and a sharp, short finish are past their prime.

A wine is defective when it smells like vinegar. A nostril-piercing, dill-pickle, sharp aroma usually signals excessive volatile acidity (VA) normally accompanied by ethyl acetate. Leave a few ounces of good red wine in a bottle, stored in a warm place for about two weeks and smell the wine. You should know what I mean.

Any wine that smells of sulfur dioxide, the smell of a burned match, is a candidate for rejection. If the aroma persists, rather than dissipates quickly, the wine should be rejected. Sulfur dioxide is a universally used anti-oxidant in winemaking; excessive amounts, however, constitute a flaw.

A smell similar to rotten eggs indicates that the wine is tainted with hydrogen sulfide. It should be refused. Hydrogen sulfide develops often enough today through sloppy winemaking or from over-sulfured grapes.

Occasionally, some wines give off other aromas indicating serious flaws. Mercaptans are chemical compounds occasionally formed in vinification; their smell is similar to that of garlic or onions, though some associate the aroma with a "skunky" character. Return any wine so plagued.

Other smells to look for when evaluating a wine are acetone and moldiness. Acetone, similar to nail polish remover, is sharp and unpleasant. Mold results from poorly treated barrels or casks and more often, from grapes which were rained upon at near-ripeness and thus developed rot. Any wine that reminds you of a petrochemical, oil-refinery smell is faulty as well.

Experience which helps you detect the most common off-aromas is the best teacher. Otherwise, remember you must never expect to return a wine which you ordered out of curiosity but then did not like. When in doubt, ask the waiter to sample the wine. If he/she is confused about its merits and acceptability, then you are off the hook and another bottle should be forthcoming.

In my experience, a well-run restaurant will not quibble or get into a battle of wills with its customers. The adage — "the customer is always right" — remains a fine business policy. It's applied with food and now, more often, with wines. However, I urge all of you not to abuse the policy.

As a paying customer, and especially at the price restaurateurs get for wine, you are entitled to fair service. Here, then, are a few personal suggestions which will help assure you of getting a fair deal.

- Make sure you are shown the bottle you ordered. Check producer, type, vintage, etc.

- See that the wine arrives with cork and foil capsule intact. It is possible that a bottle may have been refilled with inferior wine or one that was returned by another patron some time ago after the capsule was removed.

- Take the time away from your friends and guests to study the bottle. Slow the sommelier/waiter down to your pace — it is your money.

- Hold the bottle and check it out for temperature. A red wine, unless it is new Beaujolais, should be at room temperature according to your definition. Make sure the red is not too warm, since that might indicate bad storage, for instance, too close to the heater or kitchen. White wines should not be freezing cold. If it is cold to the point of being iced, beware. Wines placed in temperatures which are too cold for too long a time tend to go flat (lose their life). It is better to have white wine delivered to your table at room temperature, then placed in an ice bucket —for a few minutes.

- Do not let the wine bottle be opened until you have given your official approval. Do not let it be poured into other glasses until you have tasted and accepted it. My words: "don't rush."

- Check the wine glasses for size and type. If you are not satisfied ask for others. Champagnes and sparkling wines are best served in glasses without hollow stems; flutes are preferred, but an all-purpose wine glass may be your only alternative.

- Smell the empty glass. This sounds silly, but the slightest smell of soap or detergent would ruin most Champagne and impair most table wine. If detected, ask the waiter to scrub the glasses carefully. When returned, check the glassware again — a once-over-lightly rinse won't always do the trick.

- Make certain that the capsule is cut neatly and the cork removed cleanly. (Champagnes, incidentally, should be uncorked with a minimal pop, if any.) The cork should be offered to you, and you should smell and feel it; it should not smell of vinegar or be dried out and crumble in your hands.

- The wine should smell clean and free of defects, but it should also be consistent with its type. This assumes some knowledge on your part.

- If you randomly select a wine unfamiliar to you and discover it is not to your liking, that is your problem. Live and learn.

- If you followed the sommelier's or waiter's recommendation and description and the wine does not resemble what was described, the problem is the restaurant's. You can refuse it. Put up a good fight!

A word about timing. Far too often, about the time your food arrives, you are informed that the wine you ordered is not available. Since some of us plan the meal around the wine selected, this is not good news. You can avoid this by requesting that the wine or wines be presented and brought to the table ahead of the food.

A few other aspects of restaurant wine service deserve mention. If you intend to bring an old vintage with you or are contemplating ordering a really old wine from the list, you should check ahead for several reasons. Old wines come down to old bottles of wine which suffer from enormous variations in storage. Find out if the management will stand by the quality of old bottles in his cellar. Then, too, inquire if the restaurant has the necessary decanter, glasses, and a person experienced in decanting old wines. I feel that an old wine is like a special entree: it should be ordered ahead of time, allowing the staff to begin proper preparations which include standing the bottle upright for several hours. The wine should be ready to decant when you arrive.

Decanting is much more than simply pouring wine from the bottle into another container. It should be done slowly and with care to leave the sediment in the first bottle. Having long experience with wines, I prefer to decant an old wine myself, just to be safe. Many sommeliers, some of whom are good at the task, will insist on doing it themselves. But if you feel that the requirements for proper decanting are a bit of a nuisance to the staff, go with another kind of wine.

Most wines with a little age will, to some degree, throw a deposit. Not all require decanting. It is often better to stand the bottle up when it is brought to the table and allow the sediment to fall to the bottom. The all-present wine cradle is not only pretentious, it is also self-defeating as a means of keeping the wine clear of sediment, as the sediment is usually stirred up as the wine sloshes from pouring to cradling positions.

A dining experience can easily be ruined from the beginning by smokers, who insist on spreading smoke in all directions. Similarly, those who insist on drowning themselving with perfume or cologne before going to a restaurant are not far behind. Your best bet is to request a table away from smokers; if they arrive after you've been seated or light-up afterward, you have a real touchy problem. You can always ask the waiter to request that the smokers refrain. Since the public now frowns on smoking in public places, you usually have a good chance. Unfortunately, little can be done about perfumes and colognes.

Should you tip for your wine service? Normally, I calculate the gratuity of 15 to 20 percent on the bill exclusive of the wine. Generally, the tip for the wine should be a couple of dollars, unless the service was indeed special. When you bring your own bottle, the tip should be proportionate to the wine's value. If the bottle is valued at one hundred dollars, a ten or fifteen dollar tip is very reasonable, especially if you intend to make bringing your own wine a regular practice.

WINE SHOPS & MERCHANTS

A good wine merchant is one who really knows and understands wines, and who can advise you on particular wine selections that meet your budget and complement your palate. Sadly, very few "good" wine merchants can be found, even in the biggest wine-consuming markets. It has been my experience that the major talent of the general wine merchant lies in arranging pretty window displays and in ringing up quick sales at the cash register. The only wines he pushes are those purchased at big discounts. The average merchant does not know the difference between Cabernet Sauvignon and Merlot any more than he knows the difference between blended and unblended Scotch.

Many merchants are quick to provide advice and may sound authoritative on the surface; yet many know little or nothing about the wines they stock. Those new to wine may not know how to spot a bad wine merchant. Sometimes the store's appearance can be a tip-off. Wine which is displayed standing up, often exposed to bright sunlight, is a definite sign of the merchant's lack of knowledge or nonchalant attitude toward wine. A lack of organization, either by type, region, or variety, or an arrangement which groups the prestige wines with the jugs, clearly indicates that the merchant is not sensitive to the needs of his wine-buying customers. And, of course, the merchant who carefully displays all his imported wines on their sides, yet stands up all California wines, many of which may be superior in quality to the imports, is another to be wary of. The nature of the selection and concentration on popular brands to the exclusion of superior or more interesting wines is another clue to the merchant who can't provide sound wine advice based on personal knowledge.

The signs become less obvious when you are deciding between a passable, well-stocked wine shop and a good or great one. It usually takes experience and more than just one visit before you sense whether or not the merchant deserves your trust. Willingness to assist you is important, but not in itself, evidence of knowledge or reliability. Trustworthiness is far more important — can you rely on the advice? Are you informed about new arrivals and good bargains? Do the suggestions parallel your desires and requirements? The answers will emerge over a period of time and usually with some strain on your wine budget. If the final verdict is negative, the cost is significant.

To save time and money, you might consider a few shortcuts. A wine merchant can easily be tested, and you shouldn't feel badly about asking some questions to which you know the answers. Most of us think little about auditioning sellers of other products. We all shop around for car dealers, even family doctors and lawyers, why not a wine merchant?

Here are just a few sample "test" questions to throw out. Ask about the differences between a Bordeaux and Burgundy. Or, why a bottle of French Chablis is more expensive than one from California. See how he feels about one of your favorite wine and food combinations. Or, and this can seem very useful, specify your wine need, such as a gift bottle of dry white wine for under seven dollars, and see what is suggested. Or, a Champagne for under ten dollars. By using this tactic, you are not only testing the merchant, but also beginning to develop a potentially good relationship which, if all goes well, can only prove mutually beneficial. I strongly suggest questions based on a price range particularly to indicate you are a value hunter, not a candidate for a quick, high–profit sale. If you are quickly treated as a nuisance, you'll know this merchant's attitude toward building a clientele.

The better shops usually are well-lit and organized for the shopper's convenience. All wines should be stored away from direct sunlight; those with corks must be found lying on their sides. Some merchants believe that because their stock turns over quickly they need not worry about proper storage, but that's a sign of poor merchandising that frequently results in spoiled wine.

Window dressing is a part of selling, but in sun-drenched windows, the better wine shops display empty or sample bottles which will not be sold. No good merchant will ever sell a bottle from a window display, although wines do have to be displayed, made visible, inside the shop. Most of us still like to touch and handle bottles while shopping, so in the better shops a bottle of each available wine should be found in either a large rack or stacked in such a way that by touching it, one doesn't risk starting an avalanche. The rest of the stock should be kept in perfect, temperature-controlled storage space.

The storage temperature for wine is always important. Usually, in the main area, the temperature is constant and cool. But if the entire stock is not within sight, I often check to see where the cases are stored. Sometimes, the back rooms of a shop or a central warehouse area are far from ideal in the temperature and general storage conditions, and when you purchase wines by the case, it is reasonable to want to know where the case has been kept. This applies not only to old and rare wines, but to all wines in general. Of course wine shops without air conditioners in the summer and with blazing heat in the winter should be avoided.

The way the wines are organized also separates the good from the ordinary wine shop. A well-run shop will group wines by country and wine type, and frequently by price, with rack or isle markers or signs making it easy to locate the section you want. Another useful innovation in wine merchandising is to arrange wines by similar characteristics, i.e., Red Bordeaux along with California Cabernet Sauvignon; German Rieslings with California Johannisberg Rieslings; Chardonnays and White Burgundies, and so on which makes comparative shopping easier. It also encourages comparative tastings, by type, by nationality, and by smaller regions and sub-regions.

Wine shops, like supermarkets and bookstores, try to appeal to the impulse buyer, usually, by displaying some wine near the check-out or cash register area, frequently in a large basket, halved wine barrel, or the like. Often these wines are not necessarily bargains, even when reduced in price. Outdated inventory, or close-outs from wholesalers who have little merit frequently inhabit this section.

Most wine shops offer a "chilled wine" section, featuring whites, rosés, and Champagnes, as a convenience to patrons buying on the spur of the moment for immediate drinking. If the wines have been in a chiller for days or weeks, chances are they could have lost some of their freshness or liveliness or, worse yet, may be undrinkable. Some shops have a chilling machine that will chill your wine in three or four minutes without harming it. But if this is not available, it is far better to buy a bottle and chill it yourself for about half an hour rather than take a chance with pre-chilled wine.

Another major consideration in dealing with wine shops and wine merchants is the type, range, and assortment of wines carried. Because a shop carries a staggering quantity of wine, the owner or help is not necessarily capable of providing sound advice on its wares, but frequently provides good prices and a selection wide enough to meet the needs of a selective clientele. In such a shop, a little bit of study can offer substantial rewards in terms of values to be had.

The opposite kind of shop has a too-limited selection, which neglects many important wines. Such a place may carry a large selection of several popular wines such as French Chablis, or Beaujolais and Pouilly-Fuissé, along with jugs from California's biggest producers, and perhaps a few expensive Champagnes, and big names, often from off-vintages, from Bordeaux. This is a sure sign of a merchant who hasn't taken the time or effort to learn much about wine; another example of such a merchant will be a selection limited to only well-advertised brands. Then, there is the store that carries predominantly unknown brands or producers, from importers who specialize in so called "bargain" versions of well-known wine types. While such wines could offer good drinking and value, more often than not, they will be mediocre. Why these types of stores are merchandised as they are is not important, the point is that their proprietors have not stocked wines that are worth seeking.

Some of the well-trafficked wine shops or those that are part of a chain or franchise often carry so-called private label wines which are given either the name of the establishment selling them or some registered trademark it owns. Some of the retailer-owned labels can represent good value. The merchant will buy a certain percentage of wines in bulk and have them bottled under his label. Without the prestigious name of the winery, it will often be sold much cheaper. The quality will vary however from batch to batch; but if a good merchant builds his reputation on his own his name or exclusive trademark, you should try a bottle and hope to discover a bargain.

It is almost impossible for the same merchant to satisfy your every wine need particularly as your palate develops and changes over the years. As you will want to vary your wine selections, you should consider a repertoire of places to buy wine. For special occasion wines, you will no doubt want to rely on the expertise and careful selection of the best merchant you can discover. A discount or mass merchandiser will be a good source for bargains, particularly, if you are willing to take a chance and try his unknown or private label brands. In localities where permitted, convenience stores and supermarkets will make buying everyday wine easy and inexpensive. California residents, particularly, have the lucky choice of buying direct from the winery, many of which have tasting and sales rooms, and sell by mail order to California residents. These establishments provide selections of limited-distribution wines, and good value by cutting out all the middle men. As with any product, you are on your own in discovering where to buy. I hope these hints are helpful.

WINE AT HOME

Serving wine in your home is not complicated at all. The important thing to remember is what should be done and how to look good and comfortable while doing it. At this juncture, you have selected the wine or wines. Now the bottles must be opened and the wine enjoyed. Everything you will do is founded on common sense, not on archaic ritual or incantation.

Within recent years we have seen various bottle shapes and closures used commercially. Wine can come in a traditional-shaped bottle with a cork and capsule, in a jug with a screw cap closure, a plastic pouch enclosed in a box, even in a can with a flip-top. For now we will confine our discussion to the traditional bottle and closure which is equipped with a lead foil or plastic capsule. The capsule, which also serves aesthetic purposes, protects the cork. The cork protects the wine.

In preparing to serve wines, you want to remove both capsule and cork. Lead foil can be removed either by cutting it with a knife below the lip area at the top of the bottle, or by slicing through the foil around the neck and ripping the whole darn thing off. I prefer removing it entirely, since this allows you to see the length of the cork and the amount of fill in the bottle. The plastic capsules usually come with a tab and a perforated edge, making it easy to remove the top layer.

After the capsule is off, you may find a moldy-looking substance on the cork's surface. This green-grey stuff is usually a normal, harmless build-up of cellar muck or seepage. Remove it with a damp cloth. Now on to the cork.

REMOVING CORKS

Pulling a cork should not be a task that requires the strength of Hercules or Atlas, though it does require intelligence and an instrument of some sort. For years, our options were limited to traditional corkscrews and it was easy to recommend cork-

CORKPULLERS

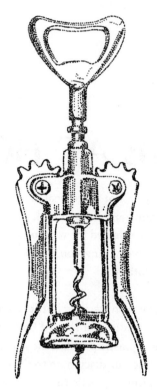

"Screwpull"

"Twin Lever"

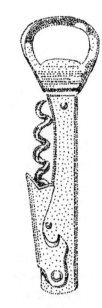

"Waiter's Corkscrew"

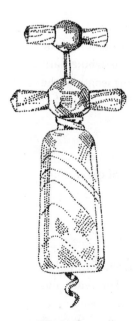

"Twin Screw"

"Ah-So" or
"Twin Blade Corkpuller"

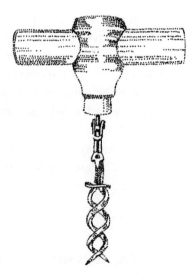

"Double Helix"

screws with some device for leverage instead of those with a screw that required physical force and plenty of grunting. Besides recommending leverage, we had two other pieces of advice: 1)That the worm (the spiral screw) be long, at least two inches; 2) That it be the helix type as opposed to the augur type with its point on the dead center. These suggestions were directed toward avoiding those moments we have all faced, whether as hosts, hostesses, waiters or waitresses, when we ended up with the bottle between our legs, pulling with all our might until we were first red, then blue in the face.

The helix-type worm works so well because it does not just cut a hole in or destroy the cork; it grips the cork firmly, making removal easier. The waiter's corkscrew, complete with leverage and a small knife, remains the most popular implement today. More recently, though, we have seen the advent of several gadgets which deserve some commentary.

The "Ah-So", or Pronged Corkpuller, is not a corkscrew at all but a two-pronged device developed in Germany. One thin leg formed of strong, tempered steel is gently pushed down until it goes below the cork, and the other leg is gently placed opposite; the cork is secured by a rocking motion and then removed by gently twisting and pulling upward. It works well for most corks, for others, not at all. The major advantage, other than reasonable ease and speed of operation, is that the cork is removed intact and can be reinserted with this device rather easily. The drawbacks are that the "Ah-So" requires some more skill than most corkscrews and is severely challenged by a dried-out cork. Also, if the cork is rather loose, the "Ah-So" pushes it into the wine before it can be gripped, a very unpleasant experience.

A fashionable item a few years ago was a device with a needle into which one pumped air to force out the cork. This clever gadget was antithetical to wine for almost every reason and should have experienced an early death. First it pumped air into the wine, which could, in an older wine, stir up the sediment. Secondly, the needle simply pushed a loose cork in. Thirdly, when a cork was no longer airtight, the air simply escaped and the cork remained in the bottle. Lastly, in a case where the cork was tight and the bottle defective, the pressure could cause the bottle to shatter. This remover may still be available and, believe me, it should still be avoided.

More recently, a company has designed a patented cork remover, called the Screwpull, that minimizes leverage pressure and has tremendous strength and durability for long-term use. It comes with a long, powerful worm and a strong, plastic design for the needed leverage. The Screwpull removes corks with little effort on your part and is self-centering, making it a breeze for even the most inept to pull any cork like a pro. My only concern is that the worm, itself, is not restrained within the plastic housing and can fall out from the case. With its razor sharp point, it can easily become a source of harm if handled by children, and I urge those who use one to place it out of their reach.

Many other corkscrews abound in the marketplace, ranging from simple pocket types encased in plastic traveling tubes to the twin-lever and twin-screw types sold in many department stores and supermarkets. Although somewhat clumsy in size, both are easy to use and employ the principle of mechanical advantage to make removing the cork easier. The twin lever works by twisting the screw into the cork, then using the two levers to pull it. The twin-screw uses one handle to screw in the cork, and another, attached to a concentric cylinder, to pull the cork with an effortless twisting motion. This type is manufactured both in wood and metal. Depending on the manufacturer, it could be excellent or awful. On the better ones, look for a sharp point and a wide helix.

Once the cork is removed and before the wine is poured, you should check a couple of things. If there is writing on the cork — a logo, brand name, and vintage date — make sure the information coincides with the label. If it does not, believe what's on the cork since it was inserted before the label was added. (Labeling mistakes are made on occasion. Hopefully, the vintage or brand is better than what is indicated on the label. If not, you have cause to demand a replacement from your wine merchant.) Also, squeeze the cork to make sure it is still somewhat sponge-like, not hard and dried out. Feel the bottom of the cork to see that it is still moist from contact with the wine. If the bottom is dry and the cork crumbly, be especially attentive to the quality of the wine since the cork may have been defective or the storage conditions hazardous to the wine's health.

Before we leave our discussion of corks, it is appropriate, here, to mention a few myths. There is a popular misconception that wine develops in the bottle because the cork allows slow breathing of air through its porous membranes. This would mean that rapid changes in temperature seriously harm a wine by increasing the rate of breathing due to expansion and contraction of the cork as the temperature rises and falls. The whole idea is outright silly.

Laboratory experiments indicate that the cork provides a hermetic seal, like a screw cap but tighter and longer lasting. Besides, air compresses easily and the expansion of the wine simply compresses the air in the bottle's headspace, although any air present when the bottle is first filled is usually absorbed by the wine, leaving a vacuum. Listen for the "whoosh" next time you open an aged bottle. However, a cork closure can dry out and permit air to enter the bottle and spoil it; a cork can also be contaminated and permit a mold to develop that can taint the taste. Wine so ruined is said to be "corked" and has a moldy taste.

The principal objection to metal caps over corks as closures for wine bottles is that they do not allow the wine to breathe. However, a little logic will prove the folly of this presumption. First of all, the cork has been scientifically proven to be a hermetic seal. However, even if a cork was porous, the capsule would impede the air. Secondly, if air did penetrate, the wine would simply oxidize early. Experiments with new types of metal screw caps and heavy-duty crown caps indicate their superiority over corks. In fact, Champagne is first aged with a metal crown cap before receiving its final cork. Thus the protestations of wine snobs and scientifically uninformed wine writers has caused fine wine producers to shy away from anything other than the cork to seal their bottles, and the public has been brainwashed into believing that only cheap wines use other closures. In actual fact, more wine is spoiled by defective corks than anything else.

WINE BREATHING

The issue of whether a wine should be allowed to breathe after being opened is more difficult to assess. Many people maintain that when exposed to air, the wine comes to life as the aroma is unleashed. In actuality, one of two things may be happening: 1) certain components in a wine may become volatile with some exposure to air; and/or 2) some odors which "block" our perception of more delicate odors dissipate, permitting the more delicate to be perceived. Breathing does allow some off-odors to dissipate. Sulphur dioxide is one specific example, among many, and in this context it seems quite certain that some unattractive elements clear with breathing. However, this is best accomplished by swirling the wine in the glass as opposed to letting the wine stand in its bottle.

Some people, however, insist the wine can be improved in other ways. They believe that younger wines are enhanced by a longer breathing time. I have never been totally convinced, even though we have, at VINTAGE, been involved in controlled experiments on several occasions. My feeling is that whatever changes occur depend on so many different variables that one simply can't postulate a rule of thumb. If you feel more comfortable with allowing a wine to breathe, I suggest you open it fifteen to twenty minutes before serving and then pour some into glasses a few minutes before you and your guests are seated. If breathing brings improvements, they will be more apt to come along in good-sized wine glasses than in the bottle with its tiny opening. Bear in mind that many old wines seem to "die" in the glass within a few minutes after the cork is pulled. Others seem to improve for hours. With these wines it's better to try them immediately after opening and enjoy them as they evolve in the glass if, luckily, they do so.

DECANTORS

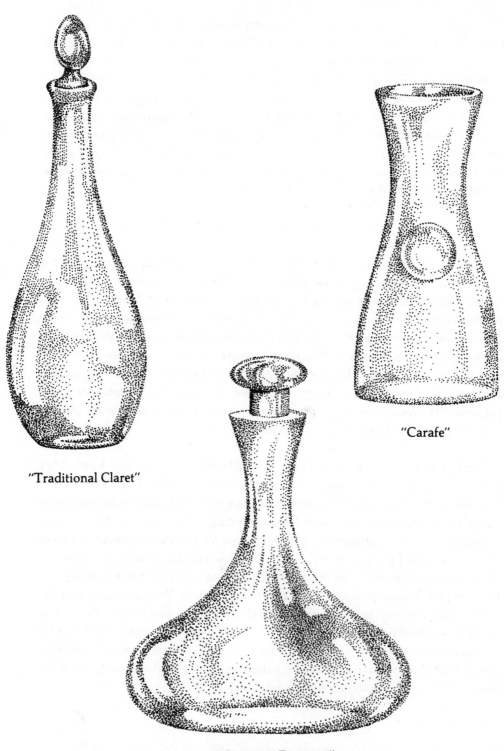

"Traditional Claret"

"Carafe"

"Captain's Decanter"

DECANTING

A deposit will be thrown in bottles of wine which have been bottle-aged for ten or more years (sometimes less). This sediment is, more often than not, bitter and when diffused into the wine, can make it bitter or mask the subtle nuances which have developed over the years. Not all wines throw deposits, by any means. Those that do were usually made with a minimum of filtering to allow the wine to develop new and more complex flavors when bottled-aged. Since wine is stored on its side, the sediment collects on the side of the bottle. So, long before serving the bottle should be placed upright to allow the sediment to fall to the bottom. Then you can decant the wine by pouring it slowly and carefully, without stopping, from the bottle into another container. This slow, steady motion will permit the sediment to remain in the bottle without being stirred back into the wine.

Incidentally, decanting also aerates the wine, but its real function is to clarify it by leaving the sediment behind. Any vessel can be used as a decanter, so long as it is clean and free from off-aromas.

When decanting, a source of light should be placed beneath the bottle's neck to enable you to see when the sediment is close to being poured. Working slowly, you stop once you see any sediment near the neck. Your poured wine is now clear. If you used a decanter with a stopper, replace it until you are ready to serve the wine. By the way, it is a pleasant touch to bring the bottle to the table so that guests can know what they are enjoying.

WINE GLASSES

Wine glasses are sometimes paid less attention than they deserve, so here I want to emphasize some of the essential requirements for the glass. Wine glasses need not be expensive crystal, but they should be clear, not colored or tinted. The stem should be a reasonable size with which most people feel comfortable. The stem is important because people should not touch the bowl as this could change the wine's temperature from the heat of the hand or leave unsightly fingerprints. The capacity should be ample. A twelve-ounce bowl is generally deemed quite adequate in an all-purpose style. When properly poured, the glass should be a little less than half full with plenty of room for swirling the wine before sniffing and tasting. This capacity allows for a good four to five ounce serving.

The actual shape of the wine glass is less important. But the rim of the bowl should curve in slightly to help capture the aroma generated by swirling. Though every household can be well-served by a set of all-purpose wine glasses — either the classic Bordeaux or Burgundy shapes will do — I'd like to suggest you have a second set, for serving a second wine or Champagne.

To appreciate the bubbly, Champagne should be poured into glasses with a high, narrow bowl like the Champagne "flute", or a similar design. Never use the typical wedding glass, the flat saucer with hollow stem, because the bubbles you paid for will fade quickly.

Wine glasses come in many shapes which provide variety and aesthetic enjoyment. The graceful Bordeaux glass is often considered the best all-purpose glass. The tall, slender Hock glass is pretty, and the big Burgundy balloon glass can also add variety, if it is not too unwieldy. The only other glassware you might consider, other than the two types mentioned, is a Sherry glass, called a *copita*. It is small, with a narrow taper and small opening. Somehow, the Sherry glass is perfectly designed to capture that wine's aroma and is also perfect for any other cordial.

Cognac glasses or brandy snifters are also most advantageous to the wine, by capturing its essence — slowly funneling it to your nose. Snifters add an elegant touch to the table, and it is agreed that the bigger the snifter, the better. Those holding sixteen ounces, even though only one or two ounces is served, really enhance the aroma. Incidentally, the use of the many contraptions for heating brandy or Cognac may add a little thrill to those who like fires, but can absolutely ruin the flavor by scorching it. Avoid them.

Along these lines, washing wine glasses requires special attention. Most experts neglect this important facet of wine enjoyment. Some simply declare that they be washed by hand *without* a strong detergent. Nothing could be farther from the truth. Wine glasses must be *absolutely* clean and *only* a good detergent can clean them thoroughly. This is true especially if the glasses have been resting in the cabinet for a time and have picked up some off-odors. It is far wiser to always wash glasses with a good dishwashing detergent prior to using them. Rinse them with fresh water several times to remove any detergent residue.

Even though a glass appears to be sparkling clean, it may not be. The best way to find out is to gently exhale into the glass and then smell it; important, because any odors that remain will come through when you pour wine into the glass. Too many wine glasses are stored upside down in a cabinet where bacteria seem to thrive. Restaurants seem to make a practice of this poor storage, so I often smell the glass even when dining out. I have had "stale" glasses at wine tastings at such prestigious restaurants as the famed Four Seasons or the Windows on the World atop the World Trade Center in New York City.

ALL-PURPOSE WINE GLASSES

"White Wine"

"Red Bordeaux"

"White Burgundy"

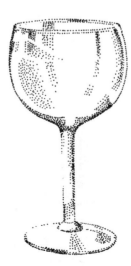

"Red Burgundy"

SPECIAL PURPOSE WINE GLASSES

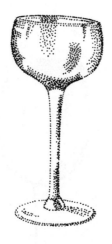

"Rhine" or "Hoch"   "Sherry"

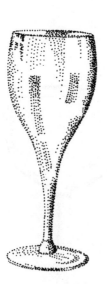

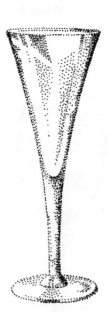

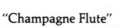

"Champagne Flute"

OPENING AND SERVING CHAMPAGNE

Serving Champagne has long been surrounded by silly rituals and unnecessary pomp when opening the bottle should be no more ceremonious than opening any other type of wine. Because the wine is bottled under tremendous pressure, several precautions should be taken to avoid accidents. Forget the rituals and misconceptions and be safe. Keep in mind that the pressure can propel a cork across the room and can seriously hurt, even maim people. Additionally, if not handled with extreme care, a defective bottle may actually explode.

An unopened bottle should be treated with the same respect as a loaded gun. It should never be pointed in anyone's direction, including your own. Hold the bottle at a forty-five degree angle away from everyone. Since temperature could possibly cause a bottle to fracture, take special care when handling iced or over chilled Champagne. For that reason, it is better to wrap the bottle in a towel or cloth napkin. The following procedures will help you enjoy your Champagne to its fullest:

- Always inspect a Champagne bottle for deep scratches or nicks. A badly scratched bottle has the potential to explode.

- Never overchill Champagne. Forty five degrees is fine. A colder temperature will increase the risk of a bursting bottle if it has deep scratches.

- Always point the neck of the bottle away from yourself and others. A flying cork may seem cute but is not worth the risk of blinding an innocent party.

- Wrap the bottle in a towel. In case the bottle explodes, the towel will prevent the spraying of glass fragments. It rarely happens but is worth the precaution.

- When removing the wire cage around the cork, always place your palm over the cork to prevent its shooting out of the bottle.

- Remove the cork by a gentle, twisting motion with your palm over the cork. There should be a barely audible pop and whisk of "smoke" when properly removed. Loud pops and gushing Champagne are vulgar and waste good wine.

- If the cork is difficult, push gently on alternate sides with your thumbs. When it begins to move cover it with your palm.

- Never attempt to remove a Champagne cork with a corkscrew. The potential for disaster is not worth the effort. Besides it looks ridiculous. Return a recalcitrant bottle to your wine store for an easier one.

- Do not pour warm Champagne over ice cubes. The bubbles will dissipate quickly and the wine will become diluted. It's a waste of good wine.

- Always remember that the excitement of Champagne lies not with a popping cork, but with the sparkle in the glass.

- I always enjoy Champagne best at home because restaurants almost always overcharge when they price Champagne; hotels and nightclubs *always* do!

KEEPING AN OPENED BOTTLE

Since it begins to deteriorate immediately, a bottle of wine is best consumed within a few hours after it is opened; but it is possible to keep it for several days without losing too many enjoyable flavors. As a general rule, the more ordinary a wine, the better it will keep. For jug wines, made with modern techniques, there is no need to transfer the contents into smaller bottles; there are no micro-organisms in the wine to culture and spoil it. With finer wines, there is more risk. As with any perishable food, wine will keep when chilled. Thus, you can keep an opened bottle for a few days upward of a week or more if you don't mind losing some of the flavor of the wine. Expensive wines, which have subtle nuances of flavor, will lose their delicacy or finesse when stored but will still have some resemblance to their original self when warmed to serving temperature. Let the chilled wine gradually return to serving temperature, never heat the wine in an oven. The best way to determine if the flavor loss is excessive is to experiment for yourself.

STORING WINE

Storing wines in your home, or "cellaring" them, if you prefer, is a part of wine serving and entertainment. You don't really need a deep, dark, hillside or underground area for wine storage. The basic requirements are a place that is away from direct sunlight, a location that is free of vibration, and a temperature that does not fluctuate dramatically over a short period of time. In regard to temperature, coolness is often over-emphasized whereas uniformity of temperature is more important. A place where the temperature will increase or decrease by 10°F within a week or two is less than ideal. Slow, incremental changes, so long as the extremes are not very extreme, will usually be sufficient. The commonplace rule that a cellar should be a constant 55°F is just an ideal, one to shoot for when selecting a spot. If your storage conditions vary in a year from, say, 50°F in the winter to a high of about 70°F in the summer, you really ought not to worry too much. However, long storage under very warm or hot conditions will seriously harm your wine. It will not only mature more rapidly, but will deteriorate before it attains peak of perfection.

WINE RACKS

How you cellar your wine depends on your needs. If you prefer to operate by having a few cases or only a few bottles on hand for occasional use, you don't need elaborate storage units or racks. Many home wine cellars are maintained for convenience over a few weeks or months to avoid having to buy a bottle at the penultimate moment. If you get into buying wines by case lots with the desire to age them for one or many years, then you might consider installing a special wine rack unit which you can either build yourself or purchase. The points to remember are first, that the wines should be stored on their sides and, secondly, that the labels or some system of identifying your bottles be visible. You don't want to jostle many bottles every time you want to find one in particular.

In convenience cellars or those intended for short-term use, the cardboard boxes or wooden cases the wine comes in are sufficient for use as storage units. These are not quite convenient for stacking, for if you stack them too high, the bottom row will collapse, leading to a possible broken bottle at worst, additional work to reorganize your cellar at best. Unfortunately, those wooden wine crates which were so sturdy and ideal for use in a home wine cellar have pretty much disappeared (although some brands do come in special wooden "wine-rack" convertible cases), leaving us with cardboard containers. If you're lucky enough to find wooden cases, by all means, use them. However, don't base your wine buying per se on the availability of the wooden crates.

Wine racks come in many sizes and configurations and are made from a variety of materials ranging from inexpensive white pine to expensive, clear lucite or polished brass. Wine racks have come into vogue in designer-decorated homes, within which a "wine wall" or built-in wine rack can cost up to several thousand dollars. But such extravagance is not necessary to store wine well and may actually be harmful. Besides, if properly located, away from bright light and heat, your wine rack will rarely be in public view.

Wine racks come in two basic configurations — the twelve-bottle rack and the larger bookcase-style. Many small racks are well-designed, enabling them to be stacked without danger of toppling. They fit easily into closets, on bookshelves, or other nooks convenient for wine storage. When buying these racks, you should check to see if they are sturdy, easy to assemble if unassembled, and have openings large enough accept a Burgundy or Champange bottle. Believe it or not, many wine racks have openings too small for many popular-sized bottles available today.

Bookshelf-style wine racks come either with openings for individual bottles, or square or diamond shaped ports which hold from six to a dozen bottles. Attractive models are available in fine furniture hardwoods, wrought iron, brass, chrome, or lucite. These are generally more expensive on a cost-per-bottle-stored basis but make a fine addition to many decorating schemes. Be sure to check that the unit is stable and will not be top-heavy when fully-loaded. Many of this type are fabricated for permanent "built-in" installation.

Completely self-contained, temperature-regulated wine cabinets are also available but are quite expensive. One company, Viking Sauna, has ingeniously converted its pre-fabricated sauna bath enclosures to wine cellars ranging in cost from approximately one thousand dollars upward to five thousand. Other firms offer a variety of sizes, styles, and finishes. Cooling units vary, some use refrigerator units, others simple air conditioners, and others still, modern solid state devices. Since vibration is a serious enemy of wine, you should determine what cooling method is used and whether the manufacturer guarantees the unit to be vibration-free. Another factor to consider is whether or not wines are stored in front of each other. This is the case in several of the Viking models, which require that the front bottles be removed to get to some of the others. Wine rack companies making these expensive units come and go. Consider the longevity of the firm, its reputation, arrangements for installation and service, its warranty, and whether or not they have local service agents in case of trouble. Personally, I would buy a unit like this only from a local department store or reputable furniture store or decorator whose visibility and reputation will help assure a hassle-free environment for my cellar.

I maintain two wine cellars. One is in a rather large cellar in a private brownstone in New York that was built to store the furs of its first occupant in a bygone era of wealth and opulence. In my opinion, its ideal, stable temperature is best used in nurturing wines. I use this cellar for long-term storage. My "working cellar" is in my apartment where I have converted a long, narrow and useless hallway into an air conditioned wine cellar lined with plastic racks stacked floor to ceiling. Many wine lovers store their wines this way, with a safe but inconvenient storage cellar away from home and a working cellar which is restocked from time to time. If you become seriously involved in wine you might consider a similar hideaway.

WINE TASTINGS

A wine tasting is basically a gathering of people for the purpose of tasting and sampling wine. It may be a serious occasion or a casual one; there are professional wine tastings that are part of one's business, and consumer wine tastings that are meant for amusement, entertainment, and education. The organizing principles and many objectives are shared by both. Holding a wine tasting can be an enjoyable experience that advances your knowledge of wine; to conduct one with aplomb, it is not necessary to be an expert.

To many people, the concept of tasting wines as part of one's profession is viewed as glamorous and exciting. Let me be the first to confess: there is little glamour in professional wine tasting; it is darn hard work. It demands mental readiness and uninterrupted concentration, often for hours at a time. The professional, whether he is a shipper, importer, wholesaler, distributor, critic, or creator, may be required to taste a few or as many as fifty or sixty different wines on one occasion. He has to sample each with the same care and attention; the fact is that some wines are awful, many mediocre, and the highlights (fine, or rarely, great wines) are often few and far between. The job can be discouraging, especially for critics who, committed to offering honest appraisals, must taste many wines that they ordinarily would pass by.

On the other hand, wine tastings held as a social function or form of entertainment with friends can be delightful and informative. A wine tasting can be either formal or informal. By formal, I mean one which is usually a sit-down affair at which the wines are presented in a prescribed order, often with their identity a secret until after the tasting and ranking, or scoring, is finished. The informal approach is one whereby a few bottles are opened and sampled at each person's own pace.

Conducting your own wine tasting is simple and merely involves selecting the wines, the wine glasses, and the people. Often, something to nibble on between wines is helpful as a palate-cleanser, but not a necessity. It is better, though, to have a theme to your wine tasting so that there is a point of comparison. For instance, you should select comparable wines, either a California varietal, or a European type, or a specific vintage or wines within a specified price range. The possibilities are almost limitless, but the wines should be selected with some method to your madness. Another alternative would be to select a certain number of red (or white) wines from different regions or countries to explore regional differences. A third idea would be to focus on wines from an emerging wine country or region.

The logistics of a wine tasting are not complicated. You can assume one bottle will easily serve twelve people, fifteen if need be. You will need a table large enough to hold several wines, (several moderate tables will do), white tablecloths to provide a proper background to view the color of the wines, (paper ones will do), and sufficient wine glasses in accordance with the theme or objective of the tasting; I suggest two per person at the least. Good-sized wine glasses are quite important to assess the bouquet. Buckets of some kind are needed for spitting-out or emptying the glasses as one goes on to taste other wines. Bright incandescent lighting is another requirement; fluorescent lights impart a bluish cast and distort the appearance of red wines by making them appear brownish.

Be very cautious in the selection of food. This applies to both the nibbles you select for the wine tasting and to any food being prepared in a nearby kitchen. Cheeses are a natural with wine, but for wine tastings, the more neutral the cheese, the better. Very aromatic cheese can clash with the wines' fragrances. The same applies to odors of food being prepared in the kitchen for enjoyment after the wine tasting. They, too, can render the results of your wine tasting useless. Plain bread or unsalted crackers are the best choices to accompany a wine tasting. Better yet, plain water will serve nicely. I prefer a neutral sparkling mineral water as it cleans the palate without imparting any offending flavors. One problem with some city water is that it is sometimes over-treated with chemicals that can affect your ability to taste.

You will want to keep a few general guidelines in mind:

- Each wine should be served at an appropriate temperature, that is, the temperature at which you would serve it with a meal. For most people, this means that whites, rosés, and Champagnes are served slightly chilled, reds at normal room temperature.

- The glasses, preferably all of the same size, should be filled to the same level, so as not to prejudice the taster by providing too much, or too little.

- Wines of the same type should be grouped and tasted together.

- Sweet wines should be tasted in progression according to sweetness. A very sweet wine, if tasted early, will make less-sweet wines seem dry.

- The number of wines being tasted should be limited. Most people can only taste ten, maybe twelve, wines and still maintain meaningful judgments.

- When mixing wines by type, sequence them so that the lighter, drier versions precede the heavier ones or, at least, that the whites and rosés are tasted before the reds.

One way to taste wines is the "blind" approach, that is, with the labels concealed and unknown. Regardless of experience, seeing a label influences one's judgment. It is simple human reasoning. If you have either been told that the label is prestigious or have sampled the wine before and liked it, you will feel foolish running counter to a consensus or your own earlier assessment. All that is required is that the bottles be covered and coded so that the tasters are unaware of what they are tasting. Wine stores have paper bags which are just the right size for a wine bottle, you might ask your wine merchant for a few. Aluminum foil works well but more easily reveals the bottle shape, which might offer a clue as to the type of wine within. Decanters are ideal, no clues here. Make a list of what wine went into what decanter, it would be a pity if you got the wines confused.

After a time, when your interest in wine tasting develops to a point where you want to discover more than which wines appeal to you, you can make the tastings more interesting and concentrate on fine-tuning your abilities through blind tastings. Often, this leaning begins long before when you unconsciously begin guessing a wine's origin, vintage, region, and winemaking style or even brand. Blind wine tastings can be used to test your expertise as a safeguard against developing personal prejudices and a false sense of security. It is really not an opportunity to show off; merely a chance to show yourself where you stand. Here are a few situations you might want to experiment with in this context.

A triangulation test is easy. It requires two wines and three glasses. The taster's task is to pick the two glasses filled from the same bottle. Sounds simple, but often even experienced tasters get mixed up. In the beginning, it will be easier if you test yourself with wines that are substantially different. As your palate develops, you will want to test yourself with wines that are increasingly similar.

Another good tasting test comes from working with pairs. Two wines with some dissimilarity are poured into four glasses; the taster has to match pairs. This exercise

WINE TASTING RECORD

Wine	Vintage Wine Name	
Country	**Region**	
Type	**Appellation**	
☐ **Producer** ☐ **Shipper**		
☐ **Importer** ☐ **Distributor**		

Evaluation	COLOR ☐AROMA TASTE BALANCE BODY PEDIGREE VA. FINISH CONT. ☐BOUQUET	**Score**
Color: Intensity	Clarity Hue	
Aroma: Intensity	Character	
Taste: Intensity	Character	
Off-flavors		
Body	**Tannins**	
Balance	**Acidity**	**Sweetness**
Structure		
Finish	**Maturity**	
Other		
	Price $ **Rated**	

COMMENTS

DATE ACQUIRED	DATE TESTED	DATE APPROVED	PRICE PAID	CATEGORY
VINTAGE ISSUE	WINE REPORTER ISSUE		TASTED BY **PHILIP SELDON**	

can be used for any number of pairs, by the way. In this exercise, the taster can be challenged by simple matching or, even by matching wines by vintage, by country, or region.

Don't make tasting a chore. Take it only as far as you want to. But if you become really serious about wines, eventually you will want to develop a scoring or ranking system through which you can catalogue particular favorites. There are several systems which professional and advanced wine buffs use, but these are somewhat complicated and require study and experience. For now, you should simply list the wines in the order you prefer them. The actual approach one follows in ranking, or scoring wines is much less important than the awareness of the differences between wines that such an organized method creates.

My feeling is that most established rating systems for wines contain their own built-in, and often unknown, fallacies and weaknesses. The best known and most often referred to scoring system was developed for wine students at the University of California, Davis. The so-called U.C. Davis Twenty Point System was devised to help future winemakers detect serious flaws and determine when a wine was below commercial acceptability. As a teaching tool, this twenty-point scoring system was, and is, extremely useful. But now it is used for purposes for which it was not intended and has been promoted by writers as "the" best wine-scoring system. It is frequently referred to by wine companies that use wine buffs to compare their wines with others. The problem is that the system is inadequate for application to fine wines, and places too much emphasis on a wine's basic chemistry as opposed to the wine's aesthetic qualities. When used at amateur wine tastings, such a system shifts the emphasis from appreciating a wine to being right or wrong in terms of a group consensus. For that reason, I have strongly objected to steering laymen to a point score system for assessing wine and have not included such a system in this book. If you are seriously interested, I have developed a very useful system and would be pleased to send it to you if you write to the address listed on page 351.

For most wine tasting purposes, I recommend that wines simply be discussed in terms of preferences. Why did you like one wine over another? Did you discern a defect in a wine? Was one wine more representative of its label than another? Wine evaluation is really a personal matter and, of course, there are no right and wrong responses or answers. It boils down to two things: what we perceive and what we like in a wine. We may very well be able to perceive a particular wine's high acidity or high residual sugar or its light or heavy body. What we like, meaning how much a wine appeals to our taste, is a matter of individual taste perception and preference.

WINE CELLAR JOURNAL

DATE ACQUIRED	WINE NAME	PRICE PAID	DATE TASTED	RATING

Comparing your own evaluations with those of others is the best way to learn about wine and your own perceptions and preferences. Understanding why another taster's preference is different than yours is more important in terms of learning about wine than knowing which wine is the better one. The best wine for you is the one you prefer. Knowing why you prefer one over another is the essential point. As you develop wine experience you will probably find that your preferences will change. This is most often the case when wine is tasted with someone whose palate and experience are more sophisticated than yours and when that person has an ability to help you isolate some subtle sensations that you may have missed. Not every experienced wine taster, however, is a good wine teacher, nor should you feel that you must adjust your preferences because one wine buff prefers a wine you don't.

Whether you are just beginning or have tasted wines for years, trying to recall a particular wine from memory can be a frustrating experience. Sometimes the situation, like an anniversary or birthday, becomes so special that the wine or wines enjoyed are difficult to recall with any accuracy at all. Therefore, for each wine, most people jot down notes, either detailed or abbreviated by symbols. Tasting notes are an invaluable aid, both to help you remember your evaluation of a wine and as a sort of record of your own wine tasting education.

There is no single, or right way, of organizing tasting notes. They can be recorded on file cards, in notebooks, or in fancy journals sold for the purpose. I've tried using many note-taking systems, but after finding most to be either too confining or too awkward or bulky to use, I've settled on the one pictured on page 304. You may want to duplicate this form or design one of your own. For me, the names of the shipper and importer are important, but they may not be to most consumers.

Those of you fortunate enough to have a wine cellar or who are in the midst of adding to one ought to consider keeping a cellar log, especially if you are building your cellar by purchasing a case or more of a particular wine to be aged. In this case, a cellar log is useful as it enables you to chart the development of your wines from the date of purchase (along with its price), on through the first sampling (with a note of when to sample next), until that particular wine remains only as a memory. The one I use is shown on page 306. Feel free to reproduce it if you wish.

The point is that one tastes wines for different reasons. For some it is professional, for others it is purely social. Some taste to purchase a bottle; others to purchase in case lots, and a few of us to monitor the progress of the wines we own or occasionally to monitor our own wine tasting progress. In any or all of the above purposes, the prevailing theme, though, is to invite some friends along simply because wine is best appreciated when shared.

THE WINE TRADE

Wine is a relatively new industry in the United States. I say this because it has only recently become big business in the "corporate" sense. Furthermore, in 1920 an era began which can best be described as a dark moment in American History; the consumption or sale of wine was illegal in the United States under the Eighteenth Amendment of the Constitution of the United States, (The Volstead Act). During Prohibition, most vineyards and wineries simply shut down. Although a few remained open to produce sacramental and medicinal wine, and some vineyards produced grapes for home winemaking, most pulled up their vines and planted another crop or simply abandoned their land.

Following Prohibition, the domestic wine industry flourished. Fortunes, typified by that of Ernest and Julio Gallo, were made by producing inexpensive, high-alcohol wines to quench America's thirst. (Until the early 1960s only a handful of wineries produced outstanding table wines in the European tradition, while fortified dessert wines dominated the market.)

Except for cheap Chianti and French Chablis, foreign wines were virtually unknown to most Americans. During the 1930s and '40s, only a handful of wine merchants stocked fine wines from France, Italy, or Germany. Yet, in the public's mind, these imported wines were synonomous with excellence, and while the best were ridiculously inexpensive (Château Lafite-Rothschild sold for about two dollars a bottle in a good vintage such as 1947), the public considered imported French wine and Champagne too expensive for their modest pocketbooks.

Under these conditions the wine trade evolved. Following Repeal in 1933, regulation of the sale of all alcoholic beverages came under the domain of each state government. Many states remained dry. Some assumed a monopoly and permitted wine and liquor to be sold only in state stores; others prohibited retail merchants from importing or buying directly from American producers. Others still, mandated minimum mark-ups at both wholesale and retail. Many states required licensing of both employees of the trade and wholesale and retail establishments, and strictly regulated where and when wine could be purchased. Other states, like California, provided virtually no restriction on wine, making it available in supermarkets, drugstores, at newsstands, etc. California wineries could, and still do, maintain tasting rooms where wine is sampled and bought by retailers without going through a wholesaler.

Although each state is different, wine in America is basically sold through what is known as the "three tier system". Wine importers and producers must sell to a distributor/wholesaler, who sells it to a retail merchant or restaurant, who in turn sells it to you. Of course, the price of the wine increases with each middleman.

Needless to say, the wine industry loves this regulation. It provides the industry with limited competition and legally-legislated, guaranteed profits. This particularly benefits the retailer in states where minimum prices are maintained. Can you blame a merchant who is protected from supermarket competition for fighting for the status quo? Unfortunately, as consumers, we pay literally millions of dollars a year for this legally legislated abuse of our rights.

Some wine merchants have discovered clever loopholes in the regulations which give them an edge over their competition and provide better value for their customers while still earning them generous profits. The most significant tactic is called "direct import." It works this way: the merchant buys wines (which are otherwise unavailable in America) abroad and arranges for an importer/wholesaler to bring these wines in for him. Although, in many states, they must be "posted" at a legal resale price, these are the merchant's wines and he sets the price. For doing the paperwork, the importer receives so much per case, usually a dollar or two. If another retailer should want these wines he is told they are out of stock, which, of course, they are since the entire shipment went to just one merchant. The wines can be sold at approximately thirty percent below the price of a comparable wine from a national importer, and frequently will be better since a merchant who would go to so much trouble will generally have a good palate and an eye for a good deal. Similar arrangements are available for domestic wines. Thus, comparative price shopping for wines can be difficult. Frequently, a higher-priced wine will be significantly lower in quality than a little known bargain brand. An experienced palate and a good book knowledge of wines are keys to finding the bargains.

After Prohibition, the liquor companies concentrated on high-profit liquor and left imported wines to smaller specialists. During this period names such as Frank Schoonmaker and Alexis Lichine became famous for their quality imported French or German wines. Lichine, for example, literally barnstormed the country, from city to city, persuading restaurants to serve French wines. He also convinced the French to package their wines to appeal to American consumers. Other wine promoters soon joined in courting American buyers.

Wines from such companies were, until recently, always guaranteed to be of superb quality, and company staffs were knowledgeable and devoted to wine. During mid-1960s and early '70s, however, giant conglomerates took a serious interest in the wine business. Lichine sold his name, but not himself, to a giant British liquor firm; Frank Schoonmaker, sold his small company to Pillsbury which subsequently lost many millions in its wine dealings; Dryfus, Ashby Co. was sold to Schenley, and Frederick Wildman and Sons, to another foreign liquor giant. The result was that liquor executives, unknowledgeable about either wine or the wine trade, were unable to exercise control over their suppliers or choose new ones with any expertise. The fabled wine importers, with a few rare exceptions, became bastardized trade names in an industry whose executives lacked the ability to evaluate quality even if they desired to. Thus, rather than offer an assurance of quality, most importers today offer a mixed bag; ironically, the names of several previously prestigious importers have become symbols of what to avoid, rather than what to buy.

Throughout this book I have focused on intelligent wine-buying through education and experience. My main point is that this country's rapidly-increased demand for wine over the last fifteen years has left the consumer in a most vulnerable position: that of being asked to pay exorbitant prices for wines of marginal quality just because they are imported.

In a strange way, the United States market has changed the perception of wine over the last few decades. The best example of this is French Chablis and, more recently, Pouilly-Fuissé. Four decades ago, when very few Americans drank wine, French Chablis, an all-purpose dry white wine almost universal in appeal, was imported because it was very inexpensive, available, and attractive to a wide range of people. As interest in imported wine increased, "Chablis" was a logical name for consumers to turn to. Over the long term, the supply of Chablis tightened, and prices increased. Today, French Chablis is priced so far above its worth as to be ludicrous.

Next, importers looked for a supply of similarly-styled, cheap, white wine they could import at a good markup. In the early 1960s, Pouilly-Fuissé became that wine, and before too long, a bottle or two was mandatory on every wine list at every restaurant that offered any kind of wine at all. Pouilly-Fuissé was an importer's dream. The regional name was neither borrowed nor bastardized then and, better yet, was ever-so-French to have tripping from one's tongue. Its fame skyrocketed despite the fact that Pouilly-Fuissé was actually just another unpretentious, dry white Burgundy made for fairly current consumption, and rarely as good as the best Chablis. But it, too, got caught up in the fancy French wine mystique, and soon commanded prices greater than that of even the best Chablis. In the 1970s, Mâcon Blanc became a French replacement for Pouilly-Fuissé which had replaced French Chablis. Prices rose with demand. Now Mâcon Blanc is frequently priced beyond its worth.

Importers, particularly those with still-strong connections to the distilled spirits trade, often buy names from French shippers without any concern for quality. But, because they offer the standard liquor brands, an enormous range of wines (usually a shipper's entire line), and can round out their offerings with other specialties, these big importing companies dominate the market.

Running counter to this general trend are a few small importing firms which select wines and particular vintages on a personal level. They maintain a tradition started years ago by the likes of Frank Schoonmaker and Frederick Wildman, along with a few others, whose interest was in wines and in bringing in the best for the United States market at a reasonable price level. These small importing houses which gained a reputation because of their integrity could be relied upon as a consistent guide. Although many small importers of this calibre exist today, to bring in fine, individually selected wines, they are usually forced to concentrate their marketing efforts in small areas of metropolitan regions.

Today, the major, visible importers are large corporations with an eye on profit through product mix and marketing muscle. Those which list a wine authority within their organization seldom give him total freedom to make the selections; some use such authorities as figureheads only. Generally, each importer concentrates its marketing efforts on one or two highly advertised popular brands, and depends on them as important profit centers. Frequently there is little incentive to bother with château or estate wines as these usually require intimate supplier relationships, an intimate knowledge of wine, and a mass of paperwork to pass these wines through the importation and distribution process. One major brand is often worth more in sales than the hundreds of individual wines that wine importers once frequently carried. Thus many of the importers known for their wide selection of fine wines are now out of the fine wine business, and concentrating on one or several mass appeal brands.

The American wine consumer has absolutely no guarantees when it comes to imported wines; certainly none regarding quality and, worse yet, none which even guarantee that the wine is what it is labeled and declared to be. The United States is totally devoid of any professional wine trade organization, formal or informal. In England, at least, importers and members of the wine trade have an accrediting organization called the Masters of Wine to which one can turn for experts. A Master of Wine (MW) must, achieve a certain level of competence. He must have apprenticed in the trade and passed written and taste examinations; furthermore, he must be well-versed in the wines of the world and in each country's wine regulations and requirements. The Vintage Foundation, of which I am a director, recently established a program called the Laureat of Wine, which hopefully will gain accept-ance within the American wine trade.

Without any equivalent or even remotely similar organization, the United States is wide-open to wine charlatans — so-called wine experts who thrive unchallenged as to their ignorance. Unfortunately for us, they often make the buying decisions for many major houses. Not all wine experts are frauds, many firms do have knowledgeable, professional wine experts, but they are outnumbered by the phonies. Mislabeled, bogus, or just poor-quality wines from abroad have recently seemed to flood the United States market. The simple reason why so many mediocre Beaujolais, Chablis, Pouilly-Fuissé, Bordeaux, and Burgundy bottlings have been targeted for United States markets is that the importers are not able to distinguish between the good and bad. The fraudulent French wines shipped to the United States, which were the subject of the recent wine scandals, could easily have been detected as inferior or unauthentic by any experienced wine amateur; yet these wines breezed by the so-called professionals without challenge or question. Few of the American companies deliberately try to cheat the public — although their lack of expertise often results in the public not getting its money's worth. The United States has been, and in my opinion will remain, the dumping ground for flawed or bogus imported wines as long we have so few wine experts in the trade.

Importers in the 1980s are likely to be faced with even more difficult supply prob-lems. Sometime in the 1970s, local producers, first in Burgundy and Germany and more recently in Bordeaux, have discovered the advantages of selling their wines directly to customers. With their reputations secure, they no longer need interna-tional sales representatives; besides, they can increase their profits by selling retail rather than wholesale. Huge amounts of Europe's finest wines are now being sold at the winery doors, and importers are being denied a supply of often-fine wines. Given the attitude of importing firms in the United States, and the rapidly dwindling supply of imported wines, the future for the best château and estate wines is hardly bright. Prices will continue to spiral, and many wines will simply not be imported into the United States because of prohibitive prices. This is already apparent with many of the finer Burgundies; many of the best are no longer available in the United States.

In the United States, wine production is dominated by a handful of large and powerful producers in California and New York State. Some of the large producers are owned by importing firms or have their own national distribution network, usually through wholesalers. These wines can be found in virtually every wine store within the United States. Gallo commands the largest share of the market, followed by Almaden, Paul Masson, United Vintners (Italian Swiss Colony) and Taylor wines. Along with several other firms, this group accounts for the vast majority of wine sold in America. It is mostly of jug or simple-premium quality and made by the most modern winemaking techniques.

California also has many small wineries called Boutique Wineries, which specialize in finer quality wines. At latest count, these number in excess of two hundred wineries, many less than ten years old. For years, many of California's finest wines rarely left the state. This was partly due to a prejudice against domestic wines on the part of consumers outside of California, and partly due to a weak or non-existent chain of distribution. But as the number of California wineries grew, the local market could not absorb all the wine produced and these wineries were not equipped to market their wines nationally. Consequently, today, many Boutique Wineries are promoted by marketing organizations which have cropped up to fill this void, or by national wine importers who have recognized these small wineries as a viable source of profit. Spotty distribution still remains a problem with many small California and New York State producers. Many simply do not have enough wine to spread around; others do not care to be involved with the regulations each state imposes on the movement and sale of wine; others simply can't afford to pay the prohibitive fees imposed by states for registering a brand for sale within its borders. Today American wine remains one of few domestically produced products that faces severe restraints in interstate trade.

America's wine producers can be grouped into several categories. Those described in the first three paragraphs that follow are generally small, private entrepreneurs specializing in premium and noble wines. Many wine enthusiasts believe that large wineries are incapable of producing very fine wines because of a "corporate" mentality. Such is nonsense. Many large wineries are producing names that rival the best of California's boutique wines or France's prestigious châteaux. These "giants" have the substantial capital to provide their winemakers with the means to develop new techniques and can at the same time absorb the cost of keeping poor vintages or winemaking "mistakes" off the market — a luxury few boutiques can afford!

1) Some wineries are operated by people with a broad knowledge of wine. They entered the business because of their love of fine wine and the desire to make wines as a means of creative fulfillment. Frequently, they left better-paying professions to

devote themselves to wine and the special quality of life found in California's wine districts. They limit what is made and also control how and where their wines are sold. They are concerned about image and reputation; they strive to produce the best wines they can in a unique style reflecting their personal wine preferences.

2) Many wineries were started by successful businessmen who became tired of the high-pressured life that brought them money but little meaning and contentment. They were attracted to the image of winemaking, and often winegrowing, because of its simplicity, its back-to-nature appeal, and their overall idealism and individualism. They began with no knowledge of wine, except for a love of drinking it; but what they brought to the wine trade was keen, business acumen. They applied that to the creation and marketing of their wines.

3) A large number of existing wineries were started by people who were enthusiastic about wine but insensitive to its subtleties, unaware of wine tradition, without technical training or experience and without the least hint of the requirements necessary to operate a winery as a business. (They can be compared to the poorly financed entrepreneur who is drawn to the restaurant profession, starts without experience, and frequently fails.) As a result, the wines they make suffer from their enthusiasm coupled with a lack of knowledge about making wine and what it should taste like. Often they produce wines which are grotesque, exaggerated in style, heavy-handed, and excessive in every possible way.

4) There also many entrepreneurs who are in the wine business primarily to make a profit. They are not interested in producing esoteric wines, but in making honest wines sold for general consumption at reasonable prices. Many of these are fairly large, family-owned wineries who carry on a family tradition of private business.

5) Finally, there are the huge, long-established wine companies such as Almadén, Paul Masson, Gallo, and the like, who specialize in producing inexpensive wines for the mass market. They are well-financed, innovative, constantly on the lookout for new and better techniques to produce good-quality everyday wine at an attractive price. Not unlike other mass marketers, most of them are sensitive to the fact that the public demands quality and maintain sophisticated quality controls, from the growing of the grape to the final sale off the retail shelf. Most are responsive to consumer complaints and monitor their wines by purchasing them in retail stores for tasting and analysis. (Not long ago a major wine company recalled fifty thousand cases of a varietal wine based on my complaint!) That is not to say that all are excellent; as in any industry, some brands are superior to others. But, as a general rule, jug and moderately priced premium wines from reputable American wineries in this category provide the best wine values in the world.

The principle difference, today, between importers and United States producers is that the former are mainly concerned with selling numerous types of wine and building brand loyalty, but are far removed from the day-to-day production of the product and its requisite quality controls. Domestic producers are "on line" all the time. And while an importer can abandon a winery or brand at will, since he rarely maintains an equity position in the property, a United States producer has a considerable investment in plant, equipment, and wine in cask.

My assessment of the future development of the Wine Trade, over-all, is optomistic. Major marketers like Pepsi and Coke have entered the wine industry in a big way bringing with them both business acumen and product awareness that should make the rest of the industry more responsive to the pulse of the market. Futhermore, I suspect that at least one prestigious Graduate School of Business will develop a program addressing the needs of this billion-dollar industry. I also suspect that importers and wine merchants will become increasingly aware of the importance of understanding their wares and will develop the ability to discern the good from the bad. The archaic federal and state regulations regarding the sale and distribution of wine should become less onerous under the pressure of consumer advocates such as myself. Tainted wines and fraudulent imports, conceivably, will be driven off the market by sound business competition and/or actions of various consumer protection agencies, or by concerned and knowledgeable consumers who bring pressure to correct abuses through the media or through the courts. All in all, I firmly believe that the refined and sophisticated taste of the American consumer, armed with a little wine education, will direct the wine trade to a bright future.

WINE ADVERTISING

The advertising of wine has suddenly become as prominent as the advertising of dish washing soap, blue jeans, and dog food. The major difference is that most Americans have been washing dishes, wearing clothes, and feeding their pets for a longer time than they have been drinking wine. Unfortunately, the public's innocence, ignorance, and naïveté have all been exploited in wine advertising, which frequently disregards the standards of ethics of the media industry. Until government agencies and the media become cognizant of these abuses, the only defense against claims of advertising "truth" is a better background and understanding of wine. Once the media powers that be (TV networks particularly) develop the sophistication to distinguish between the many deceptive wine ads and those which are accurate and fair, I am certain that many of the abuses I mention will come to an abrupt halt.

Many of the deceptive wine advertisments are guilty of erroneous logic. Let's look at just a few examples.

Several years ago (before being acquired by the Coca-Cola Company) the Taylor Wine Company had a very clever ad campaign which featured a cartoon figure called the "Answer Grape." Nothing wrong with this, but the answers frequently disregarded common ethics. In one, the voice-over asks if the consumer is confused by the different types of Chablis: *Grands Crus, Petit Chablis, Premiers Crus*, and an individual Chablis *Grand Cru* vineyard, I don't remember which one. The Answer Grape provides a reassuring way to avoid further quandaries: drink Taylor Chablis. Now, of course, the point is never made that the Chablis mentioned in the ad are all French, and by law produced from the Chardonnay grape; that the different levels (*Grands Crus*, et al) relate, rather precisely, to growing areas, vine yields, and minimum alcohol levels, and that, other than a misused name, these wines have nothing in common with the wine made in New York State. To suggest that Taylor Chablis, an American white wine which can be made from any grape variety and in any style, was a viable substitute for authentic French Chablis, is to present the consumer with blatantly deceptive and fraudulent information. Technically, the advertisement is guilty of what is known in symbolic logic as the Fallacy of Association.

Another series of wine ads based on this fallacy of logic was recently run by the Gold Seal Wine Company (before being acquired by Seagram's), which predominantly produces New York State Champagne. One of its Champagnes is made entirely from the French *vinifera* varieties which are used in authentic French Champagne. The vast majority of Gold Seal Champagne, however, is made from native American grape varieties. A voice, decidedly French, questions another Frenchman as to his drinking Gold Seal Champagne. The second Frenchman counters that the Gold Seal Champagne is made by the same methods, the same grapes, and that he, himself, was French and the actual winemaker. All these statements were true of ONE Gold Seal Champagne, but NOT the Champagne depicted in the commercial.

Another commercial claims that Gold Seal Catawba wine, an inexpensive and rather ordinary still table wine, is made from "Champagne" grapes. The point is that Gold Seal uses Catawba in its New York State Champagne. However, the Catawba is NOT a grape used in authentic French Champagne as the commerical would like its viewers to believe.

The same kind of misleading thinking can be applied to areas in which grapes are grown. Again from Taylor, we learn how its Rhine wine is made from grapes grown at the same latitude as the finest wines of Germany's Rhine Valley. Thus, the consumer appears to be informed that Taylor Rhine wine has a quality and character similar to wines grown in the Rhine region in Germany. The fact is that Taylor Rhine wine has no resemblance to authentic Rhine wines from Germany; that native American grapes were used in the Taylor product, and that the climate, despite similar latitudes, would be unsuitable for growing the German varieties even if Taylor sought to use them.

Champagnes, being somewhat festive and mysterious, come into more than a full-share of advertising abuse. The promotional logic runs by syllogism: the best French Champagnes are made by the *méthode champenoise* (fermented in the bottle), a true statement. Some domestic Champagne is made by the same procedure, (also true). Therefore, our Champagne is as good as French Champagne. Far from it! For it does not necessarily follow that an identical method of production *alone* guarantees similar quality.

Banfi, a major importer has begun to advertise "Pure and Natural" in an attempt to capitalize on the trend toward natural and organic food items. In the minds of many, this implies something better, or more healthful. As every winemaker in the world will point out, over and over again, if grapes were allowed to ferment into wine naturally, without the use of certain chemicals and techniques, the result would be vinegar. Wine is simply a mid-point in the process of producing vinegar, thus, it spoils easily. In the winery, chemicals are essential to prevent wine from continuing its development into vinegar. Without the use of pesticides and fungicides in the vineyard and without sulfur dioxide during fermentation, there would be very little palatable wine today. Certainly, some wineries use enzymes and other processes to make inexpensive wines, but all use certain basic chemicals and technical techniques; Banfi's producers do so too. In purist terms, "Pure and Natural" wine, as a claim, is total bunk! Banfi's claim is that they use less chemicals, and never use certain chemicals and techniques that their competitors use, hence *their* wines are "Pure and Natural." The theme is not just false, deceptive, and unfairly competitive, it also could be dangerous to those with restricted diets who may believe that Banfi's wines would not contain substances incompatable to special diets.

Another fallacy of association is the reference to an award won for a vintage other than that actually in the bottle. For example, Marquis de Riscal, a Spanish Rioja, pictures gold medals on its label which indicate that it was "Awarded the Gold Medal at the Paris Exposition of 1890". Resting on the laurels of an age-old accolade for an entirely different bottle of wine presumes the same quality, long-standing tradition, and success for a wine which was perhaps no longer made the same way, or is otherwise unworthy of any award. It also presumes that the award-granting standards had validity beyond commercial chicanery. Of course, the historical claim says nothing about the quality of either present-day wines or the specific wine in the bottle so-labeled. As we shall see in a moment, most wine awards are relatively meaningless and frequently deceptive when used in advertising or to grace wine labels to induce the consumer to buy the wine. I have suggested to the B.A.T.F. that all such claims be prohibited on wine labels.

Wine competitions are quite popular today, and wineries eagerly seek awards at the hundreds conducted every year. Every winery loves to be a winner and there are enough competitions with low standards to accommodate most of them. The deceit lies in the fact that the standards used to grant awards make the awards meaningless. Most wine judging competitions are *not* conducted in a professional manner in which the results could be scientifically projected to be repeatable, or would, in fact, be repeatable, using the same judges. Frequently, the judges are amateurs, who are neither instructed, no trained in what to look for, and competitions often fail to establish any criteria as to what the judges should consider worthy of merit. Furthermore, judges are rarely tested for competence; their "reputations" (frequently un-warranted) earn them invitations. There are few experts who have the competency to assess the hundreds, sometimes thousands, of wines which are sampled over a few days. The result is that even professional tasters become fatigued or are often rushed into making assessments. Wines are often scored as a result of group discussions where judges are more concerned with "looking good" rather than casting a dissen-ting vote. I could go on and on. Scholars, such as Dr. Maynard Amerine, the respected professor emeritus of the University of California's Department of Enology, at Davis, concurs with my objections and equally considers the awards granted at such events meaningless.

Many wine ads or wine labels contain the terms "premium, " "classic," or "rare," inferring that these terms have some standard of usage. Nothing could be further from true. For example, Paul Masson, which ranks among the top four wine pro-ducers in the United States, uses the term "rare" on its generic wines which are neither seldom (scarce) nor rare (exceptional). Also, Paul Masson wines are "Never sold before their time," but neither are those of their competitors. The wines in ques-tion rarely remain at the winery past the second year of their vintage.

Other brands are promoted as being "better" on the basis of being made from "one hundred percent" of something, either all of a specific grape, or all from a par-ticular locale. However, wine made from this "one hundred percent" is no guarantee that it is "better." It depends on just what the "one hundred per cent," is. Often, one hundred per cent is *not* better, for example, wines made from one hundred percent Cabernet Sauvignon, a noble grape variety, often benefit from the blending of a more mellow variety, like Merlot for added suppleness, complexity or character.

Vintage claims are often the subject of deceptive advertising. One California pro-ducer claims that "Vintage dating makes it right." The inference is that vintage dating makes it better or more desirable, which is not the case with the wines in question. As we have already seen, the vintage date only refers to when the grapes were harvested and the wine fermented, and implies nothing else with regard to a winery's standards. Several decades ago, European producers did not offer wine from a particularly bad vintage and therefore, a "vintage wine" had significance in relation to quality. Now, however, with rare exceptions, almost all wines, above jug wine quality, are released with a vintage date.

Off-vintages of world famous wines are also the subject of abuse. The implication is that a wine from a renowned wine estate is always better than less-famous wines.

Frequently these wines suffer wider swings in quality in poor vintages than their less renowned neighbors, yet they are promoted at excessive prices which, in light of the usual selling price, seem to be bargains. For example, 1965 was one of the worst vintages for Bordeaux in the Twentieth Century. Bordeaux's most famous wine, Château Lafite-Rothschild, produced one of its worst wines during that vintage. In more ethical times it would have been sold-off for regional blending. Instead, it was bottled and highly promoted by several reputed New York City wine merchants as a rare opportunity to experience this "excellent" wine at bargain prices. Because of their reputation for bottling wines under their own name only during meritorious vintages, the proprietors of Château Lafite-Rothschild had, in effect, deceived the public into believing that they were buying something considerably better than what was actually in the bottle. Incidentally, a nearby château bottled a small quantity of 1965 and recalled it shortly thereafter. It was considerably better than the Lafite.

Some advertisements attempting to capitalize on a notion that was, at one time, true for certain French wines from Bordeaux and Burgundy, claim that "Estate Bottling" makes their wines better. The original purpose of this statement was to prevent fraudulent labeling of wines which were in limited supply. For most wines which are "estate bottled," today, such labeling is not a concern and merely indicates that the wine was made and bottled under certain legal controls. It is no guarantee that the wine is any better for it.

A recent wrinkle in wine promotion is the growing use of comparative advertising which depends on groups or so-called wine experts to endorse the wine based on the results of tastings against similar wines from other producers. It has proven to be the most effective way to build a new wine brand. Such comparisons have the potential to deceive if the methods used for the comparative tastings lack a scientific basis, or the so-called experts lack real expertise. There is nothing wrong with comparative advertising; it is used for many other products, and I strongly advocate it as beneficial to the consumer in terms of price competition and providing an incentive to the wine industry to improve the quality of its wines. But in order to be accurate, such comparisons must be based on scientifically acknowledged testing methods. For wine, this means blind tastings, repeated numerous times and statistically analyzed to guarantee that the results would be repeated every time the test was given to prevent conclusions based on a fortuitous accident.

Taylor California Cellars, a relatively new brand of the Taylor Wine Company, used comparative advertising to build its brand using "experts" as tasters. But, their advertising was deceptive both in content and context. Taylor's methods of comparing wines failed to meet industry tasting standards. Their results did *not* scientifically prove that their experts actually would choose the Taylor wines consistently if the test was repeated.

Taylor's tasters became "experts" because of reputation, often self-promoted, or because of some professional involvement that may not signify any special training or professional in winetasting. Taylor failed to test the knowledge or tasting expertise of their experts to determine whether their experts were, indeed, qualified.

WRITERS ON WINE

Throughout this book I have alluded to the mass of misinformation; elitist attitudes, and lack of conceptual thinking that permeate wine literature. Much of this relates to the fact that wine writing has not attracted a wealth of erudite writers who devote their major efforts to the subject. When you come down to the facts, I suppose this void relates to economics: The media doesn't consider the subject of wine to be of great interest, and wine publications can't afford large fees; therefore, wine writing for periodicals is not a lucrative profession. Wine books are rarely well-promoted; few sell in sufficient quantities to support their authors, and consequently writers desiring an affluent lifestyle shy away from wine.

But there are many writers on wine. The latest count is well over two hundred. This includes a local wine afficionado, or a newspaper reporter on another beat, who also gets to write the wine column and becomes a self-styled wine expert relying primarily on book knowledge and self-learned tasting techniques. There is nothing wrong with this; but frequently, these individuals are more concerned with prestige rather than expertise. Many wine columnists, particularly on smaller newspapers, are local wine hobbyists who write for fun and little or no remuneration. Major newspapers prefer to use staff which, I suppose, justifies making a newspaper's financial writer or society editor the resident wine expert. Thus, there are few well-paying media outlets for the professional winewriter who devotes his full time and effort to his subject.

A reporter need not be an expert on a subject to write about it, but he should exercise the same care and concern as he would with serious news. Frequently, though, little thought or effort goes into newspaper wine columns. Columnists frequently accept what industry spokesmen tell them without question or corroboration. Public Relations agencies thrive on this sad state of affairs. A wine writer who shapes opinions on the basis of his own personal expertise must be more than a reporter. He must be an expert. Yet in few cases is he ever provided with the luxury of the requisite time to become an expert.

Although there is no excuse for blind reporting or sloppy research, I'm not sure the blame for bad wine writing lies solely on the writer's shoulder. As you know from reading this book, which really only covers the most rudimentary essentials, learning everything about wine is an exhausting, time consuming process. Real mastery of the subject takes years to acquire, and few if any wine writers have the energy and money to become professional wine experts before they become wine writers. Unless he has been fortunate enough to be friends with one of the really great wine experts of the world, the wine writer's only other alternative is to pour through the mass of sometimes technical, frequently inaccurate books that now exist and learn as he earns. Because this material is often biased or inaccurate, the wine writer cultivates wine prejudices and snobbisms which he then transfers to his readers. This is the state of much of today's wine writing.

Many years ago when the "white with fish, red with meat, rosé every other time" philosophy of wine dominated American perceptions, this kind of reporting may have sufficed. However, with today's growing interest in wines, a plethora of choices and inflated prices, the American wine buyer needs good, sound information on which to rely.

Several things can happen when a wine writer is not wine expert.

- He can recycle wrong or misleading information supplied by distributors, or importers through press releases.

- He can become victim to the P.R. hype designed by marketing mavens to spur consumer interest in products that, without the hype, would not really be very noteworthy.

- Although he may, indeed, do comparative tastings of wines, unless he has a well-developed palate, there is no guarantee that his recommendation is not merely an amateur's opinion of the best in a bad bunch of wines.

- Lastly, I am sad to admit, there is a group of wine writers who exploit the wine industry by insisting on "perks" for including mention in their articles or columns. While many wine writers feel obligated repay PR "junkets" with some kind of favorable coverage, this group but can be counted on for repaying pampering with major stories in influential publications. Several of these writers lead luxurious lives of constant travel and regal wining and dining that would be beyond the means of anyone but the most wealthy.

This chapter is not meant to be an indictment of wine writers, but rather to point the reader in the direction of good solid information. Once you are able to identify and isolate particular qualities and/or flaws in wines, and develop your own preferences, you can pit your own judgement against one or more writers' evaluations and begin to find a favorite of your own on whom you can rely. The following are brief assessments of this country's most published writers along with few of the best known foreign ones who, either frequent the pages of magazines and newspapers on a relatively large scale or who have books currently in print with a major publisher.

LEON D. ADAMS is a wine historian without rival. His book, *The Wines of America*, is the standard backgrounder for United States wines. Adams is an excellent researcher and has a way of organizing and expressing wine history that make for fine reading.

GERALD ASHER has been the wine writer for *Gourmet* Magazine for several years now. He is British and has long been involved in the wine trade. Today, he is an importer and sales agent. Seldom critical, sometimes quite thought-provoking, Asher's essays are generally well-wrought, polished, and enchanting to read.

ROBERT LAWRENCE BALZER lives in Southern California, writes for the *Los Angeles Times*, offers a syndicated wine column, and publishes his *Private Guide to Wine and Food.* He has also written several books, including the first, in 1948, on California's fine wines. Balzer is a well-respected figure. He has tremendously wide experience and a fine palate.

ALEXIS BESPALOFF entered the wine trade after earning an MBA at Harvard. He is the author of several wine books and also writes regularly for *New York* magazine. Bespaloff has a good, wide knowledge of wines, and a much better than average palate. His writing style is pleasantly facile and he is able to simplify difficult subjects and write for a popular audience.

ANTHONY DIAS BLUE began as a restaurant reviewer and expanded into wine reporting quickly, writing for *Bon Appetit*, the *San Francisco Chronicle*, and numerous freelance outlets. He knows his wine and has an exceptional "taste memory." He also covers wine and food on a popular weekly program for CBS network radio.

MICHAEL BROADBENT is a British wine authority who has become a legend in the wine world. As Director of the Wine Department of Christie's, the prestigious London auction house, he has tasted more old vintage wines than anyone. He has an impeccable palate and an extraordinary ability to describe the attributes of rare wine in a thoroughly engrossing and enchanting way. His *Wine Tasting* is the best book on the subject and his most recent work *The Great Vintage Wine Book* has quickly found its place as a classic in the literature of wine.

JOEL P. BUTLER is a wine merchant in Berkeley, California and a regular contributor to *Vintage*. He began his wine career by importing Italian wines. His writing is directed toward providing a solid reference point and a critical evaluation. He is a thorough, conscientious taster with an ever-improving palate.

CREIGHTON CHURCHILL has been writing about wines for years. He is the author of *The Notebook on the Wines of France*, the *Great Wine Rivers* (both out of print), and *The Wines of the World*. Churchill occasionally contributes articles to magazines, but concentrates most of his efforts as the wine consultant to American Airlines. He has an exceptionally good palate, wide knowledge of wine, and a marvelous writing style. Unfortunately we do not see enough of him in print.

NATHAN CHROMAN is the weekly columnist for the *Los Angeles Times*, and the Chairman, for many years, of the L.A. County Wine Judging. He is a full time attorney and a full time wine lover. His writing style is engaging, and easy-to-read.

SCOTT CLEMENS has worked in various capacities within the wine industry for a decade. He appears regularly in *Vintage* magazine writing the results of the *Vintage* Tasting Panel's critical wine assessments as "Special Reports." He is a thorough researcher, has a good palate, and writes in a lucid style.

WILLIAM CLIFFORD lives in Connecticut and writes for several magazines. Though it is rarely apparent in his writings, Clifford has, probably, the most extraordinary wealth of wine knowledge of any American-born writer. His memory is photographic; his note taking copious, and his recall amazing. For many years he has syndicated a wine column.

BARBARA ENSRUD is an up-and-coming wine writer appearing in the *New York Daily News* and occasionally in several large-circulation magazines. She travels extensively through the wine regions and has developed a good basic wine knowledge. Her tasting assessments, particularly of new French vintages, are, on occassion, at odds with the opinions of the recognized authorites on the subject. She writes well and is most competent when writing about the people and places of the wine world.

ROBERT FINIGAN is another Harvard graduate who went west in the late 1960s to eventually fall into wine reporting. He publishes a private guide to wines published under his name. He regularly travels to France to report on current developments.

EUNICE FRIED began as a travel writer and moved into wine and other subjects as a popular writer. Fried remains a popular generalist, rarely critical, and is unwilling or unable to separate the hype from the truth. She travels extensively and has been referred to as the "press-junket queen" of the wine world. Allegedly, she has been known to repay these "free trips" with enchanting articles even when the wines of the region are unworthy of attention.

EMMANUEL AND MADELINE GREENBERG are husband and wife who appear together as well as individually in large circulation magazines such as *Playboy* writing about wines and spirits on a popular level. As serious wine writers thay have appeared in *Vintage* magazine demonstrating good palates and superb command of wine tasting nomenclature.

ROY ANDRIES DE GROOT is a masterful food writer who has ventured into the wine arena claiming to be an expert. In his latest book on American wine he expounds his personal "classification" of the two hundred supreme wineries of America based on twenty years of research which included studying their soil and weather, evaluating their "efficiency" and tasting some 128,500 bottles using the "tasting standards" of the "Classification of 1855 of Bordeaux." There were no such standards! Such is De Groot's wine expertise. Enough! In my evaluation of wine experts he ranks supreme only as winedom's foremost bunco artist.

RICHARD PAUL HINKLE is a freelance writer contributing to several wine publications, including *Vintage*. He is a fine researcher and interviewer, and writes in a very ingratiating style. His forte lies in human interest stories and history. He also contributes columns to the *San Francisco Examiner and The Wine Spectator*.

HUGH JOHNSON is an Englishman, graduate of Cambridge. He has a marvelous talent to absorb information and then use it to convey important facts to a wide audience. This applies to his books about both wines and about gardening. His wine books — *Wine, The World Atlas of Wine,* and *The Pocket Encyclopedia of Wine* — likely rank among the top ten best-selling wine books. Though he does have a fine palate, he does not critique individual wines in his writing.

ALEXIS LICHINE is one of the most knowledgeable men on the subject of wine. As an importer he educated America to fine French wine encouraging fine restaurants and liquor retailers to carry the finest wines of France. He is presently proprietor of Chateau Priere-Lichine, one of the classified growths of Bordeaux. His *Wines and Vineyards of France* and *Encyclopedia of Wines & Spirits* are the best on the subject. They are revised regularly and continue to be best-sellers. Lichine's palate is truly professional; his wine knowledge awesome. He writes in an authoritive as well as engaging style.

WILLIAM MASSEE was once a leading wine writer advancing the cause of California wine long before many of the current wine writers were old enough to drink. He wrote well and had a good basic wine knowledge. Although some of his books can still be found in bookstores he is virtually a forgotten wine figure today.

ROBERT J. MISCH has been a fixture in wine journalism for many years on a very popular level. His books are basic primers on how-to approach wine; books, all written in the "quick guide" format. He contributes regularly to magazines writing at a popular level in a jaunty style.

OLKEN (CHARLES) AND SINGER (EARL) are co-editors of *The Connoisseurs' Guide to California Wines*, a bi-monthly newsletter. Both men were wine lovers before launching their wine newsletter. The authors claim totaste wine everyday. Olken admits to not evaluating his palate prior to tasting claiming that he never has a bad "tasting day," a claim no professional would make. As such, his ratings may lack consistency.

FRANK PRIAL is the wine columnist for the *New York Times*. Before serving as *Times* wine columnist, he was a general news reporter, and an excellent one at that. Prial learned on the wine beat and developed a reasonably well-respected palate.

PETER QUIMME is a pen name for a husband and wife team, best known for the *Signet Book of American Wines*. They are good researchers and adept at covering wide territory in condensed fashion. They have reasonably good palates and wine backgrounds; and a better than average writing style. They are currently wine editors for the *International Review of Food and Wine*.

TERRY ROBARDS was the wine columnist for the *New York Times* until he was removed from his column for violating the *Times'* ethics regarding "commercial tie-ins" and "conflict of interest." Although he is a seasoned reporter and writes in a lucid style, his *Times* columns have contained many errors of fact, sloppy reporting and ill-founded conclusions. It is said that his premature assessment of the 1980 French vintage as a disaster assassinated that vintage. Important consumer issues were rarely covered and he buried an important *Vintage* magazine exposé regarding fraudulent dealings at the 1980 Heublein Wine Auction. Presently he is the wine columnist for the *New York Post* where his column retains the style, flavor and content it had at the *Times*.

HANK RUBIN is Managing Editor of *Vintage* magazine and is also a regular contributor to *Vintage*. His knowledge and curiosity range widely into all subjects related to wine. As a former restaurateur and now a gourmet cook, he has an extremely good palate, but prefers neither to report critical rankings, nor to get involved in wine judgings.

ROBERT SCHOOLSKY is primarily a businessman specializing in computer data processing. As a wine enthusiast he became the wine columnist for *Newsday*, the leading Long Island (New York) daily newspaper. He is also Eastern Editor of *Winestate* magazine. As a relative newcomer to wine writing he has a basic book knowledge and is learning critical wine tasting "on the job."

PHILIP SELDON is Publisher and Editor of Vintage Magazine. He founded the Wine Magazine industry in America with his launching of *Vintage* Magazine in 1971. As this critique is autobiographical let it be said that several recognized authorities attest to his consistency and expertise as a wine taster and critic. His frank candor, and his hard-hitting investigative reporting has caused him to be considered as "controversial" by many in the wine trade. He has exposed more than one wine scandal. Seldon assesses his writing style as adequate; his secret desire is to attain the eloquent prose style of other writers he holds in high regard.

PETER SICHEL heads a leading German wine firm bearing his family name. He has been a long time resident of the United States and is one of the leading wine figures on the international wine scene. His book *Which Wine?* was well received. He recently revised the late Frank Schoonmaker's *Wines of Germany* making it one of the most authoritative and honest, yet understandable, works on this difficult subject. He has a exceptional palate and an extraordinary knowledge of German wine.

HARVEY STEIMAN, a newspaper reporter, has covered sports, and food, and is now the food and wine editor with the San Francisco *Examiner.* His style is well-above average for newspaper reporting..

CHARLES L. SULLIVAN is a full-time teacher whose serious hobby is wine history. He contributes frequently to *Vintage* and other wine and historical publications. He has a smooth style, and is always well-documented and researched.

BOB THOMPSON has written *The California Wine Book,* the popular *Sunset Guide to California's Wine Country*, and, more recently, *The Pocket Encyclopedia to California Wines*. Thompson favors offering background (historical, personal, or whatever) as opposed to offering his own judgments and wine opinions. He writes in a down-to-earth, homey, and very accessible style.

SHELDON AND PAULINE WASSERMAN are a husband and wife team who specialize in the wines of Italy and the Rhone district of France. They are good researchers going directly to the source for intensive study of their subjects. They write well and have good command of their subject though their writing occasionally tends to become mired with excessive detail. They have authored several books and contribute regularly to *Vintage* magazine.

WINE BOOKS

Now that you have read this far you are ready to further your wine education. There have been many wine books published to aid you in this pursuit. Those listed are currently in print or can still be found on the shelves of bookstores. If you can't find a particular title you may write *Vintage* magazine at the address listed on page 351 for a suitable source.

GENERAL COVERAGE

WINE: AN INTRODUCTION FOR AMERICANS by M.A. Amerine & V. L. Singleton, 532 pp. A popular textbook written by two of the top wine "academics" in America. Covers grapes, wine varieties, wine production, etc. Scholarly in its approach, as it is an undergraduate level college introductory text for those who will enter the winemaking profession. $7.95

COMMONSENSE BOOK OF WINE by Leon Adams, 228 pp. A good beginner's primer. Breezy style and some solid information. Wine recommendations are too vague to be of much use. Enjoyable reading. Paperback. $5.95

ON WINE by Gerald Asher, 222 pp. Thirty of the author's *Gourmet* magazine essays have been updated, revised and put into this book. Asher explains about wines, not as a text, but rather leads the way to learning with charm and wit. $15.95

THE GREAT VINTAGE WINE BOOK, by Michael Broadbent, 432 pp. This is a well-written, informative and massive compilation of tasting notes spanning centuries of wines from Bordeaux, Burgundy, Champagne, Germany and Portugal, among others. The tasting notes are rounded out by vintage evaluations, a glossary of tasting terms and a set of full color pages depicting the effect of aging on a wine's color. This is a singular volume, bound to please the venophile. $25.

WINE TASTING by Michael Broadbent, 96 pp. This is the standard reference for the wine enthusiast. Covers tasting techniques, appreciation and assessment, wine tasting terms in English, French and German. This is an important book no serious student of wine should be without. Paperback. $10.

THE JUG WINE BOOK by Robert Burger, 153 pp. A rather ridiculous book which attempts to explain jug wines, but overwhelms the reader with the author's attempt to prove his knowledge of the best wines of the world. Paperback. $4.95

THE GREAT WINE RIVERS by Creighton Churchill, 222 pp. An enchantingly written personal tour of the most famous wine regions which straddle the rivers of France and Germany. Covers Bordeaux, Burgundy, the Rhône and Loire regions of France and the Mosel and Rhine regions of Germany. Skillfully written, accurate, with an emphasis on expensive wines. Unfortunately now out of date, but well worth reading for Churchill's delightful prose. Published at $14.95.

LAROUSSE DICTIONARY OF WINES OF THE WORLD by Doctor Gerard Debuigne, 272 pp. This full color, lavishly illustrated book from the famous French publisher provides rather useless alphabetical entries covering the major wines, producing areas, and vinicultural practices. Text shows little effort or interest on the part of its publisher to do more than fill space between illustrations. $14.95

THE JOYS OF WINE by Clifton Fadiman & Sam Aaron, 450 pp. The most lavish wine book ever published. Opulent paper, die cut binding and magnificent photos in a large format. Written by two men who have a way with words and a love for wine. Delightful as a collector's book, for the arm chair reader who loves the romance of wine, or as a study of the mystique. Its information is somewhat dated and the book is out of print. Worth looking for to add panache to your wine library. Published at $45.

PLAYBOY'S BOOK OF WINE by Peter and Paul Gillette, 252 pp., many color plates. The original version seriously and inaccurately libeled a prominent Italian wine firm. Playboy quickly recalled the book and replaced the offending pages. Such is the caliber of this book. Worthwhile only for its color plates. $19.95

GROSSMAN'S GUIDE TO WINES, BEERS & SPIRITS by Harold J. Grossman; revised by Grossman's disciple Harriet Lembeck, 564 pp. Ponderous in content and style. Interesting similarities to the text of *Alexis Lichine's Encyclopedia of Wines and Spirits*, to which it is no equal. Includes information on operating a wine shop or bar. Best suited as a training manual for the retail trade. $17.95

WINE by Hugh Johnson, 254 pp. A classic that is must reading for Johnson's beautiful prose, if not for its solid and comprehensive information. Current edition is somewhat out of date, particularly in its coverage of California wines, but it is impeccably accurate in its information. Johnson's love of the subject is stimulating and infectious. $15.95

HOW TO TEST AND IMPROVE YOUR WINE JUDGING ABILITY by Irving H. Marcus, 96 pp. Attempts to cover the subjective art of wine tasting. Fails in its execution. Paperback. $3.95

WINE SECRETS by Dennis Overstreet, 181 pp. A pretty coffee table book which contains some useful information, but is filled with nonsense on astrology, sophomoric humor, and condescending kitsch. Reads more like a gossip column than a winebook. $25.

THE TASTE OF WINE by Pamela Vandyke Price, 192 pp., color photos. A popular book written primarily for a British audience. Its author is a well-known figure in the British food and wine establishment. Well written, but of limited use to Americans. $14.95

THE GREAT WINE GRAPES AND THE WINES THEY MAKE by Bern C. Ramey, 256 pp., full color photos. A large-format salute to the classic wine grapes and the wines they produce written in an attractive popular style accompanied by magnificent full color photographs of each variety. Printed as a collector's book with high grade paper and binding.

THE NEW YORK TIMES BOOK OF WINE by Terry Robards, 128 pp. This book, authored by the former New York Times' wine critic, appears to be a pitiful attempt to compete with Alexis Lichine's encyclopedia. It is inept in concept, poorly executed and contains many inaccuracies. $11.95

THE GREAT WINE BOOK by Jancis Robinson, 240 pp., color photographics and illustrations.York, Another coffee table book, that has much information, attractively presented. It covers France (Bordeaux, Burgundy, Chablis, Rhone, Loire, Champagne and Alsace), Germany, Italy, Spain, California, and Australia. The writing is clear and clean, the photographs are a delight, and he information accurate. This book is to be valued, and heartily recommended $29.95

WHICH WINE? by Peter M.F. Sichel and Judy Lee Allen, 242 pp. A best-selling, explicit purchasing guide to the wines of the world by a leading figure in the international trade. Author Sichel, unfortunately, fails to share his opinions on wines he tasted for the book but rejected as unworthy, since many of them grace wineshops to lure his unsuspecting readers when recommended wines are not available. Now considerably outdated. Paperback $5.95

WINES OF THE WORLD by Andre Simon, editied by Serena Sutcliffe, 630 pp., 56 full color plates. Once the bible of wine books, this compilation has been completely revised and updated. Its contributors are the leading authorities on each wine region covered. This useful and enthrallingly written classic covers all the major wine producing areas of the world, with an expanded section on North America. Contains 29 new maps. $35.

GREAT VINEYARDS AND WINEMAKERS edited by Serena Sutcliff, 256 pp., profusely illustrated. This handsome large sized coffee-table book outlines the history and winemaking of sixty-five great vineyards from France, Germany, Italy, Australia, and California. With noted authorities as contributors and Master of Wine Sutcliff as editor this book is most authorative. The vineyards are well chosen to provide a wide range of wine and winemaking techiniques. The photographs are exciting and informative and beautifully reproduced. This book deserves a place in any wine library. $25

THE WINE HANDBOOK by Serena Sutcliffe, 224pp. Published in a three ring binder (8-3/4" x 7-1/4") this is handsomely done with excellent artwork, but in an almost impossible format. Her attempt is to lead the reader through tastings and to place the knowledge learned in the process into a larger context — and at the same time have room enough in the book for tasting notes. The result is a losing compromise. There are only places for 16 wines to be noted and in the rest of the book there is a sense of compressed writing, and of omissions because of space limitation. $14.95.

WINE DIARY by Harry Waugh, 208 pp., 28 photos and illustrations. A delightful account of the travels and wine tastings by one of the wine establishment's grand figures. Waugh writes in an enchanting style, as unique as the wines he tastes. Written for the wine buff, it should entertain anyone interested in learning about the subject. Dated in terms of the wines, timeless in its charm and cachet. $16.00

WHITE WINES OF THE WORLD by Sheldon & Pauline Wasserman, 256 pp. Written to introduce the novice to the recent white wine craze. Its dictionary format is not to my liking but it does contain some very useful information. It is somewhat dated now. $8.95

HISTORY AND ROMANCE

A HISTORY OF WINE by Warner Allen, 304 pp., 28 illustrations. Covers the history of wine during the fifteen centuries following the fall of the Roman Empire. A new edition of an important classic wine book. $8.95

THE FIRESIDE BOOK OF WINE by Alexis Bespaloff, 445 pp. A unique collection of writings on wine, by some of the world's greatest wine lovers, celebrating its glories and pleasures. Provides marvelous armchair reading. $12.95

THE WINE MASTERS by Nicholas Faith, 307 pp. A comprehensive examination of the Bordeaux wine market, its history, the families, businessmen, politics and intrigues. Provides insight into the economic structure of Bordeaux, its wine booms and scandals. $12.95

FOLK WINES, CORDIALS AND BRANDIES: HOW TO MAKE THEM ALONG WITH THE PLEASURES OF THEIR LORE by Moritz Jagendorf, 414 pp. This is an unusual book, full of behind-the-scenes and how-to's of folk wines. Recipes handed down through time for wines made from fruits, berries, flowers and herbs with do-it-yourself directions. Out of print but worth searching for. Published at $12.50

JEFFERSON AND WINE, THOMAS JEFFERSON: THE WINE CONNOISSEUR AND WINE GROWER, by R. de Treville Lawrence, 200 pp., 20 illustrations. Chronicles sixty-one years of Jefferson's love of viticulture and buying, storing, and making wine. Details Jefferson's enormous effort to cultivate European vines in the New World. Paperback. $4.95

KING TUT'S WINE CELLAR by Leonard Lesko, 124 pp., color photos, maps. The author, a professor of Egyptology, provides a fascinating account of the ancient Egyptian wine industry; its wine jar labeling, vintage dating, and vineyards. Includes King Tut's wine list. Paperback. $5.00

IN CELEBRATION OF WINE AND LIFE by Richard Lamb & Ernest Mittelberger, 255 pp., over 200 photos. Displays the treasures of the Wine Museum in San Francisco in its photos, many printed in rich color. Text is beautifully written and delightful to read. A most worthwhile book detailing the history of wine in illustration and text. $14.95

CHIANTI: A HISTORY OF FLORENCE AND ITS WINES by Lamberto Paronetto, 224 pp., illustrated in color. Covers the Tuscan way of life rather than detailing its wines, but paints an accurate picture of the Tuscan landscape, its history, and its people. $6.50

THE FATHER OF CALIFORNIA WINE, AGOSTON HARASZTHY, edited by Theodore Schoenman, and foreword by Robert Balzer, 1 9 2 pp., illustrations. A reprint of the 1862 edition of *Grape Culture, Wines and Wine Making* by Agoston Harazthy, himself, with information on the origins of the California wine industry and grape varieties. Balzer's forward leaves something to be desired. Of interest to serious wine and history buffs. $10

WINEMAKING IN CALIFORNIA, The Account in Words and Pictures of the Golden State's Two-Century Adventure With Wine, by Ruth Teiser and Catherine Harroun. The long subtitle of this book describes it well. Its coverage of the history of wine in California is wide-ranging, extensive and has the smell of authenticity. It is also written with a sense of proportion. The breadth of the 222 photographs and drawings is formidable. From copies of old bills of sale, frontispieces of old catalogues to photographs and lithographs they depict visually the movement of what has happened. It is an attractive coffee-table size. $24.94

GODS, WINE AND MEN by William Younger, 516 pp. A classic and authoritative popular history of wine that traces its earliest possible origins. Many beautiful color plates. Out of print but worth searching for.

REFERENCE BOOKS

WHERE THE GREAT GERMAN WINES GROW by Dr. Hans Ambrosi, 24 pp., drawings, maps. A detailed guide best used for wine touring or specific information on an individual wine estate. Describes locations, visiting hours, cellars and tasting rooms as well as the history of each vineyard, its owner and castles. It is not intended to be a guide to German wines. $9.95

THE WINE TASTING INDEX by Bacchus Data Services, 196 pp. A wine tasting index issued annually, referencing volume and page numbers of tasting notes published in all major wine magazines and newsletters. Provides ratings as well, but is best used in conjunction with indexed publications. Published primarily for wine buffs who subscribe to the listed publications. Cites *Vintage* Magazine as first in number of wine reviews published. Journal format. $12.95

THE CONCISE ATLAS OF WINE by W. Born, 190 full color photos and maps. Interesting for its pictures and specially prepared maps and advice for travelers. Otherwise not particularly noteworthy. $10

THE POCKET GUIDE TO WINE by Barbara Ensrud, 131 pp. Were it not for Hugh Johnson's *Pocket Encyclopedia of Wine*, this book wouldn't be half-bad. It contains a good deal of factual information but is flawed by some factual inaccuracies, a few obvious misjudgements particularly with regard to individual wine and vintage ratings and a large production blunder (it's really too large to be a pocket book). More importantly it is so similar in style to the superior Johnson book that it does not represent a good value. Too bad, since Ms. Ensrud is an up and coming winewriter and should be capable of much better work - or at least something more original. $4.95

THE WINE MASTER'S GUIDE TO EUROPE by Anthony Hogg, 240 pp., photos and maps. This practical guidebook provides precise travel directions and procedures for making appointments to visit over 300 listed vineyards and cellars in France, Germany, Italy, Spain, Portugal, Austria and Hungary. Includes distilleries in Scotland for those so inclined. Paperback. $5.95

POCKET ENCYCLOPEDIA OF WINE by Hugh Johnson, illustrated. The first of the many pocket size guides. Lists many facts, abbreviated to the format of the book in individual sections for each country. Despite its title, the book isn't encyclopedic in scope, with many important terms omitted. Nevertheless it is useful and the best of its genre. $4.95

THE WORLD ATLAS OF WINE by Hugh Johnson. Original in its concept, it depicts each wine region with precise maps showing individual vineyards, wine regions, and other essential details (including many vital minor roadways) for the serious wine traveler. Its maps alone are most impressive — but also covers winemaking, label nomenclature, wine history, and wine service in a most incisive manner. $32.95

THE WHOLE WORLD WINE CATALOG by William Kaufman, 224 pp. An absurd compendium of 2,500 wine labels from all the major wine areas of the world, neglecting many important estates (like Ch. Mouton-Rothschild) who may not have sent its author a label. The book is an affrontary to the literature of wine but is typical of the author's work. Printed on poor grade newspaper stock as well. Among one of the worst wine books ever published. $5.95

ENCYCLOPEDIA OF WINES & SPIRITS by Alexis Lichine, 716 pp. This is one of the most comprehensive and most useful wine book for the serious student of wine. Well written, researched with great care, explains details in a popular, easy to read style, and comprehensive almost to a fault. The latest edition contains comprehensive coverage of American wines. This book has no peer. $25

GERMAN WINE ATLAS AND VINEYARD REGISTER by Edmund Pennig-Rowsell, 90 pp., 66 color-coded maps, 101 color photos. A useful full-color guide to all the important wine producing areas and vineyards of Germany. Includes information on soil, acreage, wine types, growers, and so forth. Paperback. $6.95

ENCYCLOPEDIA OF WINE by Frank Schoonmaker, 473 pp. Revised by Julius Wile following Schoonmaker's death. At best, it is a poor relative to the Lichine Encyclopedia. It contains many errors, provides lip-service to American wines, and includes maps which are an assault to the eye. $12.95

THE VINEYARD ALMANAC & WINE GAZETEER, 1983, Fifth Edition, 159 pp. This Almanac is a delight and chock-block full of information. Old fashioned in style with up-to-date-information with a specific focus on wine. The range is wide. The combination of a Winery Finder and a Winery Directory for the U.S. lets you find alphabetically all the wineries open to the public and how to get there. It has Vintage Reports and News, a monthly listing of sunrise and setting, the time the moon rises. Did you know that Prohibition began on January 16th, 1920 or that Ben Franklin was born on January 17th? It even has a Personal Wine Journal where you can jot down your buying or tasting notes. $3.95

AMERICA

THE WINES OF AMERICA by Leon Adams, 623 pp. A definitive history and discussion of the wineries of America, but not an explanation of its wines. Well written, opinionated, full of interesting personal experiences and anecdotes, but of limited usefulness to the wine novice. Its title is a misnomer — better titled as The Wineries of America. $14.95

WINES OF CALIFORNIA by Robert Balzer, 271 pp., 350 photos. A magnificent personal essay of California Wines from forty years of wine tasting and writing. Covers several of the most important regions and 128 of their most important wineries. The book is far from comprehensive but is worthwhile for its magnificent photographs alone. Balzer's writing style and insight are equally appealing. $25.

GREAT WINEMAKERS OF CALIFORNIA by Robert Benson & Andre Tchelistcheff, 303 pp., Great insights into the California Wine industry and the men who make its wines. A delightful and informative book for the serious wine buff. $15

TREASURY OF AMERICAN WINES by Nathan Chroman, 255 pp., 313 phots, 64 full color. A lavishly illustrated book worthwhile primarily for its photographs. Somewhat dated. $14.95

THE WINES OF CALIFORNIA, The Pacific Northwest and New York by Roy Andries De Groot, 1982, 461pp. This book may be the most outrageous wine book published in recent times if not ever! The information in it is frequently inaccurate -the author claims to have tasted wines which were never commercially made. His claims as to his intensive research are astounding! He has applied "tasting standards" that do not exist. The book is, in my opinion, a sham and an insult to the winemakers of America. $19.95

MASSEE'S GUIDE TO WINES OF AMERICA by William E. Massee, 264 pp. A seriously deficient book which was poorly researched, poorly executed, and fortunately now out of print. Still available in many bookstores. $8.95

JOYOUS ANARCHY - THE SEARCH FOR GREAT AMERICAN WINES by William E. Massee, 312 pp. The jacket of this 1978 book describes Massee as "America's foremost wine expert" and "grand master." The author's list of America's ten best wines includes Barbera and Gamay Beaujolais with no mention of Zinfandel. The book goes downhill from there. So much for expertise. Almost, but not quite, in the league of the DeGroot book. $10.95

THE CONNOISSERS' HANDBOOK OF CALIFORNIA WINES, 2nd Edition, by Charles Olken, Norman Roby and Earl Singer, 233 pp. Its comprehensive coverage of wine varieties, California vintages, wine geography, wineries and wines of California, the rest of the U.S. and Canada, and finally sections of wine language and touring are first rate. The writing is accurate and succinct and they have crammed a great deal of information into it. In the section of Wineries and Wine they cover some 400 entrees. For each winery is given its county of location, the founding date, the source of grapes, the wines that are produced and finally an evaluation of the winery and some of its wines. While some of their evaluations are unreliable, it is the best book on the subject in pocket size. $5.95

THE WINEMAKERS OF THE PACIFIC NORTHWEST by Elizabeth Purser & Lawrence Allen, 250 pp, 24 full color photos. A large format and definitive book on the new wineries and vineyards of Oregon and Washington. Opulent in its color photographs, paper and binding. $30.

CALIFORNIA WINES by Robert Thompson & editors of Sunset Books, 224 pp. A pictorial journey through California wine country about the wines and the people who make them. By the editors of Sunset Books under the direction of their wine authority, Robert Thompson. Contains many color photographs and useful information About individual wineries. $14.95

THE SIGNET BOOK OF AMERICAN WINE by Peter Quimme (pen name for John and Elen Walker), Third Edition, 324 pp. This is a practical and comprehensive introduction to American wine that compresses a mass of information in the small print and page size of a mass paperback. The Walkers know their wine and keep on top of the subject. The book covers American winemaking methods, wine catagories and grape varieties, and a brief history of the American wine industry. A capsul history is given for most of the important wineries along with comments on their wines. The book is authoritative but now is badly in need of revision. $2.50

FRANCE

SAUTERNES, by Jeffrey Benson & Allstair MacKenzie, 184 pp, 19 illustrations, 4 maps. A study of the great sweet wines of Bordeaux. Includes every important château historical information, and winemaking data as to the proportion of grape varieties used, methods of production and quantity of wine produced. Includes assessments of Sauternes vintages from 1890 to 1978. $24.95

ENCYCLOPEDIA OF THE GREAT WINES OF BORDEAUX by Michael Dovaz, 253 pp., color photos and illustrations. This is a beautifully illustrated coffee-table book (8 1/2"x 12 1/4"), covering 1855 Cru Classé wines. Each châteaux is given two pages that cover: evaluation of recent vintages , a map, the label, a few sentences on history, the land, the cultivation and vinification, the wine itself and a host of technical details such as production, geological features, duration of fermentation, percentage of press wine, percentage of varietals, aging, etc. $75

ALSACE AND ITS WINE GARDENS, CELLARS AND CUISINE by Fritz Hallgarten, 240 pp. A delightful book, written by a leading figure in the wine trade covering the history, geography, language, character, viticulture and cuisine of Alsace. Includes advice on touring. $11.95.

BURGUNDY by Anthony Hanson, 378 pp. The author, who lived and worked in Burgundy for three years tells the history of wine making in that region and describes the influence of soil, climate, vines and methods of wine-making. Now a London wine merchant, he takes a controversial look at the wine laws (which do not protect the consumer or guarantee honest wine), the quality (most Burgundy is mediocre today), and the price fetched for the wine (exhorbitant). He details the properties of each major grower, describes their winemaking methods with startling revelations, and deals with the dubious practices widely current in the region and analyses in depth the problems raised by them. This candid and outspoken work striking at hallowed ground has been long needed. It is an essential book for anyone serious about Burgundy. $24.95

GUIDE TO THE WINES AND VINEYARDS OF FRANCE by Alexis Lichine, 480 pp, 24 new maps. This is the most authoritative and readable work on the wines of

France ever published. Details each wine region; includes touring and dining information which is revised with each printing. Highly opinionated; dwells on quality standards, and the need to reform the French wine regulations. Anecdotal, revealing, and insightful to one of the leading figures in the international wine trade. Tells it like it is (most of the time). $15

MOUTON -BARONNE PHILIPPE by Joan Littlewood & Edmond Penning Rowswell, 57 pp. Published for Baron Phillippe de Rothschild by Christie's this book is a poetic tribute to this fine château named after the Baron's late wife. Edmund Penning Rowsell provides tastings notes of the vintages of the estate from 1978 back to 1945 (with the exception of 1968, 1947 and 1954 of which there was none available in the reserves of the chai). If you collect memorabilia of Bordeaux, this is worthy. $8

THE WINES OF THE RHÔNE by John Livingstone-Learmonth & Melvin C. Master, 235 pp. A detailed study on the wines of the Rhone, including many lesser known districts. A practical book for consumers and members of the wine trade. $21.95

THE WINES OF BORDEAUX by Edmund Penning-Rowsell, 320 pp. A classic which begins with a historical survey of the region, followed by a district by district analysis of its wines. Concentrates on the *Grands Crus Classés*. Fails to detail the many abuses of the wine trade and provides little advice on the less expensive wines of the regions. Once the best book on the subject; now displaced by the Peppercorn book. $10

BORDEAUX by David Peppercorn, 428 pp. The author is a British wine merchant who has made more than fifty trips to the Bordeaux region, is a Master of Wine, and presently a wine consultant. This book is up-to-date and one of the best on the subject. It covers the regions history, making the wine, classifications, four chapters on the Médoc, two on Pomerol/St. Émilion, one each on Fronsac-Bourg and Sauternes-Barsac. Finally there is an evaluation of Bordeaux vintages starting with 1798. His critique of the official 1855 Classification is quite compelling, pointing out that it is the château name that is classified, not the vineyard." $31.50

COGNAC by Cyril Ray. A witty discussion of the great brandy of the Charentes region of France. Includes section on serving, glassware, etc. Written by a leading British wine writer. $7.95

THE GREAT WINE CHÂTEAUX OF BORDEAUX, edited by Philip Seldon, 199 pp., 350 color photos. A large–format book that covers in concise, detailed text and magnificent color photos, the wines, the châteaux and the people who are involved in making France's finest wines. Collector's edition $39.95

THE WINES OF THE CÔTES DU RHÔNE by Sheldon & Pauline Wasserman, 214 pp. A reference guide to the fine wines of the Rhône. Includes history, producers, vintages and cuisine. $10.95

THE WINES OF BURGUNDY, Revised Edition by H.W. Yoxall, 192 pp. A guide to the best wines of the region which fails to reveal the current trends that have led to the decline in quality of many of the region's most renowned wines. An interesting picture of what wine lovers would like the region's wines to be, but no longer reflective of the times. Decries the need for a better book. $10

GERMANY

GERMAN WINES by S.F. Hallgarten, 397 pp. Provides an exhaustive study of German winemaking and the authors personal opinions on individual wines. Explains the new German wine laws. Its disjointed style and organization is exhausting to read but nevertheless the book provides the serious student of German wines with a wealth of accurate and vital information. Now out of print. $37.50

THE WINES OF GERMANY by Dr. Heinrich Meinard, 256 pp. A guide to the viticultural practices of each of the eleven major German wine regions. Details the unique characteristics of each along with useful information on labels, wine types and the new German wine laws. $10

THE WINES OF GERMANY by Frank Schoonmaker, Revised by Peter M.F. Sichel, $10.95. The late Frank Schoonmaker, first a journalist, then a leading importer of German wines, had an intimate knowledge of the country's wines and the winegrowers who made them. Though Schoonmaker's original work was biased by his prejudices, it was considered as the foremost work on the subject. Peter Sichel, also intimately involved in the German wine trade, has undertaken the monumental task of bringing this classic up to date. Sichel has maintained the orignial format, style and flavor of the book while removing Schoonmaker's biases. Though in the trade, he has honestly criticized aspects of the new German wine laws, rated regions, vineyards and growers making the revised edition one of the most authoritative and honest works on this complicated topic. $10.95

ITALY

VINO by Burten Anderson, 568 pp. This is probably the best book available on Italian wine. It combines a thorough approach to the wines with a multitude of in-depth interviews with winemakers plus specific vintage chart for dozens of key wines. It's well-written, enjoyable, informative and highly recommended. $19.95

ITALIAN WINES by Phillip Dallas, 336 pp., 19 maps. Covered most of the important wines of Italy and was the best book on the subject when published. Now seriously out of date. $15

ITALIAN WINE by Victor Hazan, 337 pp. The author organized this book by wine style (The Big Red Wines, The Medium-Range Reds, and the Light Reds,etc.) rather than by geography which makes for a coherent approach to what might otherwise be confusing a confusing subject. This book does not measure up to but is a good supplement to Burton Anderson's "VINO". $17.95

BRUNELLO DI MONTALCINO by Emanuel Pelluci, English Translation by Kathy Wolf Fabiani, 134 pp. This is an excellent book on a single wine. It has about a 100 photos (color and black and white) and maps. The more technical, detailed material is grouped so that the flow of the story is not interrupted. Admittedly a book of specialized interest, it nevertheless belongs in the "Italian section" of any wine library that claims any completeness. Paperback $15

CYRIL RAY: THE NEW BOOK OF ITALIAN WINES by Cyril Ray,158 pp. Back in 1964 Mr. Ray wrote the then definitive book on Italian wines. Mr. Ray's book is new new except for one chapter covering the history of wine in that nation. The author is obviously one who not only knows the wines of Italy but also loves them. The book covers, region-by-region, some six hundred plus wines, almost entirely D.O.C. He characterizes each wine well and evaluates many of them. It is a competent work of personal judgement by an experienced wine writer. While it does not overshadow Anderson's Vino, which still remains the standard, it does supplement it and would be an important part of any Italian book shelf. $30.95

THE WINES OF ITALY by Sheldon Wasserman, 212 pp. Written as a consumers' guide it contains too many details which detract from its purpose. Useful to an extent but leaves a lot to be desired in terms of format and caliber of writing. $10.

IBERIAN PENINSULA

THE WINES OF SPAIN AND PORTUGAL by Jan Read, 280 pp. The author, who has followed these wines for twenty years, describes in detail the wines from Rioja, Montilla, Alella, Valdepeñas, Tarragona, and Panadés from Spain; Vinhos Verdes, Dao, and Colares from Portugal. Port and Sherry are also covered as well as sparkling and bulk wines. Wines from the Iberian Peninsula are relatively inexpensive and provide excellent value — their history, winemaking and quality are outlined in a well organized and and easy-to-read style. $13.95

FORTIFIED WINES

PORT: An Introduction to its History & Delights by Wyndham Fletcher, 124 pp., illustrations. Provides accurate information on the Port shippers, systems in registering vineyards, allocations and other insider's data on the Port business along with a
review of vintages since 1820. $16

SHERRY — THE NOBLE WINE by Manuel Gonzales Gordon, 240 pp. Written by
the head of the Gonzales Byass wine firm who provides an immense knowledge and
detail of the wines of Jerez. A classic work on the Sherry wines of Spain. $12.95

PORT by George Robertson, 198 pp. A comprehensive work written by a leading
figure in the Port wine trade. Covers the regions, history, its land, soil, climate and a
detailed account of the production of this unique wine. Sections on selecting, serving
and cellaring Port. $12.95

GUIDE OF FORTIFIED WINES by Sheldon and Pauline Wasserman, 100 pp. This
carefully researched book covers the important fortified wines — Port, Montilla--
Moriles, Sherry, Madeira and Marsala — in very considerable detail. The wealth of
detail and the extent of the digging the authors have done is particularly manifested
in the charts they have constructed for Port. First, a Vintage Chart starting with 1811
through 1980 which tells which houses shipped vintage wine in each year; then a
check list of shippers and vintages starting with 1870 and going through 1980; a list
of shippers and the vintages that each declared. These charts are new, constructed
by the Wassermans upon the wealth of material they painstakingly uncovered. This
book will be the classic reference on the subject for years to come. Paperback $9.95

TECHNICAL WINES

TABLE WINES, THE TECHNOLOGY OF THEIR PRODUCTION by M.A.
Amerine & M.A. Joslyn. A highly technical book for professional winemakers.
Written as an advanced college text. $25

WINES: THEIR SENSORY EVALUATION by M.A. Amerine & Edward B.
Roessler, 250 pp. A technical treatise on the use of statistical techniques for
evaluating wine quality. Highly mathematical.

A PRACTICAL AMPELOGRAPHY: GRAPEVINE IDENTIFICATION by Pierre
Galet, 256 pp., full color plates, illustrations. A comprehensive guide of grapevine
identification for growers and winemakers. Includes all wine varieties including
American and French-American hybirds. $28

APPLIED WINE CHEMISTRY AND TECHNOLOGY by A. Massel, 288 pp. Covers wine chemistry from grape selection to bottling. $15

THE GREAT WINE GRAPES AND THE WINES THEY MAKE by Bern C. Ramey, 256 pp., full color photos. A large-format salute to the classic wine grapes and the wines they produce written in an attractive popular style accompanied by magnificent full color photographs of each variety. Printed as a collector's book with high grade paper and binding.

CHEMISTRY OF WINEMAKING, 312 pp. Covers thirteen different topics from *must* analysis to home winemaking delivered as speeches during an American Chemical Society Symposium. $20.50

GENERAL VITICULTURE by A.J. Winkler, James Cook, W. Klierwer & L. Lider. An advanced college text on grape growing. Highly technical. $27.50

THE WINEMAKER GUIDE by F.S. Nury, Ph. D. and K.C. Fugelsang, 106 pp., illustrations. A useful guide for the home winemaker with sound information and easy reading. $3.95

WINE COURSE CATALOGUES

GUIDE TO WINE COURSES, Society of Wine Educators, 1048 Oak Hills Way, Salt Lake City, Utah 84108. Annually. This guide covers all the wine courses given by its instructor members throughout the U.S. Many of the courses listed are conducted as part of adult education programs at local colleges; others are private ventures given at hotels and restaurants. SWE members are serious about wine education - courses given by their members are well worth looking into.

TELL ME WHAT
TO BUY

No wine guide would be complete without a listing of specific buying recommendations. The problem is that these recommendations are frequently outdated by the time a book, such as this one, is finally printed. To fill this void there are several newsletters and magazines which provide specific recommendations on an up to the minute basis for serious wine lovers who want to experience the latest vintages or review a professional evaluation before spending their hard earned money on a new wine.

These publications are relatively expensive. While writing this book I frequently wrestled with the problem of providing information that rightfully belongs in a guide like this one, but could misdirect my readers as the quality or integrity of an individual producer or importer changed, or if they had an unsuccessful vintage. My solution was to prepare a list of nationally distributed wines that I could heartily recommend, update it to keep it current, and provide it free of charge to readers of this book. In this list I also review the major importers, European shippers and producers, and current vintages in a candid and straightforward manner. The cost of printing this supplement has been included in the price of this book. To receive your copy, simply mail a self-addressed, stamped envelope to: Vintage Consumer Guide to Wine, P.O. Box 2224, New York, N.Y. 10163.

What follows is a list of the various wine periodicals currently being published in the United States. As with wine, these listings are difficult to keep up-to-date. I have also prepared a curent list which will be sent upon request. Most of the publications listed will send an examination copy without charge.

WINE MAGAZINES

VINTAGE MAGAZINE, P.O. Box 2224, New York, N.Y. 10163. Monthly, $35 per year. Vintage was recently ranked as the leading wine publication in terms of the number of wines reviewed with detailed tasting notes, and specific buying recommendations, by Bacchus Data Services, an independent research organization which surveyed both wine magazines and newsletters. Entire catagories of wines are reviewed each month with wines rated from outstanding to unacceptable. New releases are also reviewed providing the most current wine information available. *Vintage* reviews approximately two to three hundred wines each issue. In addition to reviewing wine, *Vintage* is frequently considered as controversial by the wine trade in it's coverage of the goings on in the world of wine, frequently reporting on subjects other wine publications choose to ignore. *Vintage* has exposed fraudulent dealings at the Heublien National Wine Auction, deceptive advertising by *The Wine Spectator* and dubious dealings at fund raising events sponsored by several so-called "wine charities." *Vintage* is supported primarily by its subscribers and contains limited advertising.

VINTAGE 1983. P.O. Box 2223, New York, N.Y. Annually, $20. VINTAGE 1983 is the current edition of the VINTAGE MAGAZINE ANNUAL which features articles on wines, wine personalities, wine history, reports on vintages, and current wine news. It is a non-technical full-sized, glossy 352 page "coffee-table" book, printed on fine paper illustrated with many photographs and drawings edited and designed to appeal to the wine connoisseur. It is available at better wine shops and bookstores or it can be ordered by mail from *Vintage* magazine.

FRIENDS OF WINE MAGAZINE, 2302 Perkins Place, Silver Springs, Md. 20910. Bi-monthly, $25 per year including membership in *Les Amis du Vin*, a commercial wine club. Sometimes sold at discount by Publishers Clearing House Subscription agency. Features some wine reviews, but concentrates on feature articles which avoid rating wines. Devotes considerable space to non-wine editorial material, advertising its own events, and non-wine advertising. Published for members of a Wine of the Month club which sells wine to its members through a network of retail stores. Approximately half of the magazine is advertising, Ocassionally, articles are unattributed service articles apparently published to please advertisers.

WINE WORLD, 15101 Keswick Street, Van Nuys, Ca. 91495. Bi-monthly, $14. Rather bland in its wine reviews, and feature offerings. Its wine ratings are not reliable. Accepts advertising but is not very successful in selling it.

GRAPPA, P.O. Box 221127, Carmel, Ca. 93922. Bi-monthly, $35 per year. A relatively new publication specializing in California wine. Printed on uncoated paper, does not rate wines, amateurish in its content. Accepts advertising.

THE WINE SPECTATOR, 400 E. 51st Street, New York, N.Y. 10022. Semi-monthly tabloid, $25 per year. A consumer publication in a newsprint tabloid format which contains considerable information of interest to the wine trade. This publication is ill conceived as a consumer periodical. Most of its industry news is rather dull stuff. A good portion of its articles are covered better in other magazines and in wine books. Its "Special Report" ratings of catagories of wine is mediocre covering a relatively small number of wines that hold no candle to the other publications listed here. Its articles' frequently contain "old-hat" wine info "right out of the wine books," in a headlined newspaper style apparently to provide a sense of immediacy. It is a rather useless publication for the average consumer. While it purports to be a journalistic endeavor, it frequently ignores important consumer issues; that it contains considerable advertising should be no surprise.

THE INTERNATIONAL REVIEW OF WINE AND FOOD, P.O. Box 556, Great Neck, N.Y. 11025. Monthly, $12 per year. Primarily a food magazine, but features popular wine writers who write for a mass audience. Opulent in its slick coverage of food, but rarely provides more than lip-service in its coverage of wine. Does not rate wines, and avoids controversial wine issues.

ITALIAN WINES & SPIRITS. Quarterly. $12 per year. P.O. Box 1130, Long Island City, New York, N.Y. 11101. This is the American edition of *Civiltà del bere*, the monthly Italian wine magazine. As its name implies, it deals only with Italy, covering its wines and foods superbly. This is a beautiful publication with every page in color. It contains many articles specifically written with the average wine consumer in mind, and is better written, designed and edited than most of the other wine magazines listed here. I heartily recommend it.

WINESTATE, 900 Santa Fe Avenue, Albany, Ca. 94706. Monthly, $2.00 a copy at newsstands. A slick, color, newsstand magazine which primarily reviews wines but also publishes articles on wine, food and spirits topics. Publishes only favorable reviews and appears to be quite forgiving as to quality. Wineries pay a fee to have their labels included with their reviews. Accepts advertising.

WINE COUNTRY, 4235 Park Road, Suite 4, Benicia, Ca. 94510. Monthly, $19. This is a super slick, opulent color publication about California wine county. It covers wineries, wine topics, food and travel. Its expensive paper and "art book" quality color printing are exquisite. Unfortunately it publishes editorially stylized advertisements depicting wine bottles with tasting notes (often of wines not reviewed) next to its wine reviews which at first glance appear to be part of the article. Otherwise, this is a superb "coffee table" magazine. Accepts advertising.

CONSUMER WINE NEWSLETTERS

There are many newsletters published primarily by serious wine enthusiasts. Those listed below are those which publish wine reviews and current vintage information which are reliable and worthwhile

ROBERT BALZER'S PRIVATE GUIDE TO FOOD AND WINE, 12791 Newport Avenue, Tusin, Ca. 92680. Published eleven times a year, $22.50. Author, Robert Balzer. Reviews and rates wines. Tastings are conducted specially for evaluating wines reviewed. Ratings based on author's as well as a consensus of other experienced tasters' contributions. Well-respected, well-established.

CONNOISSEUR'S GUIDE TO CALIFORNIA WINE, P.O. Box 11120, San Francisco, Ca. 94101. Bi-Monthly, $20 per year. Authors, Earl Singer and Charles Olken. Authors are serious wine amateurs employed outside the wine industry. Olken endorses Taylor wines in TV commercials. Conducted tastings for reviews. Attractive format. Detailed reviews use numerous symbols for ratings. Food recommendations as well.

ROBERT FINIGAN'S PRIVATE GUIDE TO WINES, 100 Bush Street, San Francisco, Ca. 94194. Monthly, $36 per year. Author, Robert Finigan. Reviews current vintages and recommends wines worldwide. Publishes two editions, one for California, another for the rest of the country. Witty, well written, accurate.

THE UNDERGROUND WINELETTER, P.O. Box 663, Seal Beach, Ca. 90740. Bi-monthly, $20 per year. Author, John Tilson. Tilson is a serious amateur employed outside of the wine industry. Publication concentrates on esoteric, and expensive collector's wines, both domestic and imported.

FREE WINERY NEWSLETTERS

Many wineries publish newsletters. Some are substantial in information beyond news of their latest releases, others simply announce their latest wines. These are among the best. You may write direct to the listed winery, or send your name and address to Vintage Consumer Guide to Wine, P.O. Box 2224, New York, N.Y. 10163, and your name will be forwarded to all listed.

BERINGER VINEYARDS, 2000 Main Street, St. Helena 94574
BUENA VISTA WINERY, INC., P.O. Box 182, Sonoma 95476
CAKEBREAD CELLARS, 802 E. 12 St., Oakland 94606
CASSAYRE—FORNI CELLARS, 531 Jefferson St., Napa 94558
CHATEAU MONTELENA, 1429 Tubbs Lane, Calistoga 9451

CHATEAU ST. JEAN, P.O. Box 293, Kenwood 95452
CONCANNON VINEYARDS, P.O. Box 432, Liver more 94550
CONGRESS SPRINGS VINEYARDS, 23600 Congress Springs Rd., Saratoga 95070
DAVID BRUCE WINERY, 21439 Bear Creek Road, Los Gatos 95030
DELICATO VINEYARDS, 12001 South Highway 99, Manteca 95336
DOMAIN CHANDON, P.O. Box 2470, Yountville 94599
DRY CREEK VINEYARDS, P.O. Box T, Healdsburg 95448
DUCKHORN VINEYARDS, 3027 Silverado Trails, St Helena 94574
FETZER VINEYARDS, P.O. Box 227, Redwood Valley 95470
FIELDSTONE WINERY, 10075 Highway 128, Healdsburg, CA 95448
EL FOPPIANO WINE CO., P.O. Box 606, Healdsburg 95448
GEMELLO WINERY, INC., 2003 El Camino Real, Mountain View 94040
GEYSER PEAK WINERY, P.O. Box 25, Geyserville 95441
GIBSON WINE CO., P.O. Drawer E, Elk Grove 95624
GIUMARRA FAMILY GRAPEVINE, P.O. Box 175, Edison 93220
GRAND CRU VINEYARDS, P.O. Drawer B, Glen Ellen 95442
GUNDLACH BUNDSCHU WINE COMPANY, P.O. Box 1, Vineburg 95487
HACIENDA WINE CELLARS, P.O. Box 416, Sonoma 95476
H.M.R. LIMITED, Adelaida Road, Star Route, Paso Robles 93446
HOP KILN WINERY, 6050 Westside Road, Healdsburg 95448
INGLENOOK VINEYARDS, P.O. Box 19, Rutherford 94573
JOHNSON'S ALEXANDER VALLEY WINERY, 8333 Highway 128, Healdsburg 95448
KENWORTHY VINEYARDS, Route 2, Box 2, Plymouth 95669
HANNS KORNELL CHAMPAGNE CELLARS, P.O. Box 249, St. Helena 94574
CHARLES KRUG WINERY, P.O. Box 191 St. Helena 94574
LAWRENCE WINERY, P.O. Box 1151 San Lois, Obispo, 93406
THE LUCAS WINERY, 18196 North Daris, Lodi 95240
LYTTON SPRINGS WINERY, INC., 650 Lytton Sprinrs Rd., Healdsburg 95448
MAYACAMAS VINEYARDS, 1155 Lokoya Rd., Napa 94558
MIRASSOU VINEYARDS, 3000 Aborn Road, San Jose 95135
THE MONTEREY VINEYARD, P.O. Box 780, Gon zales 93926
MONTEREY PENINSULA WINERY, 2999 Monterey-Salinas Highway, Monterey 93940
MONT LA SALLE VINEYARDS, P.O. Box 420, Napa 94558
PAPAGNI VINEYARDS, 31754 Avenue 9, Madera 93637
PAUL MASSON VINEYARDS, 13150 Saratoga Avenue, Saratoga 95070
PENDLETON WINERY, 2156 G. O'Toole Ave., San Jose 95131
RANCHO SISQUOC, 870 Market St, Rm. 1100, San Francisco 94102
ROSENBLUM CELLARS, 1775 16th St., Oakland 94612
SAN MARTIN WINERY, P.O. Box 53, San Martin 95046
SANTA BARBARA WINERY, 202 Anacapa St., Santa Barbara 93101
SANTA YNEZ VALLEY WINERY, 365 N. Fetugio, Santa Ynez 93460
SEBASTIANI VINEYARDS, P.O. Box AA, Sonoma 95476
SHERRILL CELARS, P.O. Box 4155, Woodside 94062
SOKOL BLOSSER WINERY, P.O. Box 199, Dundee, OR 97115
SONOMA VINEYARDS, P.O. Box 368, Windsor 95492
SOUVERAIN CELLARS, P.O. Box 528, Geyserville 95441
STERLING VINEYARDS, P.O. Box 365, Calistoga 94515
STONEGATE WINERY, 1183 Dunaweal Lane, Calistoga 94515
STE. CHAPELLE VINEYARDS, (Sunny Slope Press), Route 4, Caldwell, ID 83605
TOYON, 71 West North St., Suite T, Healdsburg 95448
TURGEON & LOHR WINERY, 1001 Lenzen Ave., San Jose 95126
VENTANA VINEYARDS WINERY, P.O. Box G, Soledad 93960
WEIBEL VINEYARDS, P.O. Box 3398, Mission San Jose 94538
WENTE BROS WINERY, 5565 Tesla Road, Livermore 94550
WINE AND THE PEOPLE, INC., 907 University Ave., Berkeley 94701
ZACA MESA CELLARS, P.O. Box 1255, Santa Maria 93456

A WORD OF CAUTION

Now that you have become more familiar with wine, and have, no doubt, begun to appreciate its charms, a word of caution is in order: for all its diversity and complexity, wine is, nonetheless, an alcoholic beverage. Unlike other spirits which pack an obvious punch, wine's subtle innocence masks the perception of alcohol in wines which are properly balanced. Often, when we are lost in the pleasures of the wine, it is all too easy to lose track of the fact that wine has inebriating properties. Simply said, responsible and moderate consumption of wine is beneficial to the health. Excessive consumption can be deleterious to the health and safety of both yourself and those around you.

Unlike most foods, alcohol is not digested in the digestive trace but is absorbed, through osmosis, into the bloodstream. Professionals, who spit out when tasting, often feel the effects of alcohol which has been absorbed by the tissue in the mouth. From the stomach or intestines, it makes a beeline directly to the blood stream, through which it passes to the liver, lungs, heart, and, finally, to the brain. Within a few short minutes after ingestion, alcohol reaches every part of the body.

Alcohol is then metabolized at a constant rate of approximately one-third ounce (of pure alcohol) per hour for the average person. While many people have the notion that alcohol can be quickly worked out of the system, the truth of the matter is that alcohol absorption is strictly a function of time. Exercise, coffee, cold showers, a hot sauna, and any other "old-wive's" remedy you may have heard are all in vain. The more you drink, the longer it takes to regain normalcy.

The rate of metabolism varies from individual to individual, and for each person it is a function of body weight. In layman's jargon, this means that the fatter you are, the more you can safely drink. How much can you drink per pound of body weight? That depends on genetic heredity, which explains how one person can drink another of equal weight under the table.

Because the consumption of alcohol initially produces lightheadedness and a sense of euphoria, and is at first stimulating, it is assumed by many that alcohol is a stimulant. In actual fact, it is a depressant, and as such, slows down a person's reflexes, perceptions and judgements. Up to a certain level of blood alcohol, which again varies from individual to individual, but on the average is 0.5 percent, an individual's faculties are not impaired. Once past this point, a person's ability to function normally becomes progressively impaired.

For this reason, although it is unorthodox to touch upon this subject in a winebook, I would like to discuss the responsible use of wine, or for that matter, any alcoholic beverage. I'm sure that everybody knows that driving and alcoholic beverages simply do not mix. There are many other caveats. However, you should consider the following "Thou Shall Nots" the Wine Drinkers Commandments.

- Do not drive anything; automobiles, bicycles, motorcycles, airplanes, etc. In England, which has very tough drunk driving laws, some people have resorted to riding horses.
- Do not swim, surf or waterski
- Do not participate in athletic activities requiring balance and perception such as roller skating, skiing, skateboarding, waterskiing or surfing.
- Do not use firearms or other weapons.
- Do not use power tools, particularly power saws, mowers, drills or the like.
- Do not drink wine with antihistamines or similar patent medication; drowsiness frequently results. For any others, check the label for guidelines.
- Do not drink wines with prescription medicines without first counseling your physician or pharmacist.
- Do not drink wine when under a physician's care, unless you have his explicit permission.

Unfortunately, too many hosts are considered inhospitable when they attempt to look after the health and safety of their guests. Strange, isn't it, that a host who would expose his guests to hazards on his property would be considered irresponsible, yet the host who offers his guests "one for the road" is considered a good friend. I don't think I should belabor the obvious, but let me suggest that a good policy in entertaining is to taper off the alcohol as the night progresses. If any of your guests has had too much, arrange a ride or order a cab. To do otherwise is to abrogate the responsibilities of friendship.

WINE WORDS

Acescence. Describes the impression of volatile acidity in a wine which is essential to the flavor and complexity of a fine wine. It is associated with some chemical compounds, such as acetic acid and ethyl acetate. An appropriately small amount adds to the flavor of wine — too much renders a wine sharp or disagreeable.

Acetate. Refers to the smell of ethyl acetate which is a component of the volatile acidity of a wine. When in excess it smells of nail polish remover or acetone.

Acetic. The smell of vinegar in wine. All wines contain a small amount of acetic acid, commonly called volatile acidity, which adds to the wine's complexity and character. This term is generally used when the wine has excessive volatile acidity.

Acidic. A description of wine whose total acidity is so high that it imparts a sharp feel or sour taste in the mouth.

Acidity. Refers to the non-volatile acids in a wine, principally tartaric, malic and citric. These acids provide a sense of freshness and an impression of balance to a wine. Excessive acidity provides a sharp or sour taste, too little results in a flat or flabby character.

Acute. Tasting term meaning strong or sharply defined.

Aftertaste. The lingering impression of a wine after it is swallowed. It is usually described as the "finish" of a wine. It ranges from short to lingering. A lingering aftertaste is a characteristic indicative of quality.

Aged. Describes a wine that has been cellared either in cask or bottle long enough to have developed or improved. As a tasting term it describes the characteristic scent and taste of a wine that has so developed while in its bottle.

Aggressive. Refers to the strong, assertive character of a young and powerful wine. Aggressive wines usually lack charm and grace.

Agreeable. Pleasant, easy to drink.

Astringent. A puckering, tactile sensation imparted to the wine by its tannins. A puckering quality adds to the total sense of the wine, giving it a sense of structure, style and vitality. Tannins are an essential component in red wines which are made to improve with age while in bottle. Red wines lacking in tannins are generally dull and uninteresting. Wines vinified for prolonged aging are harshly tannic when young, but mellow when the wine's age and the tannins precipitate to form a sediment in the bottle.

Atypical. Describes a wine that does not conform to its traditional character or style.

Auslese. Literally, "picked out" (i.e. selected). Under the new German wine law, wine which is subject to all regulations included in *Qualitätswein mit Prädikat* (quality wine with special attributes). Auslese wine is made entirely from selected, fully ripe grapes with all unripe and diseased grapes removed. No sugar may be added. The wine is especially full, rich and somewhat sweet.

Austere. A tasting term used to describe a wine with direct vinosity (the opposite of fruitness), high acidity, considerable tannins and little or no nuances of flavor.

Awkward. A tasting term used to describe a wine that is poorly structured or with poor balance.

Backbone. The structural framework of a wine provided by the alcohol, acids and tannins of a wine.

Back Taste. A tasting term which refers to the impression on the palate immediately prior to swallowing.

Baked. A caramelized smell inherent in wines which have grown in a hot climate; have been made from grapes improperly pasteurized, or have deliberately been baked as part of the winemaking. Usually an unattractive characteristic.

Balance. Refers to the proportion of the various elements of a wine; acid against sweetness, fruit flavors against wood, and tannic alcohol against acid and flavor.

Balanced. A pleasing sensory impression which results when all the components of a wine are in proportion to each other. This occurs when none of the flavors or tactile components of a wine override any other. Harmonious wines are said to be balanced. Imbalanced wine may be acetic, cloying, flat or flabby, harsh, heady, weak, awkward, etc.

Barrel Fermented. Refers to the fermentation of a wine in a small oak cask as opposed to a large tank or vat.

Beaujolais Primeur. The young Beaujolais, vinified to be drunk within months of the harvest. Primeur varietal wines have become popular, made with various grape varieties, particularly in California.

Beerenauslese. "Berry-selected", i.e. individual grape berries picked out (by order of ripeness) at harvest for their sugar content, quality, and their amount of Edelfäule (noble rot).

Big. A tasting term describing a wine powerful in flavor, extract, body, or alcohol. May be used to describe wine in total, or with regard to a specific component such as "big body".

Blanc de Blancs. Describes a white wine made from white grapes. The term refers to both still table and sparkling wines. The words "Blanc de Blancs" do not signify a quality better than other white wines.

Bodega. In the Spanish wine trade, a wine house, wine company, wine cellar, or even wine shop.

Body. The tactile impression of fullness on the palate caused by the alcohol, glycerine and residual sugar in a wine. The extremes of "body" are full and thin.

Bone Dry. Refers to a wine with no residual sugar. Such wines generally have à certain austerity to their taste.

Bottle Age. Refers to the time a wine has spent in its bottle. Better wines develop new and more complex flavors when so–aged.

Bottle Sick. The "dumbness", or temporary loss of a wine's flavor, which usually occurs immediately after bottling. Bottle sick wines tend to recover within several months of bottling. Wines meant for prolonged aging may become bottle sick during various periods of their development. The term is a misnomer in the sense that there is no bacteria or other factor spoiling the wine.

Bottled by. A term which refers to the individual or company that has bottled the wine. In the United States it has legal significance. When it stands alone on a bottle without the terms "grown" or "produced by", it indicates that the winery named has played a minor role in the production of the wine. It is usually made by another firm.

Botrytised. The aroma and flavor of a wine made from grapes infected by *Botrytis cinerea*, the noble mold. It imparts an unctuous, honey-like character to white wines made from certain grape varieties, particularly the Riesling and the Sauvignon Blanc, but it is an undesirable characteristic in red wines.

Botrytis Cinerea. A species of mold that attacks grapes grown in moist conditions. It is undesirable for most grape varieties, or when it infects a vineyard prior to the grapes reaching full maturity. Vineyards are treated to prevent its occurence. When it attacks fully mature grapes it causes them to shrivel, concentrating both the acidity and the sugar, and resulting in an intensified flavor and a desired sweetness balanced by acidity. This is beneficial and highly desirable for white varieties such as the Johannisberg Riesling, Sauvignon Blanc, Sémillon, and Chenin Blanc, from which unctuous, luscious and complex white wines are made in various wine regions of the world.

Bottle Fermented. Refers to the process of creating bubbles in sparkling wine by inducing a second fermentation in the bottle, as opposed to a large tank.

Bouquet. The smell of a wine after it has lost its grapy fragrances. This usually develops after a year of aging and continues as the wine matures in the bottle, developing complexity and nuances of flavors that previously did not exist.

Breed. A term used to describe the loveliest, most harmonious and refined wines that achieve what is called "classical proportions". The term is elusive to definition, but wines which deserve such acclaim are unmistakable when encountered.

Brick Red. The color of a red wine when it has reached its peak of maturity. Basically, the dark red-brown color of building bricks.

Complex. A wine offering many aromas and flavors that together deliver a pleasing harmony. Also called multifaceted or multidimensional; the opposite of wine that offers simply one flavor. This is the elusive quality that separates a great wine from a good one.

Concentrated. Refers to the flavors in a wine usually of a character more intense than would ordinarily be encountered for its type.

Cooked. A baked or cooked taste in wine. This results from grapes grown in an excessively hot climate; from wines fermented at too high a temperature, or improperly pasteurized.

Cooperage. Refers to the wooden barrels and tanks used for aging wines.

Corky. The smell and taste which results from corks infected with mold. Also referred to as "corked". A corked or corky wine does not smell of cork but of moldy cork. A wine that has spoiled due to a dried out cork generally will smell oxidized or will have turned to vinegar. This term is frequently misused even by experts.

Crackling. Refers to a sparkling wine with a slight effervescence, substantially less than that of Champagne but sufficient to remain bubbly after being poured. In France it is called *cremant*. Wines with barely perceptible effervescence are called *pétillant* or *spritzig*.

Cream. Refers to a sweet style of Sherry. Also used elsewhere to denote an excessively sweet, full-bodied wine.

Creamy. Refers to the velvety or creamy, full-bodied texture and feel of a wine when tasted.

Cross. A grape created by genetically mating two members of the same wine species to create a grape vine with specific attributes, usually the best of the two varieties selected. The term "hybrid" is usually applied to a genetic cross of two members of different wine species, hence, the term French-American hybrid.

Cru Bourgeois. Refers to red Bordeaux wines from the Haut-Medoc that rank just below the Grande Cru Classé wines of the 1855 Bordeaux classification.

Cru Classé. "Classified growth". Refers to those wines originally classified as Grand Cru Classé in the 1855 Bordeaux classification.

Crush. Commonly used to refer to the grape harvest or vintage. Most specifically refers to the breaking of the grape stems which begins a fermentation process.

Cuvé. A large vat, usually made of wood, used for the fermentation of grape juice into wine.

Cuvée. Refers to the contents of a wine vat. More loosely used to refer to all the wine made at one time or under similar conditions. Sometimes refers to a specific pressing, or batch of wine. Sometimes used as part of a brand name or trademark, or as wine label nomenclature to refer to a batch of wine.

Dosage. A small amount of sugar, champagne and brandy which is added to Champagne right after dégorgement. The final sweetness of the wine is determined by this step.

Dry. A taster's term indicating a lack of sweetness. May be modified as bone dry, off-dry (a slight sweetness) etc.

Dumb. A taster's term used to describe a wine which is showing less well than is to be expected from prior experience with it. Wines which are in their adolescence (the period between youth and maturity) are often said to be going through a dumb stage. The term dumb is only used with wines which are capable of improving significantly with bottle age.

Earthy. Describes a wine that smells like freshly-turned soil. It is generally a characteristic imparted from the peculiarities of the district from which the wine came.

Elegant. Refers to a wine which provides a sense of grace, harmony, delicate balance and beauty. This is a characteristic found only in the finest of wines.

Éleveur. Refers to a wine firm that cares for wines in their barrels and bottles them, frequently blending to provide better structure and balance. Often, this firm is also a *négociant* or shipper.

Essence. Also *Essencia*. Refers to a Late Harvest wine made from grapes which have shriveled to a raisin-like concentration. Such wines are usually quite sweet, with a balancing acidity, and are exceedingly rich in flavor.

Estate Bottled. Refers to a wine which has been bottled at the vineyard or winery in which it was made. Has legal significance in several countries, particularly France, Germany, and Italy, but is not controlled in others. Basically it connotes wine that was under the control of the winemaker from vineyard to bottle. It does not assure the excellence of a wine although it once did, as a general rule, many years ago.

Ethyl Acetate. A sweet, chemical smell that often accompanies acetic acid, which is a natural component in all wines. In small amounts it adds to the complexity of a wine; in excess, it can be offensive and is considered a defect in the wine.

Eucalyptus. The pine oil smell of eucalyptus, frequently found in Cabernet Sauvignon and Pinot Noir.

Extract. The non-sugar solids in a wine — frequently dissolved in alcohol. Adds to the weight or feel of a wine.

Extra Dry. A champagne term that in actual use refers to wine that is somewhat sweet — a grade sweeter than "brut."

Extra Sec. Extra dry.

Fat. A full-bodied wine, high in alcohol and/or glycerols, with a depth of flavor that overshadows the acidity giving a fat sensation on the palate. When the acidity of such a wine is totally insufficient the wine is said to be "flabby."

Feine, Feinste. German wine label terms referring to the producer's assessment of a particular batch of wine bottled seperately from the rest of the vintage. Since these terms were subjective and frequently abused, they are not permitted under the new German wine laws enacted in 1971.

Fermentation. The process of converting sugar into alcohol, usually by the action of yeast on the juice of fruit, such as grapes. It is a complex process in which the yeast produces enzymes which convert the sugar into alcohol, carbon dioxide and heat.

Field Crushing. The process of crushing the grapes when picked, usually by mechanical harvesters, as opposed to at the winery. Employed when the vineyards are far from the winery or when the grapes will lose certain essential qualities unless immediately protected from deterioration. Usually the juice is placed in tanks under a blanket of carbon dioxide.

Filtered. Describes a wine clarified by use of a filter to remove yeast cells, bacteria, and other solids which can detract from the quality of a wine once bottled.

Finesse. A quality of elegance which separates a fine wine from a wine which is simply good. It is a harmony of flavors and components rarely found in wine. The term is hard to define, but a wine with finesse is unmistakable when encountered.

Fining. A clarifying technique which introduces an electrolytic agent, such as egg white, powered milk, blood, diatomaceous earth (bentonite) or gelatin, to attract the solids and settle them to the bottom of a cask. Beaten egg whites or bentonite are the most frequenly used agents.

Finish. The aftertaste of a wine when it has been swallowed. Usually consists of both flavor and tactile sensations from the acidity, alcohol and tannins of the wine.

Firm. Refers to the structure of a wine in which the acidity and alcohols are in a particular balance. The opposite of flabby.

Flabby. A wine which lacks unity due to insufficient acidity to balance its alcohol, extract or residual sugar.

Flat. Refers to a wine which lacks flavor, freshness or life.

Fleshy. Refers to a wine which is full-bodied and rich in extract, giving it a chewy texture.

Flinty. A flavor associated with certain dry white wines. It is usually imparted by soil in combination with microclimate and a particular strain of yeast. Chablis is the most common example; its flavor resembles the smell of gunflint after it has been struck or rubbed.

Flor. A film of yeast or bacteria, usually in cask on top of a wine, but also found in unhygienically bottled wines. In Spain it refers to a specific yeast that grows in

Jerez and imparts a delicate, nutty quality to its wines. When Sherry is affected by this yeast, called *Saccharomyces fermentati,* it is called *fino.*

Floral/Flowery. Refers to the flowery smell and character of young white wines, mainly those made from the Riesling or its relatives. With the advent of cold fermentation, many lesser varieties have begun to show similar qualities.

Fortified. A wine to which alcohol has been added to raise its alcoholic strength. These wines usually range from 15 to 21 percent alcohol.

Foxy. Describes the strong smell of the native American grape species, the *Vitis labrusca,* which often resembles the musky smell of a caged animal. When blended with neutral wine, or otherwise treated, this distinctive flavor is diluted and can make for agreeable drinking.

Free-run Juice. The juice that is released from the grape as it is being crushed, before the pulp and skins are pressed. This juice, generally less harsh than press wine, is used for the finest wines. Free run accounts for about 60 percent of the juice available from the grape for fine wine. This juice is separated immediately from the skins for white wine but is combined with the skins and pulp for reds. It is drained off the solids prior to the pressing of the remaining grape material.

French Oak. The wood from the great oak forests of France, particularly from Nevers and Limousin, which impart a distinctive and mellow character to wine aged in barrels made from them. Also used as a term to describe the flavor imparted to wine by barrels made from this oak.

Fresh. Describes the youthful, lively qualities sought in young white and light-bodied red wines.

Fruity. Describes the fragrance or flavor of certain young wines. It is a rich, winey flavor not to be confused with the smell of fresh grape juice.

Full Bodied. Describes the feel in the mouth of a wine rich in extract or high in alcohol.

Gassy. Refers to a wine which contains unwanted CO_2, usually from fermentation in the bottle or improper treatment prior to bottling. Such a wine frequently smells and tastes of off-flavors.

Generic Wine. A broadly used wine term signifying a wine type, as opposed to a more specific name, such as a grape variety or the actual region of production. Such names have frequently been employed on American wines using famous European place names such as Chablis, Burgundy, Rhine, Champagne, or European wine types such as Claret, or Sherry.

Glycerine. A chemical compound naturally found in wine, which gives a smooth, full-bodied sensation in the mouth. Also imparts a sense of sweetness on the tip of the tongue in wines that contain no residual sugar.

Goût de Terroir. The specific taste characteristic imparted from the soil of a particular wine district.

Goût de Vieux. The distinctive taste of an old wine.

Grand Cru. Great growth. Refers to a classification of French wines considered to be superior in quality. Used in Bordeaux and Burgundy.

Grapy. The fruity aroma and flavors of fresh grapes, as opposed to the vinous flavor of wine. Often found in young wines before development with age.

Grassy. The light, fresh aroma and flavor of freshly mowed grass. Attractive in some wines, undesirable in others.

Green. Unripe. Refers to wines that taste of unripe grapes; a "stemmy" character which may detract from the flavor.

Hard. A sense of firmness or austerity in a wine. Usually refers to a young, tannic red wine before it mellows and develops full flavor with bottle age.

Harsh. A rough sensation in the mouth from wines that are too astringent because of tannins, extract, or harsh acids. Depending on the constituents contributing to this harshness, the wine may or may not mellow with age.

Hazy. Cloudy appearance in a wine. Usually due to suspended solids in the wine, which settle with time. It can also signify an unhealthy wine.

Heady. The distinct, as opposed to the harmonious, sense of alcohol in a wine. Usually refers to a wine high in alcohol but also applies to lighter wines which are imbalanced to the point where the alcohol appears excessive.

Hearty. Describes a full bodied, straightforward, high-alcohol red wine, usually of jug wine quality.

Herbaceous. An aroma and flavor evocative of herbs. Frequently found in wines made from Cabernet Sauvignon, Sauvignon Blanc or Pinot Noir.

Hot. Describes a wine so high in alcohol that it becomes unattractive or unpleasant.

Hybrids. New grape varieties genetically produced from two or more different varieties — usually defined as varieties from different species although the term is loosely used to include vines "crossed" within the same species.

Hydrogen Sulfide. A chemical compound which is a natural by-product of fermentation and imparts the smell of rotten eggs. With proper handling it dissipates prior to the finishing of a wine, but remains in poorly handled wines.

Intense. Describes a strong, concentrated flavor and aroma of a wine. The opposite of "weak."

Jug Wines. Refers to inexpensive, everyday drinking wines, usually bottled in large bottles known as jug bottles. Most wines in this category are generics, but occasionally varietals also appear in jug bottles.

Kabinett. Refers to a legally defined quality level of German wines that is governed by the German government. Kabinett wines are the lowest rank of *Qualitätswein mit Prädikat* wines, stringently defined as to geographical region of origin, natural sugar content, and other attributes.

Lactic. An off-odor that results from defects created by lactic bacteria which act on the wine during fermentation. It is a smell similar to sauerkraut or geraniums.

Late Harvest. Refers to a type of wine made from overripe grapes with a high sugar content. Generally, Late Harvest wines have been made from grapes deliberately left on the vine to achieve high sugars and concentrated flavors. White wine grapes are frequently affected by *Botrytis cinerea*, the noble mold, which further concentrates the grape and imparts its own unique honeyed character. Most Late Harvest wines are unctuously sweet, luscious in flavor and are meant to be drunk with dessert or by themselves rather than with a meal.

Leafy. Refers to a vegetative quality, evocative of fresh leaves, sometimes found in young white wines.

Lees. The sediment that results from clarifying a wine following fermentation in casks or tanks after separation from the skins and pulps. Usually consists of dead yeast cells and proteins. Wines are left on their lees to gain character and complexity; improper procedures can result in wines with unattractive flavors.

Legs. The "tears," or stream of wine, which clings to the glass after a wine is swirled. It is usually a sign of a wine with body and quality and is caused by the differences in evaporation rates of alcohol and other liquids in the wine.

Lemony. Refers to an aroma of lemons in a wine. This may occur naturally or be the result of acid adjustment through the use of citric acid.

Limousin Oak. The great white oak of the Limoges Forest in France which is considered to be among the finest oak for aging wines and brandies. It imparts a mellow, complex vanilla character, with subtle nuances particular to its species, which adds complexity and elegance to a wine aged in casks made from it.

Limited Bottling. Denotes a wine made in limited quantities. There is no legal definition of the term, thus, the quantity can range from a small lot to rather large amounts. The term is used to infer superior quality, but, in and of itself, provides no such guarantee.

Lively. Describes the character of a fresh, fruity young wine with appropriate acidity.

Lot. Wines are frequently labeled with a lot number to differentiate wines of the same type or from the same vintage thereby suggesting significant difference or superiority of one over the other. The term has no legal definition and offers no guarantees as to quality.

Maceration Carbonique. The whole-berry, intercellular fermentation by bacterial, rather than yeast action on the grapes in an airtight container. Imparts a fresh, fruity, jam-like quality to wines so treated which are light in body and meant to be consumed when young.

Maderized. Refers to a wine which has lost its freshness or has spoiled due to oxidation in the bottle, either from storage in an excessively warm area, or simply because of over-age. Maderized wines tend to smell like the wines from Madeira, hence the term. They have a sharp, yet sweet, caramelized character that is not attractive. Maderized white wines darken in color to amber or brown.

Maître de Chai. In France, refers to a winery's cellarmaster who is charged with tending the maturing casks of wine. Frequently he is also the winemaker. This position is the most important in a winery.

Malolactic Fermentation. The secondary fermentation which occurs in some wines due to the action of certain bacteria on the wine which transform the hard malic acid to softer lactic acid. It also imparts new subtle flavors which, depending on the wine type, may or may not be wanted. It is usually undesirable in white wines which require malic acid for freshness.

Metallic. Refers to a taste in wine evoking the taste of metal. It can be imparted to a wine from minerals in the soil where the grapes were grown or by contamination with metal apparatus during the winemaking process. Usually, it is an unwanted flavor in a wine.

Méthode Champenoise. The traditional method of making sparkling wine and the only one permitted in the French district of Champagne where it was invented. It is the most labor intensive and costly way to produce sparkling wine but also imparts a character and refinement, not obtainable with other methods, particularly with regard to the quality of the bubbles produced. A shortcut to the Méthode Champenoise is called the transfer process which eliminates the riddling and dégorgement steps which are the most costly and time consuming and produces wines which are sometimes indistinguishable from the more complicated method.

Meursault. The ancient wine-producing village of the Côte d'Or which gives it name to the famous white Burgundy known for its superior quality.

Middle Body. Refers to that part of the taste sensation which is experienced after the initial taste impact on the palate. It provides the core of the taste on which assessments are usually based. The first, or entry, taste and finish should both be in harmony with the middle body. A wine with a weak middle body generally gives the impression of being incomplete.

Minty. A taste of mint in a wine. Minty tastes range from eucalyptus-like to spearmint or peppermint.

Mis en Bouteilles Sur Lie. "Put in bottles on its lees," refers to the practice of bottling a wine directly from the barrel, immediately after fermentation without racking. The wine (almost always white) retains a fresh, lively quality, often with a slight petillance due to carbon dioxide absorbed during fermentation which had not completely dissipated when bottled. "Sur-lie" wines often experience a malolactic fermentation in the bottle which also contributes to the petillance or "coming alive" in the bottle in the year after bottling.

Moldy. Refers to a wine which has become flawed due to either moldy grapes or unclean cooperage that has imparted a moldy taste to the wine.

Montrachet. The most noted vineyard of Burgundy's Côte d'Or, producing a wine of great breed and finesse.

Mosel. Refers to the wine, usually delicate, flowery, light-bodied, and distinguished, which is made in the German wine district of that name.

Mountain. A loosely used term, often found on California jug wines of the lowest quality. There is no legal requirement that the grapes used in these wines come from mountain vineyards; nor is it necessarily so that mountain vineyards producing grapes for these wines are any better than grapes grown on flat areas.

Must. Refers to the unfermented grape juice produced by crushing the grapes. It is a loosely-defined word and equally defines grape juice, crushed grapes, or the juice after pressing.

Musty. Refers to the dank, mildew-like smell of a wine which comes from being stored in poorly cleaned tanks or casks, or from grapes which have been attacked by mold in the vineyards.

Qualitätswein. Literally "quality wine," which, under the German wine law, is one grade above Tafelwein ("table wine") and one grade below Qualitätswein mit Prädikat (quality wine with special attributes). Quality wine must come from a single district, and among other qualifications, be of a minimum alcoholic strength.

Racking. Refers to the traditional way of clarifying a wine by transferring it from one cask to another and leaving the precipitated solids behind.

Residual Sugar. Refers to the unfermented sugar remaining in a wine. It is usually described in terms of the percentage by weight, and is detectable when it exceeds three quarters of one percent. Above two percent it tastes quite sweet.

Rich. Describes the rich, full flavors of a wine's aroma or taste.

Ripe. Describes the smell and flavor of wine made from fully mature grapes that contribute a depth of flavor, or richness, to a wine.

Robe. Refers to the color of a wine in general, and, more specifically, to the wine's color when the glass is tipped at an angle.

Robust. Describes the character of a full-bodied, full-flavored wine that is heavy and pleasingly coarse.

Rotten Egg. Describes the smell of hydrogen sulfide (H_2S), an undesirable effect in wine.

Round, Rounded. Describes the smooth, gentle feel of a wine with a particular alcohol/acid balance that smooths the sharpness of the acidity and makes a wine feel "round" in the mouth rather than "sharp-cornered."

Sauternes. Refers to the sweet wines produced in the district of that name in the Bordeaux region of France. Also used as a generic name for California sweet wine, but seen less frequently in recent years.

Sec. Literally means "dry," and refers to a dry wine. Its use is not legally defined, and it frequently appears on wine labels of wines which are off-dry or even somewhat sweet.

Sediment. Refers to the deposit precipitated by a wine which has aged in the bottle.

Short Finish. Describes a fleeting or abrupt aftertaste of a wine.

Silky. Describes the silky smooth tactile impression of a wine that is smooth but not oily in its texture.

Simple. Describes a straightforward character of a wine which has no nuances of flavor or complexity.

Solera. Refers to the traditional Spanish blending system used in making Sherry. The Solera, itself, is a series of Sherry casks containing wines of various ages which are fractionally blended by transferring part of the contents of a younger cask into an older one.

Sparkling. Refers to a wine which, under pressure, has absorbed sufficient carbon dioxide to bubble, or "sparkle" when poured into a glass.

Spätlese. In German nomenclature, refers to a wine made from fully ripe grapes.

Spicy. Describes a wine with an aroma and taste which evoke an impression of spices.

Spritzig. Refers to a light, prickling effervescence in the mouth caused by a slight amount of absorbed carbon dioxide in a wine.

Spumante. Refers to Italian sparkling wines.

Stale. Describes a wine which has lost its lively, fruity, or vinous personality.

Stalky-Stemmy. Describes the taste of stems or sap in a wine which is usually harsh, bitter, and herbaceous.

Steely. Describes a hard acidic quality in white wines. It is usually used to describe French Chablis.

Structure. Describes the overall character of a wine and the interrelationships of all its components together with the olfactory and tactile impressions which they create in the mouth.

Stuffing. Refers to the body and extract of a wine. Usually used to describe a wine with a heavy character.

Sturdy. Describes a full-bodied wine with high alcohols, acids, and tannins which should improve with age.

Supple. Describes the tactile impression of a wine which has a softness of fruit and flavor, yet is firm in structure with sufficient acids, tannins, and alcohol to age. This is an indication that the mature wine will be delicate and complex.

Sweet. Refers to a wine with residual sugar. A wine with less than 0.5% residual sugar is dry, i.e., lacks any discernible sweetness. Slightly sweet wine has 0.5 to 1.5% residual sugar; medium sweet, 1.5 to 3.0%, and sweet, above 3%.

Tanky. Describes the musty or dank character of a wine which has aged too long in large wooden tanks.

Tannin. Refers to an astringent acid, derived from the skins, seeds, and wooden casks, which causes a puckering sensation in the mouth. Tannin is an essential preservative for quality wines. A moderate puckering sensation caused by the tannins adds to the pleasurable character of a red wine.

Tart. Refers to the flavor sensation caused by a wine's high acidity. Frequently, when appropriate to the wine, this is pleasing to the palate.

Tears. Refers to the viscous drippings that cling to the side of a glass after the wine is swirled. The same as legs.

Tired. A wine that has become over-aged in the bottle, and lacks freshness or vinosity.

Tonneau. A Bordeaux measure of wine, equivalent to four barrels, or one hundred cases of wine.

Topping. Refers to the practice of adding wine to casks of aging wine to replace evaporation losses. This step is essential to prevent the intrusion of oxygen, which could turn the wine into vinegar.

Transfer Process. Refers to a shortcut method of making bottle fermented Champagne. In this process, the wine is filtered rather than riddled and disgorged.

Trockenbeerenauslese. The highest Prädikat a German wine can carry. It signifies that the wine is made entirely from late-picked, individually-selected grape berries which have been allowed to shrivel on the vine, usually after being attacked by the *Botrytis cinerea*, the noble rot, which imparts a special quality to the finished wine.

Truffles. Refers to the scent of a wine which resembles or evokes the earthy aroma of black truffles.

Unbalanced. Describes a wine which lacks harmony in its components. This is apparent in the wine's impression in the mouth.

Unctuous. Describes a wine with a dense, heavy body resulting from a high glycerol or residual sugar content.

Unfiltered. Refers to a wine which has been bottled without being clarified or stabilized by filtration. Such a wine might be clarified by fining, however. When bottled without any cellar treatment, such a wine is labled as "Unfiltered and Unfined."

Unfined. Refers to a wine which has not been fined as part of its cellar treatment. Also infers that the wine has not been filtered and has received a minimum of treatment.

Unresolved. Refers to the impression of a wine that has not yet harmonized its various components in order to create a smooth or harmonious impression with ageing.

Vanillin. Refers to the vanilla extract of new oak barrels. Wines aged in these barrels take on the flavor of the oak, frequently tasting of vanilla, which adds complexity and smoothness to the wine.

Varietal. Refers either to a wine named after a grape variety, or one which is made entirely from a single grape variety. As legally defined (and until 1983, when the minimum requirement will be raised to 75%), such a wine need be made only from 51% of the named grape.

Varietal Character. Refers to the recognizable flavor and structure of a wine made from a particular variety of grape.

Velvety. Refers to the tactile feel of a wine which is rich in extract and smooth in its acids and tannins. Similar to, but less smooth than, silky. A desirable attribute of full bodied, or highly-perfumed wines.

Vinegary. Refers to the aroma of acetic acid and ethyl acetate — a wine's volatile acidity.

Vinifera, *Vitis vinifera.* Refers to that species of grape varieties known as "the wine bearers," which are responsible for all the finer wines of the world.

Vin Ordinaire. Refers to the lowest quality of wine. Usually quite ordinary, frequently poorly made or unpalatable.

Vinosity. Refers to the characteristic flavor of a wine as a result of fermented grape juice. It is distinct from any other flavors such as those of the unfermented grape, oak cask, or other flavor components.

Vinous. The winey character of a wine, but distinct from grapy.

Viticultural Area. A delimited region in which common geographic or climatic attributes contribute to the definable characteristic of a wine. Although it is called by different names in various countries, it isusually referred to as an Appellation of Origin. In the United States, such an appellation is called a viticultural area, and will be defined by geography alone, as opposed to requirements regulating the varieties of grapes grown, yield, or nature of wine produced.

Vitis Labrusca. Refers to a species of native North American grape varieties which are used to make some domestic wines but are predominantly used for producing grape juice, jams and jellies. Labrusca grapes are characterized by a strong, pungent aroma and a taste often described as "foxy," or similar to the sweat of a wild animal. The Concord grape is a typical example.

Volatile. Refers to a chemical compound which is capable of evaporating in normal ambient temperature. Thus, a volatile substance can be detected by smell.

Volatile Acid. Refers to the acid component of a wine which is can be detected in the aroma. In wine this is acetic acid, the acid of vinegar. It is always present in wine, usually undetectable or at low levels which add to the complexity and appeal of a wine. When excessive it is an undesirable defect.

Weedy. Refers to a smell or scent evocative of weeds or dried grass.

Woody. Refers to the aroma and flavor of a wine which has a dominant flavor of the cask in which it was aged. Usually refers to that part of the flavor which is reminiscent of sawdust or wood, as opposed to the vanilla character of new oak.

Yeasty. Refers to the smell or taste of yeast in a wine. In young table wines, it refers to the smell of live yeast, an undesirable characteristic which dissipates as a wine ages. In sparkling wine, most particularly French Champagne, it refers to the character imparted by the dead yeast cells through the process of autolysis, which is complex, pleasing and desirable. This "yeastiness" is quite distinct from the character of fresh yeast.

APPENDIX

APPENDIX I

THE WINES OF BORDEAUX

THE 1855 CLASSIFICATION OF GREAT GROWTHS OF THE MÉDOC (GRAND CRU CLASSÉ)

FIRST GROWTHS
(Premiers Crus)

Château Lafite-Rothschild *(Pauillac)*
Château Latour *(Pauillac)*
Château Margaux *(Margaux)*
Château Mouton-Rothschild *(Pauillac)*
Château Haut-Brion* *(Pessac, Graves)*

* *This wine, although a Graves, is classified as one of the four First Growths of the Médoc in recognition of its outstanding quality..*

SECOND GROWTHS
(Deuxièmes Crus)

Château Rausan-Ségla *(Margaux)*
Château Rauzan-Gassies *(Margaux)*
Château Léoville-Las Cases *(Saint-Julien)*
Château Léoville-Poyferré *(Saint-Julien)*
Château Léoville-Barton *(Saint-Julien)*
Château Durfort-Vivens *(Cantenac-Margaux)*
Château Lascombes *(Margaux)*
Château Gruaud-Larose *(Saint-Julien)*
Château Brane-Cantenac *(Cantenac-Margaux)*
Château Pichon-Longueville-Baron *(Pauillac)*
Château Pichon-Lalande *(Pauillac)*
Château Ducru-Beaucaillou *(Saint-Julien)*
Château Cos d'Estournel *(Saint-Estèphe)*
Château Montrose *(Saint-Estèphe)*

THIRD GROWTHS
(Troisièmes Crus)

Château Giscours *(Labarde-Margaux)*
Château Kirwan *(Cantenac-Margaux)*
Château d'Issan *(Cantenac-Margaux)*
Château Lagrange *(Saint-Julien)*
Château Langoa-Barton *(Saint-Julien)*
Château Malescot-Saint-Exupéry *(Margaux)*

Château Cantenac-Brown (*Cantenac-Margaux*)
Château Palmer (*Cantenac-Margaux*)
Château La Lagune (*Ludon*)
Château Desmirail (*Margaux*)
Château Calon-Ségur (*Saint-Estèphe*)
Château Ferrière (*Margaux*)
Château Marquis d'Alesme-Becker (*Margaux*)
Château Boyd-Cantenac (*Cantenac-Margaux*)

FOURTH GROWTHS
(*Quatrièmes Crus*)

Château Saint-Pierre (*Saint-Julien*)
Château Branaire (*Saint-Julien*)
Château Talbot (*Saint-Julien*)
Château Duhart-Milon-Rothschild (*Pauillac*)
Château Pouget (*Cantenac-Margaux*)
Château La Tour-Carnet (*Saint-Laurent*)
Château Lafon-Rochet (*Saint-Estèphe*)
Château Beychevelle (*Saint-Julien*)
Château Prieuré-Lichine (*Cantenac-Margaux*)
Château Marquis-de-Terme (*Margaux*)

FIFTH GROWTHS
(*Cinquièmes Crus*)

Château Pontet-Canet (*Pauillac*)
Château Batailley (*Pauillac*)
Château Grand-Puy-Lacoste (*Pauillac*)
Château Grand-Puy-Ducasse (*Pauillac*)
Château Haut-Batailley (*Pauillac*)
Château Lynch-Bages (*Pauillac*)
Château Lynch-Moussas (*Pauillac*)
Château Dauzac-Lynch (*Labarde-Margaux*)
Château Mouton-Baronne Pauline (*Pauillac*)
(*formerly known as Mouton-Baron Philippe*)
Château du Tertre (*Arsac-Margaux*)
Château Haut-Bages-Libéral (*Pauillac*)
Château Pédesclaux (*Pauillac*)
Château Belgrave (*Saint-Laurent*)
Château Camensac (*Saint-Laurent*)
Château Cos Labory (*Saint-Estèphe*)
Château Clerc-Milon-Rothschild (*Pauillac*)
Château Croizet-Bages (*Pauillac*)
Château Cantemerle (*Macau*)

SAINT—ÉMILION:
1955 OFFICIAL CLASSIFICATION

In mid 1955 the best Saint-Émilion wines were officially classified by the Institut National des Appellations d'Origine as First Great Growths and Great Growths.

FIRST GREAT GROWTHS
(Saint-Émilion—Premiers Grands Crus Classés)

These two are considered the equal of the First Growths of the Médoc and are in a class by themselves as Saint-Émilions.

Château Ausone
Château Cheval-Blanc

Château Beauséjour-Becot
Château Beauséjour Duffau Lagarosse
Château Belair
Château Canon
Château Figeac
Clos Fourtet
Château La Gaffelière
Château Magdelaine
Château Pavie
Château Trottevieille

GREAT GROWTHS
(Saint-Émilion—Grands Crus Classés)

Château l'Angélus
Château l'Arrosée
Château Baleau
Château Balestard-la-Tonnelle
Château Bellevue
Château Bergat
Château Cadet-Bon
Château Cadet-Piola
Château Canon-la-Gaffelière
Château Cap de Mourlin
Château Chapelle Madeleine
Château-le-Chatelet
Château Chauvin
Château Coûtet
Château Couvent-des-Jacobins
Château Croque-Michotte
Château Curé-Bon
Château Dassault

Château Faurie-de-Souchard
Château Fonplégade
Château Fonroque
Château Franc-Mayne
Château Grand-Barrail-Lamarzelle-Figeac
Château Grand-Corbin
Château Grand Corbin-Despagne
Château Grand-Mayne
Château Grand-Pontet
Château Grandes-Murailles
Château Guadet-Saint-Julien
Château Haut-Corbin
Clos des Jacobins
Château Jean Faure
Château La Carte
Château La Clotte
Château La Cluzière
Château La Couspaude
Château La Dominique
Clos La Madeleine
Château La Marzelle
Château La Tour-Figeac
Château La Tour-du-Pin-Figeac
Château La Tour-du-Pin-Figeac
Château Laniotte, Château Chapelle-de-la-Trinité
Château Larcis-Ducasse
Château Larmande
Château Laroze
Château Lasserre
Château Le Couvent
Château Le Prieuré
Château Matras
Château Mauvezin
Château Moulin du Cadet
Château L'Oratoire
Château Pavie-Decesse
Château Pavie-Macquin
Château Pavillon Cadet
Château Petit-Faurie-de-Souchard
Château Ripeau
Château Saint Georges-Côte Pavie
Clos Saint-Martin
Château Sansonnet
Château Soutard
Château Tertre-Daugay
Château Trimoulet
Château Trois-Moulins
Château Troplong-Mondot
Château Villemaurine
Château Yon-Figeac

RECOMMENDED WINES OF POMEROL

The wines of Pomerol have never been classified. However these personal recommendations include wines which are among the best and can be found in the American market.

Château Pétrus is considered to be in a class by itself and in many vintages is considered equal or superior to Chateau Lafite-Rothschild which is recognized as consistantly the best wine of the Médoc. In recent times Château Pétrus has commanded the highest price of any wine in Bordeaux.

NOBLE

Château Pétrus

SUPER PREMIUM
(*Exceptional Growths*)

Château Beauregard
Château Certan-de-May
Château Gazin
Château La Conseillante
Château Lafleur
Château La Fleur-Pétrus
Château Lagrange
Château Latour-Pomerol
Château La Pointe
Clos L'Église
Château L'Évangile
Château Le Gay
Château Nénin
Château Petit-Village
Vieux-Château-Certan

GRAVES:
1959 OFFICIAL CLASSIFICATION

CLASSIFIED RED WINES

Château Haut-Brion (*Pessac*)
Château Bouscaut (*Cadaujac*)
Château Carbonnieux (*Léognan*)
Domaine de Chevalier (*Léognan*)
Château de Fieuzal (*Léognan*)
Château Haut-Bailly (*Léognan*)
Château La Mission-Haut-Brion (*Pessac*)
Château La Tour-Haut-Brion (*Talence*)
Château La Tour-Martillac
    (Kressman La Tour) (*Martillac*)
Château Malartic-Lagravière (*Léognan*)
Château Olivier (*Léognan*)
Château Pape-Clément (*Pessac*)
Château Smith-Haut-Lafite (*Martillac*)

CLASSIFIED WHITE WINES

Château Bouscaut (*Cadaujac*)
Château Carbonnieux (*Léognan*)
Domaine de Chevalier (*Léognan*)
Château Couhins (*Villenave-d'Ornon*)
Château La Tour-Martillac
    (Kressman La Tour) (*Martillac*)
Château Laville-Haut-Brion (*Talence*)
Château Malartic-Lagravière (*Léognan*)
Château Olivier (*Léognan*)
Château Haut-Brion (*Pessac*)

APPENDIX II

BURGUNDY

CÔTE D'OR RED WINES
(Best known classified wines)

CÔTE DE NUITS

Commune	Grand Cru - Tête de Cuvé	Premiere Cru
Fixin	Clos de la Perrière	Clos du Chaptire
		Les Hervelet
Gevrey-Chambertin	Le Chambertin	Latricières-Chambertin
	Le Clos de Bèze	Mazys-Chambertin
		Mazoyères-Chambertin
		Ruchottes-Chambertin
		Chapelle-Chambertin
		Charmes-Chambertin
		Griotte-Chambertin
		Clos Saint-Jacques
		Les Combottes
Morey-St.-Denis	Clos de Tart	Clos de la Roche
	Clos des Lambreys	Clos St.-Denis
	Bonnes-Mares	Clos Morey
Chambolle-Musigny	Le Musigny	Les Amoureuses
		Les Charmes
Vougeot	Musigny du Clos	Le Cras
	de Vougeot	Clos de la Perrière
	Clos de Vougeot	
Flagey-Échézeaux	Les Grands Échézeaux	Clos St.-Denis
	Les Échézeaux	
Vosne-Romanée	Romanée-Conti	Romanée St.-Vivant
	La Romanée	Les Beaux-Monts
	La Tâche	or Beaumonts
	Le Richebourg	Les Malconsorts
	Les Gaudichots	La Grand Rue
		Les Suchots
		Les Reignots

Nuits-St.-Georges	Les St.Georges	Les Chaignots
	Les Boudots	Les Perrières
	Les Cailles	Les Poulettes
	Les Porrets	Les Richemonnes
	Clos des Porrets	Les Thoreys
	Les Pruliers	
	Les Vaucrains	
	Les Cras	
	Les Murgers	
	Clos de Thorey	

CÔTE DE BEAUNE

Commune	Grand Cru - Tête de Cuvé	Premiere Cru
Pernard-Vergelesses	Ile-de-Vergelesses	
Aloxe-Corton	Le Corton	Cuvée Dr. Peste
	Charlemagne	Les Maréchaudes
	Les Bresandes	Charlotte Dumay
	Le Clos du Roi	Les Perrières
	Les Renardes	Les Grèves
	Les Chaumes	La Vigne-au-Saint
		Les Pougets
		Le Roguet
		Les Vergennes
		Château Corton—Grancey
Savigny-les-Beaune	Les Vergelesses	
	Arthur Girard	
	Les Marconnets	
	Les Jarrons	
Beaune	Les Grèves	À l'Écu
	Les Fèves	Cuvée Nicolas Rollin
	Les Marconnets	Les Perrières
	Les Bresandes	Les Cent-Vignes
	Les Clos-des-Mouches	Les Epenottes
	Le Clos-de-la-Mousse	Les Bucherottes
	Les Cras	Les Theurons
	Les Champs-Pimonts	
	(Champimonts)	

Commune	Grand Cru - Tête de Cuvé	Premiere Cru
Pommard	Les Grands Épenots	Dames de la Charité
		Les Pézerolles
	Les Rugiens	Les Petits-Épenots
	Les Clos Blanc	Clos de la Commeraine
		Les Jarollières
		Château de Pommard
Volnay	Les Angles	Clos de Chênes
	Les Caillerets	Clos des Ducs
	Les Champans	
	Santenots	
Monthélie		
Auxey-Duresses	Les Duresses	Les Grands-Champs
		Les Reugnes
	Le Clos St.-	
	Jean-Morgeot	(Abbaye de) Morgeot
		La Romanée
Santenay	Les Gravières	Le Cailleret
		Clavoillons

CÔTE D'OR WHITE WINES

(Best known classified wines)

CÔTE DE BEAUNE

Commune	Grand Cru - Tête de Cuvé	Premiere Cru
Aloxe-Corton	Corton-Charlemagne	
	Le Corton Blanc	
Beaune		Clos-des-Mouches-Blanc
Meursault	Clos des Perrières	Les Genevrières
	Les Perrières	La Goutte d'Or
		Cuvée Jehan Humblot
		Les Charmes
		Les Santenots
		Les Bouchères
		Cuvée Albert Grivault
		(Meursault-Charmes)
		Le Porusot-Dessus

Commune	Grand Cru - Tête de Cuvé	Premiele Cru
Puligny-Montrachet	Le Montrachet	Le Chevalier-Montrachet
		Bâtard-Montrachet
		Bienvenues-Bâtard-Montrachet
		Le Cailleret
		Les Combettes
		Les Pucelles
		Clavoillons
Chassagne-Montrachet		Criots-Bâtard-Montrachet
		Les Ruchottes
		Morgeot

CHABLIS

(Best known classified wines)

Grand Cru	Premier Cru
Blanchots	Beugnons
Les Clos	Les Forêts
Grenouilles	Fourchaume
Valmur	Vaillons
Vaudésir	
Bourgros	
La Moutonne	
Les Preuses	

CRU OF BEAUJOLAIS

Brouilly	Côtes de Brouilly
Chénas	Chiroubles
Fleurie	Juliénas
Morgon	St.-Amour
Moulin-à-Vent	

APPENDIX III

THE BEST KNOWN WINES OF GERMANY

MOSEL-SAAR-RUWER
BEREICH: Bernkastel, Obermosel, Saar-Ruwer, Zell

Bereich: Bernkastel

GROSSLAGE:	GENERIC NAME	EINZELLAGE
Badstube	Bernkasteler Badstube	Bernkastel Bratenhöfchen
		Bernkasteler Doctor
		Bernkasteler Graben
		Bernkasteler Lay
		Bernkasteler Matheisbildchen
Kurfürstlay	Bernkastler Kurfürstlay	Bernkasteler Rosenberg
		Bernkasteler Schlossberg
		Brauneberg Juffer
		Brauneberg Juffer-Sonnenuhr
		Brauneberg Klostergarten
Michelsberg	Piesporter Michelsberg	Piesporter Falkenberg
		Piesporter Goldtröpfchen
		Piesporter Günterslay
		Piesporter Treppchen
		Trittenheimer Altärchen
		Trittenheimer Apotheke
Münzlay	Graacher Munzlay	Graacher Domprobst
		Graacher Himmelreich
		Graacher Josephshöfer
		Wehlener Klosterberg
		Wehlener Nonnenberg
		Wehlener Sonnenuhr
		Zeltingener Deutschherrenberg
		Zeltingener Himmelreich
		Zeltingener Schlossberg
		Zeltingener Sonnenuhr
Nactarsch	Kröver Nactarsch	Kröver Burglay
		Kröver Herrenberg
		Kröver Kirchlay
		Kröver Letterlay
		Kröver Paradies
		Kröver Steffensberg

GROSSLAGE	GENERIC NAME	EINZELLAGE
Schwarzlay	Erdener Schwarzlay	Erdener Busslay
		Erdener Busslay
		Erdener Herrenberg
		Erdener Prälat
		Erdener Treppchen
		Trarbacher Hühnerberg
		Trarbacher Königsberg
		Trarbacher Schlossberg
		Trarbacher Ungsberg

Bereich: Saar Ruwer

GROSSLAGE	GENERIC NAME	EINZELLAGE
Romerley	Trierer Romerley	Kaseler Hitzlay
		Kaseler Kehrnagel
		Haseler Nieschen
		Maximin Grünhauser Abtsberg
		Maximin Grünhauser Bruderberg
		Maximin Grünhauser Herrenberg
Scharzberg	Wiltinger Scharzberg	Ayler Herrenberg
		Ayler Kupp
		Hanzemer Altenberg
		Hanzemer Sonnenberg
		Oberemmeler Altenberg
		Oberemmeler Rosenberg
		Ockfener Bockstein
		Ockfener Geisberg
		Ockfener Happenstein
		Ockfener Herrenberg
		Serriger Würtzberg
		Wiltingener Braune Kupp
		Wiltingener Kupp
		Scharzhofberger

Bereich: Zell

GROSSLAGE	GENERIC NAME	EINZELLAGE
Schwarze Katz	Zeller Scharzer Katz	

THE NAHE
BEREICH: Kreuznach, Schloss Böckelheim

Bereich: Kreuznach

GROSSLAGE	GENERIC NAME	EINZELLAGE
Kronenberg	Kreuznacher Kronenberg	Kreuznacher Hinkelstein
		Kreuznacher Krötenpfuhl
		Kreuznacher Narrenkappe

Bereich: Schloss Böckelheim

Burweg	Neiderhausener Burweg	Niederhausener Hermannshöle
		Niederhausener Herrmannsberg
		Schlossböckelheimer Felsenberg
		Schlossböckelheimer Königsfels
		Schlossböckelheimer Kupfergrube
Rudesheim	Rudesheimer Rosengarten	

RHEINGAU
BEREICH: Johannisberg

Bereich: Johannisberg

GROSSLAGE	GENERIC NAME	EINZELLAGE
Geisenheim	Rüdesheim Burgweg	Burgweg
		Geisenheimer Fuchsberg
		Geisenheimer Mäuerchen
		Geisenheimer Mönchspfad
		Geisenheimer Rothenberg
		Rüdesheimer Berg Roseneck
		Rüdesheimer Berg Rottland
		Rüdesheimer Berg Schlossberg
		Rüdesheimer Berg Schlossberg
		Rüdesheimer Bischofsberg
		Rüdesheimer Drachenstein
		Rüdesheimer Kirchenpfad
		Rüdesheimer Klosterberg
		Rüdesheimer Klosterlay
		Rüdesheimer Magdalenendreuz
		Rüdesheimer Rosengarten

Erntebringer	Johannisberger Erntebrigner	Geisenheimer Kilzberg
		Geisenheimer Klaus
		Geisenheimer Kläuserweg
		Geisenheimer Schlossgarten
		Johannisberger Goldatzel
		Johannisberger Hansenberg
		Johannisberger Hölle
		Johannisberger Klaus
		Johannisberger Mittelhölle
		Johannisberger Schwarzenstein
		Winkeler Dachsberg
Gottesthal		Oestrich Doosberg
		Oestrich Lenchen
		Schloss Reichartshausen
Merhrhölzchen		Hallgartener Hendelberg
		Hallgartener Jungfer
		Hallgarten Schönhell
Honigberg		Schloss Vollrads
		Winkeler Bienengarten
		Winkeler Hasensprung
Dutelsberg	Hattenheimer-Deutelsberg	Hattenheimer Engelmannsberg
		Hattenheimer Hassel
		Hattenheimer Heiligenberg
		Hattenheimer Mannberg
		Hattenheimer Nussbrunnen
		Hattenheimer Pfaffenberg
		Hattenheimer Schützenhaus
		Hattenheimer Wisselbrunnen
		Steinberg
Heiligenstock		Keidricher Sandgrub
		Kiedrich Wasseros
Steinmächer	Rauenthaler Steinmächer	Eltviller Langenstück
		Eltviller Sandgrub
		Eltviller Sonnenberg
		Eltviller Taubenberg
		Rauenthaler Baiken
		Rauenthaler Gehrn
		Rauenthaler Langenstück
		Rauenthaler Nonnenberg
		Rauenthaler Rothenberg
		Rauenthaler Wülfen

Daubhaus	Hochheimer Daubhaus	Hochheimer Berg
		Hoccheimer Domdechaney
		Hochheimer Herrnberg
		Hochheimer Hofmeister
		Hochheimer Hölle
		Hochheimer Kirchenstück
		Hochheimer Königin Viktoriaberg
		Hochheimer Reichesthal
		Hochheimer Sommerheil
		Hochheimer Stein
		Hochheimer Stielweg

RHEINHESSEN

BEREICH: Bingen, Nierstein, Wonnegau

Bereich: Bingen

GROSSLAGE	GENERIC NAME	EINZELLAGE
Sankt Rochuskapelle	Bingener Sankt- Rochuskapelle	Bingener Buberstück
		Bingener Kapellenberg
		Bingener Kirchberg
		Bingener Osterberg
		Bingener Pfarrgarten
		Bingener Rosengarten
		Bingener Scharlachberg
		Bingener Schelmenstück
		Bingener Schlossberg-- Schwätzerchen

Bereich: Nierstein

Gütes Domtal	Niersteiner Gütes Domtal	
Güldenmorgen	Oppenheimmer- Güldenmorgen	Deinheimer Falkenberg
		Dienheimer Herrenberg
		Dienheimer Höhlchen
		Dienheimer Kreuz
		Dienheimer Siliusbrunnen
		Dienheimer Tafelstein
		Oppenheimer Daubhaus
		Oppenheimer Gutleuthaus
		Oppenheimer Herrengerg
		Oppenheimer Kreuz
		Oppenheimer Sackrager
		Oppenheimer Zuckerberg
Krötenbreunnen	Oppenheimer- Krötenbrunnen	Dienheimer Herrengarten
		Dienheim Schloss
		Oppenheimer Herrengarten
		Oppenheimer Schloss

Rehbach	Niersteiner Rehbach	Niersteiner Brudersberg
		Niersteiner Hipping
		Niersteiner Pettenthal
Spiegelberg	Niersteiner Spiegelberg	Niersteiner Bildstock
		Niersteiner Brückchen
		Niersteiner Findling
		Niersteiner Hölle
		Niersteiner Klostergarten
		Niersteiner Paterberg
		Niersteiner Rosenberg

RHEINPFALZ (PALATINATE)

BEREICH: Sudliche Weinstrasse, Mittelhaardt-Deutsche Weinstrasse

Bereich: Mittelhaardt-Deutsche Weinstrasse

GROSSLAGE	*GENERIC NAME*	*EINZELLAGE*
Gafenstück	Bockenheimer Gafenstück	Bockenheimer Schlossberg
		Bockenheimer Sonnenberg
		Bockenheimer Vogelsang
Hochmess	Dürkheimer Hochmess	Dürkheimer Michelsberg
		Dürkheimer Rittergarten
		Dürkheimer Spielberg
Hofstück	Deiderheimer Hofstück	Ruppertsberger Hoheburg
		Ruppertsberger Nussbien
		Ruppertsberger Reiterpfad
		Ruppertsberger Spiess
Mariengarten	Foster Mariengarten	Deidesheimer Hohenmorgen
		Deidesheimer Kieselberg
		Deidesheimer Leinhöle
		Deidesheimer Mäushöhle
		Deidesheimer Paradiesgarten
		Forster Jesuitengarten
		Forster Kirchenstück
		Forster Ungeheuer
		Hochenheimer Böhlig
		Hochenheimer Gerümpel
		Hochenheimer Goldbächel
		Hochenheimer Rechbächel
Schenkenböhl	Wachenheimer Schenkenböhl	Wachenheimer Königswingert
		Wachenheimer Mandelgarten
		Wachenheimer Odinstal
		Wachenheimer Schlossberg

WINE CELLAR JOURNAL

DATE ACQUIRED	WINE NAME	PRICE PAID	DATE TASTED	RATING

WINE CELLAR JOURNAL

DATE ACQUIRED	WINE NAME	PRICE PAID	DATE TASTED	RATING

INDEX

A

Aaron, S. Jay, 339
Aaron, Sam, 329, 336
Abbocato, 253
Abfüller, 251
Abfüllung, 251
Abruzzi, 81
A.C. *see* Appellation d'Origin Contrôlée (A.C. or A.O.C.)
Acetic acid, 43, 265
Acetobacter xylimim, 43
Achaia-Clauss (producers), 75
Acidity, 17, 27
    correction, 41-42
Adams, Leon D., 329, 335, 344
Advertising, 319-24, 328
    wine columns, 328
Aeration, 44, 45
Aftertaste (generally), 139, 146, 267
Aging, 192, 194, 220, 244
    barrel, 27, 143
    bottle, 26, 157, 167
    Brunello di Montalcino, 189
    Chianti, 188, 189
    legislation, 117
    process, 5, 139, 141
    wines unimproved by, 127-35, 205
Aglianico grape, 190, 191
Aglianico del Vulture (red), 82
Ah-So (cork puller), 287
Alameda County, 88
Alba, 185
Alcoholic content:
    bottle color and, 238
    listing requirement, 239, 245
    physiological effect, 373-74
    restrictions, 117, 219
Aleatico di Puglia, 81
Alexander Valley, 91, 194, 195, 198
Alex Bespaloff , 339
Alicante-Bouschet, 47
Aligoté, 47, 148
Allen, H. Warner, 220, 340
Allen, Judy Lee, 339
Allen, Lawrence, 345
Almadén, 90, 314, 315
Aloxe-Corton, 166, 168, 169
Alsace, 64, 65, 131, 238
    premium wines, 147
Alsace and Its Wine Gardens, Cellars and Cuisine, 341
Alsatian bottle, 235
Alsatian muscat, 54
Altitude, 173
Alto-Adige, 186
Alzey, 178
Amabile, 190, 253
Amador County, 89, 195, 198
Amarone, 188
Ambrosi, Hans, 346
American Airlines, 330
American Express Co., 352
Amerine, Maynard A., 20, 322, 335, 347
Amigne grape, 87
Amis du Vin, Les (association), 352
Amis du Vin, Les (magazine), 331
Amontillado, 224
Amoroso, 228
Amtliche Prüfungsnummer, 244, 251
Anbaugebiete. see Germany, subhead: regions
Ancient world, wine in, 9-10
Anderson, Burten, 344
Anderson Valley, Calif., 89
Anjou wines, 71, 132
"Answer Grape", 319
Antihistamines, 374
Antinori, Marchesi, 189
A.O.C., *see* Appellation d'Origin Contrôlée (A.C. or A.O.C.)
Aosta Valley, 184
A. P. (Amtliche Prüfungsnummer), *see* Amtliche Prüfungsnumer
Aperitif wines, 6
Appearance of wine, 259, 263-64
Appellation Contrôlée (A.C.), *see* Appellation d'Origine Contrôlée (A.C. or A.O.C.)
Appellation d'Origine Contrôlée (A.C. or

Á.Ö.Č.), 120-21, 241, 246, 247
Alsace, 147
    Bordeaux, 65, 120, 147, 156-60
    Burgundy, 68, 164
    Chablis, 164-65
    Champagne, 210
    Graves, 159
    Mâcon, 150
    Médoc, 67, 120, 156-58
    Pauillac, 120
    Sauternes, 160
Applied Wine Chemistry and Technology, 347
Apulia, 81-82, 190-91
Aquileia (Friuli-Venezia), 82
Argentina, 48, 53, 61
Arinto grape, 83
Arkansas, 92
Aromas, 139, 140, 265
    defective wines, 264-65, 274
    fermentation and, 32
    sensing mechanism, 260
Arvine grape, 87
Asciutto, 190
Asher, Gerald, 329
Asti, 54, 79, 185, 214
Aurora grape, 47
Aus eigenem Lesegut, 254
Auslese, 122, 171, 172, 175, 178, 180, 243, 251
Australia, 61-63
    map of wine regions, 115
    noble wines, 144
    Riesling, 52
    sherry, 228
    sparkling wines, 216
Austria, 52, 63, 132
Auxey-Duresses, 168
Awards, advertising use of, 321
Ayl, 176

B

Bacchus Data Services, 339
Bacchus grapes, 178
Bacon, Paul, 344
Baco Noir, 47
"Badacsonyi", 76
Bad Durkheim, 180
Baden region, 63, 73
Bag-in-a-Box, 61
Baiken (vineyard), 177
Balloon glasses, 292
Bandol (Côtes de Provence), 72, 149
Banfi, 320-21
Balzer, Robert Lawrence, 329, 341, 344, 353
Barbera, 47-48, 79, 133, 185
    California, 135, 154
    Italy, 151, 152
    premium, 151, 152, 154
Barbera d'Alba, 79, 185
Barbera d'Asti, 79
Barbaresco, *see* Gattinara
Bardolino (red), 134, 187
    Classico, 79
    Veneto, 79
Barolo, 54, 79, 184, 185
Barossa Valley, 62
Barrels, 141, 143, 159, 196, 251
    racking in, 44
    sherry, 224
Barsac (Bordeaux), 56, 67, 97
Basilicata region, 82, 191
Bas-Médoc, 97
Bastardo grape, 220
Bâtard-Montrachet, 169
B.A.T.F., *see* Bureau of Alcohol, Tobacco and Firearms, United States (B.A.T.F.)
Beaujolais (Burgundy), 51, 68, 70, 132, 170
    labelling, 171
    Primeur, 148
Beaujolais Villages, 170
Beaune, 168
Beerenauslese, 122, 171, 172, 178, 180, 243, 251
Benedictine (O.S.B.), 10
Benmarl Winery, 92
Benson, Jeffrey, 341

Benson, Robert, 345
Bereiche, 122, 171-81, 243, 250, 251
    Bernkastle, 130
    Johannisberg, 151
Beringer Vineyards, 354
Bernkastel (Mosel), 74, 151, 175-76
Bernkastler Kurfurstlay, 176
Bespaloff, Alexis, 329-30, 339, 340
Better Wines for Less Money, 337
Bianco, 132, 253
Bienvenue Bâtard-Montrachet, 169
Big Little Wines of France, The, 342
Bingen, 178, 179
Biondi-Santi, 189
Bitterness, perception of, 260, 262
Blanc de Blanc, 49
    California, 134
    champagne, 214
    defined, 247
Blanc de Noir champagne, 214
Blending, 48-54, 56-58, 121
    acidity correction by, 42
    Bordeaux, 157
    cépage, 53, 156, 157, 158
    cuvée, 55, 210, 211, 212, 214, 215, 247
    jug wines, 128, 129, 134
    premium wines, 141, 157, 160
    Sauternes, 160
Blind tasting, 303, 323
Blood alcohol, 374
Bloom, 30
Blue, Anthony Dias, 330
Blue Nun, 130
Boal grape, 229
Boca, 184
Bocksbeutel, 236
Bodega (winery), 224
Bodenheim (Rheinhessen), 73
"Body" described, 266
Bon Appetit, 330
Books on Wine, 335-47
Bordeaux Blanc, 131-32, 147
Bordeaux bottles, 233, 234, 238
Bordeaux glasses, 292
Bordeaux Rouge, 131, 147
Bordeaux Supérieur, 120, 132, 147
Bordeaux wines, 64, 65-66, 120, 313
    aromas, 266
    jug, 131-32
    labelling, 120, 156, 157, 158, 159, 160
    maps and charts, 97, 161-62
    Médoc, *see* Médoc
    noble, 144
    Pauillac, 17, 22, 23, 67, 157
    premium, 147
    reds, 48, 131, 147, 240
    sparkling wines, 214
Born, W., 342
Borola, 123
Botrytis cinerea (noble rot), 52, 67, 76, 160, 172, 195, 243, 251, 254
Bottling and bottles, 129, 143, 233-37, 242, 243, 247, 251, 253
    aging, 157
    caps, 237, 289
    chianti, 188
    color, 238
    corks, *see* Corks
    estate bottling, 247, 251, 253, 323
    fermentation, 44
    Fiaschi, 182, 188
    labels, *see* Labelling
    mosel, 175
    types illustrated, 234-37
Bouquet, *see* Aroma
Bourgogne, *see* Burgundy
Bourgogne Aligoté, 148
Bourgogne Blanc, 148
Bourgogne Passe-Tous-Grains, 148
Bourgueil (Loire) 71
    jug wines, 132
    premium wines, 150
Boutique Wineries, 314
Bouzy, 71
Brandy, 58, 219, 292
Brandy snifters, 292
Brauneberg, 175
"Breathing" in bottle, 288, 289
Brix, 254

Broadbent, Michael, 340
Brokers, see Negociants
Brouilly (Beaujolais), 70, 170
Brown Sherry, 224, 228
Bruce, David, Winery, 90, 354
Brunello di Montalcini, 80, 123, 189
Brunello (grape) see Sangiovese
Brut champagne, 247
Bual grape, 229, 230
Bucelas region, 83
Buena Vista Winery, 354
Bulgaria, 63
Bureau of Alcohol, Tobacco and Firearms,
    United States (B.A.T.F.), 124-25, 239,
    321, 324
Burger, Robert, 335
Burgundies
    aromas, 266
    California, 135, 192, 197
    French, see Burgundy district, wines of
    jug wines, 132
    labelling, 156
    Oregon, 91
Burgundy district, wines of, 10, 47, 64, 65,
    68, 132
    aging, 4
    imports from, 313
    labelling, 156, 171
    maps and charts, 98-99, 163
    noble wines, 144
    premium wines, 148, 164-70
    sparkling wine, 214
Burgundy bottle, 233, 235, 236
Business schools, 316
Butler, Joel P., 330
Butts, see Barrels

                        C

Cabernet Franc, 48, 186
    Bordeaux, 66, 156, 158
    California, 196
    Côtes de Provence premium, 149
    Italy, 82
    Loire Valley, 71, 150
Cabernet grape family, 240
Cabernet Sauvignon grape, 5, 44, 189
    Australia, 62
    blending, 322
    Bulgaria, 63
    California, 89, 90, 91, 154, 195-97
    Chile, 64
    France, 66, 156, 158-59
    Italy, 78
    New York, 91
    Rumania, 84
    South Africa, 84
Cakebread Cellars, 354
California, 10, 12-13, 88-91, 314
    champagnes, 216
    grape varieties, 12, 48
    jug wines, 134-35
    labelling of wines from, 88, 89
    maps of wine regions, 110-13
    noble wines, 144, 192, 195, 196, 197
    Port, 223
    premium wines, 146, 152-55, 192, 194-97
    producers, recommended (list of), 200-24
    regulations, 205, 310
    Riesling, 53
    Sherry, 228-29
    vintage date, 205
California bottle, 234, 236
California Wine Book, The, 332
California Wine List, A Consumer's Guide to
    114 Cabernet Sauvignons, 345
California Wine List, A Consumer's Guide to
    120 Pinot Chardonnays, 345
California Wines, 346
Cambas, Andrew (producers), 75
Campania, 82, 190
Canaiolo, 188
Cannellino, 190
Cantinas, 253
Cantina sociale, 253
Cap, 32
Capita (sherry glass), 292
Capsul, 245, 275, 285

color coding, 181
Carbonation, 210
Carbon dioxide, 30, 210
Carbonic maceration, 70
Carema, 184
Carignan, 48
Carignane (grape), 23
Carmignano, 189
Carneros district, 197, 198
Casa Vinicola, 253
Cascade Noir, 48
Casks, see Barrels
Cassis (Côtes de Provence), 72, 149
Castelli, 190
Catalonia, 85
Catawba grape, 12, 49, 320
Cellar logs, 307
Centrifuge use, 41, 128, 141
Caves, 247
Central Coast Wine Book, 346
Central Valley, Calif., 89
Cépage (blend), 53, 156, 157, 158, 188
Chablis, 49, 319
    California, 135
    France, 64, 68, 69, 149, 152, 164-65,
    194,
        309, 311, 319
Chai, 249
Chalonnais, 69, 171
Chambertin, 167
Chambertin-Clos de Bèze, 167
Chambolle-Musigny, 167
Chambre, 249
Champagne, 49, 64, 65, 70-71, 209
    advertising, 320
    American, 49, 50, 54, 215-16, 320
    French, 49, 55, 243
    labelling, 210, 213, 243
    making, 54-55, 210-12
    service of, 295-96
Champagne bottle, 234, 246
Champagne corks, 237
Champagne glasses, 292
Champigny (Loire), 71, 132, 150
Chancellor Noir, 49
Chapman, Joseph, 12
Chaptal, Jean, 40
Chaptalization, 40-41, 171
Charbono, 49
Chardonnay, 16, 44, 49, 191
    Australia, 62
    Bulgaria, 63
    Burgundy, 69, 148, 164, 240
    California, 89, 90, 91, 152, 192, 194
    Chablis, 164, 219
    Champagne, 90, 210, 213
    Italy, 82
    Mâcon, 150, 169-70
    New York, 91, 92
    Rumania, 84
    Washington, 91
Charlemagne, 74, 169
Charmat process, 212, 215
Chassagne, 10, 169
Chassagne Montrachet, 168, 169
Chasselas grape, 87
"Chateau Bottled", 121, 157, 247
Chateau (defined), 247
Château d'Yquem, 160
Chateau Greysac, 100-101
Château-Grillet, 58
Château Haut-Brion, 159
Château Lafite-Rothschild, 15, 66, 309, 323
Château La Mission-Haut-Brion, 159
Château Latour, 15, 66
Château Margaux, 66
Chateau Montelena, 354
Château Mouton-Rothschild, 15, 66
Châteauneuf-du-Pape, 52, 57, 72, 100-101,
    170
Chateau St. Jean, 91, 354
Chateau wines, 313
Chauché Gris, see Grey Riesling
Cheese, 302
Chelois, 49
Chemicals, use of, 321
Chénas (Beaujolais), 70, 170
Chenin Blanc, 49, 62, 132
    California, 88, 135, 153

Loire, 71
    Washington, 91
Chevalier-Montrachet, 169
Chianti, 78, 79, 182, 184, 188-89, 309
    California, 135
    Classico, 188, 189
    D.O.C., 80
    jug, 134
    premium, 151
Chianti: A History of Florence and Its
    Wines, 341
Chianti bottles, 151, 182, 188, 235, 236, 253
Chiavennasca, 186
Chicago (magazine), 330
Chicago Sun, 330
Chile, 48, 64
Chilling machines, 281
Chinon (Loire), 71, 132, 150
Chiroubles (Beaujolais), 70, 170
Chroman, Nathan, 330, 345
Church, Ruth Ellen, 336
Churchill, Creighton, 330, 336
Cinsault, 50, 84
Citric acid, 42
Claret, California, 135
Clarification, 143, 291
Clarity, 263
"Classico", 244, 253
    legal definition, 123
Classification des Grands Crus Rouges de
    Bordeaux, 158
Clicquot, Mme., 210
Clifford, Williams, 328, 330
Clifford's disease, 328
Climate, 2, 15, 16-17, 20, 127-28, 142, 173
    ideal, 17, 142
    vintage date and, 206
Clinton, 92
Cloning, 23
Clos, 247
Clos de Vougeot, 164
Clubs, wine tasting, 265
Coca-Cola Company, 316, 319
Coda di Volpe grape, 82
Cognac, 58, 292
Cognac (book), 342
Cognac glasses, 292
Colares region, 83
Colli Aretini (Chianti), 80
Colli Fiorentini (Chianti), 80
Collio (Friuli-Venezia), 82
Colli Orientali del Friuli, 82
Colli Pisane (Chianti), 80
Colli Senesi (Chianti), 80
Color, 263-64
Columnists, 327
Combettes, Les, 169
Commonsense Book of Wine, The, 329, 335
Commune labels, 171
Competitions, 321
Complete Book of Wines, Vineyards and
    Labels, The, 338
Concannon Vineyards, 354
Concise Atlas of Wine, The, 342
Concord grape, 12, 50
Condrieu, 58
Connoisseurs' Guide to California Wines,
    The, 331, 353
Consorzio, 253
Constancia, 84
Containers, 61
Coonawarra, 62-63
Cooperage, see Barrels
Co-operative Wine Growers' Association, 84,
    251, 253
Cooperatives, winegrowers', 84, 251, 253
Corbières (Languedoc-Roussillon), 72
Cordial glasses, 292
Cordorniu (Spanish producer), 85
Corfu, 75
Corkage fee, 272
"Corked" wine, 288
Corks, 237, 285, 287-89
    champagne, 211-12
Corkscrews, 285, 287-88
Cornas (Rhône Valley), 71
Cortaillod, 87
Cortez, Hernando, 10
Corton, 168

Corton-Bressandes, 168
Corton-Charlemagne, 49, 169
Corton-Clos du Roi, 168
Corvina grape, 79
Corvo Brut, 191
Côte, definition of, 247
Côte, La, region, 87
Coteaux Champenois, 71
Coteaux de Layon (Loire), 49, 71
Côte de Beaune (Côte d'Or), 68, 144, 166, 168-69, 171
Côte de Beaune-Villages, 166, 168
Côte de Brouilly (Beaujolais), 70, 170
Côte de Nuits (Côte d'Or), 68, 166-67
    map, 98-99
Côte de Nuits-Villages, 166, 171
Côte d'Or (Burgundy), 68-69, 171, 197
    map, 98-99
    noble wines, 144
    premium wines, 165
Côte Rôtie (Rhône Valley), 57, 71-72, 170
Côtes de Provence, 72, 149
Côtes de Roussillon-Villages, 72
Côtes du Rhône, 52, 71
    jug wines, 132
    map, 100-101
    premium wines, 150-51
Côtes du Rhône-Villages:
    jug wines, 132
    premium wines, 150
Country of origin, 239, 245
Cream Sherry, 54, 84, 224, 228
Crete, 75
Criadera, 225
Croatia, 93
Cross, Gilbert, 338
Crown caps, 289
Crozes-Hermitages (Rhône Valley), 71, 170
Crus (growths), 120, 247
Crus Bourgeois 158, 247
Crus Classé 242, 247
Crus Exceptionnel, 158, 247
Crushing, 128
Crusted Port, 221
Crystallization, 41
Cultivars, see Grapes
Cuneo, 185
Cuvées, 55, 210, 211, 212, 214, 215, 247
Cyprus, 64, 223, 228

D

Dali, Salvador, 336
Dallas, Phillip, 344
Dao region, 83, 135
Davaye, 170
David Bruce Winery, see Bruce, David, Winery
Debuigne, Gerard, 336
Decanting, 276, 291
Defective wines, 264-64, 274
Dégorgement, 211
Deidesheim (Rheinfalz), 73, 180, 181
Delaware (grape), 50
Demi-sec, 249
Denominaçao de Origem, 82
Denominazione di Origine Controllata
    (D.O.C.), 78, 79, 80, 81, 82, 123, 132, 133, 182, 184, 187, 188, 244, 253
    A.O.C. compared, 182, 184
Denominazione di Origine Controllata e
    Guarantita (D.O.C.G.), 123, 184, 244, 253
Deposits, see Sediment
Dessert wines, 5, 13, 135
    Madeira, 229-30
    Marsala, 230
    port, see Port
Devlin Wine Cellars, 354
Diamond, 50
Diary of a Wine Taster, 339
Diner's Guide to Wines, The, 337
Direct import, 310
Disease of plant, 19-20
    Phylloxera, 12, 83
Displaying wines, 279, 280, 281
D.O.C., see Denominazione di Origine
    Controllata (D.O.C.)

D.O.C.G., see Denominazione di Origine
    Controlata e Garantita (D.O.C.G.)
Docter (vineyard), 175-76
Dokter (vineyard), 175-76
Dolce, 190, 253
Dolcetto, 185
Dôle, 55, 87
Domain Chandon, 215
Domaine, 247
Domdechaney, 176
Dom Perignon (Champagne), 215
Donnaz, 184
Dosage, 211
Douro region, 220
Doux, definition of, 247
Drainage requirements, 22
Driving, drinking and, 374
Dry Creek Valley, 91, 194, 195, 198
Dry states, 309
Dryfus, Ashby Co., 311
Duff Gordon, 228
Duro River region, 84
Dutchess, 50

E

Échezeaux, 167
Edenkbener, 180
Edna Valley, 90
Egri Bikavér, 76
Einzellage, 122, 171, 243, 250, 251
Eiswein, 172-73, 251
Eitelsbach, 74, 176
Eleveur, see Negociant
Eltville, 177
Emerald Riesling, 23, 50
Emilia-Romagna, 82, 133, 151
Emmery, Lena, 345
Encyclopedia of Wine, 343
Encyclopedia of Wines and Spirits, 337, 343
Ensrud, Barbara, 330, 343
Entertaining, see Home service
Entertaining with Wine, 336
Entre-Deux-Mers, 97
Erbach, 177
Erden (Mosel), 74
Erickson, Leif, 12
Errors by wine writers, 327, 328
Erzeugerabfüllung (bottler), 243, 251
Estate bottling, 247, 251, 253, 323
Estate wines, 313
Est! Est!! Est!!!, 133, 152
Est! Est!! Est!!! di Montefiascone, 81
Estufagem, 229
Eszencia, 76
Ethyl acetate, 43
Etna wines, 81, 191
Etruscans, 9
Experts, 328

F

Fadiman, Clifton, 329, 336
Fagan, Patrick, 330
Fair trade laws, 309-10
Faith, Nicholas, 340
Fass, 251
Father of California Wine,
    Augustine Harasthy, The, 341
Fazi-Battaglia, 190
Fendant grape, see Chasselas grape
Fermentation, 32, 42, 43-44, 128, 140, 142
    by-products, 44
    fortified wines, 219
    malolactic, 43-44, 192
    rate of, 34, 140
Fetzer Vineyards, 89, 354
Fiano di Avellino, 190
Fiasco, (Fiaschi), 151, 182, 188, 235, 236, 253
Fiddletown, California, 89
Filtration, 40, 41, 291
    champagne-making, 212
    jug wines, 128, 129
Finger Lakes region, 92
Finigan, Robert, 330-31, 353
Fining (clarification), 143
Finos, 224, 225

Fino sherry, 85
Firearms, 374
Fireside Book of Wine, The, 340
Firestone Vineyards, 90
Fitow (Languedoc-Roussillon), 72
Fixin, 10, 166
Flagey-Échezeaux, 167
Fletcher, Wyndham, 347
Fleurie (Beaujolais), 70, 170
Flor yeast, 224, 228
"Flute" (champagne glass), 292
Foch (grape), 51
Folk Wines, Cordials and Brandies: How to
    Make Them Along with the Pleasures of
    Their Lore, 337
Fonte, Ron, 331
Foods, suitability with 5, 302
Foppiano Grape Tidings, 354
Forst (Rheinpfalz), 73, 180, 181
Fortified wines, 5, 40, 219-30, 239, 253, 309
    Marsala, 81
    Moscatel de Setúbal, 83
    Muscat, 54
    Port see Port
Four Seasons (restaurant), 292
Foxy aroma, 266
France, 9-10, 12
    (See also: individual regions)
    importing from, 310, 311-13
    jug wines, 130-32
    labelling requirements, 119-21, 156-60,
        164-70, 171, 205, 241-42, 246, 247
    maps of wine zones, 96, 97, 98-99,
        100-101, 102,103
    noble wines, 144
    premium wines, 146, 147-51
    regions (generally), 64-72, 96-103, 171
    vintage date, 205
Franconia region, 73, 171
Franken Riesling, 57
Franken Wines, 53, 130
Frascati, 81, 133
    premium, 151, 152, 190
Fratelli D'Angelo, 191
Free-run juice, 42
Freixenet (Spanish producer), 85
French Colombard, 50, 135
French Revolution, 10
Freshness, vintage date as guide to, 205
Fried, Eunice, 331
Friends of Wine Magazine, 352
Friuli-Venezia, 82, 186-87
Frizzante, 253
Frost, 20
Fruit wines (non-grape), 5
Fruity aroma, 265
Fuder, 251
Fuissé, 170
Fumé Blanc, 56, 91, 153, 194
Fungicides, 321
Furmint (grape), 76

G

Galet, Pierre, 347
Gallo, Ernest and Julio, 309, 314, 315
Gallo nero, 188
Gamay, 51, 70, 87, 135
Gamay Beaujolais, 51, 135
Game of Wine, The, 338
Garganega (grape), 79
Garnacha, see Grenache
Gattinara (Barbaresco) 54, 78, 123, 184, 185
Gebiet, 251
Gemello Winery, Inc., 354
Gerard, Max, 336
German Wines, 346
German Wine Atlas and Vineyard Register, 343
Germany, 174
    importing from, 313
    labelling, 121-23, 174, 205, 242-44, 250, 251
    maps and charts, 106-9, 174
    noble wines, 144, 172, 173, 176, 177, 180
    premium wines, 146, 151, 171-73, 175-76,

177-81
regions (Bereiche), 122, 171-81, 243, 251
  Anbaugebiete, 171
  Enzellagen, 122, 171, 243, 251
  Grosslagen, 122, 171, 175-77
Riesling defined, 243
sparkling wines, 214-215
Tafelwein, 130, 151, 172, 242, 251
vintage date, 205
Gevrey-Chambertin, 166-67
Gewürztraminer, 16, 28, 51, 179, 180, 181, 186
  Alsace, 65
  California, 89, 135, 153, 238
  Washington, 91
Geyser Peak Winery, 354
Ghemme, 184
Gigondas, 52, 100-101, 170
Gillette, Peter and Paul, 336
Gimmeldingen, 180
Giumarra Family Grapevine, 354
Glasses, 275, 289, 291-92, 302
Gods, Wine and Men, 341
Golden Chasselas, *see* Palomino
Gold Rush, California, 13
Gold Seal Wine Company, 92, 320
Gontron (King of Burgundy), 10
Gonzales Byass, 228, 347
Good-will, legislation and, 117-18
Gordon, Manuel Gonzales, 347
Gourmet (magazine), 329
Graach (Mosel), 74, 176
Grafenberg, 177
Grafting, 12, 18, 19
Grand Cru, 171, 242, 247, 319
Grand Crus Classes, 158
Grand Échezeau, 167
"Grand Marks" Champagnes, 213
Grand Travers, Mich., 92
Grape Culture, Wines and Wine Making, 341
Grape Escape—Bicycle Tours of the Wine Country, The, 345
Grapes, 2, 15-16, 28, 30, 47-58, 141-43
  (*See also:* Viticulture)
  advertising claims concerning, 320
  development, 20-22, 28, 30
  hybrid, 23, 47- 50, 51, 53, 56, 57, 58, 84
  labelling, 240, 250, 251, 252, 254
  regulations concerning, 117
  seeds, 141
  skins, 143
Grave del Friuli, 82
Graves (Bordeaux) 66, 67, 97, 132, 144, 159
Great Book of Wine, The, 335
Great Vintage Wine Book, The, 340
Great Western, 92
Great Wine Châteaux of Bordeaux, The, 342
Great Wine Grapes and the Wines They Make, 346
Great Winemakers of California, 345
Great Wine Rivers, 330, 336
Greco du Tufo, 190
Greece, 9, 75
Green Hungarian (grape), 52
Grenache, 51, 71
Grey Riesling, 52, 135
Grignolino, 52, 134, 152
Grosslagen, 122, 171, 175, 243, 250, 251
Gros Plant, 132
Grossman, Harold J., 337
Grossman's Guide to Wines, Beers and Spirits, 337
Growing season, 20-22
Grumello, 186
Grüner Veltliner, 63, 130
Guide to California Wines, 345
Guide to Inexpensive Wine, Alex Bespaloff's, 339
Guide to the Wines and Vineyards of France, 341
Guide to Vintage Wine Prices, 339
Gundlach Bundschu Wine Company, 354
Guntersblum, 179

H

Haardt mountains, 180
Hacienda Wine Cellars, 354
Halbtrocken wines, 181, 251

Hallgarten, S. F. (Fritz), 177,341, 346
Handpicking, 30
Hanns Kornell Champagne Cellars, 354
Haraszthy, Count Ágoston, 12-13, 341
Hargrave Vineyards, 93
Harvesting, 30, 142, 206-7
Harvey's (sherry), 228
Hattenheim, 177
Haut-Médoc, 97, 156-57
Hautvillers, Abbey of, 10
Heat, 28, 280-81
  measurement, 20-21
  summation units, 20-22
Heitz, Joseph (winery), 196
Hermitage (grape), *see* Syrah
Hermitage (Rhône Valley), 57, 71, 72, 100-101, 170
Herxheim, 180, 181
Hillman, Howard, 337
Hinkle, Richard Paul, 331
History of Wine, A, 340
History of winemaking, 9-10
Hochheim, 176
Hock bottle, 233, 236
Hock glasses, 292
Hoffman Mountain Ranch Vineyards, 90, 354
Hogg, Anthony, 337
Hölle, 176
Holzgang, David, 345
Home service, 274, 285-99
Hop Kiln Winery, 354
"House wine" prices, 270
Hudson River Valley, 92-93
Huexl grape, 178
Humagne grape, 87
Hungary, 76
Hunter River Valley, 62, 63
Hybrid grapes:
  Aurora, 47
  Bacchus, 178
  Baco Noir, 47
  Cascade Noir, 49
  Chancellor Noir, 49
  Chelois, 49
  Emerald Riesling, 50
  Foch, 51
  Huexl, 178
  Kerner, 53, 178
  Müller-Thurgau, 53
  Pinotage, 84
  Riesling types, 53, 56
  Ruby Cabernet, 56
  Scheurebe, 178
  Seyval Blanc, 57
  Vidal Blanc, 58
Hydrogen sulphide, 44, 45, 264

I

Imbottigliato del produttore, 253
Imbottigliato nello stabilimento della ditta, 253
Imbottigliato nel'origine, 253
Importers, 245, 310-13, 316
Inferno (red), 186
In Celebration of Wine and Life, 340
Infiascoto alla fattoria, 253
Inglenook Vineyards, 354
Instituto do Vinho do Porto, 82
International Album of Wine, The, 344
International Review of Food and Wine, 332
Interstate trade, 314
Ion exchange, 42
Irrigation, 20, 89
Isonzo (Friuli-Venezia), 82
Italian Riesling, 76
Italian Swiss Colonies (United Vintners), 314
Italian Trade Commission, 124
Italian Wines, 344
Italy, 77-82, 123-24
  Cabernet Sauvignon, 48
  jug wines, 132-34, 184, 185, 187
  labelling, 123-24, 182, 184, 244, 252, 253
  map, 104
  noble wines, 144, 182, 184, 188, 190
  premium wines, 146, 151-52, 182, 184-91
  sparkling wines, 214

J

Jagendorf, Moritz, 337
Jefferson, Thomas, 12
Jefferson and Wine, Thomas Jefferson: The Wine Connoisseur and Wine Grower, 340
Jeffs, Julian, 337
Jemsheed (King of Persia), 9
Jerez, 54, 223
Jerez de la Frontera, 85
Johannisberg (White) Riesling, 50, 52, 74, 176, 177
  California, 135, 194-195
  Schloss Johannisberg, 74, 177
  Switzerland, 87
  Washington, 91
Johnson, Hugh, 331, 332, 337, 343, 344
Johnson's Alexander Valley Winery, 355
Joslyn, M. A., 347
Joys of Wine, The, 329, 330, 336
Judges of wines, 322
Jug Wine Book, The, 335
Jug wines, 81, 127-35, 184, 215
  characteristics, 4, 26
  production, 5, 34-35, 38-39, 41-43
  storage, 297
Juice, *see* Must
Juliénas (Beaujolais), 70, 170
Junta Nacional do Vinho, 82

K

Kabinett wines, 122, 171, 172, 175, 177, 181, 243, 251
Kaufman, William I., 343
Keller, Gayle, 345
Keller (cellar), 251
Kellstadt, 180
Kerner (grapes), 53, 130, 172, 173, 178
Kiedrich, 177
Kimmeridge clay, 70
King City, California, 89
King Tut's Wine Cellar, 340
Kokkineli, 75
Königsbach, 180
Korbel, 215
Kornell Champagne Cellars, Hanns, 215, 354
Korshin, Nathaniel, 337
Kosher wine, 50
Krems, Austria, 63
Kurfurstlay, 175

L

Labelling:
  Austria, 63
  France, 65, 67, 68, 71, 120-21, 130, 147, 148, 150, 156-59, 160, 164, 171, 241-42, 246, 247
  Germany, 74-75, 121-23, 181, 242-44, 250, 251
  Hungary, 76
  Italy, 78, 79, 80, 81, 82, 132, 133, 182, 188, 244, 252, 253
  neck labels, 245
  Portugal, 82
  private labels, 181, 282
  South Africa, 84
  Spain, 85
  terminology, 171, 245-54
  trademark violations, 119
  United States, 134, 239, 240-41, 245, 254
  vintage date, 205
  volume indicated, 245
Labrusca, *see* Vitis labrusca
Lacryma Christi, 133
Lacryma Christi del Vesuvio, 82
Lactobacillus, 43
Lagrein, 186
Lake County, 89, 154
Lake Leelanan, 92
Lamb, Richard, 340
Lambrusco,82, 133, 151
Lancers, 135

Langenlois, Austria, 63
Langenstruck (vineyard), 177
Languedoc, 52, 65, 72
Larousse Dictionary of Wines of the World, 336
Late Bottled Vintage Port, 221
Late Harvest, 195, 254
Latisana (Friuli-Venezia), 82
Latium region, 81, 190
Laureat of wine, 313
Lavaux region, 87
Lawrence, R. de Treville, 340
Laws, *see* Labelling; Legislation
Lazio, *see* Latium
Lead foil, *see* Capsul
Leaves, role of, 19
Lees, 42
Legislation, 117-25
    labelling requirements, *see* Labelling
    state, 309-10, 316
Lembeck, Harriet, 337
Leon, Jean (Spanish producer), 85
Lesko, Leonard, 340
Lessona, 184
Licensing employees, 310
Lichine, Alexis, 13, 158, 310, 311, 337, 341, 343
Liebfraumilch, 73, 75, 130, 151, 178, 251
Liquoroso, *see* Fortified wines
Lirac (Rhône Valley), 72, 100-101
Livermore Valley, 88
Livingstone-Learmonth, John, 341
Ljutomer district, 94
Loeb, O. W., 339
Loire Valley, 64, 71
    jug wines, 132
    map, 102
    noble wines, 144
    premium wines, 149-50
    sparkling wines, 213, 214
Lombardy, 78, 186
London Company, 12
Long Island, 91, 92
Lugana (white wine), 78
Lytton Springs Winery, Inc., 355

M

Macedonia, 93
Mackenzie, Alistair, 341
Mâcon (Burgundy) 68, 69, 132, 150, 169-70, 171
Mâcon Blanc, 312
Mâcon Villages, 150
Madeira, 220, 229-30
Magazines, 353-54
Maikammerre, 180
Mainz, 179
Malbec, 53, 82
Malic acid, 43
Malmsey, 230
Malolactic (second) fermentation, 43-44, 192
Malvasia grape, 188, 189, 229, 230
Manzanilla, 85, 224, 225
Marches, The (Italy), 82, 190
Marcobrunn estate, 177
Marcus, Irving H., 339
Margaux (Bordeaux), 67, 157
Marino region, 81
Marquis de Riscal, 321
Marsala, 81, 191, 220, 230
Massee, William E., 337, 345
Massee's Guide to Wines of America, 345
Massee's Wine Handbook, 337
Massel, A., 347
Masson, Vineyards, Paul, 90, 314, 315, 322, 355
Master, Melvin C., 341
Masters of Wine, 313
Mastroberardino, Antonio, 190
Mateus, 135
Mavrodaphne, 75
Maximin Grünhaus, 74, 176
Medicinal uses of wine, 309
Medicines, drinking and, 374
Médoc (Bordeaux), 22-23, 53, 66, 120, 156-59
    map of, 97

Médoc Noir, 76
Meet Delicato, 354
Meiers Wine Cellars, 93
Meinard, Heinrich, 347
Melon grape, 71
Melville, J., 345
Mendocino, 89,152-53, 154, 155, 195, 197, 198
Mendoza region, 61
Menning, 176
Mercaptan, 44-45, 185
Meredyth Vineyards, 93
Merlot grape, 16, 48, 53, 322
    Bordeaux, 66, 67, 156, 158, 159
    California, 154-55, 196-97
    Chile, 64
    Hungary, 76
    Italy, 78, 186, 191
    Switzerland, 87
    Yugoslavia, 93
Messo in bottiglia nel'origine, 253
Metabolization of alcohol, 373-74
Méthode champenoise, 210, 211, 215-16, 247, 320
Meunier, *see* Pinot Meunier
Meursault, 10, 49, 169, 194
Michelsberg, 175
Michigan, 92
Microclimates, 173, 178
Mildews, 20
Mineral requirements, 22
Mineral water, 302
Minervois (Languedoc-Roussillon), 72
Mirassou Vineyards, 90, 355
Misch, Robert J., 331
Mis en Bouteilles au Château, 242, 247
Mis en Bouteilles au Domaine, 242, 247
Mis en Bouteilles dans la Region de Production, 242, 247
Mis en Bouteilles dans nos Caves, 242, 247
Mise au Domaine, 247
Mission grape, 89
Mississippi, 92
Missouri, 92
Mittelberger, Ernest, 340
Mittlehaardt Deutsche Weinstrasse, 180
Mittlemosel, 175
Moët et Chandon, 215
Molds, 20
Monopole, 247
Montalbano (Chianti), 80, 189
Montalcino, 189
Montepulciano, Vino Nobile di, 80, 189
Montepulciano d'Abruzzo (red), 81
Monterey, 89-90, 152, 153, 192, 194, 195, 196, 198
Monterey Peninsula Winery, 357
Monterey Vineyard, The, 355
Monthly Review of Wine and Food, The, 352
Montilla, 54, 85
Montrachet, 49
Morgan, J., 345
Morgon (Beaujolais), 70, 170
Moscatel de Setúbal, 83
Moscato, 54
Moselblümchen, 251
Mosel bottle, 233, 235
Moselle (book), 339
Mosel region, 52, 73, 74, 130, 171, 175-76
    map, 107
Moulin-à-Vent (Beaujolais), 70, 170
Mt. Eden Vineyards, 90
Mousseux, *see* Sparkling wines
Müller-Thurgau, 23, 53, 63, 73, 74, 87, 172, 173, 178, 179, 180, 186
Munzlay, 175, 176
Muscadelle, 54
Muscadet (Loire), 71, 132, 149-50
Muscadine, 92
Muscat Blanc, 54
Muscat d'Alsace, 54, 131, 147
Muscat de Frontignan, 54
Muscatel, 54
Muscat grape, 50, 54, 65, 79, 191, 214
    Moscatel de Setúbal, 83
    Portugal, 83
    Romania, 84

South Africa, 84
Spain, 86
Muscat of Alexandria, 54
Must, 30, 32, 40, 122, 128
Muté (sweet reserve), 40-41
Mythology, 9

N

Nachenheim, 179
Nahe region, 73, 108, 171, 178
Nanovic, John, 338
Napa Gamay, *see* Gamay
Napa County, 192, 194, 195
Napa Valley, 88, 90, 153, 154, 155, 196, 197, 198
    climatic conditions, 17, 18
    map, 112
Napa Valley Wine Book, 346
Nazem, 176
Nebbiolo, 54, 78, 184, 186
Nebbiolo D'Albas, 134, 184, 185
Negociants (shippers) 157, 246, 250, 252, defined, 242, 247
Nero (color), 253
Neuchâtel, 87
Neustadt, 180
Neutral spirits, 219
Nevers Forest, 159
Newsletters, 355
    winery, 356-57
New York (magazine), 329
New York (state), 91, 92-93, 215, 314
New York Daily News, 330
New York Times, 331, 332
New York Times Book of Wine, The, 332, 338
New Zealand, 223, 228
Niagara (grape), 54
Nierstein (Rheinhessen), 73, 178-79
"Noble" grapes, 16
Noble rot, *see* Botrytis cinerea
Noble wines, 4, 26, 140, 142-44
    California, 144, 192, 195, 196, 197
    France, 144
    Germany, 144, 172, 173, 176, 177, 180
    Italy, 144, 182, 184, 188, 190
Nonneberg (vineyard), 177
North Coast, 152, 153
"Nose", 265, 266
Nostrano, 87
Notebook on the Wines of France, 330
Nuits-Saint-Georges, 168

O

Oak, use of, 143
Oakville, California, 196
Oberemmel, 176
Ockfen, 176
Odors, *see* Aromas
Oeil de Perdrix (rosé), 87
Ohio, 93
Olfactory bulb, 260
Olivella grape, 82
Olken, Charles, 331, 353
Olorosos, 224, 225, 228
1,001 Questions and Answers about Wine, 338
Oporto, Portugal, 220
Oppenheim (Rheinhessen), 73, 178, 179
Oregon, 91
Organoleptic examination, 254, 265
Orvieto, 58, 80, 133, 151, 152
Orvieto Classico, 133
Overstreet, Dennis, 338
Oxidation, 264
    aeration, 44, 45

P

Paarl region, 84
Pair tests, 303, 305
Palatinate, *see* Rheinpfalz
Palomino grape, 54, 223
Panadés region, 85

Pantellaria, 191
Papagni Vineyards, 355
Parducci, 89
Paronetto, Lamberto, 341
Paso Robles, 90, 198
Passito, 253
Pasteurization, 129
Pauillac (Bordeaux), 17, 22, 23, 67, 120, 157
Paul Masson Vineyards, see Masson Vineyards, Paul
Pedro Domecq, 228
Pedro Ximénex grape, 54, 223, 228
Penning-Rowsell, Edmund, 342, 343
Pepsi-Cola Co., 316
Perfume wearers, 276
Pérignon, Dom, (O.S.B.), 10, 209, 210
Perlwein, 251
Pesticides, 321
Petillant, 247
Petit Chablis, 132, 149, 319
Petit-Dôle, 87
Petite Sirah, 54-55, 135
Petit Verdot, 48, 66, 156
Phylloxera vastatrix, 12, 83, 117
Picking grapes, 30, 142, 206-7
Picolit (dessert wine), 82
Piedirosso grape, 82
Piedmont region, 78, 184
Piesport (Mosel), 74, 130
Piesporter Michelsberg, 175
Pino Gregio, 78
Pinot Grigio, 186
Pinotage grape, 84
Pinot Bianco, see Pinot Blanc
Pinot Blanc, 55, 65, 82, 133, 153, 186
Pinot Chardonnay, 150
Pinot d'Alba, see Pinot Blanc
Pinot Gris, 55, 63, 76, 87, 130, 131, 179
    Tokay d'Alsace, 131, 147
Pinot Meunier, 55
    Champagne district, 70, 213
Pinot Noir (Nero), 16, 44, 55-56
    Alsace, 65
    Australia, 62
    Burgundy, 68, 148, 164-65
    California, 90, 155, 197-98
    Champagne, 70, 210, 213
    clones, 51
    Côte d'Or, 165
    Italy, 78, 186, 191
    New York, 91
    Oregon, 91
    Rumania, 84
    Switzerland, 87
Pinot St. George, 56
Plavac grape, 93
Playboy's Book of Wine, 336
Pocket Encyclopedia of California Wine, 343
Pocket Encyclopedia of Wine, 343
Pocket Encyclopedia to California Wines, 332
Pocket Encyclopedia to Wine, The, 331, 343
Pocket Guide to Wine, The, 343
Pomerol, 53, 67, 97
Pomice, 42
Pommard, 168
Port, 57, 82, 84, 220-23
    California, 13, 135
    crusted, 221
Port (book), 347
Port: An Introduction to Its History and Delights, 347
Port Bottles, 234, 235
Portugal, 82-84, 105, 135
    Port, 220-23
Potassium sorbate, 129
Pouilly-Fuissé (Mâcon), 69, 169-70, 311-12
Pouilly-Fumé (Loire) 56, 71, 132, 150
Power Tools, 374
Practical Ampelography: Grapevine Identification, A, 347
Prejudices, 328
Premier Cru, 171, 242, 247, 319
Premium and noble wines (generally) 4, 26, 136-70
    noble, see Noble wines
    production, 34-35, 36-37
    simple, 140, 145
    super premium, 140, 145-46

Preservatives, 25, 129
Pressing, 141, 142, 143
    champagne, 213
Press wines, 42
Prial, Frank, 331-32
Price, Pamela Vandyke, 338
Prices, 146, 273, 310, 313
    restauraunt, 269-70

                        R

Racking, 41, 44, 143
Racks for storage, 297-98
Rainbird, George, 338
Rainwater Madeira, 230
Ramay, Bern C., 346
Ranking wines, 305
Rauenthaler, 177
Ray, Cyril, 342
Recioto, 188
Récolte, see Vintage dates
Records:
    cellar logs, 307
    tasting, 307
Regaleali region, 81
Rejection of defective bottle, 273-74
Remuage, 211
Repeal of Prohibition, 309
Residual sugar, 254
Restaurants, 269-77
    bringing wine, 273
    prices, 269-70, 273
    tipping, 273, 277
    wine lists, 269, 270-73
Retail sales, 310
Retsina, 75
Rèze grape, 87
Rheingau region, 73, 74, 108, 171, 176-77, 178
Rheinhessen region, 73, 109, 171, 177-80
Rheinpfalz, (Palatinate),52, 73, 171, 178, 180-81
Rhine region, 73
Rhine Riesling, 52, 130
Rhine wine bottle, 235
Rhodes, 75
Rhône Valley, 64, 71-72, 132, 150-51
    map, 103
Richebourg, 167
Ridge Winery, 90
Rieslings, 16-18, 52, 56, 57
    Alsace, 65
    aromas, 266
    Australia, 62
    Austria, 43, 130
    bottles used for, 238
    California, 89, 90, 91, 135, 154, 194-95
    Chile, 64
    Emerald, 52
    Germany, 73, 74, 172-73, 175, 176, 178, 180, 181, 243
    Grey, 52, 135
    Hungary, 76
    hybrids, 50, 53
    Italy, 78, 186
    Johannisberg, 50, 52, 74, 87, 91, 135
    New York, 91, 92
    noble, 144
    Oregon, 91
    Rumania, 84
    soft, 154
    South Africa, 84
    Trockenbeerenauslese, 52, 122, 243, 251
    Washington, 91
    Yugoslavia, 93
Rioja, 51, 84, 86, 321
Riserva, 123, 244, 253
Riunite, 133
Robards, Terry, 332, 338
Robert Balzer's Private Guide to Food and Wine, 353
Robert Finigan's Private Guide to Wines, 353
Robertson, George, 347
Roessler, Edward B., 347
Romanée, La, 17, 167
Romanée-Conti, La, 167
Romanée Saint-Vivant, 167
Roman Red, 81

Romans, 9
Roman White, 81
Rondeau, René, 332
Rootstocks, 18, 19
Rosato, see Rosé wines
Rosé wines (Rosato), 49, 50, 51-52, 69, 71-72, 82, 87, 132, 133, 144, 149, 150
    labelling, 247, 253
Rosso, 132, 253
Rosso Conero, 82
Rosso di Sava, 82
Rotclevner, see Pinot Noir (Nero)
Rotwein, 251
Roussillon, 72
Rubin, Hank, 332
Ruby Cabernet, 23, 56
Ruby Port, 221
Rufina (Chianti), 80
Rühr region, see Ruwer region
Rülander, see Pinot Gris
Rumania, 84
Rumello (red), 78
Ruppertsberg (Rheinpfalz), 73, 180, 181
Russian River Valley, 91
Rutherford, California, 196
Ruwer region, 74, 171, 175-76

                        S

Saar region, 74, 171, 176
Saar-Ruwer, 175-76
Saar Bur, 176
Saccharo myces fermenti, see Flor yeast
Sacramental wines, 10, 13, 309
Safety precautions for drinkers, 374
Saint-Amour (Beaujolais), 70, 170
St. Bénigne, Abbey, 10
Ste. Chapelle Vineyards, 355
Saint-Émilion, see Trebbiano
Saint-Estèphe (Bordeaux), 22-23, 67, 157
St. Helena, Calif., 196
Saint-Joseph (Rhône Valley), 71
Saint-Julien (Bordeaux), 67, 157
St. Michael Grosslagen, 175
St. Nicholas wine, 173
Saint-Véran (Mâcon), 69, 150
Salinas Valley, Calif., 89
Samos, 75
San Benito County, 90
Sancerre (Loire), 66, 71, 132, 150
San Diego, 194
San Francisco Chronicle, 330
San Francisco Examiner, 331, 332
Sangiovese, 56, 188, 189
    clones, 51
    Brunello di Montalcino, 80
Sanlúcar region, 85
San Luis Obispo, 90, 192, 195, 198
    Gewürztraminer, 153
San Martin Winery, 355
Santa Barbara, 90, 192, 195
    Gewürztraminer, 153
    Riesling, 154
Santa Clara County, 90
Santa Cruz, 90, 197, 198
Santa Maria region, 85
Santa Ynez Valley, 90, 194, 197, 198
Santenay, 166, 168
Sardinia, 81
Sasella (red wine), 78, 186
Sassicaia, 189
Sauternes, 56, 57, 67, 97, 160, 341
    noble, 144
Sauvignon Blanc, 16, 28, 56, 66, 71, 91, 93, 160, 186
    California, 88, 89, 135, 153, 194
Savigny-les-Beaunes, 168
Scents, see Aromas
Scharzberg (Saar), 74, 176
Scharzhofberg (Saar), 74
Schenley Corporation, 311
Scheurebe, 130, 173, 178
Schloss definition of, 251
Schloss Eltz, 176
Schloss Johannisberg, 74, 177
Schloss Vollrads, 177
Schneider, Seven J., 344
Schoenman, Theodore, 341

Schoonmaker, Frank, 13, 310, 311, 312, 343
Schramsberg, 215
Schwarzer Heergott, 181
Schwarzlay, 175
Screw caps, 237, 289
Screwpull (cork puller) 287-88
Scoring wines, 305
Scuppernong grape, 12, 57
Sebastiani Vineyards, 355
Secco, 190, 253
Sec defined, 247
Sediment, 276, 291
Seeds, 32
Sekt, 214-15, 251
Seldon, Philip, 342, 353
Semillon, 57, 62, 66, 88, 160, 194
Senses, use of, 259-67
Serbia, 93
Sercial grape, 229
Serra, Father Junipéro, 10
Serrig, 176
Servi Chambre, 247
Servi Frais, 247
Sèvres et Maine (Loire), 71, 149
Seyval Blanc, 57
Shenandoah Valley, Calif., 89
Sherrill Cellars, 355
Sherry, 54, 220, 223-29
    Australian, 62
    California, 13, 135
    cream, 84
    Fino, 85
Sherry bottle, 235
Sherry glasses, 292
Sherry Lehman, 329
Sherry—The Noble Wine, 347
Shippers, see Negociants (shippers)
Shiraz, see Syrah
Sichel, Peter M. F., 339
Sicily, 81, 191
Signet Book of American Wines, 332
Simi Winery, 355
Simon, André, 338
Singer, Earl, 331, 353
Singleton, V.L., 335
Sissano, 184
Skins contact with, 28, 30, 32, 141, 143, 196
Slovenia, 93
Smell, sense of, 260, 262-64
    (See also: Aromas)
Smoking, 262-63, 276
Snifters, 292
Snobbishness, 328
Soave, 58, 79, 133, 187
    premium, 151, 152
    Veneto, 79
Soil, 2, 15, 16-17, 18, 22, 173
Sokol Blosser Winery, 355
Solera, 224, 225, 229
    Madeira, 229
    Marsala, 230
Solutré-Pouilly, 170
Sommelier, see Wine steward
Sommerheil, 176
Sonneberg, 177
Sonoma, 91, 153, 154, 155, 192, 193, 194, 195, 197, 198
    map, 113
Sonoma and Mendocino Wine Book, 346
Sonoma Vineyards, 355
Sousao grape, 57, 220
South Africa, 84
    port, 223
    Riesling, 52
    sherry, 228
South America, 114
    (See also: individual countries)
    Cabernet Sauvignon, 48
    Riesling, 52
    sparkling wines, 216
Souverain Cellars, 355
Spain, 84-86, 105
    noble wines, 144
    sherry, 223-28
    sparkling wines, 215
Spanna, see Barolo
Sparkling wines, 5, 47, 49, 54, 85, 92, 93, 188, 191, 209-16
    champagne, see Champagne

France, 209-10, 212-14
    Spumante, 54, 79, 214, 253
    vin mousseux, 210, 214, 247
Spätburgunder, see Pinot Noir
Spätlese, 122, 171, 172, 177, 181, 243, 251
Spoiled wines, smell of, 264-65
Sports, 374
Spritzenwein, 177
Spumante, see Sparkling wine
Stag's Leap, Calif., 196
State stores, 309
Stätswein, 251
Steiman, Harvey, 332
Steinberger vineyard, 177
Steinberg estate, 177
Steinwein, 64, 251
Stellenbosch region, 84
Stems, inclusion of, 28, 141, 143
Stemware, 291
Sterling Vineyards, 355
Stonegate Winery, 355
Storage, 297-99
    open bottle, 297
    racks, 297-98
Stravecchio, 253
Sudliche Weinstrasse, 180, 181
Sugar content, 17, 40-41, 122, 171, 254
Sullivan, Charles L., 332
Sulphur dioxide smell, 264, 265, 289, 321
Sunset Guide to California's Wine Country, 332
"Superiore", legal definition, 123, 187
Sur Lie (out-of-the-cask), 149, 247
Sweetness, perception of, 260, 262
Swirling technique, 263, 265-66, 291
Switzerland, 86
Sylvaner, 56, 57
    Alsace, 65
    Austria, 63
    France, 131
    Germany, 73, 172, 173, 178, 179, 180
    Hungary, 76
    South Africa, 84
    Yugoslavia, 93
Syrah (Shiraz), 48, 54, 57, 62, 84
Szamorodni, 76

T

Table wines, 5, 239
Table Wines, The Technology of Their Production, 347
Tâche, La (vineyard), 17, 167
Tafelwein, 122, 130, 172, 242, 251
Tannin, 27, 30, 145
Tardive, 249
Tarragona region, 85, 86
Tartaric acid, 41
Taste, sense of, 2, 260, 262-63, 266-67
    testing by, 32, 118, 123, 124
Tastings, 301-7, 323
    blind, 323
    competitions, 321
    wine writers, by, 328
Taste of Wine, The, 338
Taubenberg, 177
Taurasi, 190
Tavel (Rhône Valley), 52, 72, 100-101, 170
Tawny Port, 221, 223
Taxes, 239
Taylor, Sally, 345
Taylor California Cellars, 324
Taylor Wine Company, 92, 314, 319, 320, 324, 353
Tchelistcheff, André, 345
Temperatures, 20-22, 28, 32
    fermentation, 32
    serving, 247
    storage and selling, 280-81
Tenuta, 253
Tepusquet area, 90
Thresholds of sensations, 260, 262-63
Thompson, Robert, 332, 346
Thompson seedless, 57-58
Tignatello, 189
Tigrovo Mljeko (Tiger's Milk), 93
Tilson, John, 353

Time-Life Book of Wine, 330
Tinta Cao grape, 220
Tinta Francisca grape, 220
Tinta Madeira grape, 220
Tipping, 276
Titulus (producer), 190
Titus, Sebastian, 346
Tokay, see Pinot Gris
Tokay d'Alsace, 131, 147
Torre Quarto, 82
Torres (Spanish producer), 85
Touiga grape, 220
Trademarks, 119, 245, 250
Traminer, 58, 186
    (See also: Gewürztraminer)
    clones, 51
Transdanubia, 76
Treasury of American Wines, 330, 345
Trebbiano, 48, 58, 67, 79, 80, 81, 97, 133, 188, 189
Trellising, 18, 19
Trentino-Alto Adige region, 78, 186
Triangulation tests, 303
Trocken, 251
Trockenbeerenauslese, 122, 171, 172, 178, 243, 251
Trocken wines, 181
Tuscany, 80, 188-89
Tunisia, 223, 228
Types of wines, 5

U

U.C. Davis Twenty Point System, 305
Ugni Blanc, see Trebbiano
Ukiah, Calif., 89
Umbria, 80
Umpqua Valley, 91
Underground Wineletter, The, 353
Ungstein, 180
United States, 124-25,
    (See also: individual states)
    labelling requirements, 239, 240-41, 245, 254
    maps of wine regions, 110-13
United Vintners (Italian Swiss Colonies), 314
Upper Monterey County, 197
Ürzig (Mosel), 74

V

Valais, 86, 87
Valdepeñas, 86
Valencia, 86
Valgella, 186
Valpantena, 187
Valpolicella, 79, 134, 187-88
    Classico, 187
Valtellina, 78, 186
Varietal wines, 5, 239-40
    regulations, 124
Vaud, 86, 87
Vaudois Chablais, 87
V.D.S.Q. see Vins Délimités de Qualité Superieure (V.D.S.Q.)
Vendammia, see Vintage date
Vendage, 247
Veneto region, 79, 187-88
Ventana Vineyards Winery, 355
Verdelho grape, 229, 230
Verdicchio (white), 82, 152, 190
Verdicchio bottle, 235
Vergine wines, 191
Vermouth, 5, 79, 86, 191, 230
Verona, 187
Vibration, 299
Victoria, Australia, 63
Vidal Blanc, 58
Vignes, Jean-Louis, 12
Viking Sauna, 299
Vin de cuvée, 210
Vin de France, 241
Vin de Glacier, 87
Vin de Marque, 131
Vin de pays, 120, 121, 241
Vin de Table, 241
Vinegar, 43, 44

Vines, 28
    culture, see Viticulture
    grapes, see Grapes
    yield, 117, 119, 121
Vineyards, labelling, 171
Vin grande, 127
    (See also: Premium and noble wines)
Vinhos Verdes, 83, 135
Vinification, premium wine requirements,
    140, 142-44
Vin mousseux, see Sparkling wines
Vino (book), 344
Vino da Tavola, 253
Vino Nobile di Montepulciano, 123, 189
Vin ordinaire, 4, 27, 127-35
    (See also: Jug Wines)
Vinprom, 63
Vin Rosé, see Rosé wines
Vins Délimités de Qualité Superieure
    (V.D.S.Q.), 120, 121, 130, 241, 247
Vintage (publication), 289, 330, 331, 332,
    339, 351-52
Vintage Consumer Guide to Wine, 354
Vintage dates, 124, 205-7, 241, 322-23
    climate and, 206
    label, 245, 246, 247, 250, 251, 252,
    253, 254
    legal requirements, 205
Vintage Foundation, 313
Vintage Image, Inc., 331
Vintage Port, 220-21
Vintagewise, 345
Vintner, 1-2, 3, 15, 25-26, 314-15
    (See also: Viticulture)
Viognier (grape), 58
Virginia, 93
Virus infections, 19
Viti, 87
Viticulture, 2, 15, 16-17, 18, 20-22, 127-28,
    140, 142, 144, 206-7
Vitis labrusca, 12, 16, 50, 54, 92, 93, 266
    (See also: individual American grape
    varieties)
Vitis vinifera, 2, 12, 16, 47-58
    (See also: individual grape varieties)
    hybrid, 47-50, 51, 53, 56, 57, 58, 84
Volnay, 168
Volstead Act, 309
Vougeot, 167
Vouvray (Loire), 71, 150, 213, 214

                        W

Wachau, Austria, 63
Wachenheim (Rheinpfalz), 73, 180, 181
Wagenvoord, James, 339
Walker, Henry, 338

Wallace, Forrest, 338
Walschriesling, 76
Washington, George, 12
Washington (State), 91
Wasserman, Pauline, 338, 342
Wasserman, Sheldon, 338, 342, 344
Wasseros, 177
Waugh, Harry, 339
Wawer, 176
Weather, see Climate
Wehlen (Mosel) 74, 176
Weibel Vineyards, 355
Weimer, Glenora & Herman J., 92
Weingut, 253
Weinhändler, 251
Weinkellerei, 251
Weinstrasse, 73
Weissburgunder, see Pinot Blanc
Weisswein, 251
Wente Bros. Winery, 355
Where the Great German Wines Grow, 346
Which wine?, 339
White Burgundy, 240
White Graves, 56, 147
White Port, 223
White Riesling, see Johannisberg Riesling
White wines (generally), 3, 34, 264
White Wines of the World, 338
Wholesalers, 310
Whole World Wine Catalog, The, 343
Wiedekehr, 92
Wildman & Sons, Frederick, 311
Wildman, Frederick S., 312, 342
Wile, Julius, 343
Willamette Valley, 91
Windows on the World (restaurant), 292
Wine, 331, 337
Wine: An Introduction, 335
Wine: An Introduction for Americans, 335
Wine Buyer's Guide, 336
Wine cellar, 297
Wine components, 27
Wine Handbook, The, 338
Wine lists, 269, 270-73
Winemakers, see Vintners
Winemakers of the Pacific Northwest,
    The, 345
Wine Masters, The, 340
Wine Master's Guide to Europe, The, 337
Wine merchants, 279-82, 309-16
    employees, 310
    state monopoly, 309
    regulation of, 309-10
Wine of the Month Club, 352
Wine Reporter, The, 353
Wineries, buying direct from, 282
Winery flow chart, 34-39
Wines: Their Sensory Evaluation, 347

Wine secrets, 338
Wines of America, The, 329, 344
Wines of Bordeaux, The, 342
Wines of Burgundy, The, 342
Wines of California, 344
Wines of Europe, The, 337
Wines of Gala, The, 336
Wines of Germany, The, 347
Wines of Italy, The, 344
"Wines of Origin" Seal, 84
Wines of the Côtes du Rhône, The, 342
Wines of the Rhône, The, 341
Wines of the World, 338
Wine Spectator, The (periodical), 352
Wine steward, 269, 273, 276
    tipping, 277
Winetasters Choice, 339
Wine Tasting Index, The, 339
Wine tastings, see Tastings
Wine Tour Book, Vol I: Napa Valley, 346
Wine Tour of France, A, 342
Wine World (periodical), 352
Winkle (Rheingau), 177
Winkler, Professor, 20
Winzergenossenschaft, 251
Winzerverein, 251
Woltner & Co. (importers), 332
Wonnegau, 178, 179
Woon, Basil, 342
World Atlas of Wine, The, 331, 344
World wine zones, chart of, 94-95
Worm (corkscrew), 287
Worms, Wonnegau, 178
Writers on wine, 327-32, 335-47
Wulfen (vineyard), 177

                        Y

Yakima Valley, 91
Yeasts, 30, 40, 44, 128, 141, 143, 165, 196
    champagne making, 211, 212, 214
Younger, William, 341
Yountville, Calif., 196
Yoxall, H. W., 342
Yugoslavia, 53, 93

                        Z

Zaca Mesa Cellars, 355
Zell, Rheinpfalz, 181
Zeller Schwarz Katz, 151
Zeltingen-Rachtig (Mosel), 74, 176
Zinfandel, 16, 48, 58, 155
    California, 89, 90, 91, 155, 198